THE CHARLTON STANDARD CATALOGUE OF
ROYAL DOULTON
BESWICK JUGS

FIFTH EDITION

S0-ABB-313

BY
JEAN DALE

INTRODUCTION BY
LOUISE IRVINE

W.K. CROSS
PUBLISHER

The Charlton Press
TORONTO, ONTARIO BIRMINGHAM, MICHIGAN

Canadian Cataloguing In Publication Data

The National Library of Canada has catalogued this publication as follows:

Main entry under title:

The Charlton standard catalogue of Royal Doulton jugs

Biennial
1st ed. ([1991]) –
Issues beginning with 3rd ed. have title: Charlton standard catalogue of Royal Doulton Beswick jugs.
ISSN 1183-711X
ISBN 0-88968-221-6 (5th ed.)

1. Royal Doulton character jugs – Catalogs.

NK4695.C518C442   738.8'0294   C92-030326-9

EDITORIAL

Editor	Jean Dale
Graphic technician	Davina Rowan

Cover illustration supplied by U.K. International Ceramics

SPECIAL THANKS

The publishers would like to thank Louise Irvine for writing the introduction to the *The Charlton Standard Catalogue of Royal Doulton Beswick Jugs*. Louise Irvine is an independent writer and lecturer on Royal Doulton's history and products and is not connected with the pricing of this catalogue.

CONTRIBUTORS TO THE FIFTH EDITION

The following contributors graciously supplied photographs, price lists, data and other valuable information for the fifth edition, for which we offer a profound thank you:

Our thanks also go to the staff at Royal Doulton (U.K.) Limited who have helped with additional technical information, especially Valerie Baynton, Julie McKeown, Maria Murtagh, Gill Walters, Josie Hunt of Lawleys By Post, and Ian Howe of the Royal Doulton Visitors Centre.

Dealers

Anthony Cross, Anthony Cross and The Englishman, Blackburn, England; **William T. Cross**, William Cross Antiques and Collectibles, Burnaby, B.C.; **Margaret and Arnold Krever**, Marnalea Antiques and Collectibles, Campbellville, Ontario; **Mark Oliver**, Phillips, London, England; **Ed Pascoe**, Pascoe and Company, Miami, Florida

Collectors

Jim Adams; Mrs. H. W. Babchyck, Dedham, Massachusetts; **Tom Crook**, Swansea, England; **Tom Duenes**, Portland, Oregon; **R. Feather**, Sutton Coalfield, England; **Barry and Valerie Lee**, Barnsley, S. Yorkshire, England; **Malcolm Navias**, New York, N.Y.; **Scott Reichenberg**, North Smithfield, Rhode Island; **Sandy and Ed. Seward**, Tampa, Florida; **Elsie Shankard**, Manchester, England; **Betty Wheeler**, Pittsburgh, Pennsylvania

A SPECIAL NOTE TO COLLECTORS

We welcome and appreciate any comments or suggestions you may have regarding The Charlton Standard Catalogue of Royal Doulton Beswick Jugs. If you would like to participate in pricing or in supplying new data, such as information on unlisted jugs or varieties, please contact Jean Dale at (416) 488-1418.

**Printed in Canada
in the Province of Winnipeg**

The Charlton Press

Editorial Office
2040 Yonge Street, Suite 208, Toronto, Canada. M4S 1Z9
Telephone (416) 488-1418 Fax: (416) 488-4656
Telephone: (800) 442-6042 Fax: (800) 442-1542
www.charltonpress.com e-mail: chpress@charltonpress.com

HOW TO USE THIS CATALOGUE

THE PURPOSE

As with the other catalogues in Charlton's Royal Doulton reference and pricing library, this publication has been designed to serve two specific purposes: first, to furnish collectors with accurate and detailed listings that will provide the information needed to build a rich and rewarding collection; second, to provide collectors and dealers with an indication of the current market prices for Royal Doulton and Beswick jugs.

STYLES AND VARIATIONS

On the pages that follow, Royal Doulton and Beswick jugs are listed, illustrated and described in alphabetical order within their categories.

STYLES: When two or more jugs have the same name but different physical modelling characteristics, they are listed as **Style One**, **Style Two**, and so on. Such jugs will also have different D numbers.

VARIATIONS: A change in colour is a variation.

When known, the jug's modeller or **Designer** is listed next. What follows is a description of the jug's **Handle**.

The actual **Colour** (or colours) of the jug is then listed.

The pricing table gives the **D number** assigned to the jug, the date (or dates) when the jug was **Issued**, and the **Price** (the current market value) of the jug described. The price appears in U.S. dollars, Canadian dollars and pounds sterling.

Although the publisher has made every attempt to obtain and photograph all jugs and their varieties, several pieces, naturally, have not come into the publisher's possession.

A WORD ON PRICING

The purpose of this catalogue is to give readers the most accurate, up-to-date retail prices for Royal Doulton and Beswick jugs in the United States, Canada and the United Kingdom.

To accomplish this, The Charlton Press continues to access an international pricing panel of experts who submit prices based on both dealer and collector retail-price activity, as well as current auction results in the U.S.A., Canada and the U.K. These market prices are carefully averaged to reflect accurate valuations for jugs in each of these markets.

The prices published herein are for jugs in mint condition. Collectors are cautioned that a repaired or restored piece may be worth as little as 25 percent of the value of the same jug in mint condition.

A necessary word of caution: no pricing catalogue can be, or should be, a fixed price list. This catalogue, therefore, should be considered a guide only, showing the most current retail prices (based on market demand within a particular region) for the various jugs.

Current jugs are priced according to the manufacturer's suggested retail price in each of the market regions. Please be aware that price or promotional sales discounting is always possible and can result in lower prices than those listed.

One exception, however, occurs in the case of current jugs or recent limited editions issued in only one of the three markets. Since such items were priced by Doulton only in the country in which they were to be sold, prices for the other markets are not shown.

A further word on pricing: as mentioned previously, this is a catalogue giving prices for jugs in the currency of a particular market (U.S. dollars for the American market and sterling for the U.K. market). The bulk of the prices given herein are determined not by currency exchange calculations, but by actual market activity in the market concerned.

THE INTERNET AND PRICING

The Internet is changing the way business is done in the collectable market. It links millions of collectors around the world to one another, allowing communication to flow freely among them. Chat rooms, antique and collector malls, Internet auctions and producer Web sites all promote the new e-commerce.

Three major effects that e-commerce will have on the collectable market are as follows:

1. Collectors will deal with collectors. They will also continue with their customer/dealer relationships, but the dealer's margin will come under pressure.

2. The information on new issues, new finds, and new varieties will spread faster — and the bad news will spread even faster. Collectors' wants will be made known instantly to a wide universe of dealers and collectors.

3. Prices will be affected on two fronts:
   (a) Price differentials will disappear between global market areas as collectors and the delivery services team up to stretch the purchasing power of the collectable dollar/pound.
   (b) As margins come under pressure, overheads being low in virtual operations, prices of the common to scarce collectable items will adjust downward to compensate. The rare and extremely rare items will move up as a result of their increased exposure.

YEAR CYPHERS

The cypher for 1998 was a folded umbrella and the cypher for 1999 is the Top Hat as worn by Sir Henry Doulton.

CONTENTS

THE ORIGINS OF THE TOBY JUG
Louise Irvine

Pottery jugs in the image of human beings have been made since the dawn of civilisation, and some impressive examples have survived from Greek and Roman times, as well as from the ancient cultures of South America. In Medieval England, potters poked fun at their contemporaries by creating figurative jugs, and these primitive vessels also provide interesting precedents for the toby jug, which first appeared in the Staffordshire Potteries in the late 18th century.

The toby jug traditionally represents a seated drinking character with a pot of foaming ale balanced on his knee. He is dressed in typical costume of the period, with a long coat and knee breeches, and his large tricorn hat forms the spout of the jug. There are several theories as to the origin of his name. Some suggest a connection with Shakespeare's convivial character Sir Toby Belch, others believe the notorious Yorkshire toper Henry Elwes was the model. He died in 1761 having consumed some 2,000 gallons of Stingo, a particularly strong ale, and was known as "Toby Fillpot." Potters might also have been inspired by an old English drinking song, *The Brown Jug*, written by the Reverend Francis Fawkes, which paid tribute to Toby Fillpot, "a thirsty old soul" who excelled in boozing. The popular verses were first published in 1761 and were soon distributed in print form, accompanied by a caricature of an enthusiastic drinker with a ruddy complexion and a huge beer belly.

Admiral Lord Nelson figure jug produced at the Doulton and Watts factory

By the early years of the 19th century, the Staffordshire potters were producing many variations on the original toby type, including standing figures flourishing pipes, sporting squires, jolly sailors and even female characters. Toby jugs were also made in other parts of England, notably London, where the Lambeth potteries used their favoured brown salt-glaze stoneware material to produce genial tobies astride barrels.

DOULTON LAMBETH JUGS

Brown stoneware tobies were amongst the earliest products of the Doulton and Watts factory, which was established on the banks of the river Thames in London in 1815. As well as complete figure jugs, the company also produced face jugs of famous personalities. The most impressive and best known is their portrait of the great naval hero Lord Nelson. Two different models are marked with the company's early trademark, Doulton and Watts. The complete bust stands 11¾" tall and the smaller head and shoulder design was made in three different sizes, the largest 7½" tall. Replicas of both these models, clearly marked as such, were later made to celebrate the centenary of the Battle of Trafalgar in 1905, but even these are difficult to find today.

Stoneware portrait jug of Theodore Roosevelt modelled by Leslie Harradine

Nelson's great antagonist Napoleon has also been portrayed as a stoneware jug, and there are similar tributes to Wellington, the Iron Duke, but these are unmarked and could have been made by any of the London potters, as they frequently copied each other's ideas. The Doulton pottery went on to honour many other military heroes, politicians and statesmen on flasks, jugs and vases, but the idea of the face jug was not revived until the early 1900s, when the celebrated modeller Leslie Harradine produced a stoneware portrait jug of Theodore Roosevelt, the 26th President of the United States. This was followed by a curious pair of Veteran Motorist jugs, an ugly Highwayman, a beaming Old King Cole and a humorous caricature of Mr. Pecksniff, from Dickens's *Martin Chuzzlewit*. The pattern books also refer to a Wee Mac jug in 1908, but to date this has not materialised and there may well be others still to come to light. Harradine left the Lambeth studio in 1912, but his colleague Mark

Marshall occasionally dabbled in the toby tradition, producing a Soldier toby jug and a face jug, which bears a strong resemblance to John Barleycorn, the first character jug made at Royal Doulton's other factory in Burslem, Stoke-on-Trent.

Old King Cole modelled by Leslie Harradine

Charles Noke, the Burslem art director, was a regular visitor to Lambeth and was undoubtedly influenced by the achievements of the stoneware modellers. He was particularly impressed with the work of Harry Simeon, who contorted Toby Fillpot into a variety of useful shapes, including three styles of toby jugs, tobacco jars, ashpots, inkwells, candlesticks, decanters and even a teapot. A publicity leaflet of the mid 1920s indicates that the Simeon toby jugs were available in several sizes with modelling variations and alternative colourways. In addition the waistcoat could be coloured in a bright red enamel for a surcharge of 25 percent on the list price.

Simeon's toby wares all feature the full seated figure, with the exception of one model that depicts a happy smiling face on the marriage day, but when it is turned upside down, scowling features reveal what happens after marriage. The Marriage mug was made in three sizes and was included in the publicity leaflet for the rest of the stoneware toby collection. Although most of the Lambeth tobies were made of slip cast stoneware and produced in small editions, they are very hard to find today and count amongst the rarest of the Royal Doulton jugs.

BURSLEM CHARACTER AND TOBY JUGS

The Doulton family extended their business to Burslem, Stoke-on-Trent, in 1877, but initially they concentrated on the production of tablewares and other useful wares for the Victorian home. Gradually an art studio was developed, and

in 1889 Charles Noke, who had trained at the Worcester factory, was appointed as a modeller of ornamental vases, mainly for exhibition purposes. Before long Noke was also producing figure models and had embarked on a mission to revive the Staffordshire figurative tradition. In 1913, following the launch of his famous HN collection of figures, he was promoted to art director, and he soon turned his attention to the revival of the toby jug.

His first models were quite different in style from the traditional smoking topers with brimful tankards of ale. In 1918, he introduced a portrait of the great silent movie star Charlie Chaplin in the form of a large toby jug, and this was followed a few years later by a similar portrait of George Robey, the popular music-hall comedian. In both models the characters' bowler hats come off to reveal the jugs underneath. George Robey, the "Prime Minister of Mirth," visited the Burslem factory in 1925, and the toby jug was probably made at that time.

The Kingsware Huntsman modelled by
Charles Noke, 1919

Another early toby jug depicts a huntsman in scarlet, D4090, and this 1919 model was re-launched in more subdued colours as part of an extensive collection of tobies in 1950. The Huntsman was also issued in Kingsware, a distinctive treacle-brown ware which was developed by Noke in the early 1900s and used primarily for whisky flasks. A Kingsware Squire toby jug was also produced and a face jug of a Highlander was made around 1930 for D & J McCallum distillers in Edinburgh. It may have been this commission which gave Noke the idea for a collection of face jugs, for by 1933 he had modelled two designs, John Barleycorn, the personification of barley, and Old Charley, a typical night watchman, and they were launched the following year.

With the help of his chief modeller, Harry Fenton, Noke quickly introduced more personalities from literature, legend, folk-lore and song, and by 1935 the first models were also available in a small size (around 4") as an alternative to the original large size (around 6½"). A miniature size (around 2½") was added to the range by 1939, and the following year the first tinies (1¼") were launched. These became the four standard sizes for the character jug range, although the dimensions have altered over the years, with some large-size jugs now measuring over 7½". There have also been occasional medium- or intermediate-size jugs (around 4½"), as with the Dickens, Wild West and Beatles collections and an extra-large Tony Weller character jug, but these are exceptions to the usual sizes.

Although Charles Noke was in his mid seventies when he introduced character jugs, his fertile imagination was still working overtime, and by 1939 he had adapted the most popular personalities from the range to create a collection of useful gift items now known as the derivatives; for example, musical jugs, wall vases, tobacco jars, ashtrays, sugar bowls and teapots. He also developed a new range of toby jugs, several of which were closely based on early models by Harry Simeon at Doulton's Lambeth factory, in particular Double XX, Honest Measure and The Squire.

The bombing of the Burslem studio during the Second World War briefly interrupted Noke's creative output, but the conflict gave him an opportunity to pay tribute to the great war leader Winston Churchill, the first contemporary personality to be portrayed as a character or toby jug. Unfortunately Noke's character jug portrait, an unusual two-handled model in white, was not considered a good likeness and was quickly withdrawn from the range. It was the first character jug to be discontinued, and because of its brief production period, it is now very sought after. Early in 1941 Noke made a couple of attempts to remodel and colour the portrait, but only prototypes of these experiments are known to exist. Harry Fenton had considerably more success with his toby jug portrait of Churchill, which was launched in 1940 and remained in production for 50 years.

Charles Noke died in 1941, at the age of 83, and for several years Harry Fenton was the sole modeller. He continued to create excellent likenesses of contemporary characters, such as Monty and Smuts, but he was equally at home with historical or fictional characters, for example the Samuel Johnson and Robin Hood jugs which impart a vivid sense of reality. In 1949 Max Henk, who had been appointed as a tableware modeller, became interested in character jugs and his Uncle Tom Cobbleigh was introduced in 1952. When Fenton died in 1953, Henk was able to step into the breach and he soon set a new style for character jugs, which is most obvious in his approach to their handles. He fully exploited the handle's potential for elaborating on the story of the character portrayed; thus Scaramouche has his guitar and the handle of The Ugly Duchess is a flamingo, which she used as a croquet mallet in the story of Alice in Wonderland. Henk obviously loved delving into literature and legend for symbolic allusions such as these, and they add a new dimension to character jugs for the curious collector.

Apart from his own work, Henk had responsibility for training the next generation of artists. Geoff Blower was generally regarded as Henk's protégé and even before he had completed his five-year apprenticeship, he was contributing to the character jug range. His first jug in 1952 was Lord Nelson, and he followed this with several other popular models, such as Rip Van Winkle, which was in production for 40 years. Blower left the Burslem studio in 1956 to take up a career in teaching, but on his retirement he began modelling character jugs again and worked on the Collecting World series. His former colleague Garry Sharpe also started his career at Doulton but moved overseas in 1960, by which time he had modelled some of the best-selling character jugs in the range, including Old Salt and Merlin (style one). Perhaps his success had something to do with Fenton's modelling tools, which Henk gave him in 1953 with the challenging remark, "If there is any of Harry's magic left in these modelling tools, you certainly need it!"

Henk's third apprentice was David Biggs, who joined the team in 1958 after an art school training. Working on his first jug, the Town Crier, he soon found out how difficult it is to create one face which typifies a profession or a hobby, but he then went on to specialise in this field, modelling the Golfer, the Yachtsman, the Punch and Judy Man and many other representative characters. When stuck for a particular expression, he would often reach for a mirror and manoeuvre his own face to achieve the desired effect.

To make way for all the exciting jugs from this new generation of modellers, around 30 early models were withdrawn from production in 1960. A few years later, Royal Doulton decided to discontinue the traditional earthenware body and make all the jugs in the newly developed English Translucent China. David Biggs was given the task of making all the new, more detailed models of existing jugs, which were required for the new process, and several more jugs were withdrawn at this stage to avoid all the costly remodelling. The changeover took place between 1968 and 1970, but the fine china jugs were only made for a few years before earthenware production was resumed in 1973 at the newly acquired John Beswick factory. The fine china jugs are therefore highly valued by collectors and can be recognised most easily by the slight difference in size. Biggs continued to model new character jugs until the early 1970s, and for the next 20 years he concentrated on tableware modelling, occasionally reviving his character jug design skills, notably for W.C. Fields and Louis Armstrong in the Celebrity series. In recent years some of his models for the character jug range include H. G. Wells, Quasimodo, and the Character Jug of the Year for 1998, Lewis Carroll.

In 1972 a special studio was established for the development of figures and character jugs, and Eric Griffiths was appointed the new head of sculpture, ultimately becoming art director. Griffiths was a portrait painter by training and he particularly enjoyed modelling famous people for the jug range, notably Henry VIII, Mark Twain and Ronald Reagan. He also portrayed John Doulton, the founder of the company, as the first character jug especially for members of the Royal Doulton International Collectors Club, which was founded in 1980. There have been many more exclusive commissions for members in the intervening years, including a revival of the tiny size for the Beefeater and Old King Cole jugs.

The 1980s was an exciting time for character jug fans. The club provided a lot of useful information on the subject, stimulating many new collections, and the first major reference book by Desmond Eyles had just been published in 1979. Another informative book was produced by Jocelyn Lukins to celebrate the 50th anniversary of character jugs in 1984, and there were a number of price guides reflecting the buoyant market. New record prices were continuously being set in the sale rooms and amongst the most exceptional was the Toby Gillette jug, which was modelled by Eric Griffiths in a limited edition of three for a popular British TV show, "Jim'll Fix It." The jug sold for over £15,000 at Christie's auction rooms in 1984 to raise money for charity.

Several limited edition collections of character jugs were launched during the 1980s, beginning with the novel two-faced portraits for the Antagonists series by Michael Abberley, a young Royal Doulton figure painter who taught himself to model jugs in his spare time. The Antagonists were extremely popular, and the edition of 9,500 was soon over-subscribed. Abberley followed his first success with another two-faced collection, the Star-Crossed Lovers, and he also worked on some unlimited series, including the Wives of Henry VIII and characters from Shakespeare.

Such was the popularity of character jugs by the mid 1980s that many independent companies requested special designs for advertising purposes. This was not a new idea, as famous firms such as Charringtons had commissioned specially branded tobies in the 1930s and in 1956 the American industrialist Cliff Cornell even had a toby jug made in his own image to impress his customers. Thirty years later another American firm, Quaker Oats, ordered a character jug of Mr. Quaker and Pick Kwik Wines and Spirits of Derby purchased a large range of character jug containers for their liquor during the 1980s. Mail order companies, fair organisers and leading retailers all wanted exclusive jugs for promotional events and colourways of existing jugs were sold in special editions. At first the very small editions were snapped up , as with the colourway of the Mad Hatter made to commemorate the opening of the Royal Doulton Shop at Higbees of Cleveland in 1985, but collectors eventually became jaded with the number of colourways, and the company concentrated resources on new subjects instead.

Since the 1980s most new character jug subjects have been conceived as part of sets, thus creating interesting themes for collectors. In response to the demand for American subjects, Royal Doulton introduced the Wild West and the Celebrity series. The 50th anniversary of the Second World War led to several commemorative series, the Heroic Leaders, the Armed Forces and Heroes of the Blitz, and other important historical events have inspired individual jugs, notably Columbus, which was produced to mark the 500th anniversary of his famous voyage to the New World. Established themes have also been developed to create new series; for example, the Beefeater was joined by lots of other London characters, and Henk's early characters from *Alice's Adventures in Wonderland* were joined by The Red Queen and The March Hare. To date this is the only animal character in the range, but the designer Bill Harper has also considered a grinning Cheshire Cat and White Rabbit, so it will be interesting to see if any others appear in the future. Harper

is perhaps best known as a figure modeller, but he has produced a number of character jugs, as well as the amusing Doultonville collection of 25 small-size tobies, which were produced between 1983 and 1991.

Since 1992 there have also been limited-edition toby jugs of traditional characters, such as the Jester and the Clown. These were designed by Stan Taylor, a retired art teacher from Bristol, and he has been responsible for the majority of character jugs introduced since 1982. His subjects are extremely diverse, ranging from portraits of circus performers to typical characters encountered on a journey through Britain, such as a postman and a policeman. He also allowed his imagination to run riot for his Witch and Genie jugs. These are now in demand, having only been in production for six months because of the extensive withdrawal of character jugs at the end of 1991. The range was reduced from 157 models to 59 — all the early toby jugs were withdrawn and the miniature-size jug was discontinued altogether.

The rationalisation of the character jug range coincided with the appointment of a new art director, Amanda Hughes-Lubeck, who is in charge of all the Royal Doulton design studios. She continues to commission character jugs from Stan Taylor and Bill Harper but other younger modellers from the John Beswick studio, notably Martyn Alcock and Warren Platt, have also been encouraged to try their hands at modelling jugs. They work under the guidance of studio manager Graham Tongue, who has several advertising jugs to his credit, including the superb portrait of William Grant.

As well as all this new talent, recent marketing initiatives have also been well received by collectors. The Character Jug of the Year concept has proved very successful, with huge sales for Winston Churchill, the 1992 exclusive. The prestige limited-edition jugs with two or more handles have also been popular, notably the Henry VIII and William Shakespeare designs. After a brief period of concern about wide-ranging withdrawals and colourways, the future now looks very bright for character jug collectors.

BUILDING A COLLECTION

Collections start in many different ways. Often a surprise gift will be responsible for starting a life-long enthusiasm or it could be a legacy that starts an instant collection. Perhaps a chance discovery in an antique market might also spark off a new collector's curiosity and hunting for more will become an absorbing hobby. One thing is certain, the first acquisition is rarely alone for long.

A few dedicated collectors have acquired all the Royal Doulton character and toby jugs in the standard range and then gone on to add rare prototypes, colourways, modelling variations and unusual backstamps. However, this goal requires considerable time and energy as well as substantial financial resources. Most collectors are content to concentrate on specific themes, sizes or types of jugs and can build some fascinating collections in this way.

Collecting By Type

Lambeth Stoneware Jugs

The scarcity of the early jugs from the Lambeth factory has meant that they are not as widely publicised as the Burslem models. However, there is a committed group of collectors who specialise in English stonewares and seek out the Doulton tobies and face jugs along with other brown salt-glaze stoneware products, such as reform flasks, hunting jugs, bottles, mugs and jars. Competition is stiff, therefore, to include representative examples in Doulton jug collections. A little more accessible are the Lambeth toby wares, modelled by Harry Simeon, which were made in small editions during the 1920s. A number of collectors have specialised in this field, delighting in all the ingenious uses devised for Toby Fillpots, be it a candlestick, tobacco jar, ink pot or traditional jug. One of the largest collections, built up over ten years, included more than 75 examples in various sizes and colour schemes. Collectors' discoveries have added greatly to the archive information over the years, but it is still impossible to produce a definitive list, which is part of the fun of collecting these Simeon tobies.

Toby Jugs

The term "toby" is frequently used to describe all Royal Doulton jugs, but strictly speaking it should only be applied to jugs in the form of a full seated or standing figure. Although Royal Doulton began by producing toby jugs at their Burslem factory, they are better known for their character jugs, which feature only the head and shoulders. Nevertheless, there is a lot of scope for collectors in the toby jug range alone.

George Robey (c.1925) and Charlie Chaplin (1918)
designed by Charles Noke, Art Director

Two of the earliest Burslem tobies are also the rarest, the large portraits of Charlie Chaplin and George Robey, which stand around 11" tall. Most of the traditional tobies, with their tankards of foaming ale, were introduced in 1939, and the majority remained in production for over 50 years, so they are relatively easy to find. The best-selling toby portrait of Winston Churchill is also readily available in three different sizes and should not be confused, as has often happened, with the rare Churchill character jug. Also confusing is the similarity between the Winston Churchill toby and the toby of Cliff Cornell. This American industrialist was a great admirer of Churchill, and in 1956 he commissioned a portrait toby of himself in the image of the great statesman — even smoking a cigar. Three different colourways were produced in two sizes, with Cornell wearing either a brown, blue or tan suit and various matching ties. The base was suitably inscribed to promote his Cleveland Flux company, and he sent them to his friends and associates as Thanksgiving gifts. Today they are becoming hard to find, particularly the tan suit variation, which was made in smaller quantities than the others. Advertising toby jugs were also commissioned by Charrington's to promote their Toby Ale, and three versions with different inscriptions have been recorded from the 1930s.

Completely different in style from the rest of the range are the little Dickens tobies (4½" high), which verge on caricature. There are six characters to find in this desirable collection, which was produced between 1948 and 1960, and there is a lot of competition from Dickens fans. This whimsical style of toby jug was revived by Bill Harper for his Doultonville collection in 1983. He created 25 larger-than-life characters from the imaginary town of Doultonville for this appealing set and all have appropriate comical names. One of the rarest is Albert Sagger, the Potter, which was only made for a six-month period especially for Collectors Club members.

In 1992 Royal Doulton launched their first limited-edition toby jugs in a new style and size (5½"). The collection has grown rapidly and their instant popularity has inspired a revival of interest in Royal Doulton tobies. The subjects have varied from traditional characters, like the Jester and the Clown, to unusual double-sided designs like The Judge and Thief.

In 1994, Royal Doulton launched a new tiny size for their toby jugs, reinterpreting some of the first toby designs, such as Old Charley and Happy John, in this miniature scale. The set of six tiny tobies has been well received and it will be interesting to see if more follow.

Character Jugs

The standard character jug range has included around 300 different subjects, not to mention all the different sizes which have been available, so there is a lot of scope for collectors. It is the ambition of many keen collectors to find all of them, but as the range expands, so the task becomes more daunting and choices have to be made.

The most accessible jugs are the ones in current production, which can be purchased in local china shops or by mail order through specialist dealers. The Doulton catalogues currently list around 40 different subjects, some of which are available in large size, some in small size and some in both. There are also limited editions, subject to availability, and a few special commissions from Lawleys By Post and other companies. This number changes every year as new designs are added and models are withdrawn from production.

Once a piece has been discontinued in the Doulton catalogues, it is only available on the secondary market. Prices will depend on the demand for the retired model, which is often influenced by how long it was in production. Obviously there will be lots of Bacchus jugs around, as it was made for over 30 years before being discontinued in 1991, whereas the Genie and the Witch jugs were in production for less than a year before being caught up in the sweeping withdrawals of 1991.

There are different styles of discontinued character jugs, and it may be that a specific era or the work of a particular artist appeals. Harry Fenton, who was active in the 1930s and 40s, modelled rugged, wrinkly faces (with warts and all!), whereas in the 1950s and 60s his successor, Max Henk, favoured smoother complexions with exaggerated features. It was Henk and his assistants who saw the potential of the character jug's handle which had been mostly plain and functional in the early years, and many collectors delight in the creativity and ingenuity of the designs, which have included animals, birds, boats, various weapons, sporting equipment, musical instruments and even parts of buildings. Miniature faces or figures have often been incorporated in the handle and the latest representation of Henry VIII features all six of his wives on two handles — seven portraits in one jug! There has even been a prestigious three-handled jug recently, King Charles I. Occasionally new handles have been modelled for promotional purposes or just to ring the changes, and in the case of the Santa Claus and Father Christmas jugs, several different handles have been issued over the years.

Themes and Series

Part of the fun of collecting character jugs is researching the symbolism of the handles and finding out more about the characters behind the jugs. For bookworms there have been lots of characters from literature, beginning with the novels of Charles Dickens, a particular favourite of the art director, Charles Noke. Just looking for all the different Dickens character jugs, tobies, derivatives and limited-edition jugs could keep a collector very busy for several years. Those interested in England's past will find an abundance of kings and queens, colourful London characters and military heroes to create a historical pageant of jugs. As an island nation, the sea has been particularly important in British history, and not surprisingly there are many seafaring characters which could form part of a nautical collection. Patriotic Americans can look out for all the presidents, Civil War generals, Williamsburg pioneers, Hollywood film stars and Wild West cowboys represented in the collection. In many cases these have been presented in themed sub-collections, some in limited editions, and issued on an annual basis by Royal Doulton. A list of all the

different self-contained series is listed on pages 655 to 658 for easy reference.

Collecting by Size

Potential display space is one of the factors to consider when embarking on a collection of character jugs as many subjects have been available in four different sizes — large, small, miniature and tiny. Some keen collectors purchase their favourite jugs in all the sizes along with the toby version and the various derivatives, and in the case of Sairey Gamp, that makes 12 different portraits of her to collect!

The majority of collectors look out for one specific size of character jug and the large has tended to be the most popular. In the past Royal Doulton always launched the large size first and, if it was well received, smaller versions would follow within a few years. Sometimes the subject never appeared in the small or miniature sizes, much to the chagrin of those who were collecting these. In recent years, the Royal Doulton International Collectors Club has commissioned a number of small-size jugs exclusively for their members, and Lawleys By Post, the mail-order division of the company, also prefers the small size for their special series, and these are not produced in any other size.

The smaller the jug, the less detail it is possible to achieve, and the costs do not decrease in proportion to the scale, which has tended to make the miniature-size character jug the least popular choice. In 1992 Royal Doulton discontinued this size jug altogether, so there are now set limits to a miniature character jug collection. However, some models will be hard to find, notably Trapper and Lumberjack, which were not officially launched, yet some examples have appeared on the market. On several occasions miniature prototypes were developed many years before they were put into production, as with The Golfer, where the miniature followed 15 years after the large size, or Old Salt, where there was an interval of 23 years.

To date Royal Doulton have only produced 40 tiny-size character jugs, making this a diminutive collection in more ways than one. Their obvious appeal is reflected in the high prices commanded by the original set of 12, which are out of all proportion to their Lilliputian scale. The tinies require expert decorating skills, and the artists have to balance the minute jugs on the end of their little fingers, which is very time consuming and consequently expensive. Such tiny jugs are also difficult to display in china shops, which has meant that models have tended to be special commissions; for example, a set of Kings and Queens of the Realm characters for Lawleys By Post customers and the tiny Beefeater and Old King Cole jugs for members of the RDICC.

LIMITED AND SPECIAL-EDITION CHARACTER AND TOBY JUGS

Limited-edition jugs are comparatively recent developments, as the first character jug was not commissioned until 1978 and the first toby in 1992. It was Michael Doulton's first American tour that inspired the reproduction of the company's very first jug, John Barleycorn, and it was issued in a limited edition of 7,500, appropriately numbered and marked on the base. A few years later, in 1983, the first limited-edition collection was launched with Grant and Lee as the initial pair of Antagonists. The novel two-faced design proved to be very popular, and the edition of 9,500 was quickly sold out. The other three jugs in the series were also very successful, and so they were quickly followed in 1985 by the Star-Crossed Lovers, another two-faced collection.

In 1984 Royal Doulton had the honour of designing a character jug portrait of President Ronald Reagan as a fund-raiser for the Republican National Committee, and number one of the edition of 2,000 was presented to the President at the White House. This prestigious commission was followed by many other requests for special character jugs to promote various companies, products and events. A character jug of Mr. Quaker was produced in a limited edition of 3,500 to mark the 85th year of Quaker Oats Limited in 1985, and the restricted distribution amongst this company's customers and employees has made this a very desirable jug today. Pick-Kwik Wines and Spirits of Derby commissioned a range of small-size character jugs, some adapted as liquor containers, to promote their various whiskies. As well as the traditional pre-announced limited editions, they also issued collectors editions and special editions — new terms coined to describe commissions by independent companies that are not individually numbered limited editions in the strictest sense. Special editions have included colourways (discussed in the section on colour variations) and entirely new jugs, such as the Collecting World Series for Kevin Francis and the Great Generals series for UK International Ceramics.

There have also been occasional special commissions, which are limited by time and distribution rather than by numbers. For example, in 1984 only members of the Royal Doulton International Collectors Club could purchase a small- size Henry Doulton character jug, and in 1986 the offer was a small Doultonville toby of Albert Sagger, the Potter. Similarly, only customers attending Michael Doulton's special appearances in 1988 and 1989 could buy the character jug portrait of him. In 1991 Royal Doulton launched their new Character Jug of the Year concept, which limits the model to one year's production, and this has proved very popular.

In the last few years there has been a new approach to limited character jugs with the launch of several exceptionally complex and detailed models in low editions at premium prices. Some of these prestige jugs had two handles, or even three, and gold or silver embellishments. The first of this type was Henry VIII, issued in 1991 in a limited edition of 1,991 to mark the 500th anniversary of his birth. The edition was quickly oversubscribed, endorsing collectors' very positive reactions to these ambitious designs. Another recent development which has generated a lot of interest is the collection of limited-edition toby jugs, which began in 1992 with the Jester.

PROTOTYPES AND VARIATIONS

Once all the standard range jugs have been acquired, the ultimate challenge for many serious collectors is to find as many prototypes and variations as possible. This usually requires a very healthy bank balance, as huge sums of money can change hands for these rare pieces.

Prototypes

Prototype jugs are the samples taken from the master mould, and they are often described as pilots or trials. Usually two or three jugs are cast at this early stage, any more would wear down the detail in the master mould, and they are given different decorative treatments. If one of the prototypes is approved, then lots of production moulds will be made, but if it is rejected, the model will only exist in prototype form. There have been lots of character jugs and at least a few toby jugs that did not get past the prototype stage for various reasons.

In the 1920s Charles Noke modelled a toby jug of John Wesley, the founder of Methodism, but when the prototypes came from the kiln, he had misgivings about the propriety of portraying a strict abstainer as a toby. He therefore abandoned the project, giving one of the prototype jugs to the decorator Ted Eley, another was later presented to the Museum of the Wesley Church in Tasmania.

Prototype of The Maori modelled by Harry Fenton in 1939

During the 1930s most of the jugs that were modelled seem to have gone into production, but the war interrupted several plans. In the Royal Doulton archives there are references to an Old Scrooge jug and one called Red Wing, but no illustrations have survived. Harry Fenton modelled two portraits of a New Zealand Maori, one of which was approved in July 1939, but it did not subsequently go into the general range. A few examples survive in private collections around the world, and the last one to come on the market in 1998 sold for £21,000. No records survive for the Buffalo Bill jug, which presumably also dates from the war years and was modelled by Fenton.

The 1950s seem to have passed with only two casualties. The Scarlet Pimpernell, which was submitted by Geoff Blower, surfaced in 1987 and changed hands for over £15,000. Blower's colleague Garry Sharpe remembered his portrait of Alice in Wonderland being turned down in 1959 because of copyright restrictions, but no examples have come to light, so perhaps it did not get beyond the clay stage.

During the 1960s a rejected Village Blacksmith was rescued from a Doulton rubbish skip by a factory labourer, and his family sold it, in 1993, at Phillips Auction rooms in London for over £7,000. It is probably the work of design manager Max Henk, and it was given a pattern number D6549 in 1961, so it is strange that it was never launched.

David Biggs was responsible for many of the successful character jugs produced during the 1960s, but several of his prototypes were rejected at the end of the decade, possibly because of the re-appraisal of the collection and the change-over to bone china production, which took place at that time. He remembers submitting a Racing Driver, but this has not come to light. However, his models of of a Fisherman (1968), John Gilpin (1968) and two colourways of The Baseball Player (1971) are in private collections, and his ambitious Pilgrim Father was discovered at Royal Doulton in 1988.

Several new modellers joined the design department in the 1970s, and inevitably some of their early work was not accepted for production. Robert Tabbenor's character jug of Uncle Tom Cobbleigh was rejected in 1975 and Peter Gee's Jester toby in 1977. Although both artists later produced popular jugs, they made figure modelling their speciality. Michael Abberley's Cabinet Maker of Williamsburg, which he modelled in 1979, caused a lot of confusion, as it was publicised in the 1981 catalogue but was not launched then, as it was decided to discontinue the Williamsburg range. In August 1995 it finally joined the collection at the RDICC convention in Williamsburg to mark the 15th anniversary of the club. Bill Harper's first character jug of a pirate was rejected in 1976, but he has gone on to contribute a wide range of subjects to the range. Unfortunately his admirable portrait of Pierre Trudeau (1986) missed the boat as the Canadian Prime Minister had left office before the jug was ready to be launched. In 1987 Bill was keen to produce a Canterbury Tales series of jugs but it was felt that the Miller and The Wife of Bath were not sufficiently well-known internationally, and so they remain in prototype form in Royal Doulton's own collection. Bill also submitted a portrait of Elvis Presley for the Celebrity collection, but it was not approved by the singer's estate. Several stars in this hapless series did not get beyond the prototype stage, but they have found their way on to the market. In 1992 one of the Marilyn Monroe prototypes was auctioned in Canada for $17,500 and a Humphrey Bogart prototype has also changed hands for a significant sum. A portrait of Clark Gable had got beyond the prototype stage and several hundred had been made in 1984 before it was recalled for copyright reasons, so although not unique, it is still a rare model.

A few more jugs "got away" in the late 1980s, including a portrayal of Robin Hood by Eric Griffiths, Uncle Sam by Harry Sales and a Prison Warder by Stan Taylor, and no doubt there will be more in the future, although the art director's ideal is not to reach the expensive prototype stage until all the production problems have been ironed out. For this reason original clay models are smashed or left to dry out and crumble to dust if they do not come up to scratch.

Often the design of the character jug is basically acceptable, but there are reservations about the handle. Usually this is resolved at the clay stage, as with the Collectors Club jug of Henry Doulton, which originally incorporated a drainpipe in the handle to symbolise the firm's original achievements. It was felt that this was too mundane a reminder and the vase motif was emphasised instead. Occasionally alternative handles have been moulded, and for the Catharine of Aragon character jug two different designs featuring a cornet and a scroll were considered before the version with the tower was agreed upon.

It is not only aesthetic considerations which lead to modifications, cost is also an important factor and handles occasionally need to be simplified. For example, the prototype of Groucho Marx included the other Marx brothers peeping out from behind his cigar, and they were subsequently removed for the production model. Eagle-eyed collectors have often noticed other minor modifications. The original version of the Fireman character jug, which was used for publicity purposes, featured the badge of the London Fire Brigade, but this was changed when permission to use it was not granted. Discrepancies such as these have always had a particular fascination for jug collectors, and premium prices are paid when original-version prototypes come up for sale.

Modelling Variations

If a character jug is altered once it has gone into production, it can no longer be described as a prototype, but there is still a lot of interest in such modelling variations, and there are more of them around for collectors to find. The Anne of Cleves character jug is a celebrated example. When it was launched in 1980, the ears on the horse handle were erect, but as these were easily chipped they were soon remodelled to lie flat. A premium is now paid for the first "ears up" version. Similarly with the original handle of the Macbeth jug, the large protruding noses on the witches were prone to damage and consequently the heads were turned inwards. It would appear that only a few of the original jugs had been made before modification, so the "noses out" version is extremely rare.

Some of the early character jugs have also been modified, although the reasons for the changes are not so apparent. Harry Fenton's Granny, which was introduced in 1935, was revamped within a few years. The proportions of her face were altered and a white frill was added to the front of her bonnet, but the most significant addition was a prominent front tooth. This resulted in the original version being dubbed the "Toothless Granny," and she commands considerably more in the marketplace than the second version, which continued in production until 1983. Fenton's Cavalier also exists in two versions; the original from 1940 features a goatee beard, which is missing from the later version, but it now makes a big difference in price if he is bearded.

The war years seem to have been a period of change and reappraisal generally. Apart from the modifications already mentioned, Drake acquired a plumed hat, making the original, hatless version something of a rarity, and Pearly

Style One: Hatless Drake

Boy lost his relief-modelled buttons to become plain 'Arry. His companion, Pearly Girl, was not remodelled, but was decorated differently to become 'Arriet. The original Pearly Boy and Girl character jugs are now amongst the rarest production models to find.

Colour Variations

Changes of colour can make a significant difference to the desirability of jugs, as has been seen with the Pearly Girl. The presence of a lime green and pink hat, as opposed to the drab green worn by 'Arriet, will attract a substantial premium. Pearly Boy has also worn different coloured outfits, and the blue version is considered to be much rarer than the brown. Another expensive variation is Fenton's Old King Cole. The original, which dates from 1939, has a yellow crown, and the second common version an orange one. There are also slight modelling variations in the ruff, but the colour differences are the most pronounced.

The Clown character jug features the most radical of the early colour changes. In the first version, introduced in 1937, he has a white painted face with bright red hair, whilst the post-war version has natural flesh tones with white hair. There is also a brown-hair variation, which is contemporary with the red-haired model. All the clowns are desirable additions to a collection, but the red and brown-haired versions are priced higher.

In the early years alternative colour schemes for character jugs were unusual, but from the mid 1980s it became standard practice to offer the most popular models in different outfits. A few of these went into the general range, but most were special commissions in limited editions. The first, in 1985, was a colourway of the large-size Mad Hatter, which was produced in an edition of 250 to celebrate the opening of the Royal Doulton room at Higbees department store in the US, and it sold out on the day of issue. Many

more special colourway editions followed this early success, but their appeal gradually diminished until ultimately the practice ceased at the end of the decade.

During long production runs, colours have frequently been altered for technical reasons, and the results of the new recipes are often noticed by serious collectors. The most obvious in recent years was the Beefeater, who received an on-glaze red jacket in 1987 instead of the early underglaze maroon shade. There have also been other modifications to this long-lived jug. In the first year or so of production, the Royal Cypher GR was picked out in gold, and this is now very rare. When Queen Elizabeth was crowned in 1953, the handle was altered again to feature her cypher ER.

Character and toby jugs are all painted individually by different artists, and so inevitably there will be slight variations in colour between one and another, even though everybody is following the same standard. Occasionally mistakes are made, colours might be reversed or omitted, and they can cause a lot of interest amongst collectors when they slip through the system. An interesting error was spotted in 1984, when the first Custer and Sitting Bull character jugs left the factory. The Indian chief was depicted with grey eyes and, when it was pointed out that this was genetically unlikely, the eyes were altered to brown. There are no prizes for guessing which variation is the most sought after! Around the same time a small quantity of Henry V jugs left the factory without the on-glaze red and gold decoration, and initially they caused some excitement in the marketplace before it was realised they were seconds. Colour variations do not always command premium prices, but it is still fun looking out for them.

DERIVATIVES

Novelty coupled with practicality became Charles Noke's maxim during the 1930s, as his fertile imagination contorted many of his favourite character jug personalities into all sorts of useful items, including teapots, tobacco jars, ashtrays and wall vases. Collecting these derivatives, as they are known, can add another dimension to Doulton displays. It is possible to find Old Charley in 15 different guises, including character jugs, tobies and derivatives, and Sairey Gamp comes a close second in the variety of her appearances, so putting together displays of these characters alone could be fun.

It may be that Noke was given the idea for the derivatives from the novel toby wares made by Harry Simeon at the Lambeth studio, and it is probably not a coincidence that the Burslem factory was also commissioned to model character decanters for Aspreys and Co. The resulting Scotsman and Irishman whisky containers were issued in 1934 and can be considered forerunners of the derivatives. Bookends, busts and napkin rings of Dickens personalities followed, and although they have more in common with Noke's figures from the HN series, they are still sought after by jug enthusiasts.

The first true character jug derivatives were the ashtrays of 1936, which are essentially miniature-size jugs with trays added. These must have been successful, for larger ashbowls and tobacco jars were soon added to the range. Generally only minor modifications were required to suit the character

Complete set of Sairey Gamp character jugs together with a sugar bowl and bust

jugs for their new purposes. The musical jugs, for instance, had an extended hollow base to accommodate the Thorens Swiss movement which played the appropriate tune. In contrast, Harry Fenton's creative powers were fully stretched to incorporate Sairey Gamp, Tony Weller and Old Charley into teapots! Although it is highly unlikely that these figurative teapots were used, they soon had matching sugar bowls. Perhaps milk jugs would have followed if it had not been for the outbreak of war, which abruptly curtailed production of all these whimsical gift items. Consequently all the early derivatives are considered rare.

It was not until the late 1950s that designers were once again able to turn their attention to the novelty gift market. A range of table lighters in the form of jug personalities was launched in 1958, and some of these now prove elusive. As well as the 14 lighters recorded in the catalogues, a prototype Granny lighter has also made an appearance in the market. Most of the post-war derivatives have been liquor containers made to order for various distillers and bottlers, including W. Walklate, Pick-Kwik and William Grant, and perhaps there will be more in the future. The Royal Doulton International Collectors Club has also played its part in keeping the derivatives in focus by reviving the potty teapot tradition. In 1988 they commissioned the Old Salt Teapot especially for members, and this led to the introduction of several new character teapots of The Old Balloon Seller, Long John Silver and Falstaff. As they were only in the range for a brief period, they will eventually become as hard to find as some of the early derivatives.

LIMITED-EDITION LOVING CUPS AND JUGS

A few years before the successful launch of character jugs, Charles Noke and Harry Fenton had already collaborated on a spectacular range of limited-edition loving cups and jugs. These large, colourful pieces are vigorously modelled in low relief, and they feature many of the characters who were later portrayed as jugs. Thus in terms of subject and style, they are closely related to character and toby jugs, and consequently many keen collectors seek them out as display centrepieces. Unfortunately they are not easy to find, as most

were only made for a short period during the 1930s, and they were produced in very small editions of 300 to 1,000, some of which were never completed. Also it is inevitable that some have been broken in the intervening years, so not surprisingly, they are expensive when they do appear on the market.

These loving cups and jugs were Royal Doulton's very first limited-edition pieces and, as such, represent the zenith of Noke's achievements as art director. The accompanying certificates of authenticity are almost as splendid as the items they describe, with elaborate illustrations, ribboned seals and Noke's signature written in ink. Understandably many collectors have these documents framed as works of art in their own right. Further authentification and the unique number of the loving cup or jug appears on the base, which is usually equally decorative, with appropriate motifs or symbols. Perhaps the most novel is the treasure chart on the base of The Treasure Island jug.

Wandering Minstrel Loving Cup

The majority of the loving cups and jugs stand around 10 inches high, and the scene unfolds in relief, painted in glowing underglaze colours. The handles are often ingeniously linked to the subject; for instance, the John Peel loving cup has a riding crop and fox head, whilst the Guy Fawkes jug has a flaming torch. It is interesting that symbolic handles such as these later became a major feature of the character jug range.

Many of the subjects reflect Noke's literary interests, which he regularly explored in the series ware, figures and character jug collections, in particular the writings of Dickens and Shakespeare and popular adventure stories such as The Three Musketeers and Treasure Island. The exploits of real-life seafaring heroes, such as Drake, Nelson and Cook, were also celebrated in the range.

Noke realised at an early stage that these prestige pieces were ideal for commemorating important historical and royal events, and so the bicentenary of the birth of George Washington in 1932 was marked with a patriotic American jug, bedecked in stars and stripes, whilst the anniversary of the founding of New South Wales was recalled by the launch of the Captain Phillip jug. There was no shortage of royal events to celebrate during the 1930s, and loving cups with portraits of the monarchs, emblazoned with flags and regalia, were issued for the Silver Jubilee of George V and the coronation of George VI. There are even three different coronation loving cups for Edward VIII, who, of course, was never crowned, but some of the editions had been sold before his abdication. Years later these ceremonial loving cups were revived for the Coronation and Silver Jubilee of Queen Elizabeth II in 1953 and 1977 respectively, and perhaps they will be used again for important royal occasions in the future.

In 1982 the Royal Doulton International Collectors Club commissioned a loving cup in traditional style depicting Pottery in the Past, and as it was only made in small numbers for members, it is becoming increasingly difficult to find.

Collecting all the limited-edition loving cups and jugs will prove to be something of a challenge, and as with all Royal Doulton wares, there are also some tantalising prototypes and variations. To date nobody has found the trials of Roger Solemel, Cobbler, and I.T. Wigg, Broom-man, but one lucky collector has a prototype George Washington presentation jug with a different stars and stripes handle. This variation was not recorded in the Royal Doulton archives, and there may well be others to be found, so happy hunting.

MAKING CHARACTER AND TOBY JUGS

Each Royal Doulton character and toby jug goes through the hands of many skilled and experienced individuals. From ÿthe designer to the painter to the kiln manager, each person is responsible for ensuring the quality of the finished article.

Today the diverse ideas for new jugs usually originate in the company's marketing department, and following discussions with the design managers, the modeller is briefed about the required subject. A great deal of research goes into the initial concept. If a historical personality is to be depicted, contemporary paintings, photographs and other records are studied to ensure accuracy in features and costume. For a fictional character, the designer needs to read the relevant book and consider any illustrations before embarking on sketches. Some Royal Doulton artists submit drawings of their proposed subject, others prefer to work directly with the modelling clay to visualise their ideas.

A careful balance must be achieved between portraiture and caricature, good humour and dignity, to create a jug suitable for the Royal Doulton range. The symbolism of the handle, which is now such an important element of the design, also requires a lot of thought and ingenuity. When the modeller is completely satisfied with his work, it goes for approval to the art and marketing directors, who occasionally suggest modifications to improve the design or avert potting problems. It is vital that everybody is happy with the jug at this stage, because the lines and details of this master model will determine the exact appearance of the finished piece.

The mould-maker then takes over and carefully disects the original to create plaster of Paris moulds of each part. Usually a four-part mould is required, for the head and the handle are moulded separately. A few sample jugs, known as prototypes, will be cast from the master mould for further discussion and colour trials. Ideally only two or three prototypes are produced, as with each casting the intricate detail of the mould is gradually worn away. If the prototype is approved at one of the design conferences, a rubber working "case" is made from the master mould, and it is from this case that all the subsequent plaster of Paris production moulds are made.

In the casting department a liquid clay mixture known as slip is poured into the production moulds through a hole in the top. The porous plaster absorbs the water in the slip and a layer of solid clay is formed in the interior of the mould. When this has reached the required thickness, the excess slip is drained away and the mould is taken apart for the various cast sections to be extracted. The separate parts of the jug are assembled using slip as an adhesive and the rough edges and seams smoothed away in a process known as fettling.

After drying at a controlled temperature, the jugs are ready to receive their first firing in the electric tunnel kiln. This is known as the "biscuit" firing because of the texture of the jug when it emerges from the kiln. On completion the fragile clay body has shrunk by about an eighth of its original size, becoming hard and durable.

The white biscuit jug is then taken to the decorating studio, where special pigments suitable for underglaze painting are used. Painting directly onto the porous biscuit body gives the rugged character lines and wrinkles required in many jug subjects. Considerable care and expertise is required at this stage, as some colours can change during the fixing process in the hardening — on kiln.

After this second, low-temperature firing, the jug is ready to be glazed, and this is done by either spraying it with a liquid glass mixture or dipping it into a vat of the same mixture. The glossy, protective finish is achieved by firing the jug again, this time in a glost kiln. In many cases, this completes the process, but some brightly coloured jugs have a further coat of paint applied on top of the glaze, and they need to be fired a fourth time to seal the colours permanently. Before leaving the factory, the finished jugs are inspected by the quality control staff to ensure there are no flaws, and they are then packed for despatch all over the world.

BODIES AND GLAZES

Stoneware

The first Doulton jugs were produced at the Lambeth factory in London, and these were made of salt-glaze stoneware, a high-fired ceramic body which is literally glazed with salt thrown into the kiln at peak temperatures. Bodies range from a plain buff to a rich brown, which is sometimes dipped in a darker coloured slip to create a two-tone effect. Muted colours can be achieved in this high-temperature process, but only the Simeon toby wares were additionally coloured with a bright red on-glaze enamel colour.

Earthenware, Kingsware and China

The first character and toby jugs produced at Royal Doulton's factory in Nile Street, Burslem, were mostly made of white earthenware, although the treacle-coloured Kingsware body was used for some early commissions. For a brief period, between 1968 and 1973, character jugs were made in English Translucent China, a porcelain body pioneered by Doulton chemists in 1959. All the jugs had to be remodelled for this process, and so collectors will notice differences in detail between earthenware and ETC jugs. However, the most obvious variation is the size, as the china body fires about a half- inch smaller than the earthenware.

Following Royal Doulton's acquisition of the John Beswick factory, it was decided to concentrate the production of jugs at this location in Longton, and the earthenware body was revived. Consequently, since 1973 new models have been produced in earthenware and painted under the glaze, although some recent designs also have on-glaze decoration, particularly to achieve bright reds, blues or metallic effects.

In the early 1980s there was some research at the Nile Street factory to revive the china body for character jugs, in order to cope with the demand for the Antagonists and Beatles collections, and although the experiment was short-lived, occasional china examples come on to the market.

White Jugs

From time to time, white-glazed versions of standard character jugs appear on the market, and these are highly valued by collectors. Most were made from the late 1930s to the early 1950s when wartime restrictions prohibited the production of decorated china for the UK market. It is believed that white biscuit jugs with slight flaws, which could not be decorated for the export market, were glazed for sale to company employees.

These white substandard jugs should not be confused with the white character jug portrait of Winston Churchill, which was originally conceived undecorated, no doubt because of the UK embargo. Examples are rare because it did not remain in production for long.

During the 1930s D&J McCallum, the whisky distillers, commissioned a white version of their Highlander jug, as well as the better-known Kingsware variety. Numbers were limited to around 1,000 and they are hard to find today. Fifty years later Pick-Kwik Wines and Spirits of Derby commissioned two undecorated variations in their extensive range of promotional jugs. Only 100 of each were made of the Micawber character jug and spirit container for internal promotional use.

Occasionally modern white character jugs have turned up at local auctions and markets, but it would appear that these have "escaped" from the factory in an undecorated state and been glazed to cater for the strong market demand for white jugs.

CARE AND REPAIR

Character and toby jugs are relatively robust and easy to look after. The glaze seals and protects the colours permanently, and occasional dusting will maintain the shiny finish. If the jugs are displayed on open shelves, it is a good idea to fill the interior with crumpled tissue paper, as this catches the dust and can be replaced easily at cleaning times. When necessary, jugs can be washed in luke-warm water using a mild detergent, then rinsed thoroughly and dried naturally or buffed with a soft cloth. Care should be taken not to knock jugs against the tap or each other – the rims and handles are the most vulnerable parts. If an accident does happen, there are professional restorers who can make "invisible" repairs to chips and cracks, even hairlines.

Obviously when buying on the secondary market, it is advisable to check very carefully for restorations such as these, as they are not immediately obvious to the naked eye. Expert dealers have many different ways of spotting repairs. Rarely do they carry an ultraviolet lamp that will highlight problem areas, instead they become sensitive to the different vibrations given by the softer restored areas when tapped with a metallic object or even bitten with the teeth! Reputable dealers will stand by any guarantees they give regarding restorations. Prices should reflect the level of damage sustained and the quality of the ÿrestoration.

Occasionally old jugs have been used as containers, and these can appear at flea markets quite dirty and stained. If washing fails, petroleum jelly will usually remove stubborn rust marks. It is worth persevering — apparently the rare, coloured Churchill character jug, which made over £16,000 at auction in 1989, had originally been used as a storage jar under the kitchen sink.

A GUIDE TO BACKSTAMPS AND DATING

The marks on the base of a character jug can be a useful guide for dating the piece, particularly if it has been in production for a while. However, it is impossible to be precise, as stocks of old-style backstamps continued to be used up after changes had been implemented. Nevertheless, jugs can usually be placed in a specific time period and, very occasionally, if there is a date code, an exact year of manufacture can be determined.

The Royal Doulton Trademark

Most prominent on the base is the Royal Doulton factory mark, which has featured a lion standing on a crown ever since the company was awarded the Royal Warrant in 1901. It is unusual for a jug not to have a Royal Doulton trademark, but occasionally prototypes have been found with a blank base, and these have been authenticated by the company in Stoke-on-Trent.

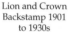

Lion and Crown Backstamp 1901 to 1930s   Made in England was added in the 1930s

The early Royal Doulton trademark is found on some of the first Burslem toby jugs, such as Charlie Chaplin, and on the McCallum character jugs. By the early 1930s, the words "Made in England" had been incorporated in the lion and crown trademark, and this style of backstamp has been recorded, with no other information, on some of the first character jugs. Most of the toby jugs issued between 1939 and 1950 are marked with this backstamp and the title of the character portrayed. Copyright information was either nonexistent or kept to a minimum, unlike the character jugs.

The 1930s

In order to protect their designs from being copied, Royal Doulton registered them at the UK patent office, and the resulting registration number (e.g. RdNo782778 for John Barleycorn) is often printed underneath the backstamp. The year the jug was registered can be worked out from the table of numbers published by the patent office. Usually registration was a year before the jug went into production, but on occasion the number was not issued in time and the words "Reg. applied for" were added to the backstamp (this has also been found misspelt "Registeration"). It should be noted that the registration number does not give the date of manufacture for a specific piece, only when the design was first protected.

Around 1938 Royal Doulton also began to register their designs in Australia, and the information "Regd in Australia" was added to the backstamp.

By the late 1930s, the name of the jug in inverted commas was usually included above the registration number (e.g. "The Cavalier"). Jugs produced during the 1930s might also have a hand-painted D pattern number, which was added by the decorator when the jug was completed. This practice continued until the Second World War.

Registered trademak below backstamp. Printed numeral '14' stands for 1941   Regd in Australia. Name in inverted commas

All the above details will help date a piece to the 1930s, but the only way to determine the exact year of manufacture is with the date code, if it has one. This numbering system began in 1928 with the number one. The date-code number is immediately to the right of the lion and crown symbol, and the year of manufacture can be calculated by adding it to 1927. Thus the code number 11 will give a date of 1938, and 15 indicates 1942. This code system can be found on character jugs from the 1930s and 40s.

The 1940s and 1950s

A capital A on the left of the lion and crown symbol is known as the A mark and it is a kiln control mark denoting a specific type of earthenware body known as Georgian. Sometimes an A mark appears on a character jug without any other information. It was used on a variety of Royal Doulton products between 1939 and 1955, so its presence on character jugs will date the piece to within that time period.

'A' to the left of the Lion and Crown   Copyright mark

After the war Royal Doulton found it necessary to register their designs in more of their main export markets, and a new style backstamp was devised in 1947. This gives a copyright date for Doulton and Co Limited and four different registration numbers for the UK, Australia, South Africa and New Zealand. A few jugs introduced in 1950 only have three registration numbers.

From circa 1952 a printed D pattern number appears above the copyright date, and a few years later the inverted commas around the character's name were dropped. Several different typefaces appear to have been used.

The 1960s and 1970s

New UK copyright laws in 1966 gave protection in each country without separate design registrations. Protection was extended to articles previously registered, and as the period of registration ran out, the relevant numbers were withdrawn from the backstamp. By circa 1973 the lists had disappeared altogether and a new copyright symbol was adopted, "C" in place of "Copr." From 1975 the company's new name, Royal Doulton Tableware Ltd, began to appear in the copyright notice, and many collectors were puzzled by this reference to tableware on gift items.

The 1980s and 1990s

A large elegant script was adopted for the character names in the early 1980s, and by 1983 the first reference to hand made and hand decorated had been included underneath. The new Doultonville tobies also adopted this improved style. An entirely new design of backstamp was introduced in 1984, featuring the new styling for the company name, Royal Doulton, the subject of the jug in bold capitals, the modeller's facsimile signature and the words "Hand made and hand decorated" forming an arch around the lion and crown. These changes were implemented in order to acknowledge the talents of individual artists and to seek public recognition of the specialist production skills involved. Initials or dots and dashes on the base are decorator's marks, but no records exist to identify these.

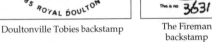

Doultonville Tobies backstamp	The Fireman backstamp

In the last ten years backstamps have become increasingly interesting and attractive, as evocative images and typefaces are chosen to capture the spirit of the subject matter; for example, the Journey through Britain series has lots of novel backstamp motifs, including a hose for the Fireman jug and postage stamp for the Postman. The Celebrity collection has a Hollywood-billboard typeface and relevant quotes from the characters portrayed. This is not a completely new idea, as one of the earliest jugs, Mephistopheles, was inscribed with a quotation about the devil by Rabelais. Not all the jugs carry this inscription, however, and keen collectors are prepared to pay a slight premium for this feature.

Promotional and Commemorative Backstamps

There are many other interesting backstamp variations which ardent collectors will seek out. During the 1930s several independent companies commissioned standard character jugs with their name printed on the base for promotional purposes, and this can now add to the value of the jug. Amongst the names to look for are Coleman's, Bentall's, Darley and Sons and the Salt River Cement Works. In 1967, to celebrate the Canadian Centenary, the North American Indian and Trapper jugs were launched with a special backstamp in North America only, and this was deleted for worldwide sales the following year. The presence of this commemorative backstamp will double the price of these jugs.

This practice of pre-releasing has continued in recent years for Royal Doulton's important customers. For example, the first two jugs in the Celebrity series, W.C. Fields and Mae West, were produced in a premier edition for American Express, and a small premium is payable for this backstamp.

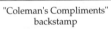

"Coleman's Compliments" backstamp	"Winston Churchill Prime Minister of Great Britain 1940"

Generally speaking the backstamps on toby jugs do not excite collectors, the exception being the portrait of Winston Churchill, which originally had a backstamp commemorating "Winston Churchill Prime Minister of Great Britain 1940." This was deleted after 1940, and so jugs with this mark are very rare and consequently expensive.

Other Guides to Dating

Much can obviously be gleaned from the backstamp as to the age of a character jug, but occasionally there are some other clues. It used to be the practice with large-size jugs to continue painting inside the rim, and this is referred to by collectors as bleeding. As this method was discontinued by 1973, it is possible to date jugs with this trait before then. Having checked the rim, look into the character's eyes! It is not as strange as it sounds, for early-style modelling was to indent the iris, and this continued until the early 1960s. For a few years between 1968 and 1973, character jugs were produced in a type of porcelain known as ETC, so pieces in this body must have been made during this short period.

Other clues are specific to certain models; for example, early versions of Auld Mac have "Owd Mac" on the backstamp and also impressed in the tammy. Toby Philpots was spelt with a double t until circa 1952, so those spelt Toby Philpotts date from the 1930s or 40s. The Beefeater has a couple of unique clues. Until circa 1953 it was called "Beefeaters" on the backstamp, and following the coronation of Queen Elizabeth in 1953, the handle was remodelled with a new Royal cypher (see Modelling Variations).

ROYAL DOULTON COLLECTORS CLUB AND GUILD

Royal Doulton International Collectors Club

Founded in 1980, the Royal Doulton International Collectors Club provides an information service on all aspects of the company's products, past and present. A club magazine, *Gallery*, is published four times a year with information on new products and current events that will keep the collector up-to-date on the happenings in the world of Royal Doulton. Upon joining the club, each new member will receive a free gift and invitations to special events and exclusive offers throughout the year.

To join the Royal Doulton Collectors Club, please contact your local stockist, or contact the club directly at the address or telephone numbers below:

Royal Crown Derby Collectors Guild

The Royal Crown Derby Collectors Guild was established in 1994 to establish closer contact with Royal Crown Derby Collectors. Membership entitles the collector to a yearly subscription to the quarterly *Gallery* magazine, *Royal Crown Derby News*, membership gifts and free admission to the Royal Crown Derby Visitor Centre.

To join the Royal Crown Derby Collectors Guild, please contact the guild at the address or telephone number below:

Minton House
London Road, Stoke-on-Trent
Staffordshire ST4 7QD, England

Telephone:
U.K.: (01782) 292127
U.S.A. and Canada: 1-800-747-3045 (toll free)
Australia: 011-800-142624 (toll free)
Fax: U.K.: (01782) 292099
Attn.: Maria Murtagh

Caithness Glass Paperweight Collectors Society
Caithness Glass International Paperweight Collectors Society

Formed in 1997, by Colin Terris, the society is the clearing house for all information on Caithness Glass Paperweights. Membership of the society entitles the collector to receive *Reflections*, the society's twice yearly magazine, plus three newsletters and a personal tour of the paperweight studios in Perth, Scotland, if you are ever in the area. An annual International Convention is held in Scotland in October.

To join the Caithness Glass Paperweight Collectors Society, please contact the society at one of the addresses or telephone numbers below:

In the U.K. and International
Caithness Glass Paperweight Collectors Scoiety
Caithness Glass Inc.
Inveralmond, Perth PH1 3TZ, Scotland
Tel.: (44) (0) 1738 637373
Fax: (44) (0) 1738 622494

In the U.S.A.
Caithness Glass Paperweight Collectors Society
Caithness Glass Inc.
141 Lanza Avenue, Building No. 12
Garfield, N.J. 07026, U.S.A.
Tel.: 973-340-3330
Fax: 973-340-9415

COLLECTOR CLUB CHAPTERS

Chapters of the RDICC have formed across North America and are worthy of consideration in those areas.

Detroit Chapter
Frank Americk, President
1771 Brody, Allen Park, MI 48101

Edmonton Chapter
Mildred's Collectibles
6813 104 Street, Edmonton, AB

New England Chapter
Charles Wood, President
Charles Briggs, Secretary
21 Walpole Street, Norwood, MA 02062
Tel.: (781) 784-8121

Northern California Chapter
Donald A. Blubaugh, President
P.O. Box 3665, Walnut Creek, CA 94598
Tel.: (925) 945-1687 Fax: (925) 938-6674
Blubaugh@usa.net

Northwest, Bob Haynes, Chapter
Alan Matthew, President
15202 93rd Place N.E., Bothell, WA 98011
Tel.: (425) 488-9604

Ohio Chapter
Reg Marvis, President
Dick Maschmeier, Treasurer
5556 White Haven Avenue,
North Olmstead, Ohio 44070
Tel.: (216) 779 5554

Rochester Chapter
Judith L. Trost President
103 Garfield Street, Rochester, N.Y. 14611
Tel.: (716) 436-3321

Western Pennsylvania Chapter
John Re, President
9589 Parkedge Drive, Allison Park, PA 15101
Tel.: (412) 366-0201 Fax: (412) 366-2558

ROYAL DOULTON VISITOR CENTRES

Royal Doulton Visitor Centre

Opened in the summer of 1996, the Royal Doulton Visitor Centre houses the largest collection of Royal Doulton figurines in the world. The centre also is home to the Minton Fine Art Studio, which specializes in hand painting and gilding. Demonstration areas offer the collector a first hand insight on how figurines are assembled and decorated. Also at the Visitor Centre is a cinema showing a 20 minute video on the history of Royal Doulton, plus a restaurant, and a retail shop offering both best quality ware and slight seconds.

Factory tours may be booked, Monday to Friday, at the Visitor Centre.

Nile Street, Burslem
Stoke-on-Trent, ST6 2AJ, England
Tel.: (01782) 292434
Fax: (01782) 292424
Attn.: Yvonne Wood

Royal Doulton John Beswick Studios

Tours of the John Beswick Factory and Museum are available Monday to Thursday by appointment only. Please book in advance.

Gold Street, Longton
Stoke-on-Trent, ST3 2JP, England
Tel.: (01782) 291213
Fax: (01782) 291279
Attn.: Joan Barker

Royal Crown Derby Visitor Centre

Opened in the spring of 1998, the Visitor Centre was created to provide an insight into the tradition, history and skills that go into making Royal Crown Derby collectables. The centre houses the largest collection of Royal Crown Derby seen anywhere in the world, a demonstration area for skilled Royal Crown Derby artists and crafts people, restaurants, and shops.

Factory tours may be booked Monday to Friday at the centre, with advance bookings suggested.

194 Osmaston Road
Derby, DE23 8JZ, England
Tel.: (01332) 712841
Fax: (01332) 712899
Attn.: Stella Birks

Caithness Glass Visitor Centre

The Visitor Centre is home to the largest public display of Caithness Glass paperweights. Over 1200 designs are on display. A special viewing gallery enables visitors to watch the complete paperweight making process.

Inveralmond
Perth, PH1 3TZ, Scotland
Tel.: (44) (0)1738 637373
Fax: (44) (0)1738 622494

Factory Shops

Royal Doulton Visitor Centre
Nile Street, Burslem
Stoke-on-Trent, England
Tel.: (01782) 292451

Royal Doulton Group Factory Shop
Lawley Street, Longton, England
Stoke-on-Trent ST3 2PH
Tel.: (01782) 291172

Royal Doulton Factory Shop
Minton House, London Road
Stoke-on-Trent, ST4 7QD, England
Tel.: (01782) 292121

Royal Doulton Factory Shop
Leek New Road, Baddeley Green,
Stoke-on-Trent ST2 7HS, England
Tel.: (01782) 291700

Royal Doulton Factory Shop
Victoria Road, Fenton,
Stoke-on-Trent ST4 2PJ, England
Tel.: (01782) 291869

Beswick Factory Shop
Barford Street, Longton,
Stoke-on-Trent. ST3 2JP, England
Tel.: (01782) 291237

Web Site and E-mail Addresses

Sites: www.royal-doulton.com
www.caithnessglass.co.uk
E-mail:
Clubs: icc@royal-doulton.com
Visitor Centre: Visitor@royal-doulton.com
Consumer Enquiries: enquiries@royal-doulton.com
Museum Curator: heritage@royal-doulton.com
Lawleys by Post: lbp@royal-doulton.com

WHERE TO BUY

Discontinued Doulton collectables can be found in Antique shops, Markets, Auctions, Shows and Fairs. Specialist dealers in Royal Doulton collectables attend many of the events listed below.

For Auction happenings it is necessary to subscribe to Auction Houses that hold 20th Century or Doulton Auctions.

UNITED KINGDOM
Auction Houses

BBR Auctions
Elsecar Heritage Centre
Nr. Barnsley,
South Yorkshire, S74 8HJ, England
Tel.: (01226) 745156
Fax: (01226) 351561
Attn: Alan Blakeman

Bonhams
65-69 Lots Road, Chelsea,
London, SW10 0RN, England
Tel.: (0171) 393-3900
Fax: (0171) 393-3906
www.bonhams.com
Attn: Neil Grenyer

Christie's South Kensington
85 Old Brompton Road
London, SW7 3LD, England
Tel.: (0171) 581 7611
Fax: (0171) 321-3321
www.christies.com
Attn: Michael Jeffrey

Potteries Specialist Auctions
271 Waterloo Road
Stoke-on-Trent
Staffordshire, ST6 3HR, England
Tel.: (01782) 286622
Fax: (01782) 213777
Attn: Steve Anderson

Louis Taylor
Britannia House
10 Town Road, Hanley,
Stoke-on-Trent, ST1 2QG
England
Tel.: (01782) 21411
Fax: (01782) 287874
Attn: Clive Hillier

Phillips
101 New Bond Street
London, W1Y 0AS, England
Tel.: (0171) 629-6602
Fax: (0171) 629-8876
www.phillips-auctions.com
Attn: Mark Oliver

Sotheby's
34-35 New Bond Street
London, W1A 2AA, England
Tel.: (0171) 293-5000
Fax: (0171) 293-5989
www.sothebys.com
Attn: Christina Donaldson

Sotheby's Sussex
Summers Place
Billingshurst, Sussex, RH14 9AF
England
Tel.: (01403) 833500
Fax: (01403) 833699

Thomson Roddick & Laurie
60 Whitesands
Dumfries, DG1 2RS
Scotland
Tel.: (01387) 255366
Fax: (01387) 266236
Attn: Sybelle Medcalf

Peter Wilson Auctioneers
Victoria Gallery, Market Street
Nantwich, Cheshire, CW5 5DG
England
Tel.: (01270) 623878
Fax: (01270) 610508
Attn: Stella Ashbrook or
        Robert Stone

Antique Fairs

Doulton and Beswick Collectors Fair
National Motorcycle Museum, Meriden, Birmingham,
Usually March and August
For information on times and dates:
Doulton and Beswick Dealers Association
(0181) 303 3316

Doulton and Beswick Collectors Fair
The Queensway Hall Civic Centre, Dunstable,
Bedfordshire. Usually in October.
For information on times and location:
UK Fairs Ltd. 10 Wilford Bridge Spur,
Melton,Woodbridge, Suffolk, IP12 1 RJ
901394) 386663

20th Century Fairs
266 Glossop Road, Sheffield S10 2HS, England
Usually the last week in May or the first week in June.
For information on times and dates:
Tel.: (0114) 275-0333
Fax: (0114) 275-4443

International Antique & Collectors Fair
Newark, Nottinghamshire
Usually six fairs annually.
For information on times and dates:
International Antique & Collectors Fair Ltd.
P.O. Box 100, Newark, Nottinghamshire, NG2 1DJ
(01636) 702326

West London Wade Beswick & Doulton Fair
Brunel University, Kingston Lane,
Uxbridge, Middlesex
For information on times and dates:
B & D Fairs, P.O. Box 273, Uxbridge,
Middlesex, UB9 4LP
(01895) 834694 or 834357

Yesterdays Doulton Fair
Usually November.
For information on times and location:
Doulton and Beswick Dealers Association
Tel.: (0181) 303-3316

London Markets

Alfie's Antique Market
13-25 Church Street, London
Tuesday - Saturday

Camden Passage Market
London
Wednesday and Saturday

New Caledonia Market
Bermondsey Square, London
Friday morning

Portobello Road Market
Portobello Road, London
Saturday

UNITED STATES
Auction Houses

Christie's East
219 East 67th Street
New York, NY 10021
(212) 606-0400
www.christies.com
Attn: Timothy Luke

Sotheby's Arcade Auctions
1334 York Avenue
New York, NY 10021
(212) 606-7000
www.sothebys.com
Attn: Andrew Cheney

Collectable Shows

Atlantique City
New Atlantic City Convention Centre
Atlantic City, NJ
Usually March and October
For information on times and dates:
Brimfield and Associates
P.O. Box 1800, Ocean City, NJ 08226
(609) 926-1800
www.atlantiquecity.com

Florida Doulton Convention & Sale
Sheraton Inn
1825 Griffin Road
Dania, Florida
Usually mid-January
For information on times and dates:
Pascoe and Company, 101 Almeria Avenue,
Coral Gables, Florida 33134. (305) 44503229
Charles Dombeck, 29720 Rich Walk Court
Davie, Florida 33328. (954) 452-9174

O'Hare National Antiques Show & Sale
Rosemont Convention Centre,
Chicago, IL.
Usually April, August and November
For information on times and dates:
Manor House Shows Inc.
P.O. Box 7320, Fort Lauderdale, Florida 33338
(954) 563-6747

Royal Doulton Convention & Sale
John S. Knight Convention Centre
77 E. Mill Street, Akron, Ohio 44308
Usually August.
For information on times and dates:
Colonial House Productions
182 Front Street, Berea, Ohio 44017
(800) 344-9299

CANADA
Auction Houses

Maynards
415 West 2nd Avenue, Vancouver, BC V5Y 1E3
Tel.: (604) 876-1311

Ritchie's
288 King Street East, Toronto, Ontario. M5A 1K4
Tel.: (416) 364-1864   Fax: (416) 364-0704
Attn: Caroline Kaiser

Collectable Shows

Canadian Art & Collectibles Show & Sale
Kitchener Memorial Auditorium, Kitchener, Ontario.
Usually early May.
For information on times and location:
George or Jackie Benninger
P.O. Box 130, Durham. Ont. N0G 1R0. (519) 369-6950

Canadian Doulton & Collectable Fair
Toronto, Ontario.
Usually early September.
For information on times and location:
George or Jackie Benninger
P.O. Box 130, Durham, Ont. N0G 1R0. (519) 369-6950

FURTHER READING

Storybook Figurines

The Charlton Standard Catalogue of Bunnykins by Jean Dale and Louise Irvine
Cartoon Classics and other Character Figures by Louise Irvine
Royal Doulton Bunnykins Figures by Louise Irvine
Bunnykins Collectors Book by Louise Irvine
Beatrix Potter Figures and Giftware edited by Louise Irvine
The Beswick Price Guide by Harvey May

Animals, Figures and Character Jugs

Royal Doulton Figures by Desmond Eyles, Louise Irvine and Valerie Baynton
The Charlton Standard Catalogue of Beswick Animals by Diane & John Callow
              and Marilyn & Peter Sweet
The Charlton Standard Catalogue of Royal Doulton Animals by Jean Dale
The Charlton Standard Catalogue of Royal Doulton Beswick Figurines by Jean Dale
The Charlton Standard Catalogue of Royal Doulton Beswick Jugs by Jean Dale
Collecting Character and Toby Jugs by Jocelyn Lukins
Collecting Doulton Animals by Jocelyn Lukins
Doulton Flambé Animals by Jocelyn Lukins
The Character Jug Collectors Handbook by Kevin Pearson
The Doulton Figure Collectors Handbook by Kevin Pearson

General

The Charlton Standard Catalogue of Beswick Pottery by Diane and John Callow
Discovering Royal Doulton by Michael Doulton
The Doulton Story by Paul Atterbury and Louise Irvine
Royal Doulton Series Ware by Louise Irvine (Vols. 1-5)
Limited Edition Loving Cups by Louise Irvine and Richard Dennis
Doulton for the Collector by Jocelyn Lukins
Doulton Kingsware Flasks by Jocelyn Lukins
Doulton Burslem Advertising Wares by Jocelyn Lukins
Doulton Lambeth Advertising Ware, by Jocelyn Lukins
The Doulton Lambeth Wares by Desmond Eyles
The Doulton Burslem Wares by Desmond Eyles
Hannah Barlow by Peter Rose
George Tinworth by Peter Rose
Sir Henry Doulton Biography by Edmund Gosse
Phillips Collectors Guide by Catherine Braithwaite
Royal Doulton by Jennifer Queree
John Beswick: A World of Imagination. Catalogue reprint (1950-1996)
Royal Doulton by Julie McKeown

Magazines and Newsletters

Rabbitting On (Bunnykins Newsletter) Contact Leah Selig: 2 Harper Street, Merrylands 2160
              New South Wales, Australia. Tel./Fax 61 2 9637 2410 (International), 02 637 2410 (Australia)
Collect It! Contact subscription department at: P.O. Box 3658, Bracknell, Berkshire RG12 7XZ
              Telephone: (1344) 868280 or e-mail: collectit@dialpipex.com
Collecting Doulton Magazine, Contact Doug Pinchin, P.O. Box 310, Richmond, Surrey TW9 1FS, England
Doulton News, published by Thorndon Antiques & Fine China Ltd., edited by David Harcourt
              P.O. Box 12-076 (109 Molesworth Street), Wellington, New Zealand
Beswick Quarterly (Beswick Newsletter) Contact Laura J. Rock-Smith: 10 Holmes Ct., Sayville,
              N.Y. 11782-2408, U.S.A. Tel./Fax 516-589-9027

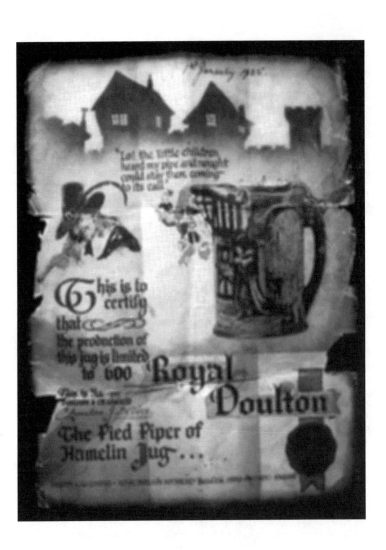

DOULTON
LAMBETH
JUGS

ADMIRAL LORD NELSON

STYLE ONE: NELSON MODELLED TO THE CHEST

The Admiral Lord Nelson jug was produced in the 1820s by Doulton and Watts in Lambeth. Although originally called a figure mug, this jug must be considered one of the first character jugs. This jug was reissued in 1905 to commemorate the 100th anniversary of the Battle of Trafalgar in which Nelson defeated the French fleet.

Backstamp B - Doulton & Watts

Backstamp C - Doulton & Watts Replica

Designer:	Unknown
Handle:	Rope
Colourway:	Saltglaze; light tan

Backstamps:	**A.** Doulton & Watts
	B. Doulton & Watts, Lambeth Pottery London
	C. Doulton & Watts Replica

Model Number	Size	Backstamp	Height	Intro.	Discon.	Current Market Value U.K. £	U.S. $	Can. $
—	Large	A and B	6 - 7 ½"	1821	1830	700.00	1,100.00	1,350.00
—	Large	C	6"	1905	Unknown	475.00	675.00	800.00
—	Small	A and B	5"	1821	1830	600.00	900.00	1,100.00
—	Miniature	A and B	2 ½"	1821	1830	425.00	700.00	800.00

ADMIRAL LORD NELSON

STYLE TWO: NELSON MODELLED TO THE WAIST

The inscription around the base of this jug is Nelson's famous words spoken before the Battle of Trafalgar, "England Expects Every Man to do his Duty." As in style one, this jug was reproduced in 1905 to commemorate the 100th anniversary of the Battle of Trafalgar.

Backstamp B - Doulton Burslem

Designer: Unknown	**Backstamp: A.** Doulton & Watts
Handle: Hair tied with a bow	Lambeth Pottery, London
Colourway: Saltglaze; light brown	**B.** Doulton Burslem

Model Number	Size	Backstamp	Height	Intro.	Discon.	Current Market Value U.K. £	U.S. $	Can. $
—	Large	A	11 ¾"	1845	Unknown	1,500.00	2,750.00	3,000.00
—	Large	B	11 ¾"	1905	1905	1,250.00	2,250.00	2,500.00

THE BEST IS NOT TOO GOOD

STYLE ONE: SMILING FACE; EYES OPEN; LEFT HAND HOLDING A PIPE
15 BUTTONS

Issued circa 1925, this jug by Harry Simeon was the forerunner of The Best is not too Good by Harry Fenton. It is wider and darker than the later version. The character has white hair, a closed mouth, a dark waistcoat with 15 light-coloured buttons, a smooth face and his whole hand encloses the pipe. The Harry Fenton jug is lighter, and the character has dark hair, white teeth on a smiling face, no tie, a dark waistcoat with 11 buttons, his face is detailed and his index finger holds the pipe.

The Best is Not Too Good, Style One

The Best is Not Too Good, Tobacco Jar

Designer: Harry Simeon
Handle: Plain
Colourway: Slate blue jacket, brown waistcoat and breeches

Backstamp: Doulton Lambeth

Model Number	Size	Backstamp	Height	Intro.	Discon.	Current Market Value		
						U.K. £	U.S. $	Can. $
8598	Small	Doulton	4 ½"	c.1925	Unknown	500.00	1,000.00	1,250.00

Derivatives of Style One

Designer: Harry Simeon
Colourway: Lidded Jar — Slate blue jacket, grey shirt, olive green breeches
Inscription around base "Ye Olde Cock Tavern 22 Fleet St Founded 1549"
Tobacco Jar — Slate blue jacket, grey shirt, olive green breeches

Model Number	Item	Height	Intro.	Discon.	Current Market Value		
					U.K. £	U.S. $	Can. $
8598	Lidded jar	5"	c.1925	Unknown	1,000.00	2,000.00	2,500.00
8598	Tobacco jar	4 ½"	c.1925	Unknown	1,000.00	2,000.00	2,500.00

THE BEST IS NOT TOO GOOD

STYLE TWO: SMILING FACE; LEFT EYE WINKING; LEFT HAND HOLDING A PIPE; 15 BUTTONS

The Best is Not Too Good, Style Two

the Best is Not Too Good, Liquor Flask

Designer: Harry Simeon
Handle: Plain
Colourway: Slate blue jacket; white waistcoat; brown breeches

Backstamp: Doulton Lambeth

Model Number	Size	Backstamp	Height	Intro.	Discon.	Current Market Value U.K. £	U.S. $	Can. $
8588	Small	Doulton	3"	c.1925	Unknown	400.00	800.00	900.00

Derivatives of Style Two

The neck of this flask is hallmarked sterling silver. The outer edge of the flask is blue.

Designer: Harry Simeon
Colourway: Slate blue jacket; orange waistcoat; olive-green breeches
Inscription: No inscription around base

Backstamp: Doulton Lambeth

Model Number	Item	Height	Intro.	Discon.	Current Market Value U.K. £	U.S. $	Can. $
—	Liquor flask	8 ½"	c.1925	Unknown	1,500.00	3,000.00	3,500.00

Note: See page 35 for the continuation of this jug in china.

THE BEST IS NOT TOO GOOD

STYLE THREE: SOMBRE FACE; SQUINT EYES; LEFT HAND HOLDING LONG PIPE; 12 BUTTONS

Photograph not
available
at press time

Designer: Harry Simeon **Backstamp:** Doulton Lambeth
Handle: Plain
Colourway: Slate blue jacket; red waistcoat; brown breeches

Model Number	Size	Backstamp	Height	Intro.	Discon.	U.K. £	U.S. $	Can. $
						Current Market Value		
8588	Small	Doulton Lambeth	4 ½"	c.1925	Unknown	425.00	800.00	900.00

Derivatives of Style Three

Designer: Harry Simeon **Backstamp:** Doulton Lambeth
Colourway: Slate blue jacket; orange waistcoat; olive-green breeches
Inscription: No inscription around base

Model Number	Item	Height	Intro.	Discon.	U.K. £	U.S. $	Can. $
					Current Market Value		
8593	Lidded jar	5"	c.1925	Unknown	1,000.00	2,000.00	2,500.00

THE BEST IS NOT TOO GOOD

STYLE FOUR: SMILING FACE; EYES OPEN; LEFT HAND HOLDING LAPEL; 13 BUTTONS

Designer: Harry Simeon   **Backstamp:** Doulton Lambeth
Handle: Plain
Colourway: Variation No. 1 — Slate blue jacket; orange waistcoat; brown breeches
Variation No. 2 — Slate blue jacket olive green waistcoat; brown breeches

Model Number	Variation	Backstamp	Height	Intro.	Discon.	Current Market Value U.K. £	U.S. $	Can. $
8588	Var. 1	Doulton Lambeth	4"	c.1925	Unknown	500.00	1,000.00	1,200.00
8588	Var. 2	Doulton Lambeth	4"	c.1925	Unknown	500.00	1,000.00	1,200.00

THE BEST IS NOT TOO GOOD

STYLE FIVE: SOMBRE FACE; EYES OPEN; LEFT HAND HOLDING LAPEL;
13 BUTTONS

Designer: Harry Simeon   **Backstamp:** Doulton Lambeth
     Handle: Plain
Colourway: Variation No. 1 — Slate blue jacket; white waistcoat; olive-green breeches
                    Variation No. 2 — Olive green jacket; white waistcoat; blue breeches; black hat

Model Number	Variation	Backstamp	Height	Intro.	Discon.	Current Market Value U.K. £	U.S. $	Can. $
8584	Var. 1	Doulton Lambeth	3 ¾"	c.1925	Unknown	425.00	900.00	1,100.00
8584	Var. 2	Doulton Lambeth	3 ¾"	c.1925	Unknown	425.00	900.00	1,100.00

Derivatives of Style Five

Designer: Harry Simeon   **Backstamp:** Doulton Lambeth
Colourway: Slate blue jacket; white waistcoat;
                    olive green breeches

Model Number	Item	Height	Intro.	Discon.	Current Market Value U.K. £	U.S. $	Can. $
8593	Tobacco jar	4 ½"	c.1925	Unknown	1,000.00	2,000.00	2,500.00

THE BEST IS NOT TOO GOOD

STYLE SIX: SMILING FACE; EYES OPEN; 16 BUTTONS

Derivative of Style Six

Designer: Harry Simeon   **Backstamp:** Doulton Lambeth
Colourway: Slate blue jacket with red edging and gold apaulettes;
white waistcoat; olive green breeches; white stockings

Model Number	Item	Height	Intro.	Discon.	Current Market Value		
					U.K. £	U.S. $	Can. $
—	Teapot	4 ¾"	c.1925	Unknown	1,000.00	2,000.00	2,500.00

HIGHWAYMAN

This design by Leslie Harradine could very well be interpreted as the forerunner of the Doulton line of character jugs.

Designer: Leslie Harradine
Handle: Strands of hair
Colourway: Saltglaze

Backstamp: Doulton Lambeth

Model Number	Backstamp	Height	Intro.	Discon.	Current Market Value U.K. £	U.S. $	Can. $
—	Doulton Lambeth	Unknown	c. 1912	Unknown		Extremely rare	

HONEST MEASURE

Ink Pot
(Removable Head)

Designer: Harry Simeon
Colourway: Variation No. 1 — Olive-green jacket; orange waistcoat; slate blue breeches
Variation No. 2 — Brown jacket; white waistcoat; black breeches
Backstamp: Doulton Lambeth

Model Number	Variation	Backstamp	Height	Intro.	Discon.	Current Market Value		
						U.K. £	U.S. $	Can. $
8583	Var. 1	Doulton Lambeth	2 ¾"	c.1925	Unknown	600.00	1,100.00	1,400.00
8583	Var. 2	Doulton Lambeth	2 ¾"	c.1925	Unknown	600.00	1,100.00	1,400.00

Ash Pot
(Removable Hat)

Designer: Harry Simeon
Colourway: Variation No. 1 — Olive-green jacket; dark green waistcoat; black breeches
Variation No. 2 — Olive-green jacket; orange waistcoat; slate blue breeches
Variation No. 3 — Brown jacket; saltglazed waistcoat; blue breeches
Variation No. 4 — Cream jacket; blue waistcoat; brown breeches
Backstamp: Doulton Lambeth

Model Number	Variation	Backstamp	Height	Intro.	Discon.	Current Market Value U.K. £	U.S. $	Can. $
8584	Var. 1	Doulton Lambeth	4"	c.1925	Unknown	600.00	1,150.00	1,400.00
8584	Var. 2	Doulton Lambeth	4"	c.1925	Unknown	600.00	1,150.00	1,400.00
8583	Var. 3	Doulton Lambeth	2 ¾"	c.1925	Unknown	600.00	1,150.00	1,400.00
8583	Var. 4	Doulton Lambeth	2 ¾"	c.1925	Unknown	600.00	1,150.00	1,400.00

MARRIAGE DAY

This saltglaze jug was issued with the words "Marriage Day" and "After Marriage" inscribed atop either a smiling or frowning face resulting in two variations.

Designer: Harry Simeon
Handle: Plain
Colourway: Blue, brown and white

Backstamp: Doulton Lambeth

Doulton Number	Size	Description	Height	Intro.	Discon.	Current Market Value		
						U.K. £	U.S. $	Can. $
8595	1/2 pint	Frown upright	4 ¾"	c.1925	Unknown	500.00	1,100.00	1,400.00
8595	1/2 pint	Smile upright	4 ¾"	c.1925	Unknown	500.00	1,100.00	1,400.00
8596	1/4 pint	Frown upright	3 ½"	c.1925	Unknown	450.00	1,000.00	1,300.00
8596	1/4 pint	Smile upright	3 ½"	c.1925	Unknown	450.00	1,000.00	1.300.00
8595	Miniature	Frown upright	2"	c.1925	Unknown	950.00	1,400.00	1,750.00
8595	Miniature	Smile upright	2"	c.1925	Unknown	950.00	1,400.00	1,750.00

Note: A plain white stoneware jug exists (model number X7590).

MR PECKSNIFF

VARIATION No. 1:   Colourway — Ivory

Variation No. 1 - Ivory   Variation No. 2 - Treacle Glaze

Designer: Leslie Harradine   **Backstamp:** Doulton Lambeth
Handle: Plain
Colourway: Variation No. 1 — Ivory
Variation No. 2 — Treacle glaze

Model Number	Variation	Backstamp	Height	Intro.	Discon.	Current Market Value		
						U.K. £	U.S. $	Can. $
15354	Var. 1	Doulton Lambeth	7 ½"	c.1912	Unknown	1,750.00	23,000.00	3,750.00
15354	Var. 2	Doulton Lambeth	7 ½"	c.1912	Unknown	1,750.00	2,750.00	3,500.00

OLD KING COLE

Designer: Leslie Harradine   **Backstamp:** Doulton Lambeth
Handle: Plain
Colourway: Saltglaze stoneware

Model Number	Size	Backstamp	Height	Intro.	Discon.	Current Market Value		
						U.K. £	U.S. $	Can. $
—	Large	Doulton Lambeth	Unknown	c.1910	Unknown		Extremely rare	

SAILOR

Designer: Harry Simeon
Handle: Rope design
Colourway: Saltglaze stoneware

Backstamp: Doulton Lambeth

Model Number	Backstamp	Height	Intro.	Discon.	Current Market Value U.K. £	U.S. $	Can. $
—	Doulton Lambeth	6"	Unknown		Extremely Rare		

SEATED MAN
MATCH HOLDER

Designer: Harry Simeon
Colourway: Blue-green jacket; white waistcoat, cuffs, stockings and hari; green breeches; brown barrel and base; blue wells

Backstamp: Doulton Lambeth

Model Number	Backstamp	Height	Intro.	Discon.	Current Market Value U.K. £	U.S. $	Can. $
—	Doulton Lambeth		c.1925	Unknown	400.00	900.00	1,100.00

SEATED TOBY

STYLE ONE: KNEES TOGETHER

Seated Toby Jug

Derivative - Candlestick Holder

Designer: Harry Simeon
Handle: Plain
Colourway: Variation No. 1 — Slate blue jacket; orange waistcoat; olive green breeches
Variation No. 2 — Slate blue jacket; olive green waistcoat; white breeches
Backstamp: Doulton Lambeth

Model Number	Variation	Backstamp	Height	Intro.	Discon.	Current Market Value U.K. £	U.S. $	Can. $
8599	Var. 1	Doulton Lambeth	3 1/8"	c.1925	Unknown	500.00	900.00	1,000.00
8599	Var. 2	Doulton Lambeth	3 1/8"	c.1925	Unknown	500.00	900.00	1,000.00

Seated Toby Derivative

Designer: Harry Simeon   **Backstamp:** Doulton Lambeth
Colourway: Slate blue jacket; orange breeches

Model Number	Item	Height	Intro.	Discon.	Current Market Value U.K. £	U.S. $	Can. $
8559	Candlestick Holder	3 ¾"	c.1925	Unknown	600.00	1,000.00	1,300.00

SEATED TOBY

STYLE TWO: KNEES APART

Designer: Harry Simeon
Colourway: Slate blue jacket; olive green waistcoat; brown breeches
Backstamp: Doulton Lambeth

Model Number	Size	Backstamp	Height	Intro.	Discon.	Current Market Value		
						U.K. £	U.S. $	Can. $
8594	Tiny	Doulton Lambeth	2 ½"	c.1925	Unknown	750.00	1,400.00	1,750.00
8588	Tiny	Doulton Lambeth	2"	c.1925	Unknown	750.00	1,400.00	1,750.00

Seated Toby Derivative

Designer: Harry Simeon
Colourway: Variation No. 1 — Slate blue jacket; white waistcoat
Variation No. 2 — Cream jacket; tan waistcoat
Variation No. 3 — Slate blue jacket; brown waistcoat
Variation No. 4 — Slate blue jacket; olive green waistcoat; olive green breeches
Backstamp: Doulton Lambeth

Model Number	Variation	Item	Height	Intro.	Discon.	Current Market Value		
						U.K. £	U.S. $	Can. $
8594	Candlestick	Var. 1	2 ½"	c.1925	Unknown	450.00	900.00	1,200.00
8594	Candlestick	Var. 2	2 ½"	c.1925	Unknown	450.00	900.00	1,200.00
8594	Candlestick	Var. 3	2 ¾"	c.1925	Unknown	450.00	900.00	1,200.00
8594	Candlestick	Var. 4	2"	c.1925	Unknown	450.00	900.00	1,200.00

SEATED TOBY

STYLE THREE: ARMCHAIR VARIETY

Variation No. 1

Variation No. 6

Liquor Flask

Designer: Harry Simeon
Colour: Variation No. 1 — Blue jacket; cream waistcoat; dark brown breeches
Variation No. 2 — Brown jacket; orange waistcoat; dark brown breeches
Variation No. 3 — Royal blue jacket; burgundy waistcoat; green breeches
Variation No. 4 — Slate blue jacket; orange waistcoat; brown breeches
Variation No. 5 — Blue jacket, white waistcoat, brown breeches
Variation No. 6 — Green jacket; rust waistcoat; black breeches
                Advertisement for "Ye Olde Cock Tavern 22 Fleet Street Founded 1549"
Backstamp: Doulton Lambeth

Model Number	Variation / Description	Height	Intro.	Discon.	Current Market Value U.K. £	U.S. $	Can. $
8586	Var. 1 / Blue, white, brown	4"	c.1925	Unknown	475.00	900.00	1,200.00
543	Var. 2 / Brown, orange, blue	4"	c.1925	Unknown	475.00	900.00	1,200.00
543	Var. 3 / Royal blue, burgundy	4"	c.1925	Unknown	475.00	900.00	1,200.00
543	Var. 4 / Slate blue, orange	6"	c.1925	Unknown	600.00	1,100.00	1,400.00
551	Var. 6/ Green, rust, black	6"	c.1925	Unknown	600.00	1,100.00	1,400.00

Seated Toby Derivative

Designer: Harry Simeon

Colourway: Green jacket; orange waistcoat; brown breeches

Backstamp: Doulton Lambeth

Model Number	Item	Height	Intro.	Discon.	Current Market Value U.K. £	U.S. $	Can. $
543	Ash - Var. 5	4 ¼"	c.1925	Unknown	750.00	1,400.00	1,750.00
543	Ash - Var. 5	6"	c.1925	Unknown	750.00	1,400.00	1,750.00
543	Liquor Flask	6"	c.1925	Unknown	750.00	1,400.00	1,750.00

SOLDIER BOY

Designer: Mark Mitchell
Handle: Plain
Colourway: Saltglaze stoneware

Backstamp: Doulton Lambeth

Model Number	Size	Backstamp	Height	Intro.	Discon.	Current Market Value		
						U.K. £	U.S. $	Can. $
—	Large	Doulton Lambeth	Unknown	c.1910	Unknown		Extremely rare	

THE STANDING MAN

STYLE ONE: SMILING FACE

Designer: Harry Simeon
Handle: Plain
Colourway: Variation No. 1 — Slate blue jacket; orange waistcoat; brown breeches; waistcoat buttons are either white or gold
Variation No. 2 — Slate blue jacket; olive green waistcoat; olive green breeches
Issued: c.1925 — Unknown
Backstamp: Doulton Lambeth

Model Number	Size	Variation — Description	Height	Current Market Value		
				U.K. £	U.S. $	Can. $
8572	Large	Var. 1 — White waistcoat buttons	8 ¾"	500.00	950.00	1,150.00
8572	Large	Var. 1 — Silver rim, white waistcoat buttons	8 ¾"	600.00	1,100.00	1,400.00
8572	Medium	Var. 1 — White waistcoat buttons	8 ¾"	500.00	950.00	1,150.00
8572	Medium	Var. 1 — Gold waistcoat buttons	7"	475.00	900.00	1,100.00
8572	Medium	Var. 1 — Silver rim, white waistcoat buttons	7"	600.00	1,100.00	1,400.00
8572	Medium	Var. 1 — Silver rim, gold waistcoat buttons	7"	600.00	1,100.00	1,400.00
8572	Medium	Var. 1 — White waistcoat buttons	7"	475.00	900.00	1,100.00
8572	Medium	Var. 1 — Silver rim, white waistcoat buttons	7"	600.00	1,100.00	1,400.00
8572	Medium	Var. 1 — White waistcoat buttons	6 ¼"	475.00	900.00	1,100.00
8572	Medium	Var. 2 — Slate blue; olive green	6"	475.00	900.00	1,100.00
8572	Small	Var. 1 — White waistcoat buttons	4 ½"	450.00	850.00	1,000.00

Note: Large and medium size jugs are found with sterling silver rims hallmarked Birmingham, 1928 or 1929.

THE STANDING MAN

STYLE TWO: SOMBRE FACE

The sombre-face, standing-man variety has two buttons on the left lapel of his jacket.

Designer: Harry Simeon
Handle: Plain
Colourway: Slate blue jacket; brown waistcoat;
brown breeches; white or gold waistcoat buttons
Issued: c.1925 - Unknown

Backstamp: Doulton Lambeth

Model Number	Size	Variation \ Description	Height	Current Market Value		
				U.K. £	U.S. $	Can. $
8572	Large	White waistcoat buttons	8 ¾"	550.00	1,000.00	1,300.00
8572	Large	Gold waistcoat buttons	8 ¾"	600.00	1,100.00	1,400.00
8572	Medium	White waistcoat buttons	6 ¼"	500.00	900.00	1,200.00
8572	Small	White waistcoat buttons	4 ½"	400.00	700.00	1,000.00
8572	Tiny	White waistcoat buttons	2 ¾"	750.00	1,400.00	1,950.00

THEODORE ROOSEVELT

Designer: Leslie Harradine
Handle: Plain
Colourway: Saltglaze stoneware

Backstamp: Doulton Lambeth

Model Number	Size	Backstamp	Height	Intro.	Discon.	Current Market Value		
						U.K. £	U.S. $	Can. $
—	Large	Doulton Lambeth	Unknown	c.1910	Unknown		Extremely rare	

TOBY XX

HAND HOLDS JUG OF ALE, WITH HANDLE

STYLE ONE: SALTGLAZE STONEWARE

Designer: Unknown
Handle: Hair tied with a bow
Colourway: Variation No. 1 — Light brown overall glaze; no dark brown overglaze
Variation No. 2 — Light brown overall glaze, different sections with dark brown overglaze
Variation No. 3 — Light brown overall glaze; "XX" is replaced with "W. Dow & Co. India Pale Ale" on barrel
Backstamp: Doulton Lambeth

Model Number	Variation	Backstamp	Height	Intro.	Discon.	Current Market Value U.K. £	U.S. $	Can. $
6365	Var. 1	Doulton Lambeth	14 ½"	1863	Unknown	1,000.00	1,800.00	2,200.00
6365	Var. 1	Doulton Lambeth	8 ½"	1863	Unknown	500.00	1,000.00	1,300.00
6365	Var. 2	Doulton Lambeth	12 ½"	1863	Unknown	800.00	1,500.00	1,900.00
6365	Var. 2	Doulton Lambeth	10 ½"	1863	Unknown	650.00	1,200.00	1,500.00
6365	Var. 2	Doulton Lambeth	8 ½"	1863	Unknown	500.00	1,000.00	1,300.00
6365	Var. 3	Doulton Lambeth	14 ½"	1891	Unknown	Rare		

Note: 1. Some examples carry a registration number 169753, which is a design registration by Doulton, circa 1891.
2. Some of the above jugs are found with sterling silver rims, usually hallmarked Birmingham, 1928 or 1929. These jugs will command a premium of 10% to 20% over the catalogue price.

TOBY XX

HAND HOLDS JUG OF ALE, WITH HANDLE

STYLE TWO: SALTGLAZE COLOURED STONEWARE

Designer: Harry Simeon
Handle: Strands of hair
Colourway: Variation No. 1 — Slate blue jacket; brown waistcoat; green breeches
Variation No. 2 — Slate blue jacket; orange waistcoat; green breeches
Variation No. 3 — Slate blue jacket; brown waistcoat; brown breeches
Variation No. 4 — Slate blue jacket; orange waistcoat; olive-green breeches
Variation No. 5 — Slate blue jacket; green waistcoat; olive-green breeches
Variation No. 6 — Black jacket; olive-green waistcoat; slate blue breeches
Variation No. 7 — Slate blue jacket; white waistcoat; brown breeches
Backstamp: Doulton Lambeth

Model Number	Variation	Backstamp	Height	Intro.	Discon.	Current Market Value U.K. £	U.S. $	Can. $
8590	Var. 1	Doulton Lambeth	8"	c.1925	Unknown	500.00	1,000.00	1,300.00
8590	Var. 2	Doulton Lambeth	8"	c.1925	Unknown	500.00	1,000.00	1,300.00
8592	Var. 3	Doulton Lambeth	8"	c.1925	Unknown	500.00	1,000.00	1,300.00
8589	Var. 4	Doulton Lambeth	6 ¾"	c.1925	Unknown	450.00	900.00	1,200.00
8589	Var. 5	Doulton Lambeth	6 ¾"	c.1925	Unknown	450.00	900.00	1,200.00
8589	Var. 6	Doulton Lambeth	6 ¾"	c.1925	Unknown	450.00	900.00	1,200.00
8589	Var. 7	Doulton Lambeth	6 ½"	c.1925	Unknown	450.00	900.00	1,200.00

Toby XX Derivative

This liquor container is supported by a silver-plated stand, produced by Finnigans Limited, Manchester.

Designer: Harry Simeon
Handle: None
Colourway: Slate blue jacket; orange waistcoat;
brown breeches

Backstamp: Doulton Lambeth

Model Number	Item	Height	Intro.	Discon.	Current Market Value U.K. £	U.S. $	Can. $
8589	Liquor container	10 ¼"	c.1925	Unknown	1,100.00	2,000.00	2,500.00

TOBY XX

HANDS REST ON KNEES, WITHOUT HANDLE

STYLE ONE: SALTGLAZE STONEWARE

Designer: Unknown
Handle: None
Colourway: Variation No. 1 — Light brown overall glaze; no dark brown overglaze
Variation No. 2 — Light brown overall; different sections with dark brown overglaze
Backstamp: Doulton Lambeth
Doulton Lambeth, Phillips Oxford St. London

Model Number	Variation	Backstamp	Height	Intro.	Discon.	Current Market Value U.K. £	U.S. $	Can. $
8547	Var. 1	Doulton Lambeth	5 ¾"	c.1925	Unknown	500.00	900.00	1,200.00
8547	Var. 2	Lambeth/Phillips	5 ¾"	c.1925	Unknown	500.00	900.00	1,200.00

TOBY XX

HANDS REST ON KNEES, WITHOUT HANDLE

STYLE TWO: SALTGLAZE COLOURED STONEWARE

Designer: Unknown
Handle: None
Colourway: Variation No. 1 — Olive-green jacket; white waistcoat; olive-green breeches
Variation No. 2 — Slate blue jacket; orange waistcoat; brown breeches
Variation No. 3 — Slate blue jacket; green waistcoat; green breeches
Backstamp: Doulton Lambeth

Model Number	Variation	Backstamp	Height	Intro.	Discon.	Current Market Value U.K. £	U.S. $	Can. $
8591	Var. 1	Doulton Lambeth	5 ¾"	c.1925	Unknown	450.00	800.00	1,000.00
8591	Var. 2	Doulton Lambeth	5 ½"	c.1925	Unknown	450.00	800.00	1,000.00
547	Var. 3	Doulton Lambeth	5 ½"	c.1925	Unknown	450.00	800.00	1,000.00

VETERAN MOTORISTS

Designer: Leslie Harradine
Handle: Plain
Colourway: Saltglaze stoneware

Backstamp: Doulton Lambeth

Model Number	Size	Style	Height	Intro.	Discon.	Current Market Value		
						U.K. £	U.S. $	Can. $
—	Large	Style one	Unknown	c.1905	Unknown	Extremely rare		
—	Large	Style two	Unknown	c.1905	Unknown	Extremely rare		

Note: Both style one and style two have sterling silver hallmarked rims dated 1906.

WEE MAC

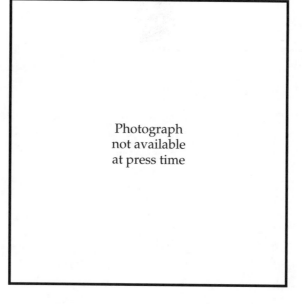

Photograph
not available
at press time

Designer: Unknown
Handle: Unknown
Colourway: Saltglaze stoneware

Backstamp: Doulton Lambeth

Model Number	Backstamp	Height	Intro.	Discon.	Current Market Value		
					U.K. £	U.S. $	Can. $
—	Doulton Lambeth	Unknown	c.1908	Unknown		Extremely rare	

ALBERT SAGGER THE POTTER

THE DOULTONVILLE COLLECTION
ONE OF 25
ROYAL DOULTON INTERNATIONAL COLLECTORS CLUB SERIES

This jug was issued for the Royal Doulton International Collectors Club in 1986.

Designer: William K. Harper
Handle: Plain
Colourway: Brown apron; white shirt; dark green cap; light green vase

Backstamp: Doulton/RDICC

Doulton Number	Size	Backstamp	Height	Intro.	Discon.	Current Market Value		
						U.K. £	U.S. $	Can. $
D6745	Small	Doulton/RDICC	4"	1986	1986	85.00	150.00	225.00

ALDERMAN MACE THE MAYOR

THE DOULTONVILLE COLLECTION
ONE OF 25

Designer: William K. Harper
Handle: Plain
Colourway: Red coat trimmed with gold; white collar and scarf;
black hat trimmed with gold and white feathers

Backstamp: Doulton

Doulton Number	Size	Backstamp	Height	Intro.	Discon.	Current Market Value		
						U.K. £	U.S. $	Can. $
D6766	Small	Doulton	4"	1987	1991	60.00	100.00	150.00

THE BEST IS NOT TOO GOOD

STYLE TWO: BURSLEM, 11 BUTTONS

This jug was modelled on an earlier Harry Simeon Lambeth design of about 1920. There are, however, several obvious differences on this later piece. See page 5 for an outline of these differences.

For the tiny version of this jug see Tiny Tobies set page 102.

The Best is not too good.

Designer: Harry Fenton	**Backstamp:** Doulton
Model No.: 8338	
Handle: Plain	
Colourway: Green jacket; burgundy trousers; mustard waistcoat with double row of black buttons; brown hat with gold trim	
Inscription: "The Best is not too Good"	

Doulton Number	Size	Backstamp	Height	Intro.	Discon.	Current Market Value U.K. £	U.S. $	Can. $
D6107	Small	Doulton	4 ½"	1939	1960	300.00	575.00	800.00

BETTY BITTERS THE BARMAID

THE DOULTONVILLE COLLECTION
ONE OF 25

Designer: William K. Harper   **Backstamp:** Doulton
Handle: Plain
Colourway: Green blouse; burgundy skirt; yellow hair

| Doulton Number | Size | Backstamp | Height | Intro. | Discon. | Current Market Value | | |
						U.K. £	U.S. $	Can. $
D6716	Small	Doulton	4"	1984	1990	50.00	100.00	125.00

CAP'N CUTTLE

DICKENS TOBIES
ONE OF SIX

Designer: Harry Fenton
Handle: Plain
Colourway: Light brown suit; blue highlights on
jacket lapels and waistcoat

Backstamp: Doulton

Doulton Number	Size	Backstamp	Height	Intro.	Discon.	Current Market Value		
						U.K. £	U.S. $	Can. $
D6266	Small	Doulton	4 ½"	1948	1960	150.00	250.00	350.00

CAPTAIN PROP THE PILOT

THE DOULTONVILLE COLLECTION
ONE OF 25

Designer: William K. Harper
Handle: Plain
Colourway: Brown coat and gloves; grey cap; cream scarf

Backstamp: Doulton

Doulton Number	Size	Backstamp	Height	Intro.	Discon.	Current Market Value		
						U.K. £	U.S. $	Can. $
D6812	Small	Doulton	4"	1989	1991	80.00	130.00	200.00

CAPT. SALT THE SEA CAPTAIN

THE DOULTONVILLE COLLECTION
ONE OF 25

Designer: William K. Harper
Handle: Plain
Colourway: Blue-black coat; blue-black cap trimmed
with yellow

Backstamp: Doulton

Doulton Number	Size	Backstamp	Height	Intro.	Discon.	Current Market Value		
						U.K. £	U.S. $	Can. $
D6721	Small	Doulton	4"	1985	1991	60.00	100.00	150.00

CHARLES DICKENS

The 125th anniversary of the death of Charles Dickens was commemorated in 1995 with this toby jug of Dickens. The jug, issued in a limited edition of 2,500, was available through Lawleys By Post.

For the toby jug Charles Dickens see page 185.

Designer: Stanley J. Taylor
Handle: Plain
Colourway: Black

Backstamp: Doulton

Doulton Number	Size	Backstamp	Height	Intro.	Discon.	Current Market Value U.K. £	U.S. $	Can. $
D6997	Small	Doulton	5"	1995	Ltd. ed.	125.00	200.00	250.00

CHARLIE

This figure of Charlie Chaplin has a removable bowler hat. He stands on a green base and the name "Charlie" is incised around the base.

Designer: Unknown	**Backstamp:** Doulton
Handle: Plain	

Colourway: Black suit and bowler hat; green and red plaid waistcoat; red-brown tie; green base

Doulton Number	Size	Backstamp	Height	Intro.	Discon.	Current Market Value U.K. £	U.S. $	Can. $
D —	Large	Doulton	11 ¼"	1918	Unknown	2,500.00	5,000.00	6,000.00

CHARLIE CHEER THE CLOWN

THE DOULTONVILLE COLLECTION
ONE OF 25

Designer: William K. Harper
Handle: Plain
Colourway: Orange jacket; blue tie; green cap; yellow hair; pink sausages

Backstamp: Doulton

Doulton Number	Size	Backstamp	Height	Intro.	Discon.	Current Market Value		
						U.K. £	U.S. $	Can. $
D6768	Small	Doulton	4"	1987	1991	75.00	125.00	175.00

CHARRINGTON & CO. LTD.

According to the Bass Museum, Burton-on-Trent, Staffordshire, these jugs originated from Hoare & Co., a London brewery which had been purchased by Charrington, another London brewery. The original Charrington toby jugs were made by Doulton, but there are no records of the numbers manufactured. The three variations below were made as promotional pieces for Charrington & Co., Mile End, London. They differ only in the wording on their bases and were in production from the 1930s. Charrington closed Hoare & Co. in 1933.

Variation No. 2 "One Toby Leads to Another"

Variation No. 3 "Charrington's Toby"

Designer: Unknown
Handle: Plain
Colourway: Black hat; green coat; maroon trousers

Backstamp: Doulton

VARIATION No. 1: Inscription around base — "Toby Ale"

| Doulton Number | Variation | Inscription | Height | Intro. | Discon. | Current Market Value | | |
						U.K. £	U.S. $	Can. $
D8074	Var. 1	Toby Ale	9"	1934	1938	375.00	650.00	800.00

VARIATION No. 2: Inscription around base — "One Toby Leads to Another"

| Doulton Number | Variation | Inscription | Height | Intro. | Discon. | Current Market Value | | |
						U.K. £	U.S. $	Can. $
D8074	Var. 2	One Toby	9"	1937	1938	500.00	900.00	1,200.00

VARIATION No. 3: Inscription around base — "Charrington's Toby"

| Doulton Number | Variation | Inscription | Height | Intro. | Discon. | Current Market Value | | |
						U.K. £	U.S. $	Can. $
D8074	Var. 3	Charrington's	9 ¼"	1938	1939	500.00	900.00	1,200.00

CLIFF CORNELL

In 1956 an American industrialist commissioned these toby jugs as gifts to friends and associates. The inscription on the base reads, "Greetings Cliff Cornell 'Famous Cornell Fluxes' Cleveland Flux Company." Approximately 500 pieces were issued for the large size blue and dark brown jugs and 375 pieces for the small sizes. The number of light brown jugs produced is unknown.

Variation No. 1

Variation No. 2

Variation No. 3

VARIATION No. 1:   Colourway — Tan suit

Designer: Unknown
Handle: Plain
Colourway: Light brown suit; brown and cream striped tie

Backstamp: Doulton

Doulton Number	Size	Variation	Height	Intro.	Discon.	Current Market Value U.K. £	U.S. $	Can. $
D —	Large	Var. 1	9"	1956	1956	300.00	650.00	800.00
D —	Small	Var. 1	5 ½"	1956	1956	1,250.00	2,000.00	2,500.00

VARIATION No. 2:   Colourway — Dark blue suit; red tie with cream polka dots

Doulton Number	Size	Variation	Height	Intro.	Discon.	Current Market Value U.K. £	U.S. $	Can. $
D —	Large	Var. 2	9"	1956	1956	200.00	350.00	525.00
D —	Small	Var. 2	5 ½"	1956	1956	200.00	325.00	475.00

VARIATION No. 3:   Colourway — Dark brown suit; green, black and blue design on tie

Doulton Number	Size	Variation	Height	Intro.	Discon.	Current Market Value U.K. £	U.S. $	Can. $
D —	Large	Var. 3	9"	1956	1956	200.00	325.00	475.00
D —	Small	Var. 3	5 ½"	1956	1956	200.00	350.00	525.00

THE CLOWN

This jug was issued in a limited edition of 3,000.

Royal Doulton®
THE CLOWN
D 6935
Modelled by
Stanley James Taylor
© 1992 ROYAL DOULTON
ISSUED IN A LIMITED
EDITION OF 3,000.
THIS IS N° 129

Designer: Stanley J. Taylor
Handle: Plain, black
Colourway: Green shirt; blue trousers; yellow bow tie with blue polka dots; yellow and red drum

Backstamp: Doulton

Doulton Number	Size	Backstamp	Height	Intro.	Discon.	Current Market Value		
						U.K. £	U.S. $	Can. $
D6935	Medium	Doulton	5 ½"	1993	Ltd. ed.	70.00	200.00	235.00

DR. JEKYLL AND MR. HYDE

Designer: Stanley J. Taylor
Handle: Plain
Colourway: Black, white and brown

Backstamp: Doulton

Doulton Number	Size	Backstamp	Height	Intro.	Discon.	Current Market Value		
						U.K.	U.S.$	Can.$
D7024	Small	Doulton	5"	1996	1998	75.00	150.00	225.00

DR. PULSE THE PHYSICIAN

THE DOULTONVILLE COLLECTION
ONE OF 25

Designer: William K. Harper
Handle: Plain
Colourway: Light brown jacket; grey hair

Backstamp: Doulton

Doulton Number	Size	Backstamp	Height	Intro.	Discon.	Current Market Value U.K. £	U.S. $	Can. $
D6723	Small	Doulton	4"	1985	1991	50.00	90.00	100.00

FALSTAFF

Backstamp B - Falstaff

Designer: Charles Noke
Model No.: 8328
Handle: Plain
Colourway: Burgundy clothes; black hat with burgundy feathers

Backstamps: **A.** Sir John Falstaff
B. Falstaff

Doulton Number	Size	Backstamp	Height	Intro.	Discon.	Current Market Value		
						U.K. £	U.S. $	Can. $
D6062	Large	Doulton	8 ½"	1939	1991	85.00	150.00	200.00
D6063	Small	Doulton	5 ¼"	1939	1991	60.00	100.00	125.00

FAT BOY

DICKENS TOBIES
ONE OF SIX

Designer: Harry Fenton
Handle: Plain
Colourway: Brown

Backstamp: Doulton

Doulton Number	Size	Backstamp	Height	Intro.	Discon.	Current Market Value		
						U.K. £	U.S. $	Can. $
D6264	Small	Doulton	4 ½"	1948	1960	175.00	300.00	400.00

FATHER CHRISTMAS

A holly wreath is incorporated into the backstamp of the Father Christmas toby jug. Produced in a limited edition of 3,500, each jug is issued with a certificate of authenticity.

Designer: William K. Harper
Handle: Plain
Colourway: Red and white

Backstamp: Doulton

Doulton Number	Size	Backstamp	Height	Intro.	Discon.	Current Market Value		
						U.K. £	U.S. $	Can. $
D6940	Small	Doulton	5 ½"	1993	Ltd. ed.	85.00	175.00	250.00

THE FIRE KING and THE ICE QUEEN

This is the first-ever matched pair of toby jugs. Both characters hail from the realm of the mystica, the imaginative. He holds his book of ancient rites for passing judgments; she can rely on her flask of 'snow gems' to deal with wrongdoers by turning them into frozen statues of ice. Embellished with 22 carat gold and platinum, these jugs were issued by Lawleys By Post, numbered and sold as a pair, in a limited edition of 1,500.

Designer:	Martyn C. R. Alcock	**Backstamp:**	Doulton
Handle:	Plain		
Colourway:	Fire King — Red, yellow, orange and gold		
	Ice Queen — Blue, pink, white and gold		

Doulton Number	Name	Backstamp	Height	Intro.	Discon.	Current Market Value U.K. £	U.S. $	Can. $
D7070	Fire King	Doulton	5"	1998	Ltd. ed.	195.00	—	—
D7071	Ice Queen	Doulton	5"	1998	Ltd. ed.	Pair		

FLORA FUCHSIA THE FLORIST

THE DOULTONVILLE COLLECTION
ONE OF 25

Designer: William K. Harper
Handle: Plain
Colourway: Light blue uniform; brown hair;
red, yellow and white flowers

Backstamp: Doulton

Doulton Number	Size	Backstamp	Height	Intro.	Discon.	Current Market Value		
						U.K. £	U.S. $	Can. $
D6767	Small	Doulton	4"	1987	1990	80.00	150.00	200.00

FRED FEARLESS THE FIREMAN

THE DOULTONVILLE COLLECTION
ONE OF 25

Designer: William K. Harper
Handle: Plain
Colourway: Dark blue uniform with green buttons;
yellow helmet

Backstamp: Doulton

Doulton Number	Size	Backstamp	Height	Intro.	Discon.	Current Market Value		
						U.K. £	U.S. $	Can. $
D6809	Small	Doulton	4"	1989	1991	70.00	125.00	175.00

FRED FLY THE FISHERMAN

THE DOULTONVILLE COLLECTION
ONE OF 25

Designer: William K. Harper
Handle: Plain
Colourway: Light brown coat; tan hat; grey fish and net

Backstamp: Doulton

Doulton Number	Size	Backstamp	Height	Intro.	Discon.	Current Market Value		
						U.K. £	U.S. $	Can. $
D6742	Small	Doulton	4"	1986	1991	60.00	100.00	125.00

GEORGE ROBEY

George Robey, a star of the British Music Hall, entertained thousands during his long career. The hat on this jug is detachable, and his name is incised on the base.

Designer: Charles Noke
Handle: Plain
Colourway: Black suit and hat; grey shirt; green base

Backstamp: Doulton

Doulton Number	Size	Backstamp	Height	Intro.	Discon.	Current Market Value		
						U.K. £	U.S. $	Can. $
—	Large	Doulton	9 ¾"	c.1925	Unknown	2,500.00	5,500.00	6,500.00

HAPPY JOHN

For the tiny version of Happy John, see Tiny Tobies, page 102.

HAPPY JOHN

Designer: Harry Fenton
Handle: Plain
Colourway: Black hat; light green coat; yellow scarf with blue polka dots; orange breeches

Backstamp: Doulton

Doulton Number	Size	Backstamp	Height	Intro.	Discon.	Current Market Value		
						U.K. £	U.S. $	Can. $
D6031	Large	Doulton	8 ½"	1939	1991	85.00	150.00	200.00
D6070	Small	Doulton	5 ¼"	1939	1991	60.00	100.00	125.00

HONEST MEASURE

For the tiny version of Honest Measure, see Tiny Tobies, page 102.

Honest Measure

Designer:	Harry Fenton	**Backstamp:** Doulton
Handle:	Plain	
Colourway:	Green coat; orange waistcoat with black buttons; burgundy trousers; brown hat with gold trim	
Inscription:	"Honest Measure: Drink at Leisure"	

Doulton Number	Size	Backstamp	Height	Intro.	Discon.	Current Market Value U.K. £	Current Market Value U.S. $	Current Market Value Can. $
D6108	Small	Doulton	4 ¼"	1939	1991	75.00	125.00	175.00

THE HUNTSMAN

Variation No. 1   Variation No. 2

VARIATION No. 1: Burslem
                 Colourway — Bright orange coat

Designer: Charles Noke   **Backstamp:** Doulton Burslem
Handle: Plain
Colourway: Bright orange coat; yellow waistcoat;
            silver rim around top of hat

Model Number	Size	Variation	Height	Intro.	Discon.	Current Market Value		
						U.K. £	U.S. $	Can. $
4090	Large	Var. 1	8"	c.1919	Unknown		Extremely rare	

VARIATION No. 2: Burslem
                 Colourway — Red coat

This variation may be found with or without the sterling silver rim around the hat. The variety recorded has a silver rim.

Designer: Charles Noke   **Backstamp:** Doulton Burslem
Handle: Plain
Colourway: Red coat with yellow buttons;
            yellow waistcoat; white shirt

Model Number	Size	Variation	Height	Intro.	Discon.	Current Market Value		
						U.K. £	U.S. $	Can. $
4090	Large	Var. 2	7 ¾"	c. 1919	1930		Extremely rare	

| Variation No. 3 | Variation No. 4 | Variation No. 4 backstamp |

VARIATION No. 3: Doulton Kingsware
Colourway — Browns

Designer: Charles Noke   **Backstamp:** Doulton
Handle: Plain
Colourway: Browns

Doulton Number	Size	Variation	Height	Intro.	Discon.	Current Market Value		
						U.K. £	U.S. $	Can. $
—	Large	Var. 3	7 ¼"	1910	c.1927	800.00	1,400.00	1,500.00

VARIATION No. 4: Doulton
Colourway — Black hat; maroon coat

This is the Harry Fenton adaption of Noke's original design.

Designer: Harry Fenton   **Backstamp:** Doulton
Handle: Plain
Colourway: Black hat; maroon coat; white shirt;
gold waistcoat; grey trousers

Doulton Number	Size	Variation	Height	Intro.	Discon.	Current Market Value		
						U.K. £	U.S. $	Can. $
D6320	Large	Var. 4	7"	1950	1991	90.00	150.00	200.00

THE JESTER

STYLE ONE: JESTER HOLDING PUNCH

The Jester jug was issued in 1992 in a limited edition of 2,500.

Designer: Stanley J. Taylor
Handle: Plain, black
Colourway: Mauve and brown costume with yellow bobbles

Backstamp: Doulton

| Doulton Number | Size | Backstamp | Height | Intro. | Discon. | Current Market Value | | |
						U.K. £	U.S. $	Can. $
D6910	Medium	Doulton	5"	1992	Ltd. ed.	150.00	235.00	300.00

THE JESTER and THE LADY JESTER

STYLE TWO: JESTER HOLDING BALLOON

These jugs, in a green and pink colourways which resembles the parianware Jester figure (HN 3922), was issued, numbered and sold as a pair in a limited edition of 1,500 by Lawleys By Post.

Designer: David B. Biggs   **Backstamp:** Doulton
Handle: Plain
Colourway: Pale green and pink, gold bobbles

Doulton Number	Name	Backstamp	Height	Intro.	Discon.	Current Market Value U.K. £	U.S. $	Can. $
D7109	Jester	Doulton	5"	1997	Ltd. ed.	195.00	—	—
D7110	Lady Jester	Doulton	5"	1997	Ltd. ed.	Pair		

JOHN WESLEY

PROTOTYPE

Designer: Charles Noke   **Backstamp:** Doulton
     Handle: Plain
Colourway: Black

Doulton Number	Size	Backstamp	Height	Intro.	Discon.	Current Market Value		
						U.K. £	U.S. $	Can. $
—	Large	Doulton	Unknown	c.1925	Unknown	Only two known		

JOLLY TOBY

For the tiny version of Jolly Toby, see Tiny Tobies, page 102.

Designer: Harry Fenton   **Backstamp:** Doulton
Handle: Riding crop
Colourway: Variation No.1—Black hat; burgundy coat; yellow vest; white pants
                   Variation No.2—Black hat; burgundy coat; yellow vest; blue pants

Doulton Number	Colourway/Description	Height	Intro.	Discon.	Current Market Value		
					U.K. £	U.S. $	Can. $
D6109	Var. 1/White pants	6"	1939	1991	80.00	135.00	200.00
D6109	Var. 2/Blue pants	6"	Unknown	Unknown	350.00	575.00	750.00

THE JUDGE AND THIEF

This is a double-sided toby jug with the caricatures of a stern judge and a smirking thief.

Designer: Stanley J. Taylor
Handle: Plain
Colourways: Red, white, black and brown

Backstamp: Doulton

Doulton Number	Size	Backstamp	Height	Intro.	Discon.	Current Market Value U.K. £	U.S. $	Can. $
D6988	Medium	Doulton	5 1/4"	1995	1998	75.00	200.00	275.00

KING AND QUEEN OF CLUBS

SUITES FROM PLAYING CARDS
ONE OF FOUR

This is the second jug issued in this series. It was produced in 1995 in a limited edition of 2,500.

Designer: Stanley J. Taylor
Handle: Plain
Colourway: King in red; Queen in blue; both wear yellow crowns

Backstamp: Doulton

Doulton Number	Size	Backstamp	Height	Intro.	Discon.	Current Market Value		
						U.K. £	U.S. $	Can. $
D6999	Small	Doulton	5"	1995	Ltd. ed.	100.00	200.00	300.00

KING AND QUEEN OF DIAMONDS

SUITES FROM PLAYING CARDS
ONE OF FOUR

This is one of a series of four tobies illustrating the four suites of playing cards. This is the first double-sided toby jug in this series, and it was issued in a limited edition of 2,500.

Designer: Stanley J. Taylor
Handle: Plain
Colourway: King in red; Queen in blue; both wear yellow crowns

Backstamp: Doulton

Doulton Number	Size	Backstamp	Height	Intro.	Discon.	Current Market Value		
						U.K. £	U.S. $	Can. $
D6969	Small	Doulton	5"	1994	Ltd. ed.	100.00	200.00	300.00

KING AND QUEEN OF HEARTS

SUITES FROM PLAYING CARDS
ONE OF FOUR

This is the third jug in this series. It was issued in 1996 in a limited edtion of 2,500.

Designer: Stanley J. Taylor
Handle: Plain
Colourway: King in red, Queen in blue; both wear yellow crowns

Backstamp: Doulton

Doulton Number	Size	Backstamp	Height	Intro.	Discon.	Current Market Value		
						U.K. £	U.S. $	Can. $
D7037	Small	Doulton	5"	1996	Ltd. ed.	100.00	200.00	300.00

KING AND QUEEN OF SPADES

SUITES FROM PLAYING CARDS
ONE OF FOUR

This is the fourth and last jug in this series. It was issued in 1997 in a limited edtion of 2,500.

Designer: Stanley J. Taylor
Handle: Plain
Colourway: King in red, Queen in blue; both wear yellow crowns

Backstamp: Doulton

Doulton						Current Market Value		
Number	Size	Backstamp	Height	Intro.	Discon.	U.K. £	U.S. $	Can. $
D7087	Small	Doulton	5"	1997	Ltd. ed.	100.00	200.00	300.00

KING HENRY VIII

Commissioned by Lawleys By Post in a limited edition of 2,500, this piece was issued singly or with the six wives on a presentation stand. For the Six Wives of Henry VIII series, see page 478.

For Henry VIII see page 295, for King Henry VIII (style one) see page 327 and for Henry VIII (style two) see Kings and Queens of the Realm, page 328.

Designer: William K. Harper
Handle: Plain
Colourway: Black, white, yellow and gold

Backstamp: Doulton

Doulton Number	Size	Backstamp	Height	Intro.	Discon.	Current Market Value		
						U.K. £	U.S. $	Can. $
D7047	Miniature	Doulton	3 ½"	1996	Ltd. ed.	75.00	175.00	200.00

LEN LIFEBELT THE LIFEBOATMAN

THE DOULTONVILLE COLLECTION
ONE OF 25

Designer: William K. Harper
Handle: Plain
Colourway: Yellow life jacket and sou'wester;
blue sweater; white life preserver

Backstamp: Doulton

Doulton Number	Size	Backstamp	Height	Intro.	Discon.	Current Market Value		
						U.K. £	U.S. $	Can. $
D6811	Small	Doulton	4"	1989	1991	60.00	100.00	150.00

LEPRECHAUN

This jug was issued in a worldwide limited edition of 2,500. It was sold out in 1994.

Royal Doulton®
LEPRECHAUN
D 6948
Modelled by
Stanley James Taylor.
© 1993 ROYAL DOULTON
LIMITED EDITION OF 2,500
THIS IS NO. 370

Designer: Stanley J. Taylor
Handle: Plain
Colourways: Light and dark green and brown

Backstamp: Doulton

Doulton Number	Size	Backstamp	Height	Intro.	Discon.	Current Market Value		
						U.K. £	U.S. $	Can. $
D6948	Medium	Doulton	5"	1994	Ltd. ed.	90.00	150.00	225.00

LEWIS CARROLL

The centenary of the death of Lewis Carroll, author of *Alice in Wonderland,* was commemorated by the issue of this toby jug. The jug was commissioned by Lawleys By Post in a limited edition of 1,500.

For the character jug Lewis Carroll see page 334.

Designer: David Biggs
Handle: Plain
Colourway: Red, black, white and grey

Backstamp: Doulton

Doulton Number	Size	Backstamp	Height	Intro.	Discon.	Current Market Value U.K. £	U.S. $	Can. $
D—	Medium	Doulton	6 ½"	1997	Ltd. ed.	100.00	200.00	300.00

MADAME CRYSTAL THE CLAIRVOYANT

THE DOULTONVILLE COLLECTION
ONE OF 25

Designer: William K. Harper
Handle: Plain
Colourway: Green headscarf; burgundy skirt;
mauve shawl with blue fringe

Backstamp: Doulton

Doulton Number	Size	Backstamp	Height	Intro.	Discon.	Current Market Value		
						U.K. £	U.S. $	Can. $
D6714	Small	Doulton	4"	1984	1989	60.00	100.00	125.00

MAJOR GREEN THE GOLFER

THE DOULTONVILLE COLLECTION
ONE OF 25

Designer: William K. Harper
Handle: Plain
Colourway: Light brown waistcoat; yellow shirt; green cap

Backstamp: Doulton

Doulton Number	Size	Backstamp	Height	Intro.	Discon.	Current Market Value U.K. £	U.S. $	Can. $
D6740	Small	Doulton	4"	1986	1991	75.00	125.00	200.00

MANSION HOUSE DWARF
SON

The inspiration for this jug was derived from London's Mansion House Dwarves in Tudor times who seemed to fulfil the function of walking billboards by displaying advertising on their large hats for upcoming events. The quote on the dwarf's hat reads "Royal Doulton Potteries / There can be no better gift - call in today!". The jug was issued by Lawleys By Post in a limited edition of 1,500, along with a signed limited edition print of William K. Harper's working sketches.

Modeller: William K. Harper	**Backstamp:** Doulton
Handle: Plain	
Colourway: Black hat with pink feathers; blue and white vest with gold buttons, pink sleeves and pantaloons, white stockings, black shoes with blue bows	

Doulton Number	Size	Backstamp	Height	Intro.	Discon.	Current Market Value U.K. £	U.S. $	Can. $
D7135	Small	Doulton	4 ¾"	1998	Ltd. ed.	100.00	—	—

MIKE MINERAL THE MINER

THE DOULTONVILLE COLLECTION
ONE OF 25

Designer: William K. Harper
Handle: Plain
Colourway: Light green shirt; grey helmet;
blue scarf; light brown belt

Backstamp: Doulton

Doulton Number	Size	Backstamp	Height	Intro.	Discon.	Current Market Value		
						U.K. £	U.S. $	Can. $
D6741	Small	Doulton	4"	1986	1989	100.00	175.00	200.00

MISS NOSTRUM THE NURSE

THE DOULTONVILLE COLLECTION
ONE OF 25

Designer: William K. Harper   **Backstamp:** Doulton
Handle: Plain
Colourway: Blue uniform; white apron; blue and white cap

Doulton Number	Size	Backstamp	Height	Intro.	Discon.	Current Market Value		
						U.K. £	U.S. $	Can. $
D6700	Small	Doulton	4"	1983	1991	55.00	85.00	125.00

MISS STUDIOUS THE SCHOOLMISTRESS

THE DOULTONVILLE COLLECTION
ONE OF 25

Designer: William K. Harper
Handle: Plain
Colourway: Yellow blouse; green waistcoat; dark burgundy skirt

Backstamp: Doulton

Doulton Number	Size	Backstamp	Height	Intro.	Discon.	Current Market Value		
						U.K. £	U.S. $	Can. $
D6722	Small	Doulton	4"	1985	1989	70.00	125.00	175.00

MONSIEUR CHASSEUR THE CHEF

THE DOULTONVILLE COLLECTION
ONE OF 25

Designer: William K. Harper
Handle: Plain
Colourway: White chef's coat and hat; blue scarf

Backstamp: Doulton

Doulton Number	Size	Backstamp	Height	Intro.	Discon.	Current Market Value		
						U.K. £	U.S. $	Can. $
D6769	Small	Doulton	4"	1987	1991	75.00	125.00	175.00

MR. BRISKET THE BUTCHER

THE DOULTONVILLE COLLECTION
ONE OF 25

Designer: William K. Harper
Handle: Plain
Colourway: Pale blue shirt; white apron;
yellow hat with brown band

Backstamp: Doulton

Doulton Number	Size	Backstamp	Height	Intro.	Discon.	Current Market Value U.K.£	U.S. $	Can. $
D6743	Small	Doulton	4"	1986	1991	60.00	100.00	150.00

MR. FURROW THE FARMER

THE DOULTONVILLE COLLECTION
ONE OF 25

Designer: William K. Harper
Handle: Plain
Colourway: Dark brown coat; cream trousers; light brown hat

Backstamp: Doulton

Doulton Number	Size	Backstamp	Height	Intro.	Discon.	Current Market Value U.K. £	U.S. $	Can. $
D6701	Small	Doulton	4"	1983	1989	55.00	90.00	125.00

MR. LITIGATE THE LAWYER

THE DOULTONVILLE COLLECTION
ONE OF 25

Designer: William K. Harper
Handle: Plain
Colourway: Black robes; yellow waistcoat;
grey wig and trousers

Backstamp: Doulton

Doulton Number	Size	Backstamp	Height	Intro.	Discon.	Current Market Value		
						U.K. £	U.S. $	Can. $
D6699	Small	Doulton	4"	1983	1991	60.00	100.00	125.00

MR. MICAWBER

DICKENS TOBIES
ONE OF SIX

Designer:	Harry Fenton	**Backstamp:** Doulton
Handle:	Plain	
Colourway:	Browns	

Doulton Number	Size	Backstamp	Height	Intro.	Discon.	Current Market Value		
						U.K. £	U.S. $	Can. $
D6262	Small	Doulton	4 ½"	1948	1960	150.00	250.00	300.00

MR. PICKWICK

DICKENS TOBIES
ONE OF SIX

Designer: Harry Fenton
Handle: Plain
Colourway: Browns

Backstamp: Doulton

Doulton Number	Size	Backstamp	Height	Intro.	Discon.	Current Market Value U.K. £	Current Market Value U.S. $	Current Market Value Can. $
D6261	Small	Doulton	4 ½"	1948	1960	150.00	250.00	300.00

MR. TONSIL THE TOWN CRIER

THE DOULTONVILLE COLLECTION
ONE OF 25

Designer: William K. Harper
Handle: Plain
Colourway: Burgundy coat trimmed with gold; brown hat trimmed with gold; white scarf

Backstamp: Doulton

Doulton Number	Size	Backstamp	Height	Intro.	Discon.	Current Market Value		
						U.K.£	U.S. $	Can. $
D6713	Small	Doulton	4"	1984	1991	55.00	90.00	125.00

MRS. LOAN THE LIBRARIAN

THE DOULTONVILLE COLLECTION
ONE OF 25

Designer:	William K. Harper	**Backstamp:** Doulton
Handle:	Plain	
Colourway:	Dark green blouse trimmed with white;	
	light green skirt; yellow book	

Doulton Number	Size	Backstamp	Height	Intro.	Discon.	Current Market Value		
						U.K. £	U.S. $	Can. $
D6715	Small	Doulton	4"	1984	1989	55.00	90.00	125.00

OLD CHARLIE

For the tiny version of Old Charlie see Tiny Tobies, page 102.

Designer: Harry Fenton
Handle: Plain
Colourway: Brown hat; green coat; burgundy trousers

Backstamp: Doulton

Doulton Number	Size	Backstamp	Height	Intro.	Discon.	Current Market Value		
						U.K. £	U.S. $	Can. $
D6030	Large	Doulton	8 1/2"	1939	1960	275.00	500.00	600.00
D6069	Small	Doulton	5"	1939	1960	200.00	350.00	450.00

OLD FATHER TIME

For the first time Royal Doulton have incorporated a working clock into a toby jug. This jug was released by Lawleys By Post in a limited edition of 2,500.

Designer: David Biggs
Handle: Hour glass and hat
Colourway: Dark blue, white and brown

Backstamp: Doulton

Doulton Number	Size	Backstamp	Height	Intro.	Discon.	Current Market Value		
						U.K. £	U.S. $	Can. $
D7069	Small	Doulton	6 ½"	1996	Ltd. ed.	100.00	200.00	250.00

PAT PARCEL THE POSTMAN

THE DOULTONVILLE COLLECTION
ONE OF 25

Designer: William K. Harper
Handle: Plain
Colourway: Dark blue uniform trimmed with red; grey postbag

Backstamp: Doulton

Doulton Number	Size	Backstamp	Height	Intro.	Discon.	Current Market Value		
						U.K. £	U.S. $	Can. $
D6813	Small	Doulton	4"	1989	1991	55.00	90.00	125.00

REV. CASSOCK THE CLERGYMAN

THE DOULTONVILLE COLLECTION
ONE OF 25

Designer: William K. Harper
Handle: Plain
Colourway: Black coat; grey shirt; brown cap

Backstamp: Doulton

Doulton Number	Size	Backstamp	Height	Intro.	Discon.	Current Market Value		
						U.K. £	U.S. $	Can. $
D6702	Small	Doulton	4"	1983	1990	50.00	85.00	110.00

SAIREY GAMP

DICKENS TOBIES
ONE OF SIX

Designer: Harry Fenton
Handle: Plain
Colourway: Browns

Backstamp: Doulton

Doulton Number	Size	Backstamp	Height	Intro.	Discon.	Current Market Value		
						U.K.£	U.S. $	Can. $
D6263	Small	Doulton	4 ½"	1948	1960	150.00	250.00	300.00

SAM WELLER

DICKENS TOBIES
ONE OF SIX

Designer: Harry Fenton
Handle: Plain
Colourway: Browns

Backstamp: Doulton

Doulton Number	Size	Backstamp	Height	Intro.	Discon.	Current Market Value		
						U.K.£	U.S. $	Can. $
D6265	Small	Doulton	4 ½"	1948	1960	150.00	225.00	300.00

SGT. PEELER THE POLICEMAN

THE DOULTONVILLE COLLECTION
ONE OF 25

Designer: William K. Harper
Handle: Plain
Colourway: Blue-black uniform

Backstamp: Doulton

Doulton Number	Size	Backstamp	Height	Intro.	Discon.	Current Market Value		
						U.K.£	U.S. $	Can. $
D6720	Small	Doulton	4"	1985	1991	55.00	90.00	125.00

SHERLOCK HOLMES

The inscription on the base of this jug reads "Issued to Commemorate the 50th Anniversary of the Death of Sir Arthur Conan Doyle (1859 - 1930)."

For the character jug Sherlock Holmes, see the Sherlock Holmes Set, page 468.

Designer: Robert Tabbenor
Handle: Plain, black
Colourway: Green hat and cloak; green-brown coat

Backstamp: Doulton

Doulton Number	Size	Backstamp	Height	Intro.	Discon.	Current Market Value		
						U.K.£	U.S. $	Can. $
D6661	Large	Doulton	9"	1981	1991	90.00	175.00	200.00

SIR FRANCIS DRAKE

The inscription on the base of this jug reads "Issued to commemorate the 400th Anniversary of the circumnavigation of the world."

For the character jug Drake, see page 221, and for the character jug Sir Francis Drake, see page 471.

Designer: Michael Abberley	**Backstamp:** Doulton
Handle: Plain	
Colourway: Black hat with white feather; yellow with brown tunic; tan boots	

Doulton Number	Size	Backstamp	Height	Intro.	Discon.	Current Market Value		
						U.K.£	U.S. $	Can. $
D6660	Large	Doulton	9"	1981	1991	95.00	175.00	225.00

THE SPOOK and THE BEARED SPOOK

The Spook and Bearded Spook are based on the original figures designed by C. J. Noke. They were remodelled by Robert Tabbenor. This pair of jugs was issued, numbered and sold as a set in a limited edition of 1,500 by Lawleys By Post.

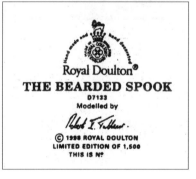

Designer: C. J. Noke
Modeller: Robert Tabbenor
Handle: Plain
Colourway: Blue-grey robes, black caps,
Brown handles and bases

Backstamp: Doulton

Doulton Number	Name	Backstamp	Height	Intro.	Discon.	Current Market Value U.K.£	U.S. $	Can. $
D7132	Spook	Doulton	5 ¾"	1998	Ltd. ed.	125.00	—	—
D7133	Bearded Spook	Doulton	5 ¼"	1998	Ltd. ed.	Pair	—	—

THE SQUIRE

Variation No. 1 - Kingsware

Variation No. 2 - Earthenware

VARIATION No. 1: Kingsware
Colourway — Browns; sterling silver rim around neck of jug

Designer: Unknown   **Backstamp:** Doulton
Handle: Plain
Colourway: Browns

Model Number	Variation	Backstamp	Height	Intro.	Discon.	Current Market Value U.K.£	U.S. $	Can. $
—	Var. 1	Doulton	6"	c.1910	Unknown	800.00	1,375.00	1,650.00

VARIATION No. 2: Earthenware
Colourway — Green coat; brown hat

Designer: Harry Fenton   **Backstamp:** Doulton
Handle: Plain
Colourway: Brown hat; green coat; mustard waistcoat with black buttons

Doulton Number	Size	Variation	Height	Intro.	Discon.	Current Market Value U.K.£	U.S. $	Can. $
D6319	Medium	Var. 2	6"	1950	1969	375.00	650.00	850.00

Note: We believe there is a possibility that an early Squire jug, issued circa 1910, exists in earthenware. If anyone has any information regarding this jug, please contact us.

TINY TOBIES

The Harry Fenton designs of the 1930s were authentically reproduced by William K. Harper in a new tiny size for 1994. The limited edition of 2,500 was sold only as a set and was available with a presentation stand.

The best is not too good
D. 6977

629

Happy John
D. 6979

629

Honest Measure
D. 6974

629

Jolly Toby
D. 6975

629

Old Charley
D. 6978

629

Toby XX
D. 6975

629

Designer: William K. Harper	**Backstamp:** Doulton
Handle: Plain	

Colourway: Best is not too Good, (The) — Green, mustard and brown
Happy John — Light green, mustard and black
Honest Measure — Geen, yellow and brown
Jolly Toby — Burgundy, yellow and black
Old Charlie — Green, brown and mustard
Toby XX — Burgundy, mustard, black and white

Doulton Number	Name	Height	Intro.	Discon.	Current Market Value U.K.£	U.S $	Can. $
D6977	Best is not too Good (The)	1 ½"	1994	Ltd. ed.	55.00	100.00	125.00
D6979	Happy John	2 ½"	1994	Ltd. ed.	55.00	100.00	125.00
D6974	Honest Measure	2"	1994	Ltd. ed.	55.00	100.00	125.00
D6976	Jolly Toby	2"	1994	Ltd. ed.	55.00	100.00	125.00
D6978	Old Charlie	2 ½"	1994	Ltd. ed.	55.00	100.00	125.00
D6975	Toby XX	2"	1994	Ltd. ed.	55.00	100.00	125.00
	Complete set with presentation stand				325.00	600.00	750.00

TOBY XX

STYLE FOUR: BURSLEM, EARTHENWARE, BURGUNDY COAT, WITH HANDLE

Style four is a modification of the 1925 design by Harry Simeon. Toby XX is also known as The Man on the Barrel and Double XX. See page 27 for the early stoneware Toby XX tobies. For the tiny version of Toby XX, see Tiny Tobies, page 102.

Designer:	Harry Fenton
Model No.:	8337
Handle:	Plain
Colourway:	Burgundy coat; orange shirt; blue bow tie; black trousers; dark brown hat; green-grey hair and Handle; cream barrel

Backstamp: Doulton

Doulton Number	Size	Backstamp	Height	Intro.	Discon.	Current Market Value		
						U.K. £	**U.S. $**	**Can. $**
D6088	Medium	Doulton	7"	1939	1969	250.00	500.00	600.00

TOWN CRIER

The Town Crier jug was issued in a limited edition of 2,500.

Designer: Stanley J. Taylor
Handle: Plain, black
Colourway: Scarlet great coat trimmed with yellow; black tricorn hat trimmed with yellow; white feather

Backstamp: Doulton

Doulton Number	Size	Backstamp	Height	Intro.	Discon.	Current Market Value		
						U.K.£	U.S. $	Can. $
D6920	Medium	Doulton	5"	1992	Ltd. ed.	125.00	250.00	275.00

WINSTON CHURCHILL

For the character jug Churchill, see page 197, for the character jug Sir Winston Churchill, see page 477 and for the character jug Winston Churchill, see page 527.

WINSTON CHURCHILL
PRIME MINISTER
OF GREAT BRITAIN
— 1940 —

Backstamp A

WINSTON CHURCHILL

Backstamp B

Designer: Harry Fenton	**Backstamps:**	**A.** "Winston Churchill Prime Minister of Great Britain 1940" Model No. 8360 B
Handle: Plain		
Colourway: Black hat; brown overcoat; black-green suit		**B.** "Winston Churchill"

Doulton Number	Size	Backstamp	Height	Intro.	Discon.	Current Market Value U.K.£	U.S. $	Can. $
D6171	Large	A. Doulton	9"	1940	1940	300.00	550.00	700.00
D6171	Large	B. Doulton	9"	1941	1991	90.00	150.00	150.00
D6172	Medium	A. Doulton	5 ½"	1940	1940	250.00	450.00	600.00
D6172	Medium	B. Doulton	5 ½"	1941	1991	60.00	100.00	100.00
D6175	Small	A. Doulton	4"	1940	1940	175.00	275.00	400.00
D6175	Small	B. Doulton	4"	1941	1991	55.00	90.00	90.00

ROYAL DOULTON
CHARACTER JUGS

JOHN BARLEYCORN
Handle Inside (left), Handle Outside (right)

ABRAHAM LINCOLN

PRESIDENTIAL SERIES
ONE OF THREE
PRESIDENTS OF THE UNITED STATES

First in a series of Presidents of the United States of America, issued in a limited edition of 2,500. The American flag and Lincoln's famous speech that begins "Four score and seven years ago..." form the handle.

Designer: Stanley J. Taylor
Handle: U.S. flag and Gettysburg Address
Colourway: Black and white

Backstamp: Doulton

Doulton Number	Size	Backstamp	Height	Intro.	Discon.	Current Market Value U.K. £	U.S. $	Can. $
D6936	Large	Doulton	6 ¾"	1992	Ltd. ed.	200.00	325.00	375.00

THE AIRMAN
(Royal Air Force)

ARMED FORCES SERIES
ONE OF THREE

This series pays tribute to those servicemen of the Royal Air Force, the Royal Army and the Royal Navy who fought in World War II. An airman belongs to the Royal Air Force, as either a pilot or another member of the crew.

STYLE ONE: HANDLE — GERMAN PLANE

VARIATION No. 1:   White scarf without cypher

Royal Doulton®
THE AIRMAN
D 6870
Modelled by

William K. Harper

© 1990 ROYAL DOULTON

Designer: William K. Harper
Handle: German fighter plane shot down in flames
Colourway: Light brown cap; dark brown flight jacket with cream collar; white scarf

Backstamp: Doulton

Doulton Number	Size	Backstamp	Height	Intro.	Discon.	Current Market Value		
						U.K. £	U.S. $	Can. $
D6870	Small	Doulton	4 ½"	1991	1996	45.00	95.00	150.00

THE AIRMAN
(Royal Canadian Air Force)

THE CANADIANS SERIES
ONE OF THREE

The Airman jug was commissioned by The British Toby of Ontario, Canada, in a limited edition of 250 pieces. It sold originally as part of a set of three at Can. $465.00.

STYLE ONE: HANDLE — GERMAN PLANE

VARIATION No. 2: Red scarf with cypher "RCAF"

Backstamp: Doulton

Designer: William K. Harper
Handle: German fighter plane shot down in flames
Colourway: Dark brown cap; flight jacket with beige collar; red scarf with cypher

Doulton Number	Size	Backstamp	Height	Intro.	Discon.	Current Market Value U.K.£	U.S. $	Can. $
D6903	Small	Doulton	4 ½"	1991	Ltd. ed.	175.00	300.00	350.00

THE AIRMAN

NATIONAL SERVICE EDITION
ONE OF THREE

Commissioned by Lawleys By Post, one could have a National Service Number incorporated within the accompanying certificate.

STYLE TWO: HANDLE — OXYGEN MASK

NATIONAL SERVICE EDITION

Royal Doulton®

THE AIRMAN

D 6982

Modelled by

William K. Harper

© 1990 ROYAL DOULTON

Designer: William K. Harper
Handle: An oxygen mask
Colourway: Cream, brown and grey

Backstamp: Doulton

Doulton Number	Size	Backstamp	Height	Intro.	Discon.	Current Market Value		
						U.K.£	U.S. $	Can. $
D6982	Small	Doulton	4 ½"	1994	Sp. ed.	65.00	150.00	200.00

ALADDIN'S GENIE

FLAMBÉ SERIES
ONE OF THREE

Issued in a limited edition of 1,500, this was the first jug to be decorated in flambé.

Designer: David Biggs
Handle: Lamp, ghost form and tassle
Colourway: Flambé

Backstamp: Doulton

Doulton Number	Size	Backstamp	Height	Intro.	Discon.	Current Market Value U.K.£	U.S. $	Can. $
D6971	Large	Doulton	7 ½"	1994	Ltd ed.	300.00	675.00	800.00

ALBERT EINSTEIN

Royal Doulton®
ALBERT EINSTEIN™
D7023
Modelled by
Stanley James Taylor
© 1995 ROYAL DOULTON
ALBERT EINSTEIN LICENSED BY
THE ROGER RICHMAN AGENCY, INC:
BEVERLEY HILLS, CA

Designer: Stanley J. Taylor
Handle: Molecule, theory of relativity, scroll $E=mc^2$
Colourway: White, blue and red

Backstamp: Doulton/Albert Einstein Licensed by The Roger Richman Agency, Inc. Beverley Hills. CA

Doulton Number	Size	Backstamp	Height	Intro.	Discon.	Current Market Value		
						U.K.£	U.S. $	Can. $
D7023	Large	Doulton	7"	1995	1997	125.00	225.00	250.00

ALFRED HITCHCOCK

This jug commemorates the achievements of Alfred Hitchcock (1899-1990) in producing superb movie thrillers. The handle features the shower curtain from *Psycho* and a bird from *The Birds*.

The original design of this jug had the shower curtain painted pink and the backstamp was the usual Royal Doulton design. This was later changed to a white shower curtain with blue shading and a backstamp that incorporated the MCA Universal Copyright.

VARIATION No. 1: Colourway — White shower curtain with pink shading

VARIATION No. 2: Colourway — White shower curtain with blue shading

Backstamp A - Doulton

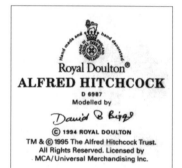

Backstamp B - Doulton/MCA
Universal Copyright

Designer: David B. Biggs
Handle: Shower curtain, bird and film
Colourway: See variations
Backstamp: A. Doulton
B. Doulton/MCA Universal Copyright

Doulton Number	Colourway	Backstamp	Height	Intro.	Discon.	Current Market Value U.K. £	U.S. $	Can. $
D6987	Var. 1/Pink	Doulton A	7 ½"	1995	1995	1,600.00	3,000.00	3,500.00
D6987	Var. 1/Pink	Doulton B	7 ½"	1995	1995	1,000.00	1,850.00	2,000.00
D6987	Var. 2/Blue	Doulton B	7 ½"	1995	1997	125.00	225.00	250.00

THE ANGEL

CHRISTMAS MINIATURE SERIES
(ONE OF SIX)

This jug was issued in the U.S.A. only, but made available to all members of the Royal Doulton International Collectors Club. This is the last jug in the Christmas Miniature Series of Santa, Mrs. Claus, The Elf, Snowman and Caroller.

Royal Doulton®
THE ANGEL
D7051
© 1996 ROYAL DOULTON

Designer: Martyn Alcock	**Backstamp:** Doulton
Handle: Harp and bells	
Colourway: White, light brown and yellow	

Doulton Number	Size	Backstamp	Height	Intro.	Discon.	Current Market Value U.K.£	U.S. $	Can. $
D7051	Miniature	Doulton	2 ¾"	1996	1997	40.00	77.50	110.00

THE ANGLER

CHARACTERS FROM LIFE SERIES
ONE OF SEVEN

STYLE ONE: HANDLE — FISH AND LURE

Designer: Stanley J. Taylor
Handle: A fish and lure
Colourway: Green jacket; brown hat; cream pullover

Backstamp: Doulton

Doulton Number	Size	Backstamp	Height	Intro.	Discon.	Current Market Value		
						U.K.£	U.S. $	Can. $
D6866	Small	Doulton	4"	1990	1995	45.00	100.00	125.00

THE ANGLER

STYLE TWO: HANDLE — FISHING NET AND REEL

Designer: David B. Biggs
Handle: Fishing net and reel
Colourway: Green jacket, yellow pullover, tan hat

Backstamp: Doulton

Doulton Number	Size	Backstamp	Height	Intro.	Discon.	Current Market Value U.K.£	U.S. $	Can. $
D7065	Small	Doulton	4 ¾"	1997	Current	53.00	145.00	285.00

ANNE BOLEYN

HENRY VIII AND HIS SIX WIVES SERIES
ONE OF EIGHT

Anne Boleyn (1502-1536) became the second wife of Henry VIII in a secret ceremony performed in January 1533. Their marriage was officially sanctioned in May by the Archbishop of Canterbury, Thomas Cranmer, and she was crowned Queen on June 1, 1533, in Westminster Hall. Unable to produce the son Henry VIII desired, Anne was imprisoned in the Tower of London on false grounds of adultery. She was beheaded with a sword on May 19, 1536, in a courtyard of the Tower of London (the modeller's use of an axe to form the handle was incorrect). Anne Boleyn was the mother of Queen Elizabeth I, born on September 7, 1533.

For Anne Boleyn, style two, see "The Six Wives of Henry VIII," page 478.

STYLE ONE: HANDLE IN FORM OF AN AXE

Designer: Douglas V. Tootle
Handle: An axe and chopping block
Colourway: Black and grey

Backstamp: Doulton

Doulton Number	Size	Backstamp	Height	Intro.	Discon.	Current Market Value		
						U.K.£	U.S. $	Can. $
D6644	Large	Doulton	7 ¼"	1975	1990	100.00	175.00	200.00
D6650	Small	Doulton	3 ½"	1980	1990	75.00	130.00	150.00
D6651	Miniature	Doulton	2 ½"	1980	1990	75.00	125.00	125.00

ANNE OF CLEVES

HENRY VIII AND HIS SIX WIVES SERIES
ONE OF EIGHT

In a political arrangement by Thomas Cromwell, Anne of Cleves (1515-1557) was chosen to marry Henry VIII. Upon seeing his dull and unattractive betrothed, whom he later referred to as his "Flanders Mare," Henry attempted unsuccessfully to break the contract. Anne became his fourth wife on January 6, 1540, for only a brief time. Henry had the marriage annulled on July 8th of that year and gave Anne a pension for life.

For Anne of Cleves, style two, see "The Six Wives of Henry VIII," page 478.

STYLE ONE: HANDLE IN THE SHAPE OF A HORSE'S HEAD

VARIATION No. 1: Handle — Horse's ears pointing up

Variation No.2, Ears flat; Variation No.1, Ears pointing up

Designer: Michael Abberley
Handle: Head of a horse; ears pointing up
Colourway: Black and red

Backstamp: Doulton

Doulton Number	Size	Variation	Height	Intro.	Discon.	Current Market Value U.K.£	U.S. $	Can. $
D6653	Large	Var. 1	7 ¼"	1980	1981	185.00	300.00	375.00

VARIATION No. 2: Handle — Horse's ears flat against head. Because the upright ears tended to break off during packaging and shipping, the design was changed so the ears lay flat against the head.

Royal Doulton
ANNE OF CLEVES
D 8653
Modelled by

© ROYAL DOULTON TABLEWARE
LIMITED 1979

Large jug, D6653, backstamp

Royal Doulton®
ANNE OF CLEVES
D 6753
Designed by M Abberley
Modelled by

PeterAGee

© 1979 ROYAL DOULTON (UK)

Small jug, D6753, backstamp

Designer: Large size: Michael Abberley
Small and miniature size: Peter Gee
Handle: Head of a horse; ears flat
Colourway: Black and red

Backstamp: Doulton

Doulton Number	Size	Variation	Height	Intro.	Discon.	Current Market Value		
						U.K.£	U.S. $	Can. $
D6653	Large	Var. 2	7 ¼"	1980	1990	100.00	175.00	225.00
D6753	Small	Var. 2	4 ¼"	1987	1990	100.00	175.00	175.00
D6754	Miniature	Var. 2	2 ½"	1987	1990	100.00	175.00	175.00

ANNIE OAKLEY

THE WILD WEST COLLECTION
ONE OF SIX

Phoebe Anne Moses (1860-1926) learned to shoot at the age of eight and helped support her family by killing game for a hotel in Cincinnati, Ohio. At 15, she defeated professional marksman Frank Butler in a shooting contest. She married him in 1876 and became a regular performer in shooting exhibitions, using the stage name Annie Oakley. She was a star of Buffalo Bill's Wild West Show from 1885 until 1901, when she was injured in a train accident and forced to retire. During World War I she trained American soldiers in marksmanship.

Backstamp: Doulton

Designer: Stanley J. Taylor
Handle: Rifle and belt
Colourway: Yellow hair; cream hat; brown tunic

Doulton Number	Size	Backstamp	Height	Intro.	Discon.	Current Market Value		
						U.K.£	U.S. $	Can. $
D6732	Mid	Doulton	5 ¼"	1985	1989	85.00	150.00	175.00

THE ANTIQUE DEALER

THE COLLECTING WORLD
ONE OF THREE

This jug was commissioned by Kevin Francis Ceramics Ltd. in 1988 in a special edition of 5,000 pieces. It is interesting to note that Kevin Francis jugs have the handle on the left side.

Designer: Geoff Blower
Handle: Flintlock handgun and candlestick
Colourway: Black hat; blue coat

Backstamp: Doulton/Kevin Frances Ceramics

Doulton Number	Size	Backstamp	Height	Intro.	Discon.	Current Market Value		
						U.K.£	U.S. $	Can. $
D6807	Large	Doulton	7 ¼"	1988	Sp. ed.	100.00	225.00	250.00

ANTONY AND CLEOPATRA

PROTOTYPE

A prototype of this character jug exists where Antony has a pudgy face, wide eyes and brown hair, and Cleopatra has lighter eye make-up, lighter beads around her neck and a dark red headdress. Only one is known to exist.

Prototype (left); Regular Issue (right)

Doulton Number	Size	Variation	Height	Intro.	Discon.	Current Market Value		
						U.K.£	U.S. $	Can. $
D6728	Large	Prototype	7 ¼"	1984	1984		Unique	

ANTONY AND CLEOPATRA

THE STAR-CROSSED LOVERS COLLECTION (TWO-FACED JUG)
ONE OF FOUR

Marcus Antonius (83-30 B.C.) was a skilled soldier and co-ruler of Rome with Caesar's nephew Octavian from 43 to 32 B.C. Cleopatra (68-30 B.C.), well known for her charm and beauty, was queen of Egypt and an ally and lover of Julius Caesar. In 41 B.C. Antony and Cleopatra met and fell in love, marrying in 37 B.C. Antony gave Cleopatra and their children a share of his Roman provinces in 34 B.C., a move which enraged Octavian, who waged war on the couple, pursuing them in their defeat to Alexandria.

Antony, hearing a false rumour of Cleopatra's death, stabbed himself in grief. He was carried to her and died in her arms. In turn, Cleopatra committed suicide by placing an asp on her chest, apparently from fear of Octavian.

The jugs were issued in 1985 in a limited edition of 9,500 pieces.

Designer: Michael Abberley
Handle: Eagle's head, dagger and shield; asp and harp
Colourway: Black, grey, brown
Backstamp: Doulton

Doulton Number	Size	Backstamp	Height	Intro.	Discon.	Current Market Value		
						U.K.£	U.S. $	Can. $
D6728	Large	Doulton	7 ¼"	1985	Ltd. ed.	85.00	135.00	150.00

APOTHECARY

CHARACTERS FROM WILLIAMSBURG
ONE OF EIGHT

Along with the other characters in the Williamsburg Series, the apothecary was central to colonial life in 18th century America.

Character Jugs from Williamsburg
Apothecary
D 6567
COPR 1962
DOULTON & CO LIMITED
Rd No 906337
Rd No 43444
Rd No 9223
Rd No 287/62

Designer: Max Henk
Handle: Mortar and pestle
Colourway: Green coat with white cravat; white wig

Backstamp: Doulton

Doulton Number	Size	Backstamp	Height	Intro.	Discon.	Current Market Value		
						U.K. £	U.S. $	Can. $
D6567	Large	Doulton	7"	1963	1983	100.00	175.00	200.00
D6574	Small	Doulton	4"	1963	1983	60.00	100.00	150.00
D6581	Miniature	Doulton	2 ½"	1963	1983	60.00	100.00	125.00

Note: This jug was also issued in English Translucent China. These jugs command a premium of 50 to 100% over the earthenware variety.

ARAMIS

THE THREE MUSKETEERS, ONE OF FOUR
NOW PART OF THE CHARACTERS FROM LITERATURE, ONE OF 11

One of the three musketeers, Aramis joined Athos, Porthos and D'Artagnan in a life of adventure in Alexandre Dumas's 19th century novel, following their code "All for one, and one for all."

The wording "One of the Three Musketeers" was included in the earlier backstamp to indicate that Aramis was one of the famous Musketeers.

VARIATION No. 1:   Colourway — Black hat; white feather; brown tunic

Backstamp B -
Doulton/"One of"

Designer:	Max Henk	
Handle:	Handle of a sword	
Colourway:	Black hat; white feather; brown tunic	

Backstamps: A. Doulton
   B. Doulton/One of the
   Three Musketeers

Doulton Number	Size	Backstamp	Height	Intro.	Discon.	U.K. £	U.S. $	Can. $
							Current Market Value	
D6441	Large	A.Doulton	7 ¼"	1956	1991	75.00	100.00	125.00
D6441	Large	B.Doulton/One	7 ¼"	1956	1970	75.00	125.00	150.00
D6454	Small	A.Doulton	3 ½"	1956	1991	60.00	60.00	65.00
D6454	Small	B.Doulton/One	3 ½"	1956	1970	65.00	75.00	80.00
D6508	Miniature	A.Doulton	2 ½"	1960	1991	50.00	60.00	65.00
D6508	Miniature	B.Doulton/One	2 ½"	1960	1970	55.00	75.00	80.00

Note: This jug was also issued in English Translucent China. These jugs command a premium of 50 to 100% over the earthenware variety.

VARIATION No. 2:   Colourway — Yellow hat; maroon tunic

This jug was commissioned by Peter Jones China Ltd., England, and issued in 1988 in a limited edition of 1,000.

Backstamp: Doulton

Doulton Number	Size	Backstamp	Height	Intro.	Discon.	Current Market Value		
						U.K. £	U.S. $	Can. $
D6829	Large	Doulton	7 ¼"	1988	Ltd. ed.	120.00	225.00	250.00

'ARD OF 'EARING

With hand held to cup his ear, this cockney gentleman is a comic representation of a deaf man. After being discontinued in 1967, this jug has increased in value and is difficult to find.

Designer: David Biggs
Handle: A hand held to the ear
Colourway: Dark purple tricorn; green, white and yellow clothing

Backstamp: Doulton

Doulton Number	Size	Backstamp	Height	Intro.	Discon.	Current Market Value U.K. £	U.S. $	Can. $
D6588	Large	Doulton	7 ½"	1964	1967	1,300.00	2,200.00	2,700.00
D6591	Small	Doulton	3 ½"	1964	1967	800.00	1,300.00	1,700.00
D6594	Miniature	Doulton	2 ½"	1964	1967	950.00	1,600.00	2,000.00

A.R.P. WARDEN

HEROES OF THE BLITZ
ONE OF THREE

The A.R.P. (Air Raids Precautions) Wardens were charged with the responsibility of insuring that people were as secure as possible during an air raid. Armed only with his whistle, he would patrol the streets enforcing the "lights out please" signal and see that all citizens took cover as quickly as possible. The Heroes of the Blitz jugs were commissioned by Lawleys By Post in a limited edition of 9,500 sets.

Designer: Stanley J. Taylor
Handle: Grey whistle
Colourway: Dark blue jacket; white helmet with black stripe and the initial W (Warden)

Backstamp: Doulton

Doulton Number	Size	Backstamp	Height	Intro.	Discon.	Current Market Value		
						U.K. £	U.S. $	Can. $
D6872	Small	Doulton	4"	1991	Ltd. ed.	115.00	190.00	275.00

'ARRIET

'Arriet is a coster or costermonger, a cockney woman who sold fruits and vegetables from a barrow in the streets of London. She is a variation of the Pearly Girl character jug (see page 398).

"'arriet."

COPR. 1946.
DOULTON & CO LIMITED
R�ᵈNº 847682
R�ᵈNº 23909.
R⁊Nº 132/46.
R⁊Nº 5195.

Designer: Harry Fenton
Handle: Hat feather
Colourway: Green hat; brown coat; yellow scarf

Backstamp: Doulton

Doulton Number	Size	Backstamp	Height	Intro.	Discon.	Current Market Value		
						U.K. £	U.S. $	Can. $
D6208	Large	Doulton	6 ½"	1947	1960	150.00	250.00	275.00
D6236	Small	Doulton	3 ¼"	1947	1960	80.00	150.00	190.00
D6250	Miniature	Doulton	2 ¼"	1947	1960	60.00	110.00	135.00
D6256	Tiny	Doulton	1 ¼"	1947	1960	125.00	225.00	250.00

Note: This jug was also issued in English Translucent China. These jugs command a premium of 50 to 100% over the earthenware variety.

'ARRY

'Arriet's husband 'Arry is also a costermonger, plying his trade in London. He is a variation of the Pearly Boy (see page 396) character jug. The original design featured the word "Blimey" across the back, but it was never produced.

Designer: Harry Fenton
Handle: Plain
Colourway: Brown hat and coat; red and yellow scarf

Backstamp: Doulton

Doulton Number	Size	Backstamp	Height	Intro.	Discon.	Current Market Value U.K. £	U.S. $	Can. $
D6207	Large	Doulton	6 ½"	1947	1960	150.00	225.00	275.00
D6235	Small	Doulton	3 ½"	1947	1960	75.00	125.00	150.00
D6249	Miniature	Doulton	2 ½"	1947	1960	65.00	100.00	125.00
D6255	Tiny	Doulton	1 ½"	1947	1960	125.00	225.00	250.00

Note: This jug was also issued in English Translucent China. These jugs command a premium of 50 to 100% over the earthenware variety.

ARSENAL (FOOTBALL CLUB)

THE FOOTBALL SUPPORTERS
ONE OF TEN

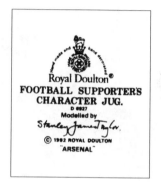

Designer: Stanley J. Taylor
Handle: Team coloured scarf
Colourway: Red and white uniform

Backstamp: Doulton

Doulton Number	Size	Backstamp	Height	Intro.	Discon.	Current Market Value		
						U.K. £	U.S. $	Can. $
D6927	Mid	Doulton	5"	1992	Unknown	60.00	125.00	150.00

ARTFUL DODGER

For the character jug Artful Dodger, see the "Charles Dickens Commemorative Set" page 185.

ASTON VILLA (FOOTBALL CLUB)

THE FOOTBALL SUPPORTERS
ONE OF TEN

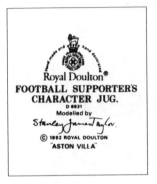

Designer: Stanley J. Taylor
Handle: Team coloured scarf
Colourway: Maroon and blue uniform

Backstamp: Doulton

Doulton Number	Size	Backstamp	Height	Intro.	Discon.	Current Market Value		
						U.K. £	U.S. $	Can. $
D6931	Mid	Doulton	5"	1992	Unknown	60.00	125.00	150.00

ATHOS

THE THREE MUSKETEERS, ONE OF FOUR
NOW PART OF THE CHARACTERS FROM LITERATURE, ONE OF 11

Under the banner of "All for one and one for all," Athos was one of the original musketeers in the 19th-century novel by Alexandre Dumas. First issued as one of four in the Three Musketeers Series, Athos is now incorporated into the larger series, Characters from Literature.

VARIATION No. 1:   Mould — Feathers along rim of hat
Colourway — Black hat; white feather; green tunic with gold trim

Backstamp A - Doulton

Backstamp B -
Doulton/"One of"

Designer: Max Henk
Handle: Upper half of a sword
Colourway: Black hat; white feather; green tunic with gold trim

Backstamps: **A.** Doulton
B. Doulton /One of the Three Musketeers
The wording "One of the Three Musketeers" was included in the early backstamp to indicate that Athos was one of the famous Musketeers.

Doulton Number	Size	Backstamp	Height	Intro.	Discon.	Current Market Value U.K. £	U.S. $	Can. $
D6439	Large	A. Doulton	7 ¼"	1956	1991	80.00	100.00	100.00
D6439	Large	B. Doulton/One	7 ¼"	1956	1991	95.00	125.00	125.00
D6452	Small	A. Doulton	3 ¾"	1956	1991	45.00	60.00	60.00
D6452	Small	B. Doulton/One	3 ¾"	1956	1991	45.00	75.00	75.00
D6509	Miniature	A. Doulton	2 ½"	1960	1991	35.00	50.00	50.00
D6509	Miniature	B. Doulton/One	2 ½"	1960	1991	40.00	70.00	70.00

Note: This jug was also issued in English Translucent China. These jugs command a premium of 50 to 100% over the earthenware variety.

VARIATION No. 2: Mould — Feather along rim of hat
Colourway — Purple hat; white feather; yellow tunic with purple trim

VARIATION No. 3: Mould — Feathers above rim of hat
Colourway — Purple hat; white feather; yellow tunic with purple trim

There were two different moulds used in the production of the Jones Colourway, variation 2 and variation 3. A total of 1,000 jugs were issued, but how many of each variation were produced is unknown.

Variation No. 2 (left); Variation No. 3 (right)

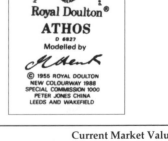

Designer: Max Henk
Handle: Upper half of a sword
Colourway: Black hat; white feather;
yellow tunic with blue trim

Backstamp: Doulton/Peter Jones China Ltd.
Commissioned by Peter Jones China Ltd.,
England. Issued in 1988 in a limited
edition of 1,000.

Doulton Number	Size	Variation	Height	Intro.	Discon.	Current Market Value U.K. £	U.S. $	Can. $
D6827	Large	Var. 2	7 ¼"	1988	Ltd. ed.	120.00	225.00	250.00
D6827	Large	Var. 3	7 ¼"	1988	(incl. in above)	120.00	225.00	250.00

THE AUCTIONEER

THE COLLECTING WORLD
ONE OF THREE

Commissioned by Kevin Francis Ceramics Ltd., The Auctioneer jug was issued in 1988 in a limited edition of 5,000. Characteristic of Kevin Francis, this is a left-handed jug.

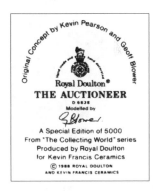

Designer: Geoff Blower
Handle: Auctioneer's gavel and The Bather (HN687)
Colourway: Green coat and bow tie; light brown cap

Backstamp: Doulton/Kevin Frances Ceramics

Doulton Number	Size	Backstamp	Height	Intro.	Discon.	Current Market Value		
						U.K. £	U.S. $	Can. $
D6838	Large	Doulton	6 ¼"	1988	Sp. ed.	125.00	250.00	300.00

AULD MAC

A song by Sir Harry Lauder, a 20th-century singer and comedian, called "Bang Went Saxpence," inspired this piece. In it a Scotsman named Mac found the prices too high in London because every time he made a move, "bang went saxpence," which is incised on the back of his tam, below "Auld Mac."

"OWD MAC" (left)' "AULD MAC" (right)

Backstamp A - "Owd Mac"

Backstamp B - "Auld Mac"

Designer: Harry Fenton
Handle: A brier
Colourway: Green tam; brown coat

Backstamps: A. Doulton/"Owd Mac"
"Owd Mac" was incised in the
tam and printed in the backstamp, c. 1937.
B. Doulton/Auld Mac
"Auld Mac" was incised in the
tam in 1938, but "Owd Mac"
continued in the backstamp
until c.1940.
C. Doulton/Auld Mac
"Auld Mac" was incised in the
tam and printed in the backstamp.

Doulton Number	Size	Backstamp	Height	Intro.	Discon.	Current Market Value U.K. £	U.S. $	Can. $
D5823	Large	A. "Owd"/"Owd"	6 ¼"	1937	c. 1937	350.00	625.00	750.00
D5823	Large	B. "Auld/Owd"	6 ¼"	1938	1940	175.00	400.00	525.00
D5823	Large	C. "Auld/Auld"	6 ¼"	1940	1986	75.00	100.00	120.00
D5824	Small	A. "Owd"/"Owd"	3 ¼"	1937	1937	275.00	500.00	600.00
D5824	Small	B. "Auld/Owd"	3 ¼"	1938	1940	125.00	150.00	200.00
D5824	Small	C. "Auld/Auld"	3 ¼"	1940	1985	35.00	65.00	85.00
D6253	Miniature	C. "Auld/Auld"	2 ¼"	1946	1985	35.00	65.00	75.00
D6257	Tiny	C. "Auld/Auld"	1 ¼"	1946	1960	110.00	235.00	275.00

Auld Mac Derivatives

Doulton Number	Item	Height	Intro.	Discon.	Current Market Value U.K. £	U.S. $	Can. $
D5889	Musical jug	6 ¼"	1938	c. 1939	575.00	1,150.00	1,350.00
D6006	Ash bowl	3"	1938	1960	100.00	175.00	175.00

Note: 1. The musical jug plays the tune "The Campbells are Coming."
2. The "Auld/Auld" variety of this jug was also issued in English Translucent China. These jugs command a premium of 50 to 100% over the earthenware variety.

AUXILIARY FIREMAN

HEROES OF THE BLITZ
ONE OF THREE

Large numbers of volunteer firemen were needed to assist the regular firemen during the World War II bombing of London and other cities of Great Britain. It was through the courage of the Auxiliary Fire Service (A.F.S.) that many of the fires of the air raids were held in check. The Heroes of the Blitz set of jugs was commissioned by Lawleys By Post in a limited edition of 9,500 sets.

Designer: Stanley J. Taylor
Handle: Hose and nozzle
Colourway: Black jacket; grey helmet
with white initials "A.F.S."

Backstamp: Doulton

Doulton Number	Size	Backstamp	Height	Intro.	Discon.	Current Market Value U.K. £	U.S. $	Can. $
D6887	Small	Doulton	4"	1991	Ltd. ed.	100.00	175.00	250.00

BACCHUS

In Greek and Roman mythology, Bacchus was the god of wine and nature, inspiring men and women to appreciate music and poetry. "Bacchanalia," the harvest celebrations to honour him, were reputed to be such orgies of excess that the Roman government had them banned.

Some of the earlier versions of the miniature jug had the leaves on the vine handle painted green. There is no current premium value for this variety.

Backstamp A - Doulton

Backstamp B - City of
Stoke-on-Trent

Designer: Max Henk
Handle: Grapevine
Colourway: Maroon robes; green leaves and purple grapes adorn the head

Backstamps: A. Doulton
   B. Doulton/City of Stoke-on-Trent Jubilee Year 1959 - 1960
   With the compliments of Lord Mayor and Lady Mayoress Alderman Harold Clowes, O.B.E., J.P. and Miss Christine Clowes

Doulton Number	Size	Backstamp	Height	Intro.	Discon.	Current Market Value U.K. £	U.S. $	Can. $
D6499	Large	Doulton	7"	1959	1991	65.00	125.00	150.00
D6499	Large	Doulton/City	7"	1959	1960		Rare	
D6505	Small	Doulton	4"	1959	1991	50.00	60.00	75.00
D6521	Miniature	Doulton	2 ½"	1960	1991	40.00	65.00	80.00

Bacchus Derivative

Doulton Number	Item	Height	Intro.	Discon.	Current Market Value U.K. £	U.S. $	Can. $
D6505	Table lighter	3 ½"	1964	1974	150.00	300.00	350.00

Note: This jug was also issued in English Translucent China. These jugs command a premium of 50 to 100% over the earthenware variety.

BAHAMAS POLICEMAN

This jug was commissioned by Island Galleria, Nassau, Bahamas, in a special edition of 1,000 jugs. The D number 6912 is also the numerical designation of The Snake Charmer.

Designer: William K. Harper
Handle: Tassle
Colourway: White and red

Backstamp: Doulton/Island Galleria

Doulton Number	Size	Backstamp	Height	Intro.	Discon.	Current Market Value		
						U.K. £	U.S. $	Can. $
D6912	Large	Doulton	7"	1992	Sp. ed.	165.00	300.00	325.00

BASEBALL PLAYER ̄

Only two of these jugs are known to exist, and each is different. They are test pieces and were never put into production.

STYLE ONE: HANDLE — BAT AND BALL

VARIATION No. 1:   Colourway — Blue-green jersey; red sleeves and cap

Designer: David Biggs   **Backstamp:** Doulton
Handle: Bat and ball
Colourway: Blue-green jersey; red sleeves and cap

Doulton Number	Size	Variation	Height	Intro.	Discon.	Current Market Value		
						U.K. £	U.S. $	Can. $
D6624	Large	Var. 1	7 ½"	1970	1970		Extremely rare	

VARIATION No. 2:   Colourway — Striped blue and black jersey and cap

Doulton Number	Size	Variation	Height	Intro.	Discon.	Current Market Value		
						U.K. £	U.S. $	Can. $
D6624	Large	Var. 2	7 ½"	1970	1970		Extremely rare	

THE BASEBALL PLAYER

CHARACTERS FROM LIFE
ONE OF SEVEN

STYLE TWO: HANDLE — BALL, BAT AND GLOVE

VARIATION No. 1: General baseball player — blue cap with lion and crown insignia

Backstamp A - Doulton

Backstamp B - Britannia Ltd.

Designer: Stanley J. Taylor
Handle: Ball, bat and glove
Colourway: Dark blue cap; white jersey with blue trim

Backstamps: A. Doulton
For general issue, 1991.
B. Doulton/Britannia Limited
Commissioned by Britannia
Limited to celebrate the fifth
anniversary of their Doulton
Convention and Sale, January
1991. Issued in a special
edition of 500 pieces.

Doulton Number	Size	Backstamp	Height	Intro.	Discon.	Current Market Value		
						U.K. £	U.S. $	Can. $
D6878	Small	Doulton	4 ¼"	1991	1998	50.00	125.00	150.00
D6878	Small	Doulton/Britannia	4 ¼"	1991	Sp. ed.	100.00	175.00	200.00

VARIATION No. 2:   Toronto Blue Jays — blue cap with Toronto Blue Jays insignia

This character jug was issued to commemorate the Toronto Blue Jays, winner of the 1992 and 1993 World Series of baseball. It was produced in limited edition of 2,500 worldwide.

Designer: Stanley J. Taylor
Handle: Ball, bat and glove
Colourway: Blue cap; white jersey with blue trim

Backstamp: Doulton/MLBPA/Blue Jays

Doulton Number	Size	Backstamp	Height	Intro.	Discon.	Current Market Value U.K. £	U.S. $	Can. $
D6973	Small	Doulton	4 ¼"	1994	Ltd. ed.	75.00	135.00	200.00

VARIATION No. 3: Philadelphia

Produced to celebrate the 125th anniversary of Strawbridge and Clothier in Philadelphia, this jug was available only through that retailer. It was issued in a limited edition of 2,500 pieces.

Royal Doulton®
THE BASEBALL PLAYER
D 6957
Modelled by
Stanley James Taylor
© 1990 ROYAL DOULTON
NEW COLOURWAY 1993

Designer: Stanley J. Taylor
Handle: Ball, bat and glove
Colourway: Red cap; white jersey with red stripes

Backstamp: Doulton
"NewColourway 1993"

Doulton Number	Size	Backstamp	Height	Intro.	Discon.	Current Market Value		
						U.K. £	U.S. $	Can. $
D6957	Small	Doulton	4 ¼"	1993	Ltd. ed.	100.00	165.00	250.00

BEEFEATER (WITH KEYS)

PROTOTYPE

This jug was designed for a proposed commission by PWC Publishing. The head was from the standard Beefeater jug, originally modelled by Harry Fenton, and Harry Sales remodelled the keys from Simon the Cellarer to form the handle. Due to cost and quantity requirements, the project was not continued.

Variation 3 was not returned to Doulton and is now in a U.S. collection.

VARIATION No. 1:   Colourway — Grey keys; blue hat

VARIATION No. 2:   Colourway — Yellow keys; blue hat; name highlighted in yellow

VARIATION No. 3:   Colourway — Yellow keys; black hat with on-glaze red and blue band

Designer: Head — Harry Fenton
Keys — Remodelled by Harry Sales
Handle: See colourway variations above
Colourway: Scarlet tunic; white ruff; black hat

Backstamp: Doulton

Doulton Number	Size	Variation	Height	Intro.	Discon.	Current Market Value U.K. £	U.S. $	Can. $
D —	Large	Var. 1	6 ½"	1988	1988		Unique	
D —	Large	Var. 2	6 ½"	1988	1988		Unique	

BEEFEATER

THE LONDON COLLECTION
ONE OF TEN

The Yeomen of the Guard and warders of the Tower of London are colloquially referred to as Beefeaters. The name "Beefeater" came from a visiting Grand Duke who was astonished by the large amounts of beef eaten by the Yeoman Guards. The monarch's cypher, GR, at the base of the handle is an abbreviation of George Rex, for King George VI. After his death in 1953, the cypher was changed to ER (Elizabeth Regina), for Queen Elizabeth II.

VARIATION No. 1: Handle — Pink with a "GR" cypher

Designer: Harry Fenton/Robert Tabbenor
Handle: Pink with a "GR" cypher
Colourway: Black hat; white ruff; pink tunic

Backstamp: Doulton/"Beefeaters"
The pluralized name was used on all three sizes of jugs from 1947 through 1953.

Doulton Number	Size	Variation	Height	Intro.	Discon.	Current Market Value U.K. £	U.S. $	Can. $
D6206	Large	Var. 1	6 ½"	1947	1953	90.00	225.00	225.00
D6233	Small	Var. 1	3 ¼"	1947	1953	60.00	125.00	150.00
D6251	Miniature	Var. 1	2 ½"	1947	1953	60.00	125.00	125.00

VARIATION No. 2:   Handle — Yellow with a "GR" cypher

Backstamp: Doulton / "Beefeaters"

Doulton Number	Size	Variation	Height	Intro.	Discon.	Current Market Value U.K. £	U.S. $	Can. $
D6206	Large	Var. 2	6 ½"	1947	1947	1,200.00	3,000.00	3,750.00
D6233	Small	Var. 2	3 ¼"	1947	1947	1,000.00	2,000.00	2,500.00
D6251	Miniature	Var. 2	2 ½"	1947	1947	Rare		

VARIATION No. 3:   Handle — Pink with an "ER" cypher

Backstamp A   Backstamp B, Large   Backstamp B, Small   Backstamp C

Backstamps: **A.** Doulton/"Beefeaters"
  The plural name was found only on early versions of the "ER" jugs.
  B. Doulton/Beefeater
  In late 1953 the backstamp was adjusted and the singular "Beefeater" name was incorporated.
  C. Doulton/Beefeater
  Fired in the last firing of a traditional Bottle Oven 1978 Longton Stoke-on-Trent, England

Doulton Number	Size	Variation	Height	Intro.	Discon.	Current Market Value U.K. £	U.S. $	Can. $
D6206	Large	Var. 3A	6 ½"	1953	1953	65.00	145.00	145.00
D6206	Large	Var. 3B	6 ½"	1953	1987	60.00	110.00	110.00
D6206	Large	Var. 3C	6 ½"	1978	1978	Rare		
D6233	Small	Var. 3A	3 ¼"	1953	1953	40.00	75.00	75.00
D6233	Small	Var. 3B	3 ¼"	1953	1987	40.00	65.00	65.00
D6251	Miniature	Var. 3A	2 ½"	1953	1953	35.00	55.00	55.00
D6251	Miniature	Var. 3B	2 ½"	1953	1987	35.00	55.00	55.00

Note: 1. Some of the early George VI (GR cypher) jugs have yellow highlights on the handle. Jugs also exist with gilt highlights on the handle, however we do not have confirmation that the gilt was factory applied.
  2. This jug was also issued in English Translucent China. These jugs command a premium of 50 to 100% over the earthenware variety.

VARIATION No. 4:

Variation 3, left; Variation 2, centre; Variation 4, right

Designer: Harry Fenton
Modeller: Robert Tabbenor
Handle: Scarlet with an "ER" cypher
Colourway: Black hat; white ruff; scarlet tunic

Backstamps: **A.** Doulton/"Beefeater"
B. Doulton/Royal Doulton International Collectors Club
In 1988 Robert Tabbenor miniaturized Fenton's design of 1947 and created a tiny Beefeater, which was offered for sale to the members of the RDICC.

Doulton Number	Size	Variation	Height	Intro.	Discon.	Current Market Value U.K. £	U.S. $	Can. $
D6206	Large	Var. 4A	6 ½"	1987	1996	55.00	110.00	125.00
D6233	Small	Var. 4A	3 ¼"	1987	1996	40.00	65.00	100.00
D6251	Miniature	Var. 4A	2 ½"	1987	1991	40.00	55.00	70.00
D6806	Tiny	Var. 4B	1 ½"	1988	1988	85.00	150.00	175.00

Beefeater Derivative

Doulton Number	Item	Height	Intro.	Discon.	Current Market Value U.K. £	U.S. $	Can. $
D6233	Table lighter	3 ½"	1958	1973	100.00	200.00	250.00

BEETHOVEN

GREAT COMPOSERS
ONE OF EIGHT

Royal Doulton®
BEETHOVEN
D7021
Modelled by
Stanley James Taylor
© 1995 ROYAL DOULTON

Designer: Stanley J. Taylor
Handle: Bar of music and quill
Colourways: Brown, white and maroon

Backstamp: Doulton

Doulton Number	Size	Variation	Height	Intro.	Discon.	Current Market Value		
						U.K. £	U.S. $	Can. $
D7021	Large	Doulton	7"	1996	Current	90.00	260.00	340.00

BENJAMIN FRANKLIN

An American publicist, scientist and statesman, Ben Franklin (1706-1790) was a signatory to the peace between Britain and the U.S.A. following the War of Independence. In 1748 he left his printing business to his foreman and devoted his life to science. His most famous discovery, that lightning is electricity, was accomplished with the simple objects of a knife and a key. It lead to the invention of the lightning rod, still used today to divert lightning harmlessly into the ground.

This jug was modelled for "The Queen's Table," Royal Doulton's exhibit at the United Kingdom Showcase at Walt Disney's Epcot Center in Orlando, Florida. It was sold exclusively to Epcot tourists visiting the exhibition during 1982, then released for general sale in 1983.

Designer: Eric Griffiths
Handle: A kite and key
Colourway: Black coat; white shirt; blue scarf

Backstamp: Doulton

Doulton Number	Size	Backstamp	Height	Intro.	Discon.	Current Market Value U.K. £	U.S. $	Can. $
D6695	Small	Doulton	4"	1982	1989	75.00	135.00	165.00

BETSEY TROTWOOD

For the character jug Betsey Trotwood, see the "Charles Dickens Commemorative Set" page 185.

BILL SIKES

One of Dickens' most memorable characters is the infamous Bill Sikes, a character from *Oliver Twist*. This jug was commissioned by Lawleys By Post in a limited edition of 2,500.

Designer: Stanley J. Taylor
Handle: Pistol and dog "Bull's-eye"
Colourway: Beige hat; green jacket; red scarf

Backstamp: Doulton

Doulton Number	Size	Backstamp	Height	Intro.	Discon.	Current Market Value		
						U.K. £	U.S. $	Can. $
D6981	Large	Doulton	7"	1994	Ltd. ed	125.00	250.00	350.00

BILL SYKES

For the character jug Bill Sykes see the "Charles Dickens Commemorative Set" page 185.

BLACKSMITH

PROTOTYPE

This large prototype of the Blacksmith jug has older features, a different hat and a different hair style. Only one copy is known to exist.

Designer: David Biggs
Handle: Hammer, anvil and pliers
Colourway: Beige, white and black

Backstamp: Doulton

Doulton Number	Size	Backstamp	Height	Intro.	Discon.	Current Market Value		
						U.K. £	U.S. $	Can. $
Not issued	Large	Doulton	7 ¼"	c. 1963		Unique		

BLACKSMITH

CHARACTERS FROM WILLIAMSBURG
ONE OF EIGHT

Designer: David Biggs
Handle: Hammer, anvil and pliers
Colourway: Salmon hat; white shirt; light brown apron

Backstamp: Doulton

Doulton Number	Size	Backstamp	Height	Intro.	Discon.	Current Market Value		
						U.K. £	U.S. $	Can. $
D6571	Large	Doulton	7 ¼"	1963	1983	65.00	100.00	135.00
D6578	Small	Doulton	4"	1963	1983	50.00	85.00	100.00
D6585	Miniature	Doulton	2 ½"	1963	1983	45.00	75.00	85.00

Note: This jug was also issued in English Translucent China. These jugs command a premium of 50 to 100% over the earthenware variety.

BONNIE PRINCE CHARLIE

James II's grandson, the "Young Pretender" (1720-1788), was born Charles Edward Stuart in Rome. He became the hopeful leader of the Jacobites, adherents to the Stuart line, and led them in an unsuccessful uprising in 1745. After being defeated at Culloden Moor in 1746, he escaped to France with the help of Flora McDonald. Charles roamed Europe, a drunkard, until settling in Rome where he passed the remainder of his life.

Backstamp: Doulton

Designer: Stanley J. Taylor
Handle: Crown atop thistles
Colourway: Blue plaid tam; red coat trimmed with yellow collar; white ruffles at the neck

Doulton Number	Size	Backstamp	Height	Intro.	Discon.	U.K. £	U.S. $	Can. $
						Current Market Value		
D6858	Large	Doulton	6 ½"	1990	1994	120.00	225.00	275.00

BOOTMAKER

PROTOTYPE

This large-size prototype of the Bootmaker jug has younger features and different hair, handle and hat designs. Only one copy is known to exist.

Designer: David Biggs
Handle: A boot and hammer, with a pair of shoes at the base
Colourway: Beige cap; white shirt; black shoes

Backstamp: Doulton

Doulton Number	Size	Backstamp	Height	Intro.	Discon.	Current Market Value		
						U.K. £	U.S. $	Can. $
D6572	Large	Doulton	7 ½"	c. 1963		Sold March 12, 1997. Sotheby's Arcade Auction, New York, $1,955.00		

BOOTMAKER

CHARACTERS FROM WILLIAMSBURG
ONE OF EIGHT

Designer: David Biggs
Handle: A boot and hammer, with a pair of shoes at the base
Colourway: Salmon cap; white shirt

Backstamp: Doulton

Doulton						Current Market Value		
Number	Size	Backstamp	Height	Intro.	Discon.	U.K. £	U.S. $	Can. $
D6572	Large	Doulton	7 ½"	1963	1983	70.00	100.00	135.00
D6579	Small	Doulton	4"	1963	1983	50.00	85.00	100.00
D6586	Miniature	Doulton	2 ½"	1963	1983	45.00	85.00	100.00

Note: This jug was also issued in English Translucent China. These jugs command a premium of 50 to 100% over the earthenware variety.

BOWLS PLAYER

CHARACTERS FROM LIFE
ONE OF SEVEN

Bowls is a British game played on a flat green in lanes. Sir Francis Drake is reputed to have been playing bowls when the Spanish Armada was sighted in the English Channel.

Designer: Stanley J. Taylor
Handle: Bowl, jack and measure
Colourway: White and yellow

Backstamp: Doulton

Doulton Number	Size	Backstamp	Height	Intro.	Discon.	Current Market Value		
						U.K. £	U.S. $	Can. $
D6896	Small	Doulton	4"	1991	1995	45.00	100.00	150.00

BUDDY HOLLY

A native of Lubbock, Texas, Buddy Holly left his mark on popular music, influencing later generations. He is best known for his song *Peggy Sue*. This jug was issued in a limited edition of 2,500 pieces.

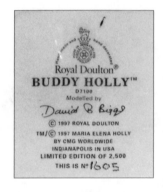

Designer:	David B. Biggs
Handle:	A guitar, records, music sheet Peggy Sue
Colourway:	Black and brown; resin glasses

Backstamp: Doulton/TM/© 1997 Maria
Elena Holly By CMG Worldwide
Indianapolis in USA

Doulton Number	Size	Backstamp	Height	Intro.	Discon.	Current Market Value		
						U.K. £	U.S. $	Can. $
D7100	Large	Doulton/CMG	8"	1998	Ltd. ed.	125.00	300.00	400.00

BUFFALO BILL

William Frederick Cody (1846-1917) was a scout, plainsman, soldier in the Civil War, hotelier, rancher and showman. His expert marksmanship as a buffalo hunter earned him his nickname Buffalo Bill. In 1883, Cody and others formed "Buffalo Bill's Wild West Show," a theatrical shooting exhibition, which became very successful and travelled through the U.S. and Europe.

STYLE ONE: "W.F. CODY BUFFALO BILL"

This jug was piloted but never put into production, and only three jugs are known to exist. "W.F. Cody Buffalo Bill" is incised on the right shoulder in raised letters.

Designer: Unknown	**Backstamp:** Doulton
Handle: A rifle and buffalo head	
Colourway: Brown hat; grey moustache and goatee	

Doulton Number	Size	Backstamp	Height	Intro.	Discon.	Current Market Value U.K. £	U.S. $	Can. $
D —	Large	Doulton	7 ½"	Unknown		Extremely rare		

BUFFALO BILL

THE WILD WEST COLLECTION
ONE OF SIX

STYLE TWO: BUFFALO BILL

Designer: Robert Tabbenor	**Backstamp:** Doulton
Handle: Buffalo head and horn	
Colourway: Light brown hat and buckskin jacket	

Doulton Number	Size	Backstamp	Height	Intro.	Discon.	Current Market Value U.K. £	U.S. $	Can. $
D6735	Mid	Doulton	5 ½"	1985	1989	60.00	100.00	125.00

THE BUSKER

PROTOTYPE

The prototype of The Busker jug had a one-man band for the handle; however, this was too complex for production and was replaced by a concertina.

Photograph
Not Available
at Press Time

Designer: Stanley J. Taylor   **Backstamp:** Doulton
Handle: One-man band
Colourway: Grey cap; green coat; yellow scarf

Doulton Number	Size	Backstamp	Height	Intro.	Discon.	U.K. £	U.S. $	Can. $
—	Large	Doulton	6 ½"	c.1988			Unique	

THE BUSKER

THE LONDON COLLECTION
ONE OF TEN

From its roots with the early wandering minstrels, entertaining in public places for money is still a way for artists to support themselves while gaining public exposure for their work.

Royal Doulton®
THE BUSKER
D 6775
Modelled by
Stanley James Taylor.
© 1987 ROYAL DOULTON

Designer: Stanley J. Taylor
Handle: An open concertina
Colourway: Grey cap; green coat; yellow scarf

Backstamp: Doulton

Doulton Number	Size	Backstamp	Height	Intro.	Discon.	Current Market Value		
						U.K. £	U.S. $	Can. $
D6775	Large	Doulton	6 ½"	1988	1991	100.00	195.00	225.00

BUZFUZ

This is an excellent example of the literary character designs of early character jugs. In Dickens' *Pickwick Papers*, Sergeant Buzfuz was the counsel of Mrs. Bardell in the breach of promise suit she brought against Mr. Pickwick.

Buzfuz Lighter

Buzfuz Bust

Designer: Leslie Harradine / Harry Fenton
Handle: Plain
Colourway: White collar; brown waistcoat; dark green coat; black robe

Backstamp: Doulton

Doulton Number	Size	Backstamp	Height	Intro.	Discon.	Current Market Value U.K. £	U.S. $	Can. $
D5838	Mid	Doulton	5 ½"	1938	1948	135.00	250.00	300.00
D5838	Small	Doulton	4"	1948	1960	75.00	135.00	165.00

Buzfuz Derivatives

Doulton Number	Item	Height	Intro.	Discon.	Current Market Value U.K. £	U.S. $	Can. $
D5838	Table lighter	3 ½"	1958	1959	175.00	325.00	350.00
D6048	Bust	3"	1939	1960	75.00	100.00	125.00

Note: This jug was also issued in English Translucent China. These jugs command a premium of 50 to 100% over the earthenware variety.

CABINET MAKER

CHARACTERS FROM WILLIAMSBURG
ONE OF EIGHT

In 1981 it was announced that a new jug in the Williamsburg series, the Cabinet Maker, would be produced. However, the series was cancelled in 1983, and the jug was not put into production at that time. In 1995 the decision was made to put the jug into production and to launch it at the 15th anniversary convention of the Royal Doulton International Collectors Club, held at Williamsburg. It was issued in a special edition of 1,500 pieces.

Designer: Michael Abberley
Handle: Brace
Colourway: Red, white and brown

Backstamp: Doulton

Doulton Number	Size	Backstamp	Height	Intro.	Discon.	Current Market Value		
						U.K. £	U.S. $	Can. $
D6659	Large	Doulton	7 ½"	1979	1979		Prototype	
D7010	Large	Doulton	7 ½"	1995	Sp. ed.	200.00	300.00	400.00

CAPT AHAB

Captain Ahab sailed the whaler, *Pequod*, in Herman Melville's great 19th-century American classic, *Moby Dick*. He lost a leg and then his life in pursuit of the great white whale, who triumphed in the chase and sunk his ship.

Capt Ahab
D 6500
COPR 1958
DOULTON & CO LIMITED
Rd No 889571
Rd No 38227
Rd No 8037
Rd No 422/58

Designer: Garry Sharpe
Handle: A grey whale
Colourway: Blue cap; black coat; white sweater

Backstamp: Doulton

Doulton Number	Size	Backstamp	Height	Intro.	Discon.	Current Market Value U.K. £	U.S. $	Can. $
D6500	Large	Doulton	7"	1959	1984	95.00	160.00	175.00
D6506	Small	Doulton	4"	1959	1984	55.00	100.00	125.00
D6522	Miniature	Doulton	2 ½"	1960	1984	45.00	90.00	110.00

Capt Ahab Derivative

Doulton Number	Item	Height	Intro.	Discon.	Current Market Value U.K. £	U.S. $	Can. $
D6506	Table lighter	3 ½"	1964	1973	225.00	400.00	450.00

CAPTAIN BLIGH

CHARACTER JUG OF THE YEAR

This character jug of the year for 1995 commemorates Captain Bligh and the *Mutiny on the Bounty*. In 1789 the crew of the *Bounty*, under the leadership of Christian Fletcher, mutinied and set Bligh adrift in an open boat. He survived a 3,500-mile voyage before reaching land.

STYLE ONE: HANDLE ON RIGHT SIDE OF JUG

Designer: Stanley J. Taylor	**Backstamp:** Doulton/Character
Handle: Navigation chart; palm tree and "Bligh of the Bounty"	Jug of the Year, 1995
Colourway: Black, cream, green, red and brown	

Doulton Number	Size	Backstamp	Height	Intro.	Discon.	Current Market Value U.K. £	U.S. $	Can. $
D6967	Large	Doulton	7"	1995	1995	125.00	200.00	300.00

CAPTAIN BLIGH AND FLETCHER CHRISTIAN

This pair of jugs was issued by Lawleys By Post, in a limited edition of 2,500.

STYLE TWO: CAPTAIN BLIGH — HANDLE ON LEFT SIDE OF JUG

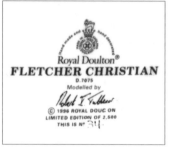

Designer:	Robert Tabbenor	**Backstamp:** Doulton
Handle:	Captain Bligh — Palm tree and lifeboat	
	Fletcher Christian — Potted sapling	
Colourway:	Captain Bligh — Black, white, yellow and brown	
	Fletcher Christian — Dark blue, white, grey and yellow	

Doulton Number	Name	Backstamp	Height	Intro.	Discon.	Current Market Value		
						U.K. £	U.S. $	Can. $
D7074	Captain Bligh		4 ½"	1997	Ltd. ed.	100.00	250.00	300.00
D7075	Fletcher Christian		4 ½"	1997	Ltd. ed.		(Pair)	

CAP'N CUTTLE

The wonderful characters of Dickens' novels were the inspiration for many early jug designs. Captain Edward Cuttle was an eccentric English gentleman in *Dombey and Son* (1846), who is best known for saying, "When found, make a note of it."

Designer: Leslie Harradine / Harry Fenton	**Backstamp:** Doulton
Handle: Plain	
Colourway: Blue-black coat; grey-green hat; white collar; green bow tie	

Doulton Number	Size	Backstamp	Height	Intro.	Discon.	Current Market Value U.K. £	U.S. $	Can. $
D5842	Mid	Doulton	5 ½"	1938	1948	135.00	250.00	250.00
D5842	Small	Doulton	4"	1948	1960	75.00	125.00	150.00

Cap'n Cuttle Derivative

Doulton Number	Item	Height	Intro.	Discon.	Current Market Value U.K. £	U.S. $	Can. $
D5842	Table lighter	3 ½"	1958	1959	175.00	350.00	375.00

Note: This jug was also issued in English Translucent China. These jugs command a premium of 50 to 100% over the earthenware variety.

CAPT HENRY MORGAN

A privateer and pirate leader in the West Indies, Morgan (1635-1688) also carried out commissions from the British authorities. His attack on Panama in 1671 violated a peace treaty between England and Spain. Sent to England to stand trial, he was instead knighted and became Lieutenant Governor of Jamaica, where he remained until his death.

Backstamp A - Doulton

Backstamp B - City of
Stoke-on-Trent

Designer: Garry Sharpe
Handle: Sails of a ship
Colourway: Black tricorn; blue collar trimmed with gold

Backstamps: A. Doulton
B. Doulton/City of Stoke-on-Trent Jubilee Year 1959-1960/ With the compliments of Lord Mayor and Lady Mayoress Alderman Harold Clowes, O.B.E., J.P., and Miss Christine Clowes

Doulton Number	Size	Backstamp	Height	Intro.	Discon.	Current Market Value		
						U.K. £	U.S. $	Can. $
D6467	Large	Doulton	6 ¾"	1958	1982	85.00	135.00	165.00
D6467	Large	Doulton/Stoke	6 ¾"	1958	1959		Rare	
D6469	Small	Doulton	3 ½"	1958	1982	35.00	60.00	75.00
D6510	Miniature	Doulton	2 ½"	1960	1982	45.00	75.00	85.00

Note: This jug was also issued in English Translucent China. These jugs command a premium of 50 to 100% over the earthenware variety.

CAPT HOOK

Captain Hook is the nemesis of Peter Pan in J.M. Barrie's famous story. Peter Pan cut off Hook's hand and fed it to a crocodile, who liked it so much he followed the captain around in hopes of eating the rest of him. Hook managed to keep eluding his predator because the crocodile had accidentally swallowed a clock that ticked inside him and ruined the element of surprise.

STYLE ONE: HANDLE — CROCODILE AND CLOCK

Designer: Max Henk / David Biggs
Handle: An alligator and clock
Colourway: Blue tricorn trimmed with yellow; green coat trimmed with yellow; white ruffles at the neck

Backstamp: Doulton

Doulton Number	Size	Backstamp	Height	Intro.	Discon.	Current Market Value		
						U.K. £	U.S. $	Can. $
D6597	Large	Doulton	7 ¼"	1965	1971	400.00	750.00	900.00
D6601	Small	Doulton	4"	1965	1971	275.00	500.00	600.00
D6605	Miniature	Doulton	2 ½"	1965	1971	300.00	525.00	650.00

Note: This jug was also issued in English Translucent China. These jugs command a premium of 50 to 100% over the earthenware variety.

CAPTAIN HOOK

CHARACATER JUG OF THE YEAR

This was the Character Jug of the Year for 1994.

STYLE TWO: HANDLE — SILVER HOOK AND CROCODILE

Designer: Martyn C. R. Alcock
Handle: Crocodile, silver hook
Colourway: Black, scarlet and grey

Backstamp: Doulton/Character
Jug of the Year, 1994

Doulton Number	Size	Backstamp	Height	Intro.	Discon.	Current Market Value		
						U.K. £	U.S. $	Can. $
D6947	Large	Doulton	7 ½"	1994	1994	135.00	250.00	350.00

CAPTAIN JAMES COOK

In a striking tribute to the famous navigator and explorer, this character jug incorporates a first-ever feature in its handle: a working compass. This jug was issued by Lawleys By Post in a limited edition 2,500 to commemorate the life and times of Captain Cook (1728-1779).

For the character jug Cook see the "Explorers Set" page 233.

Designer: William K. Harper
Handle: Map of Australia, working compass
Colourway: Naval uniform and cap, yellow trim, gold buttons

Backstamp: Doulton

Doulton Number	Size	Backstamp	Height	Intro.	Discon.	Current Market Value U.K. £	U.S. $	Can. $
D7077	Large	Doulton	6 ½"	1998	Ltd. ed.	150.00	—	—

CAPTAIN SCOTT

Captain Robert Falcon Scott (1868-1912) was the leader of the ill-fated British expedition to the South Pole in 1910. Not only were they bested by Amundsen's Norwegian expedition, but also Captain Scott and his team perished and never completed the return journey.

For the character jug Scott see the "Explorers Set" page 233.

Designer:	David B. Biggs	**Backstamp:** Doulton
Handle:	Snow, Union Jack and tent	
Colourway:	Cream balaclava, brown goggles	

Doulton Number	Size	Backstamp	Height	Intro.	Discon.	Current Market Value U.K. £	U.S. $	Can. $
D7116	Large	Doulton	7"	1998	Current	100.00	205.00	385.00

THE CARDINAL

This jug has minor colour variations in the hair. The earliest jugs had brown hair, and later jugs either grey or white hair. This jug was produced with and without pink highlighting on the raised character name.

Designer: Charles Noke
Handle: Tassle
Colourway: Scarlet robes; Purple handle

Backstamp: Doulton

Doulton Number	Size	Backstamp	Height	Intro.	Discon.	Current Market Value		
						U.K. £	U.S. $	Can. $
D5614	Large	Doulton	6 ½"	1936	1960	125.00	195.00	200.00
D6033	Small	Doulton	3 ½"	1939	1960	50.00	95.00	100.00
D6129	Miniature	Doulton	2 ¼"	1940	1960	40.00	75.00	80.00
D6258	Tiny	Doulton	1 ½"	1947	1960	150.00	275.00	300.00

Note: This jug was also issued in English Translucent China. These jugs command a premium of 50 to 100% over the earthenware variety.

THE CAROLER

CHRISTMAS MINIATURES SERIES
ONE OF SIX

This is the fifth in the Christmas Miniatures Series of jugs. Issued during 1995, the jug was commissioned and sold by Royal Doulton (U.S.A.) Limited in America, and was made available worldwide through the Royal Doulton International Collectors Club.

Designer: Martyn C. R. Alcock	**Backstamp:** Doulton
Handle: Sheet music and lantern	
Colourway: Black, white and blue	

Doulton Number	Size	Backstamp	Height	Intro.	Discon.	U.K. £	U.S. $	Can. $
						Current Market Value		
D7007	Miniature	Doulton	2 ½"	1995	1995	70.00	125.00	150.00

CATHERINE OF ARAGON

HENRY VIII AND HIS SIX WIVES
ONE OF EIGHT

Daughter of Ferdinand and Isabella of Spain, Catherine (1485-1536) was married to Arthur, Prince of Wales, in a political arrangement between the two countries. When Arthur died shortly after their wedding, she married Henry VIII to continue the arrangement. This first marriage for Henry lasted 24 years, until he became restless at the lack of a male heir and sought out Anne Boleyn. In 1527 Henry attempted to have his marriage annulled, a move that led to his excommunication by the Pope and, eventually, to the English Reformation. Catherine was banished from the royal court and lived until the age of 50, unhappy and lonely.

For Catherine of Aragon, style two, see "The Six Wives of Henry VIII" page 478.

STYLE ONE: HANDLE: A TOWER

Designer: Alan Maslankowski
Handle: A tower
Colourway: Red, gold, black and white

Backstamp: Doulton

Doulton Number	Size	Backstamp	Height	Intro.	Discon.	Current Market Value U.K. £	U.S. $	Can. $
D6643	Large	Doulton	7"	1975	1989	75.00	125.00	150.00
D6657	Small	Doulton	4"	1981	1989	95.00	165.00	175.00
D6658	Miniature	Doulton	2 ½"	1981	1989	100.00	175.00	200.00

CATHERINE HOWARD

HENRY VIII AND HIS SIX WIVES
ONE OF EIGHT

Niece to the Duke of Norfolk, Catherine Howard (1521-1542) became Henry VIII's fifth wife on July 28, 1540, in a marriage arranged by her family. In 1541 Henry accused her of adultery and had her beheaded at the Tower of London.

For Catherine Howard, style two, see "The Six Wives of Henry VIII" page 478.

STYLE ONE: HANDLE: AN AXE

Designer:	Peter Gee	**Backstamp:**	Doulton
Handle:	An axe		
Colourway:	Brown, gold and white		

| Doulton | | | | | | Current Market Value | | |
Number	Size	Backstamp	Height	Intro.	Discon.	U.K. £	U.S. $	Can. $
D6645	Large	Doulton	7"	1978	1989	100.00	175.00	200.00
D6692	Small	Doulton	4"	1984	1989	135.00	250.00	250.00
D6693	Miniature	Doulton	2 ½"	1984	1989	100.00	225.00	225.00

CATHERINE PARR

HENRY VIII AND HIS SIX WIVES
ONE OF EIGHT

Catherine Parr (1512-1548) became Henry VIII's last wife on July 12, 1543, after being twice widowed. She came to wield considerable power in the royal court, serving for a time as Queen regent in 1544 and overseeing the start of Edward VI's reign. After Henry's death in 1547, she married Baron Seymour of Sudeley, but died during childbirth the following year.

For Catherine Parr, style two, see "The Six Wives of Henry VIII" page 478.

STYLE ONE: HANDLE: A BIBLE AND PULPIT

Designer: Michael Abberley	**Backstamp:** Doulton
Handle: Bible and pulpit	
Colourway: Black, brown and gold	

Doulton Number	Size	Backstamp	Height	Intro.	Discon.	Current Market Value		
						U.K. £	U.S. $	Can. $
D6664	Large	Doulton	6 ¾"	1981	1989	125.00	250.00	350.00
D6751	Small	Doulton	4"	1987	1989	150.00	300.00	350.00
D6752	Miniature	Doulton	2 ½"	1987	1989	150.00	275.00	300.00

THE CAVALIER

The cavaliers were Royalist soldiers who fought for Charles I during the English Civil War. They became known for their gallantry and haughtiness, an attitude still described as "cavalier."

STYLE ONE: CAVALIER WITH GOATEE

Designer: Harry Fenton
Handle: Handle of a sword
Colourway: Green hat; white ruff

Backstamp: Doulton

Doulton Number	Size	Backstamp	Height	Intro.	Discon.	Current Market Value		
						U.K. £	U.S. $	Can. $
D6114	Large	Doulton	7"	1940	1950	2,000.00	4,000.00	5,000.00

THE CAVALIER

This jug was originally listed in Royal Doulton's product guide as the Laughing Cavalier, presumably after the famous Frans Hals painting.

STYLE TWO: CAVALIER WITHOUT GOATEE

Slight colour changes, along with alterations to the ruff and removal of the goatee, occurred in 1950.

Designer: Harry Fenton
Handle: Handle of a sword
Colourway: Green hat; white ruff

Backstamp: Doulton

Doulton Number	Size	Backstamp	Height	Intro.	Discon.	Current Market Value		
						U.K. £	U.S. $	Can. $
D6114	Large	Doulton	7"	1950	1960	100.00	175.00	175.00
D6173	Small	Doulton	3 ¼"	1941	1960	60.00	80.00	90.00

CELTIC (FOOTBALL CLUB)

THE FOOTBALL SUPPORTERS
ONE OF TEN

Designer: Stanley J. Taylor
Handle: Team coloured scarf
Colourway: Green and white uniform

Backstamp: Doulton

Doulton Number	Size	Backstamp	Height	Intro.	Discon.	Current Market Value		
						U.K. £	U.S. $	Can. $
D6925	Mid	Doulton	5"	1992	Unknown	65.00	125.00	150.00

CHARLES I and OLIVER CROMWELL

Commissioned by Lawleys By Post, Charles I (1600-1649) and his companion jug, Oliver Cromwell (1599-1659), form a pair which were issued in a limited edition of 2,500.

For the Charles I (style one), see the "Kings and Queens of the Realm" page 328, and for King Charles I see page 325. For Oliver Cromwell (style One), see page 391.

STYLE TWO: CHARLES I — HANDLE IS CROWN, BIBLE AND SASH
OLIVER CROMWELL — HANDLE IS SILVER MACE AND SASH

Designer:	William K. Harper	**Backstamp:** Doulton
Handle:	Charles I — Crown and bible against a red sash	
	Oliver Cromwell —Silver mace; sash	
Colourway:	Charles I — Black hat; maroon and purple jacket; cream collar	
	Oliver Cromwell — Grey and white with silver details	

Doulton Number	Name	Backstamp	Height	Intro.	Discon.	Current Market Value U.K. £	U.S. $	Can. $
D6985	Charles I	Doulton	4 ½"	1995	Ltd. ed.	75.00	175.00	225.00
D6986	Cromwell	Doulton	4 ½"	1995	Ltd. Ed	75.00	175.00	225.00
	Pair					150.00	350.00	450.00

CHARLES DICKENS COMMEMORATIVE SET

The 12 jugs in this set were issued to commemorate the 170th anniversary of the birth of Charles Dickens, and each one comes with a certificate of authenticity. A mahogany display shelf completes the set. The set was first sold by Lawleys By Post in the U.K. from 1982 to 1988, and from 1985 in North America and Australia.

STYLE ONE: CHARLES DICKENS - HANDLE PLAIN

Designers: See below		**Backstamp:** Doulton	
Height: 1 1/2"		**Handle:** Plain	
Size: Tiny		**Issued:** 1982 - 1989	
Colourways: See below			

Doulton Number	Name	Designer	Colourways	U.K. £	U.S. $	Can. $
					Current Market Value	
D6678	Artful Dodger	Eric Griffiths	Grey and black	35.00	60.00	65.00
D6685	Betsey Trotwood	Michael Abberley	Yellow, white and black	35.00	60.00	75.00
D6684	Bill Sykes	Michael Abberley	Green and dark blue	35.00	60.00	70.00
D6676	Charles Dickens, Style One	Eric Griffiths	Grey and black	60.00	165.00	175.00
D6680	David Copperfield	Michael Abberley	Dark blue and black	40.00	95.00	95.00
D6679	Fagin	Robert Tabbener	Orange and brown	40.00	85.00	95.00
D6681	Little Nell	Michael Abberley	Yellow and black	40.00	70.00	80.00
D6686	Mr. Bumble	Robert Tabbener	Yellow, dark blue and green	40.00	65.00	75.00
D6687	Mrs. Bardell	Robert Tabbener	Yellow and green	40.00	65.00	75.00
D6677	Oliver Twist	Robert Tabbener	Dark and light blue	40.00	65.00	75.00
D6683	Scrooge	Michael Abberley	Yellow and brown	40.00	65.00	75.00
D6682	Uriah Heep	Robert Tabbener	Grey and green	40.00	60.00	75.00
	Display stand for 12 tinies			65.00	45.00	50.00
	Complete Set			500.00	750.00	850.00

CHARLES DICKENS

ROYAL DOULTON INTERNATIONAL COLLECTORS CLUB

The Charles Dickens jug was commissioned by the Royal Doulton International Collectors Club in a limited edition of 7,500 pieces.

For the toby jug Charles Dickens see page 44.

STYLE TWO: HANDLE — QUILL PEN AND INK POT

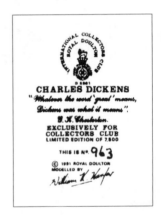

Backstamp: Doulton/RDICC

Designer: William K. Harper
Handle: Quill pen and ink pot, the book "The Old Curiosity Shop"
Colourway: Black and olive green

Doulton Number	Size	Backstamp	Height	Intro.	Discon.	Current Market Value U.K. £	Current Market Value U.S. $	Current Market Value Can. $
D6901	Small	Doulton/RDICC	4"	1991	Ltd. ed.	95.00	160.00	175.00

CHARLES DICKENS

The 125th anniversary of the death of Charles Dickens was commemorated in 1995 with a two-handled jug of Dickens, in a limited edition of 2,500.

STYLE THREE: TWO-HANDLED JUG

Designer: William K. Harper
Handle: Six of Dickens characters:
Oliver Twist, Sairey Gamp, Ebenezer Scrooge,
Little Nell, Mr. Pickwick and Little Dorritt
Colourway: Green, black, yellow and brown

Backstamp: Doulton

Doulton Number	Size	Backstamp	Height	Intro.	Discon.	Current Market Value		
						U.K. £	U.S. $	Can. $
D6939	Large	Doulton	7"	1995	Ltd. ed.	250.00	525.00	675.00

CHARLIE CHAPLIN

Issued in 1993 in a limited edition of 5,000, this jug was available through Lawleys By Post.

Designer: William K. Harper
Handle: Cane
Colourway: Black hat and jacket with green, white and
black striped tie

Backstamp: **A.** Doulton

Doulton Number	Size	Backstamp	Height	Intro.	Discon.	Current Market Value		
						U.K. £	U.S. $	Can. $
D6949	Large	Doulton	7 ¼"	1993	Ltd. ed.	135.00	250.00	300.00

THE CHEF

Designer: David B. Biggs
Handle: Wooden spoons, onions, striped tea towel
Colourway: White chef's jacket and hat, red neckerchief

Backstamp: Doulton

Doulton Number	Size	Backstamp	Height	Intro.	Discon.	Current Market Value		
						U.K. £	U.S. $	Can. $
D7103	Small	Doulton	4"	1998	Current	53.00	145.00	295.00

CHELSEA PENSIONER

THE LONDON COLLECTION
ONE OF TEN

Charles II founded the Royal Hospital in Chelsea for "worthy old soldiers broken in the wars." It was built by Christopher Wren and completed in 1692. Each year on Founders Day, the opening of the hospital is celebrated by the soldiers in full dress uniform, as worn by the gentleman depicted on this jug.

Designer: Stanley J. Taylor
Handle: Medals of honour
Colourway: Black tricorn trimmed with gold;
scarlet tunic; black collar

Backstamp: A. Doulton
For general issue, 1989.

Backstamp B - Hornes

Backstamp C - Holmes

Backstamp D - Higbee

Pre-released in the U.S.A. in 1988 at the following four stores in a limited edition of 1,000 pieces, with 250 jugs per store:

Backstamps: **B.** Doulton / Joseph Hornes / To commemorate the First Anniversary of the opening of the Royal Doulton Room Joseph Horne's, Pittsburgh, Pennsylvania, U.S.A.

C. Doulton / D. H. Holmes / To commemorate the First Anniversary of the opening of the Royal Doulton Room D. H. Holme's, New Orleans, Louisiana, U.S.A.

D. Doulton / Higbee Company / To commemorate the Third Anniversary of the opening of the Royal Doulton Room The Higbee Company, Cleveland, Ohio, U.S.A.

E. Doulton / Strawbridge and Clothier / To commemorate the Second Anniversary of the opening of the Royal Doulton Room Strawbridge and Clothier, Philadelphia, Pennsylvania, U.S.A.

Doulton Number	Size	Backstamp	Height	Intro.	Discon.	Current Market Value U.K. £	U.S. $	Can. $
D6817	Large	Var. A	6 ½"	1989	1991	100.00	200.00	275.00
D6830	Large	Var. B	6 ½"	1988	Ltd. ed.	150.00	275.00	325.00
D6831	Large	Var. C	6 ½"	1988	Ltd. ed.	150.00	275.00	325.00
D6832	Large	Var. D	6 ½"	1988	Ltd. ed.	150.00	275.00	325.00
D6833	Large	Var. E	6 ½"	1988	Ltd. ed.	150.00	275.00	325.00

CHIEF SITTING BULL
GEORGE ARMSTRONG CUSTER

THE ANTAGONISTS' COLLECTION (TWO-FACED JUG)
ONE OF FOUR

Chief Sitting Bull (1831-1890) of the Sioux Indians spent his life working for the right of his people to own and control their land. He was shot by the Indian police on a questionable charge of resisting arrest.

George Armstrong Custer (1839-1876) was the youngest general in the U.S. Army. He first saw action in the Civil War and was later stationed in the Dakota Territory during the gold rush on Sioux Land. In 1876 he led an attack against an Indian encampment at Little Big Horn. Sitting Bull and his men outnumbered Custer's regiment and easily defeated them, leaving no survivors.

This jug was issued in a limited edition of 9,500 pieces.

VARIATION No. 1:   Colourway — Multi-coloured; Sitting Bull has grey eyes.

Designer:	Michael Abberley	**Backstamp:** Doulton
Handle:	Sitting Bull — tomahawk	
	Custer —pistol	
Colourway:	Multi-coloured; Sitting Bull has grey eyes	

Doulton Number	Size	Variation	Height	Intro.	Discon.	Current Market Value U.K. £	U.S. $	Can. $
D6712	Large	Var. 1	7"	1984	Ltd. ed.	150.00	300.00	350.00

VARIATION No. 2:   Colourway — Multi-coloured; Sitting Bull has brown eyes

Variation 1 Brown Eyes (left); Variation 2 Grey Eyes (right)

Doulton Number	Size	Variation	Height	Intro.	Discon.	Current Market Value		
						U.K. £	U.S. $	Can. $
D6712	Large	Var. 2	7"	1984	1989	150.00	250.00	300.00

CHOPIN

GREAT COMPOSERS
ONE OF EIGHT

Designer: Stanley J. Taylor
Handle: Piano keyboard and scroll
Colourway: Dark blue, black, brown, white and yellow

Backstamp: Doulton

Doulton Number	Size	Backstamp	Height	Intro.	Discon.	Current Market Value		
						U.K. £	U.S. $	Can. $
D7030	Large	Doulton	7"	1996	Current	90.00	260.00	340.00

CHRISTOPHER COLUMBUS

STYLE ONE: HANDLE — MAP OF THE NEW WORLD

This jug was issued in 1991 to commemorate the 500th anniversary of the discovery of the New World.

For Columbus see the "Explorers Set" page 233.

Designer: Stanley J. Taylor
Handle: Map of the New World
Colourway: Dark blue and white

Backstamp: Doulton

Doulton Number	Size	Backstamp	Height	Intro.	Discon.	Current Market Value		
						U.K. £	U.S. $	Can. $
D6891	Large	Doulton	7"	1991	1997	75.00	150.00	250.00

CHRISTOPHER COLUMBUS

ROYAL DOULTON INTERNATIONAL COLLECTORS CLUB

This jug was issued to recognize the 500th anniversary of Columbus's voyage to America in 1492. It was created exclusively for the Royal Doulton International Collectors Club and was issued in a limited edition of 7,500. The jug was exhibited in the British Pavillion at Expo '92 in Seville, Spain.

STYLE TWO: HANDLE — THE SHIP SANTA MARIA

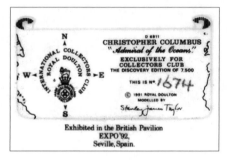

Exhibited in the British Pavilion
EXPO '92,
Seville, Spain.

Designer: Stanley J. Taylor
Handle: The ship Santa Maria
Colourway: Brown, light brown, grey and cream

Backstamp: Doulton / RDICC /
Christopher Columbus
"Admiral of the Oceans."
Exclusively For Collectors Club
The Discovery Edition of 7,500

Doulton Number	Size	Backstamp	Height	Intro.	Discon.	Current Market Value U.K. £	U.S. $	Can. $
D6911	Small	Doulton/RDICC	3 ½"	1992	Ltd. ed.	70.00	175.00	200.00

CHURCHILL

Sir Winston Leonard Spencer Churchill (1874-1965) was first lord of the Admiralty, Home Secretary and Prime Minister on three occasions. As Prime Minister during World War II, he led Britain to victory and captured the spirit of the Allies with his famous radio broadcasts. He was awarded the Nobel Prize for Literature in 1953.

For the Sir Winston Churchill character jug, see page 477. For Winston Churchill character jug, see page 527. For the Winston Churchill toby jug, see page 105.

VARIATION No. 1:   With an inscription on the base
Colourway — Cream with two black handles

WINSTON SPENCER CHURCHILL
PRIME MINISTER
OF BRITAIN
—— 1940 ——
THIS LOVING CUP WAS MADE
DURING THE "BATTLE OF BRITAIN"
AS A TRIBUTE TO A GREAT LEADER

modelled by NOKE

Designer: Charles Noke   **Backstamp:** Doulton
Handle: Plain
Colourway: Cream; two black handles

Doulton Number	Size	Variation	Height	Intro.	Discon.	Current Market Value U.K. £	U.S. $	Can. $
D6170	Large	Doulton	6 ½"	1940	1941	5,000.00	9,000.00	11,000.00

VARIATION No. 2: Modelling portrays a young Churchill
Colourway — Very lightly coloured overall, with two grey handles
Without inscription on base; green Doulton backstamp

Variation No. 1

Variation No. 3

Doulton Number	Size	Variation	Height	Intro.	Discon.	Current Market Value U.K. £	U.S. $	Can. $
D6170	Large	Var. 2	6 ½"	Unknown		Extremely rare		

VARIATION No. 3: Modelling portrays a young Churchill
Colourway — Fully decorated in natural colours, with two dark brown handles
No inscription on base

Doulton Number	Size	Variation	Height	Intro.	Discon.	Current Market Value U.K. £	U.S. $	Can. $
D6170	Large	Var. 3	6 ½"	Unknown		Extremely rare		

CITY GENT

THE LONDON COLLECTION
ONE OF TEN

Royal Doulton®
CITY GENT
D 6815
Modelled by
Stanley James Taylor.
© 1988 ROYAL DOULTON

Designer: Stanley J. Taylor
Handle: Umbrella handle
Colourway: Black and grey hat;
black coat; white shirt; grey tie

Backstamp: Doulton

Doulton Number	Size	Backstamp	Height	Intro.	Discon.	Current Market Value		
						U.K. £	U.S. $	Can. $
D6815	Large	Doulton	7"	1988	1991	60.00	175.00	200.00

CLARK GABLE

THE CELEBRITY COLLECTION
ONE OF SIX

An Ohio native, Clark Gable (1901-1960) worked in a tyre factory and as a lumberjack before he took up acting. He began his career in 1930 and appeared in over seventy films. He won an Academy Award in 1934 for his performance in *It Happened One Night*, but is perhaps best remembered as Rhett Butler in *Gone With the Wind*.

This jug was issued in the U.S.A. prior to approval from the Gable estate and had to be withdrawn when permission was denied. A small number of jugs are known to exist.

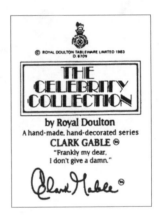

Designer:	Stanley J. Taylor
Handle:	Movie camera entwined in film
Colourway:	Brown; light brown suit; tan tie

Backstamp: Doulton

Doulton Number	Size	Backstamp	Height	Intro.	Discon.	Current Market Value		
						U.K. £	U.S. $	Can. $
D6709	Large	Doulton	7"	1984	1984	2,500.00	4,800.00	6,000.00

THE CLOWN

There are three recognised variations of The Clown without hat, those with red, brown or white hair.

STYLE ONE: CLOWN WITHOUT HAT

VARIATION No. 1: Colourway — Red hair
Handle — Multi-coloured

The Clown.
COPR. 1950.
DOULTON & CO. LIMITED.
Rᵈ Nº 28163.
Rᵈ Nº 6207.
Rᵈ Nº 92/50.

Designer: Harry Fenton
Handle: Multi-coloured
Colourway: Red hair

Backstamp: Doulton

Doulton Number	Size	Colour	Height	Intro.	Discon.	Current Market Value U.K. £	U.S. $	Can. $
D5610	Large	Red hair	7 ½"	1937	1942	2,000.00	4,000.00	4,500.00

VARIATION No. 2: Colourway — Brown hair
Handle — Plain brown

Doulton Number	Size	Colour	Height	Intro.	Discon.	Current Market Value U.K. £	U.S. $	Can. $
D5610	Large	Brown hair	7 ½"	c. 1937	1942	2,000.00	4,000.00	4,500.00

VARIATION No. 3: Colourway — White hair
Handle — Multi-coloured

Doulton Number	Size	Colour	Height	Intro.	Discon.	Current Market Value U.K. £	U.S. $	Can. $
D6322	Large	White hair	7 ½"	1951	1955	700.00	1,350.00	1,600.00

Note: A black-haired clown exists, however, its authencity as a factory release has not yet been determined.

THE CLOWN

THE CIRCUS
ONE OF FOUR

STYLE TWO: CLOWN WITH HAT

Royal Doulton®
THE CLOWN
D 6834
Modelled by
Stanley James Taylor
© 1988 ROYAL DOULTON

Designer: Stanley J. Taylor
Handle: Gloved hand touching cap
Colourway: Green cap; yellow bow tie with black spots; red nose and mouth

Backstamp: Doulton

Doulton Number	Size	Backstamp	Height	Intro.	Discon.	Current Market Value		
						U.K. £	U.S. $	Can. $
D6834	Large	Doulton	6 ½"	1989	1995	85.00	250.00	300.00

THE COLLECTOR

THE COLLECTING WORLD
ONE OF THREE

These jugs were commissioned by Kevin Francis Ceramics Ltd. The large size was issued in 1988 in a special edition of 5,000 pieces, and the small size was issued in 1991 in a special edition of 1,500 pieces. Note the Kevin Francis characteristic of the left-handed jug.

Designer: Geoff Blower
Modeller: Stanley J. Taylor
Handle: A hand holding a Mephistopheles jug
Colourway: Black hat; dark green jacket; tan shirt

Backstamp: Doulton/Kevin Francis Ceramics

Doulton Number	Size	Backstamp	Height	Intro.	Discon.	Current Market Value		
						U.K. £	U.S. $	Can. $
D6796	Large	Doulton	7"	1988	Sp. ed.	100.00	275.00	325.00
D6906	Small	Doulton	4"	1991	Sp. ed.	100.00	200.00	250.00

CONFUCIUS

FLAMBÉ SERIES
ONE OF THREE

Issued in a limited edition of 1,750, this is the second jug to be decorated in flambé.

Royal Doulton®
FLAMBÉ
CONFUCIUS
D.7003
Modelled by

© 1995 ROYAL DOULTON
LIMITED EDITION OF 1,750
THIS IS Nº

Designer:	Robert I. Tabbenor
Handle:	Yin and Yang symbol and book of his teachings, "The Analects"
Colourway:	Flambé

Backstamp: Doulton

Doulton Number	Size	Backstamp	Height	Intro.	Discon.	Current Market Value		
						U.K. £	**U.S. $**	**Can. $**
D7003	Large	Doulton	7"	1995	Ltd. ed.	250.00	700.00	850.00

THE COOK AND THE CHESHIRE CAT

ALICE IN WONDERLAND
ONE OF SIX

These are two characters from Lewis Carroll's *Alice's Adventures in Wonderland.*

Royal Doulton®
**THE COOK AND
THE CHESHIRE CAT**
D. 6842
Modelled by

© 1989 ROYAL DOULTON

Designer: William K. Harper
Handle: A Cheshire cat
Colourway: White mob cap trimmed with a blue bow

Backstamp: Doulton

Doulton Number	Size	Backstamp	Height	Intro.	Discon.	Current Market Value		
						U.K. £	U.S. $	Can. $
D6842	Large	Doulton	7"	1990	1991	175.00	350.00	400.00

COUNT DRACULA

Count Dracula was the Character Jug of the Year for 1997.

Designer: David B. Biggs
Handle: Garlic, open window and a cross
Colourway: Black, red and brown

Backstamp: Doulton/Character
Jug of the Year, 1997/
Sir Henry Doulton 18971-1997

Doulton Number	Size	Backstamp	Height	Intro.	Discon.	Current Market Value		
						U.K. £	U.S. $	Can. $
D7053	Large	Doulton	7 ¼"	1997	1997	100.00	250.00	300.00

CYRANO DE BERGERAC

Designer:	David Biggs
Handle:	Sword, quill and letter
Colourway:	Maroon jacket; white collar; black hat; white plume

Backstamp: Doulton

Doulton Number	Size	Backstamp	Height	Intro.	Discon.	Current Market Value		
						U.K. £	U.S. $	Can. $
D7004	Large	Doulton	7"	1995	1997	75.00	200.00	300.00

DaGAMMA

For the character jug DaGamma see the "Explorers Set" page 233.

D'ARTAGNAN

THE THREE MUSKETEERS, ONE OF FOUR
NOW PART OF THE CHARACTERS FROM LITERATURE, ONE OF 11

A character in Alexandre Dumas' lively 19th-century fiction, D'Artagnan came to Paris to join the celebrated band of Three Musketeers and share their adventures.

Designer: Stanley J. Taylor
Backstamp: Doulton
Handle: An extension of the feathers with a fleur-de-lis and sword at the base
Colourway: Black hat trimmed with white feathers; white lace collar

Royal Doulton
D'ARTAGNAN
D.6691
Hand made and Hand decorated
© ROYAL DOULTON
TABLEWARE LTD 1982

Doulton Number	Size	Backstamp	Height	Intro.	Discon.	Current Market Value U.K. £	U.S. $	Can. $
D6691	Large	Doulton	7 ½"	1982	1995	100.00	175.00	225.00
D6764	Small	Doulton	4"	1987	1995	60.00	125.00	150.00
D6765	Miniature	Doulton	2 ½"	1987	1991	60.00	125.00	150.00

DAVID COPPERFIELD

For the character jug David Copperfield see the "Charles Dickens Commemorative Set" page 185.

DAVY CROCKETT AND ANTONIO LOPEZ DE SANTA ANNA

THE ANTAGONISTS' COLLECTION (TWO-FACED JUG)
ONE OF FOUR

Davy Crockett (1786-1836) was a hunter and expert marksman, as well as a gregarious drinker. Antonio Lopez de Santa Anna (1795-1876) was a Mexican general who led troops on many missions into the U.S. He was finally defeated in Texas in 1837 and jailed for a year.

This jug was issued in 1985 in a limited edition of 9,500 pieces.

Designer: Michael Abberley
Handle: Crocket—Alamo, a horn, mission wall
Santa Anna—Sword, mission wall
Colourway: Yellow and brown

Backstamp: Doulton

Royal Doulton
'The Antagonists'
Collection
D.6729
The Battle of the Alamo 1836
Davy Crockett/Antonio Lopez de Santa Anna
Hand made and Hand decorated
Designed by Michael Abberley

© ROYAL DOULTON (U.K.) 1984
Worldwide Limited Edition of 9,500
This is Number 699

Doulton Number	Size	Backstamp	Height	Intro.	Discon.	Current Market Value		
						U.K. £	U.S. $	Can. $
D6729	Large	Doulton	7"	1985	Ltd. ed.	100.00	200.00	250.00

DENIS COMPTON, CBE

This jug was issued to commemorate Denis Charles Scott Compton, CBE, contribution to the sport of cricket during the 1940s and 1950s. This limited edition (9,500) character jug, commissioned by Lawleys By Post, joins the other great cricketers, Grace, Hutton, Bird and Johnston.

Designer: Stanley J. Taylor
Handle: Cricket bat, ball and wicket
Colourway: Black, white and red

Backstamp: Doulton

Doulton Number	Size	Backstamp	Height	Intro.	Discon.	Current Market Value		
						U.K. £	U.S. $	Can. $
D —	Small	Doulton	4 ½"	1997	Ltd.ed.	50.00	125.00	150.00

DENNIS AND GNASHER

Dennis the Menace is a cartoon character from the U.K. comic magazine, *The Beano*. To celebrate the 60th anniversary of *The Beano* comic in 1998 a special anniversary logo appeared on the base of the large and small jugs for that year.

Designer: Simon Ward
Handle: A bag of peas, pea shooter, Gnasher the dog
Colourway: Red, black and green

Backstamp: A. Doulton/
© D.C. Thomson & Co., Ltd.
B. 60th Anniversary logo

Doulton Number	Size	Backstamp	Height	Intro.	Discon.	Current Market Value U.K. £	U.S. $	Can. $
D7005	Large	A. Doulton	7"	1995	1999	90.00	245.00	400.00
D7005	Large	B. 60th Anniv.	7"	1998	1998	90.00	245.00	400.00
D7033	Small	A. Doulton	4"	1996	1999	55.00	145.00	230.00
D7033	Small	B. 60th Anniv.	4"	1998	1998	55.00	145.00	230.00

DESPERATE DAN

Desperate Dan is a cartoon character from the U.K. comic *The Dandy*. To celebrate the 60th anniversary of *The Dandy* comic in 1998 a special anniversary logo appeared on the base of the large and small jugs for that year.

Designer: Simon Ward
Handle: A cow pie, cactus and jug of Owl Hoot juice
Colourway: Red shirt; black vest; blue scarf; brown and black hat

Backstamp: A. Doulton/
© D.C. Thomson & Co., Ltd.
B. 60th Anniversary logo

Doulton Number	Size	Backstamp	Height	Intro.	Discon.	Current Market Value		
						U.K. £	U.S. $	Can. $
D7006	Large	A. Doulton	7"	1995	1999	90.00	195.00	225.00
D7006	Large	B. 60th Anniv.	7"	1998	1998	90.00	195.00	225.00
D7034	Small	A. Doulton	4"	1996	1999	55.00	100.00	125.00
D7034	Small	B. 60th Anniv.	4"	1998	1998	55.00	100.00	125.00

DIAMOND ANNIVERSARY SET

This set was issued in 1994 to commemorate the Diamond Anniversary of the revival of the traditional Staffordshire jugs by Charles Noke in 1934. It was issued in a limited edition of 2,500 and came with a diamond shaped wall stand.

Designer: William K. Harper	**Backstamp:** Doulton
Height: 1 ½"	**Handle:** As original model
Size: Tiny	**Issued:** 1994 in a Ltd. ed. 2,500
Colourway: See below	

Doulton Number	Name	Designer	Colourway	Current Market Value U.K. £	U.S. $	Can. $
D6951	Dick Turpin	Fenton & Noke	Brown, grey and green	50.00	90.00	125.00
D6954	Granny	Fenton & Henk	Grey and white	50.00	90.00	125.00
D6953	Jester	Charles Noke	Brown, green and yellow	50.00	90.00	125.00
D6952	John Barleycorn	Charles Noke	Browns	50.00	90.00	125.00
D6955	Parson Brown	Charles Noke	Grey and white	50.00	90.00	125.00
D6956	Simon the Cellarer	Noke & Fenton	Maroon and white	50.00	90.00	125.00
	Complete set with display stand			300.00	550.00	750.00

DICK TURPIN

Dick Turpin (1705-1739) joined forces with fellow highwayman Tom King, whom he accidentally shot. Before he died, King betrayed him. Dick Turpin was hanged in 1739 for the murder of an Epping Forest gamekeeper.

The first style of the Dick Turpin jug has the mask up on the brim of the tricorn, and a pistol forms the handle. All of the sizes should have "R.T." inscribed on the pistol grip; however, it may be more obvious on certain jugs due to the casting variations. There is no premium value whether or not the "R.T." inscription is visible.

For tiny version of the Dick Turpin character jug see the "Diamond Anniversary Set" page 214.

STYLE ONE: HANDLE — A PISTOL

Designer:	Charles Noke / Harry Fenton
Handle:	Pistol
Colourway:	Brown hat; black mask up; green coat; white cravat

Backstamps: A. Doulton
B. Doulton / Bentalls / Souvenir From Bentalls 1936

Doulton Number	Size	Backstamp	Height	Intro.	Discon.	Current Market Value U.K. £	U.S. $	Can. $
D5485	Large	Doulton	6 ½"	1935	1960	100.00	195.00	250.00
D5618	Small	Doulton	3 ½"	1936	1960	60.00	80.00	100.00
D5618	Small	Doulton/Bentalls	3 ½"	1936	1936	450.00	850.00	1,100.00
D6128	Miniature	Doulton	2 ¼"	1940	1960	45.00	60.00	75.00

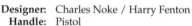

Dick Turpin Derivative

Doulton Number	Item	Height	Intro.	Discon.	Current Market Value U.K. £	U.S. $	Can. $
D5601	Match stand/ashtray	3"	1936	1960	85.00	150.00	200.00

DICK TURPIN

This second style of Dick Turpin has the mask covering the eyes, and the handle depicts a horse's head and neck.

STYLE TWO: HANDLE — NECK AND HEAD OF HORSE

Dick Turpin
D 6528
COPR 1959
DOULTON & CO LIMITED
Rd No 893841
Rd No 39649
Rd No 8313
Rd No 420/59

Designer: David Biggs
Handle: Head and neck of a horse
Colourway: Green tricorn; black mask over the eyes; red jacket

Backstamp: Doulton

Doulton Number	Size	Backstamp	Height	Intro.	Discon.	Current Market Value		
						U.K. £	U.S. $	Can. $
D6528	Large	Doulton	7"	1960	1981	85.00	135.00	160.00
D6535	Small	Doulton	3 ¾"	1960	1981	50.00	90.00	125.00
D6542	Miniature	Doulton	2 ¼"	1960	1981	50.00	85.00	110.00

Note: This jug was also issued in English Translucent China. These jugs command a premium of 50 to 100% over the earthenware variety.

DICK WHITTINGTON

The first Dick Whittington jug was styled on the character of a poor orphan boy who was employed in a London kitchen, as described in a play dated 1605. He gave his cat to his employer to sell to earn money, but then ran away to escape his evil employer's cook who mistreated him. The Bow Bells rang as he fled and seemed to say, "Turn back, Whittington, Lord Mayor of London." He obeyed and found that his cat had fetched a huge sum, making him a wealthy man.

Dick Whittington
D. 6 375.
COPR 1952
DOULTON & CO LIMITED.
Rᵈ Nᵒ 868419
Rᵈ Nᵒ 30500
Rᵈ Nᵒ 193/52.
Rᵈ Nᵒ 6649.

Designer: Geoff Blower
Handle: A stick and handkerchief
Colourway: Dark green cap and robes

Backstamp: Doulton

Doulton Number	Size	Backstamp	Height	Intro.	Discon.	Current Market Value		
						U.K. £	U.S. $	Can. $
D6375	Large	Doulton	6 ½"	1953	1960	275.00	550.00	700.00

DICK WHITTINGTON
LORD MAYOR OF LONDON

Richard Whittington (1358-1423), in actual fact, made his fortune as a textile dealer. He entered London politics as a councilman and rose to become the Lord Mayor of London in 1397, an office he held three times.

This jug was commissioned by The Guild of Specialist China and Glass Retailers and issued in 1989 in a special edition of 5,000 pieces.

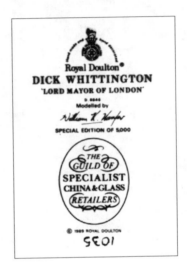

Designer:	William K. Harper
Handle:	Handle is of a signpost to London, the Bow Bells are above the signpost and a sack of gold is at the base
Colourway:	Blue tricorn hat trimmed with white feathers; blue coat trimmed with white fur; yellow chain of office

Backstamp: Doulton/Guild

Doulton Number	Size	Backstamp	Height	Intro.	Discon.	Current Market Value U.K. £	U.S. $	Can. $
D6846	Large	Doulton/Guild	7 ½"	1989	Sp. ed.	85.00	200.00	225.00

DOC HOLLIDAY

THE WILD WEST COLLECTION
ONE OF SIX

The son of a lawyer, John Henry Holliday (1852-1887) worked as a dentist in Baltimore, Maryland. At the age of 20 he learned he had tuberculosis and moved west to a warmer climate to prolong his life. He became adept at using firearms and the bowie knife and became known for his wild gambling, brawls and shootouts. He survived the famous gunfight at the O.K. Corral, but died in a sanatorium at age 35.

Designer: Stanley J. Taylor	**Backstamp:** Doulton
Handle: Pistol in a holster and dice	
Colourway: Black and grey hat; black coat	

Doulton Number	Size	Backstamp	Height	Intro.	Discon.	Current Market Value		
						U.K. £	U.S. $	Can. $
D6731	Mid	Doulton	5 ½"	1985	1989	85.00	175.00	200.00

DON QUIXOTE

CHARACTERS FROM LITERATURE
ONE OF 11

Don Quixote is the hero of the novel by Cervantes, a satirical parody of the chivalrous knight. Don Quixote leads a life of adventure, capturing many hearts along the way.

The helmet colour of the jugs varies from dark grey to light grey, with no difference in value.

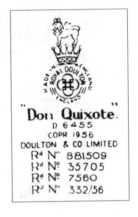

Backstamp: Doulton

Designer: Geoff Blower
Handle: A feather with a shield at the base
Colourway: Blue-grey helmet; dark green robes

Doulton Number	Size	Backstamp	Height	Intro.	Discon.	Current Market Value U.K. £	U.S. $	Can. $
D6455	Large	Doulton	7 ¼"	1957	1991	85.00	150.00	175.00
D6460	Small	Doulton	3 ¼"	1957	1991	50.00	80.00	90.00
D6511	Miniature	Doulton	2 ½"	1960	1991	45.00	75.00	95.00

Note: This jug was also issued in English Translucent China. These jugs command a premium of 50 to 100% over the earthenware variety.

DR LIVINGSTONE

For the character jug Dr Livingstone see the "Explorers Set" page 233.

DRAKE

Sir Francis Drake (1540-1596) was an English navigator and admiral. He was Queen Elizabeth I's right hand against the Spanish, going on many plundering expeditions in the Spanish West Indies. On one of these voyages, between 1577 and 1580, Drake became the first Englishman to sail around the world. He also repelled the Spanish Armada sent to invade England.

For the toby jug Sir Francis Drake see page 99, and for the character jug Sir Francis Drake see page 471.

STYLE ONE: WITHOUT HAT

VARIATION No. 1:   Colourway — White ruff; red-brown collar
The raised lettering "Sir Francis Drake" on the back of the coat is painted over

REGISTRATION
APPLIED FOR

Designer: Harry Fenton
Handle: Plain
Colourway: White ruff; red-brown collar

Backstamp: Doulton

Doulton Number	Size	Backstamp	Height	Intro.	Discon.	Current Market Value U.K. £	U.S. $	Can. $
D6115	Large	Doulton	5 ¾"	1940	1941	2,250.00	5,000.00	6,500.00

VARIATION No. 2: Colourway — White ruff; green collar
The raised lettering "Sir Francis Drake" on the back of the coat is painted white, highlighting the name

"Drake."

R⁴ Nº 838085.

Doulton Number	Size	Backstamp	Height	Intro.	Discon.	Current Market Value		
						U.K. £	U.S. $	Can. $
D6115	Large	Doulton	5 ¾"	1940	1941.	Extremely rare		

Sold Phillips Auction, London, England
October 29, 1998, £4,850.00

DRAKE

STYLE TWO: WITH HAT

Designer:	Harry Fenton	
Handle:	Rope	
Colourway:	Brown hat; green robes; white ruff; brown drum at back of handle alongside ruff	

Backstamp: Doulton

Doulton Number	Size	Backstamp	Height	Intro.	Discon.	Current Market Value		
						U.K. £	U.S. $	Can. $
D6115	Large	Doulton	5 ¾"	1940	1960	100.00	200.00	250.00
D6174	Small	Doulton	3 ¼"	1941	1960	60.00	100.00	120.00

DUKE OF WELLINGTON

THE GREAT GENERALS COLLECTION
ONE OF FOUR

Arthur Wellesley (1769-1852), first Duke of Wellington, was a British general and statesman. He led the British forces in the defeat of Napoleon at Waterloo in 1815 and also served as Prime Minister from 1828 to 1830.

This jug was commissioned by UK International Ceramics Ltd., in a special edition of 5,000.

For the character jug Wellington see "Napoleon and Wellington" page 379.

Designer: William K. Harper
Handle: Cannon above a banner reading "Waterloo"
Colourway: Blue and gold

Backstamp: Doulton

Doulton Number	Size	Backstamp	Height	Intro.	Discon.	Current Market Value U.K. £	U.S. $	Can. $
D6848	Large	Doulton	7 ¼"	1989	Sp. ed.	125.00	225.00	225.00

EARL MOUNTBATTEN OF BURMA

HEROIC LEADERS
ONE OF THREE

A British naval and military leader, Louis Francis Albert Victor Nicholas Mountbatten (1900-1979) was the last viceroy of India. Mountbatten was Governor-General of the Dominion of India from 1947 to 1948, relinquishing power to native rule in 1948. Upon his retirement from the navy in 1959, he became the principal military adviser to the Ministry of Defence. He was killed when a bomb exploded his fishing boat off the coast of Ireland.

This jug was commissioned by Lawleys By Post. It was issued in 1989 as one of a set of three, in a limited edition of 9,500 pieces.

STYLE ONE: HANDLE — NAVAL ENSIGN

Designer: Stanley J. Taylor
Handle: Naval ensign
Colourway: White naval uniform trimmed with gold

Backstamp: Doulton

Doulton Number	Size	Backstamp	Height	Intro.	Discon.	Current Market Value U.K. £	U.S. $	Can. $
D6851	Small	Doulton	3 ¼"	1990	Ltd. ed.	125.00	150.00	200.00

EARL MOUNTBATTEN OF BURMA

ROYAL DOULTON INTERNATIONAL COLLECTORS CLUB

This was the first large-size character jug to be commissioned by the Royal Doulton International Collectors Club and was issued in a limited edition of 5,000 jugs.

STYLE TWO: HANDLE — ANCHOR AND INTERTWINED ROPE

Designer:	Stanley J. Taylor	
Handle:	Anchor and intertwined rope	
Colourway:	Yellow, black and white	

Backstamp: Doulton/RDICC

Doulton Number	Size	Backstamp	Height	Intro.	Discon.	Current Market Value U.K. £	U.S. $	Can. $
D6944	Large	Doulton/RDICC	7"	1993	Ltd. ed.	150.00	275.00	300.00

THE ELEPHANT TRAINER

THE CIRCUS
ONE OF FOUR

Backstamp - Doulton

Designer: Stanley J. Taylor
Handle: Head of an elephant
Colourway: Orange turban; black coat trimmed
with green and yellow

Backstamps: **A**. Doulton
General issue, 1990.
B. Doulton/The Higbee Company/
To commemorate the Fourth Anniversary of the opening of The Royal Doulton Room
The Higbee Company, Cleveland, Ohio, U.S.A. Commissioned by the Higbee Company,
Cleveland, Ohio. Issued in 1989 in a limited edition of 250 pieces.
C. Doulton/Royal Doulton Rooms USA Strawbridge and Clothier, Hornes, Holmes/
To commemorate the anniversary of the opening of the Royal Doulton Rooms in the
United States of America. Issued in a limited edition of 250.

Doulton Number	Size	Backstamp	Height	Intro.	Discon.	Current Market Value U.K. £	U.S. $	Can. $
D6841	Large	Doulton	7"	1990	1993	125.00	275.00	300.00
D6856	Large	Higbee	7"	1989	Ltd. ed.	250.00	325.00	350.00
D6857	Large	Strawbridge	7"	1989	Ltd. ed.	250.00	325.00	350.00

ELF

CHRISTMAS MINIATURES SERIES
ONE OF SIX

The Elf miniature character jug was specially commissioned for the U.S. market. It was designed to complement the miniature Caroler (D7007), Christmas Angel (D7051), Mrs. Claus (D6922), Santa Claus (D6900) and Snowman (D6972). Although commissioned for the U.S. market, the jug was also available in other countries through the Royal Doulton International Collectors Club.

Designer: William K. Harper
Handle: Holly Wreath
Colourway: Green

Backstamp: Doulton

Doulton Number	Size	Backstamp	Height	Intro.	Discon.	Current Market Value U.K. £	U.S. $	Can. $
D6942	Miniature	Doulton	2 ¾"	1993	1993	65.00	125.00	150.00

ELGAR

GREAT COMPOSERS
ONE OF EIGHT

The Elgar jug completes the eight-piece Great Composers collection. One of England's greatest composers, Edward Elgar (1857-1934) is especially remembered for his Pomp and Circumstance marches, especially *Land of Hope and Glory*, which is traditionally part of the fitting climax to the Promenade Concerts *Last Night iof the Proms*.

Designer: Stanley J. Taylor
Handle: Organ pipes, Land of Hope and Glory
Colourway: Black, white, brown and cream

Backstamp: Doulton

Doulton Number	Size	Backstamp	Height	Intro.	Discon.	Current Market Value U.K. £	U.S. $	Can. $
D7118	Large	Doulton	7"	1998	Current	100.00	205.00	340.00

ELVIS PRESLEY

THE CELEBRITY COLLECTION

PROTOTYPE

Elvis Aaron Presley (1935-1977), the "King of Rock 'n' Roll," was the most popular artist in the history of American rock music. After his debut in 1955, he appeared in 33 films, as well as on numerous albums. This jug was not issued due to copyright problems, and while at least two prototypes are known to exist, none are known to be in private collections.

Designer: Stanley J. Taylor
Handle: Guitar and strap
Colourway: Black hair; white shirt with gold trim

Backstamp: Doulton

Doulton Number	Size	Backstamp	Height	Intro.	Discon.	Current Market Value		
						U.K. £	U.S. $	Can. $
D6730	Large	Doulton	7 ¼"	1987	1987		Extremely rare	

THE ENGINE DRIVER

JOURNEY THROUGH BRITAIN
ONE OF FOUR

Each jug in the Journey Through Britain series was given a specially designed backstamp relating to the subject of the jug. The backstamp on the Engine Driver has the wording within the outline of a locomotive engine. It was issued through Lawleys By Post in a limited edition of 5,000 pieces.

Designer: Stanley J. Taylor
Handle: A railway signal
Colourway: Black cap and coat; white shirt

Backstamp: Doulton

Doulton Number	Size	Backstamp	Height	Intro.	Discon.	Current Market Value U.K. £	U.S. $	Can. $
D6823	Small	Doulton	4"	1988	Ltd. ed.	100.00	200.00	250.00

EVERTON (FOOTBALL CLUB)

THE FOOTBALL SUPPORTERS
ONE OF TEN

Designer:	Stanley J. Taylor
Handle:	Team coloured scarf
Colourway:	Blue and white uniform

Backstamp: Doulton

Doulton Number	Size	Backstamp	Height	Intro.	Discon.	Current Market Value		
						U.K. £	**U.S. $**	**Can. $**
D6926	Mid	Doulton	5"	1992	Unknown	50.00	100.00	125.00

EXPLORERS

The Explorers collection present six tiny character jugs modelled after the great explorers who ushered in a new era in world history. Each set, issued in a limited edition of 2,500, comes complete with a wooden wall mount display stand.

Designer: Stanley J. Taylor
Handle: Globe and navigation chart showing each mans area of exploration
Colourway: See below

Backstamp: Doulton
Height: 1 ½"
Issued: 1997 in limited edition of 2,500

Doulton Number	Name	Colourway	U.K. £	U.S. $	Can. $
D7081	Columbus	Red, grey, blue and tan			
D7086	Cook	Dark blue, yellow, white and tan			
D7083	DaGamma	Green. grey and brown			
D7085	Dr. Livingstone	Yellow, brown and green			
D7084	Marco Polo	Red, brown, green and grey			
D7082	Scott	Browns	200.00	—	730.00

Current Market Value

FAGIN

For the character jug Fagin see the "Charles Dickens Commemorative Set" page 185.

THE FALCONER

Once called the sport of kings, falconry is the art of training birds of prey for the hunt. The sport began in China more than 3,000 years ago and still enjoys popularity in Europe and North America.

VARIATION No. 1: Colourway — Green with black and white striped fur hat; green coat; grey and white falcon

The Falconer
D 6540
COPR 1959
DOULTON & CO LIMITED
Rd No 893846
Rd No 39654
Rd No 8318
Rd No 415/59

Designer: Max Henk
Handle: A falcon
Colourway: Green with black and white striped fur hat; green coat; grey and white falcon

Backstamp: Doulton

Doulton Number	Size	Backstamp	Height	Intro.	Discon.	Current Market Value		
						U.K. £	**U.S. $**	**Can. $**
D6533	Large	Doulton	7 ½"	1960	1991	75.00	135.00	150.00
D6540	Small	Doulton	3 ¾"	1960	1991	50.00	85.00	100.00
D6547	Miniature	Doulton	2 ¾"	1960	1991	45.00	70.00	90.00

Note: This jug was also issued in English Translucent China. These jugs command a premium of 50 to 100% over the earthenware variety.

VARIATION No. 2:   Colourway — Dark green and brown striped fur hat; dark brown coat; ginger beard; brown falcon

Backstamp: Doulton/Joseph Horne Company /
Celebrating the opening of The Royal Doulton Room, Hornes, Pittsburgh, Pennsylvania, U.S.A.
Specially commissioned from Royal Doulton by the Joseph Horne Company, Pittsburgh, Pennsylvania,
U.S.A. Issued in 1987 in a limited edition of 250 pieces.

Doulton Number	Size	Backstamp	Height	Intro.	Discon.	Current Market Value U.K. £	U.S. $	Can. $
D6798	Large	Doulton/Horne	7 ½"	1987	Ltd. ed.	225.00	325.00	375.00

VARIATION No. 3:   Colourway — Black with maroon and white striped fur hat; red-brown coat; brown falcon

Backstamp: Doulton / Peter Jones China Ltd /
New Colourway 1987 Special Commission 1000 Peter Jones Collection Leeds and Wakefield
Commissioned by Peter Jones China Ltd, Leeds and Wakefield, England. Issued in 1987 in a
special edition of 1,000 pieces.

Doulton Number	Size	Backstamp	Height	Intro.	Discon.	Current Market Value U.K. £	U.S. $	Can. $
D6800	Large	Doulton/Jones	7 ½"	1987	Sp. ed.	125.00	225.00	300.00

FALSTAFF

CHARACTERS FROM LITERATURE
ONE OF 11

Sir John Falstaff is a fat, good-humoured braggart who figures in Shakespeare's *Henry IV* and *The Merry Wives of Windsor*. A trial piece exists in a red and dark green colourway, but it was not released for sale.

VARIATION No. 1:   Colourway — Rose tunic; black hat trimmed with rose plumes; grey beard

Falstaff
D 6287
COPR 1949
DOULTON & CO LIMITED

Designer: Harry Fenton
Handle: Plain
Colourway: Rose tunic; black hat trimmed with rose plumes; grey beard

Backstamp: Doulton

Doulton Number	Size	Backstamp	Height	Intro.	Discon.	Current Market Value U.K. £	U.S. $	Can. $
D6287	Large	Doulton	6"	1950	1995	75.00	150.00	175.00
D6385	Small	Doulton	3 ½"	1950	1995	50.00	65.00	75.00
D6519	Miniature	Doulton	2 ½"	1960	1991	55.00	75.00	90.00

Note: This jug was also issued in English Translucent China. These jugs command a premium of 50 to 100% over the earthenware variety.

VARIATION No. 2:   Colourway — Yellow tunic; black hat trimmed with yellow plumes; brown beard

Backstamp: Doulton/U.K. Fairs Ltd.
                 Produced exclusively for U.K. Fairs Ltd. in a special edition of 1,500.

Doulton Number	Size	Backstamp	Height	Intro.	Discon.	Current Market Value U.K. £	U.S. $	Can. $
D6795	Large	Doulton	6"	1987	Sp. ed.	55.00	150.00	200.00

Falstaff Derivatives

Doulton Number	Item	Height	Intro.	Discon.	Current Market Value U.K. £	U.S. $	Can. $
D6385	Table lighter	3 ½"	1958	1973	125.00	150.00	200.00
D6854	Teapot	Unknown	1989	1991	125.00	200.00	250.00

FARMER JOHN

STYLE ONE: HANDLE — INSIDE JUG

Backstamp B - Doulton/Coleman's

Designer: Charles Noke
Handle: Brown handle set within the neck of the jug
Colourway: Brown

Backstamps: **A.** Doulton
B. Doulton/Coleman's/
Coleman's Compliments

Doulton Number	Size	Backstamp	Height	Intro.	Discon.	Current Market Value		
						U.K. £	U.S. $	Can. $
D5788	Large	A. Doulton	6 ½"	1938	1960	100.00	225.00	250.00
D5788	Large	B. Coleman's	6 ½"	1938	1938	1,000.00	2,000.00	2,500.00
D5789	Small	A. Doulton	3 ¼"	1938	1960	60.00	110.00	150.00

Note: This jug was also issued in English Translucent China. These jugs command a premium of 50 to 100% over the earthenware variety.

FARMER JOHN

STYLE TWO: HANDLE — OUTSIDE JUG

Designer: Charles Noke
Handle: Brown handle set at the top of the neck.
Colourway: Brown

Backstamp: Doulton

Doulton Number	Size	Backstamp	Height	Intro.	Discon.	Current Market Value		
						U.K. £	U.S. $	Can. $
D5788	Large	Doulton	6 ½"	1938	1960	100.00	200.00	225.00
D5789	Small	Doulton	3 ¼"	1938	1960	60.00	100.00	125.00

Farmer John Derivative

Doulton Number	Item	Height	Intro.	Discon.	Current Market Value		
					U.K. £	U.S. $	Can. $
D6007	Ash bowl	3"	1939	1960	100.00	150.00	175.00

Note: This jug was also issued in English Translucent China. These jugs command a premium of 50 to 100% over the earthenware variety.

FAT BOY

Another wonderful Dickens character, Joe, the Fat Boy, was the lazy glutton who worked as servant to Mr. Wardle in *The Pickwick Papers.*

Designer: Leslie Harradine/Harry Fenton
Handle: Plain
Colourway: Blue shirt; white scarf

Backstamp: Doulton

Doulton Number	Size	Backstamp	Height	Intro.	Discon.	Current Market Value U.K. £	U.S. $	Can. $
D5840	Mid	Doulton	5"	1938	1948	150.00	275.00	325.00
D5840	Small	Doulton	4"	1948	1960	85.00	175.00	200.00
D6139	Miniature	Doulton	2 ½"	1940	1960	60.00	100.00	125.00
D6142	Tiny	Doulton	1 ½"	1940	1960	60.00	100.00	120.00

Fat Boy Derivative

Doulton Number	Item	Height	Intro.	Discon.	Current Market Value U.K. £	U.S. $	Can. $
M59	Napkin ring	3 ½"	1935	1939	300.00	600.00	750.00
—	Toothpick holder	2 ¼"	Unknown		600.00	1,100.00	1,200.00

Note: This jug was also issued in English Translucent China. These jugs command a premium of 50 to 100% over the earthenware variety.

FIELD MARSHAL MONTGOMERY

Issued for the 50th anniversary of Montgomery's victory over Rommel in North Africa in 1942, this jug was produced in a limited edition of 2,500 pieces worldwide.

For the character jug Monty see page 368, and for the character jug Viscount Montgomery of Alamein see page 518.

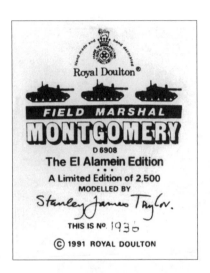

Designer:	Stanley J. Taylor	
Handle:	Baton, oak leaves, "El Alamein"	
Colourway:	Black beret; khaki uniform; purple and cream baton	

Backstamp: Doulton

Doulton Number	Size	Backstamp	Height	Intro.	Discon.	Current Market Value		
						U.K. £	U.S. $	Can. $
D6908	Large	Doulton	6 ½"	1992	Ltd. ed.	125.00	250.00	300.00

THE FIREMAN

Launched exclusively by Griffith Pottery House in 1983, The Fireman jug was then released into the general range in 1984. Varieties of the handle exist, with the nozzle ranging from dark orange to light yellow, but there is no premium value for these colourway variations.

An error in this jug exists. The red background of the helmet badge was not applied during painting, resulting in a white badge. This curiousity piece has very little premium value.

STYLE ONE: HANDLE — NOZZLE OF FIRE HOSE

Royal Doulton
The Fireman
D.6697
Hand made and Hand decorated
Designed by Jerry D.Griffith
Modelled by Robert Tabbenor
© ROYAL DOULTON
TABLEWARE LTD. 1982

Backstamp C

Designer:	Jerry D. Griffith
Modeller:	Robert I. Tabbenor
Handle:	Nozzle of fire hose
Colourway:	Black, brown and red helmet badge

Backstamps: A. Doulton/Hand made and hand decorated. No credits
B. Doulton/Hand made and Hand decorated Modelled by Robert Tabbenor
C. Doulton/Hand made and Hand decorated Designed by Jerry D. Griffith/Modelled by Robert Tabbenor

Doulton Number	Size	Backstamp	Height	Intro.	Discon.	U.K. £	U.S. $	Can. $
D6697	Large	A. Doulton	7 ¼"	1984	1991	100.00	250.00	275.00
D6697	Large	B. Doulton	7 ¼"	1984	1991	100.00	250.00	275.00
D6697	Large	C. Doulton	7 ¼"	1983	1991	100.00	250.00	275.00

THE FIREMAN

JOURNEY THROUGH BRITAIN
ONE OF FOUR

As with the other pieces in this series, the wording of the backstamp is contained within a design connected to the subject. This design is a coiled hose. Issued through Lawleys By Post in 1988, this jug was produced in a limited edition of 5,000 pieces.

STYLE TWO: HANDLE — AXE AND FIRE HOSE

Designer: Stanley J. Taylor
Handle: An axe and fire hose
Colourway: Yellow helmet; dark blue jacket

Backstamp: Doulton

Doulton Number	Size	Backstamp	Height	Intro.	Discon.	Current Market Value		
						U.K. £	U.S. $	Can. $
D6839	Small	Doulton	4 ¼"	1989	Ltd. ed.	100.00	175.00	200.00

THE FORTUNE TELLER

STYLE ONE: HANDLE — SIGNS OF THE ZODIAC

Backstamp: Doulton

Designer: Garry Sharpe
Handle: Zodiac design
Colourway: Green scarf around head; black shawl; purple handle

Doulton Number	Size	Backstamp	Height	Intro.	Discon.	Current Market Value		
						U.K. £	U.S. $	Can. $
D6497	Large	Doulton	6 ¾"	1959	1967	400.00	800.00	950.00
D6503	Small	Doulton	3 ¾"	1959	1967	250.00	500.00	600.00
D6523	Miniature	Doulton	2 ½"	1960	1967	275.00	525.00	600.00

Note: This jug was also issued in English Translucent China. These jugs command a premium of 50 to 100% over the earthenware variety.

THE FORTUNE TELLER

CHARACTER JUG OF THE YEAR

Beginning in 1991, one jug was selected as the Character Jug of the Year, produced for one year only and issued with a certificate of authenticity. The Fortune Teller was the Character Jug of the Year for 1991.

STYLE TWO: HANDLE — TAROT CARDS

Royal Doulton®
CHARACTER JUG OF THE YEAR
THE FORTUNE TELLER
D 6874
Modelled by

Stanley James Taylor

This special edition will only
be available during the year
1991
© 1990 ROYAL DOULTON

Designer: Stanley J. Taylor
Handle: Bandana and tarot cards
Colourway: Orange polka-dot bandana; light blue shirt

Backstamp: Doulton/Character
Jug of the Year, 1991

Doulton Number	Size	Backstamp	Height	Intro.	Discon.	Current Market Value U.K. £	U.S. $	Can. $
D6874	Large	Jug of the Year	7"	1991	1991	175.00	325.00	350.00

FRANCIS ROSSI and RICK PARFITT
(STATUS QUO)

Produced in a limited edition of 2,500, the Francis Rossi jug was issued in conjunction with the Rick Parfitt jug, commemorating the U.K. band, Status Quo. The Parfitt jug handle is on the left, and the Rossi handle is on the right, so they can be displayed as a pair.

Designer:	Martyn C. R. Alcock	
Handle:	Cream and brown guitar	
Colourway:	Blue and brown	

Backstamp: Doulton /
© Phantom Music Ltd.

Doulton Number	Name	Height	Intro.	Discon.	Current Market Value		
					U.K. £	**U.S. $**	**Can. $**
D6961	Francis Rossi	5"	1993	Ltd. ed.	50.00	100.00	125.00
D6962	Rick Parfitt	5"	1993	Ltd. ed.	50.00	100.00	125.00
	Pair				100.00	200.00	250.00

FRANKENSTEIN'S MONSTER

The Frankenstein character first appeared in a 19th century book written by Mary Shelley. The Hollywood film of 1931 starring Boris Karloff as Frankenstein creating his "monster" on the electric operating table carried the legend to new heights. This jug was issued by Lawleys By Post in a limited edition of 2,500.

Designer: Martyn C. R. Alcock
Handle: The monster on the electric table
Colourway: Black, brown and grey

Backstamp: Doulton

Doulton Number	Size	Backstamp	Height	Intro.	Discon.	Current Market Value		
						U.K. £	U.S. $	Can. $
D7052	Large	Doulton	6 ½"	1996	Ltd. ed	125.00	250.00	300.00

FRIAR TUCK

Fat and jolly and fond of drink, Friar Tuck joined the legendary Robin Hood and his band of rogues in Sherwood Forest as they robbed the rich to feed the poor in rural England.

Designer: Harry Fenton   **Backstamp:** Doulton
Handle: Tree trunk
Colourway: Light and dark brown robes; green oak leaves

Doulton Number	Size	Backstamp	Height	Intro.	Discon.	Current Market Value		
						U.K. £	U.S. $	Can. $
D6321	Large	Doulton	7"	1951	1960	300.00	550.00	700.00

GAOLER

CHARACTERS FROM WILLIAMSBURG
ONE OF EIGHT

Designer: David Biggs
Handle: Two keys
Colourway: Black tricorn; white shirt; red vest

Backstamp: Doulton

Doulton Number	Size	Backstamp	Height	Intro.	Discon.	Current Market Value		
						U.K. £	U.S. $	Can. $
D6570	Large	Doulton	7"	1963	1983	100.00	175.00	200.00
D6577	Small	Doulton	3 ¾"	1963	1983	55.00	100.00	125.00
D6584	Miniature	Doulton	2 ¾"	1963	1983	50.00	90.00	120.00

Note: This jug was also issued in English Translucent China. These jugs command a premium of 50 to 100% over the earthenware variety.

THE GARDENER

STYLE ONE: HANDLE — A SPADE AND VEGETABLES

VARIATION No. 1: Colourway — Red scarf; red striped shirt; brown hat

Designer: David Biggs
Handle: A spade with carrots and a marrow at the base
Colourway: Red scarf; red striped shirt; brown hat
Backstamp: Doulton

The Gardener
D.6630
©DOULTON & CO. LIMITED. 1972
REGISTRATION APPLIED FOR

Doulton Number	Size	Backstamp	Height	Intro.	Discon.	Current Market Value U.K. £	U.S. $	Can. $
D6630	Large	Doulton	7 ¾"	1971	1971		Rare	

VARIATION No. 2: Colourway — Yellow scarf; white shirt; light brown hat

Doulton Number	Size	Backstamp	Height	Intro.	Discon.	Current Market Value U.K. £	U.S. $	Can. $
D6630	Large	Doulton	7 ¾"	1973	1981	125.00	200.00	225.00
D6634	Small	Doulton	4"	1973	1981	75.00	110.00	135.00
D6638	Miniature	Doulton	2 ¾"	1973	1981	95.00	125.00	165.00

THE GARDENER

CHARACTERS FROM LIFE
ONE OF SEVEN

STYLE TWO: HANDLE — A RED FLOWERING POTTED PLANT

Designer:	Stanley J. Taylor
Handle:	A potted plant
Colourway:	Beige hat; green sweater; beige shirt
Backstamp:	Doulton

VARIATION No. 1: Mould — Younger face with hair in front

Doulton Number	Size	Variation	Height	Intro.	Discon.	Current Market Value		
						U.K. £	U.S. $	Can. $
D6867	Large	Var. 1	7 ¼"	1990	1991	100.00	200.00	250.00

VARIATION No. 2: Mould — Older face without hair in front

Doulton Number	Size	Variation	Height	Intro.	Discon.	Current Market Value		
						U.K. £	U.S. $	Can. $
D6868	Small	Var. 2	4"	1990	1995	40.00	100.00	125.00

GENERAL CUSTER

Designer: Stanley J. Taylor	**Backstamp:** Doulton
Handle: A sword and flag	
Colourway: Black, yellow and red	

Doulton Number	Size	Backstamp	Height	Intro.	Discon.	Current Market Value		
						U.K. £	U.S. $	Can. $
D7079	Large	Doulton	7"	1997	1999	100.00	245.00	410.00

GENERAL EISENHOWER

GREAT GENERALS
ONE OF FOUR

This jug was commissioned by U.K. International Ceramics in a special edition of 1,000. It commemorates the 50th anniversary of the U.S. Army's landing in Africa on November 7 and 8, 1942.

Designer:	William K. Harper
Handle:	Face — Shield "S.H.A.E.F."
	Back — U.S. flag
	Both rest on tin helmet
Colourway:	Brown uniform; cream shield;
	red and white stars and stripes

Backstamp: Doulton

Doulton Number	Size	Backstamp	Height	Intro.	Discon.	Current Market Value		
						U.K. £	U.S. $	Can. $
D6937	Large	Doulton	7"	1993	Sp. ed.	200.00	350.00	375.00

GENERAL GORDON

GREAT GENERALS
ONE OF FOUR

Charles George Gordon (1833-1885) was known as "Chinese Gordon" after he commanded the Chinese forces against Taiping rebels in 1863. As Governor-General of the Sudan, he was instrumental in closing down the slave trade. In 1884 he was ordered to rescue the Egyptian garrison at Khartoum, instead he was besieged in Khartoum and killed.

The jug was commissioned by U.K. International Ceramics and issued in 1991 in a special edition of 1,500 pieces.

Designer: William K. Harper
Handle: Camel's head and neck with Khartoum ensign
Colourway: Red, blue and gold

Backstamp: Doulton

Doulton Number	Size	Backstamp	Height	Intro.	Discon.	Current Market Value U.K. £	U.S. $	Can. $
D6869	Large	Doulton	7 ¼"	1991	Sp. ed.	125.00	250.00	275.00

GENERAL PATTON

GREAT GENERALS
ONE OF FOUR

This jug was commissioned in 1996 to commemorate the 50th anniversary of VE-Day, May 8th, 1945, by UKI Ceramics in a special edition of 1,000.

Designer: Warren Platt
Handle: Revolver, bulldog and flags
Colourways: Brown, khaki and green

Backstamp: Doulton

Doulton Number	Size	Backstamp	Height	Intro.	Discon.	Current Market Value U.K. £	U.S. $	Can. $
D7026	Large	Doulton	7"	1996	Sp. ed.	195.00	325.00	375.00

THE GENIE

MYSTICAL CHARACTERS
ONE OF THREE

Popularized through legend, the genie is said to reside in a magic lantern and to become the servant of whoever frees him.

Royal Doulton®
THE GENIE
D 6892
Modelled by

Stanley James Taylor

© 1991 ROYAL DOULTON

Designer: Stanley J. Taylor
Handle: Lamp and hair
Colourway: Grey, black, red and yellow

Backstamp: Doulton

Doulton Number	Size	Backstamp	Height	Intro.	Discon.	Current Market Value		
						U.K. £	U.S. $	Can. $
D6892	Large	Doulton	7"	1991	1991	150.00	350.00	400.00

GEOFFREY CHAUCER
LOVING CUP

This jug was issued in 1996 in a limited edition of 1,500.

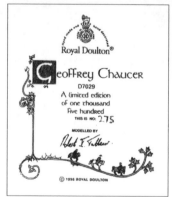

Designer: Robert I. Tabbenor
Handle: Three mounted riders either side
Colourway: Browns

Backstamp: Doulton

Doulton Number	Size	Backstamp	Height	Intro.	Discon.	Current Market Value		
						U.K. £	U.S. $	Can. $
D7029	Large	Doulton	7 ½"	1996	Ltd. ed.	300.00	800.00	1,000.00

GEORGE III AND GEORGE WASHINGTON

THE ANTAGONISTS' COLLECTION (TWO-FACED JUG)
ONE OF FOUR

George Washington (1732-1799), as commander-in-chief of the American States, led the U.S. to victory in the War of Independence. In 1789 he became the first president of the United States, governing for two terms until 1797.

King George III (1738-1820) ruled Great Britain from 1760 until his death. He led his country in the war against the American States, which he lost in 1776.

This jug was issued in 1986 in a limited edition of 9,500.

Designer: Michael Abberley
Handle: George Washington —
Declaration of Independence
George III — A cannon
Colourway: Red crown; black hat

Backstamp: Doulton

Royal Doulton®
'The Antagonists'
Collection
D.6749
The Siege of Yorktown 1781
George III/George Washington
Hand made and Hand decorated
Designed by Michael Abberley

© 1985 ROYAL DOULTON (UK)
Worldwide Limited Edition of 9,500
This is Number 3895

Doulton Number	Size	Backstamp	Height	Intro.	Discon.	Current Market Value		
						U.K. £	U.S. $	Can. $
D6749	Large	Doulton	7 ¼"	1986	Ltd. ed.	100.00	200.00	225.00

GEORGE HARRISON

THE BEATLES
ONE OF FOUR

One of the members of the legendary rock band, the Beatles, George Harrison was born in 1943 in Liverpool, England. He is a guitar player and song writer, and since the break-up of the Beatles in 1970, Harrison has pursued a solo career.

Designer: Stanley J. Taylor   **Backstamp:** Doulton
Handle: Plain
Colourway: Green tunic; orange collar and epaulettes

Doulton Number	Size	Backstamp	Height	Intro.	Discon.	Current Market Value U.K. £	U.S. $	Can. $
D6727	Mid	Doulton	5 ½"	1984	1991	125.00	275.00	300.00

GEORGE STEPHENSON

Created to mark the 150th anniversary of the death of George Stephenson, this character jug highlights his achievements. Inventor of the Rocket steam locomotive, George Stephenson is considered the father of the Railway Age that made such a change in the economic and social life of the country. This jug was issued in a limited edition of 1,848 by Lawleys By Post.

Designer: William K. Harper
Handle: Metal model of the Rocket steam locomotive. bridge structure dated 1830
Colourway: Black, maroon, white and tan

Backstamp: Doulton

Doulton Number	Size	Backstamp	Height	Intro.	Discon.	Current Market Value		
						U.K. £	U.S. $	Can. $
D7093	Large	Doulton	7"	1998	Ltd. ed.	100.00	—	—

GEORGE TINWORTH

ROYAL DOULTON INTERNATIONAL COLLECTORS CLUB

This jug was created exclusively for the Royal Doulton International Collectors Club.

Designer: William K. Harper
Handle: Tinworth sculptures
Colourway: Browns, black and grey

Backstamp: Doulton/RDICC

Doulton Number	Size	Backstamp	Height	Intro.	Discon.	Current Market Value		
						U.K. £	U.S. $	Can. $
D7000	Small	Doulton/RDICC	4 ¼"	1995	1996	85.00	150.00	175.00

GEORGE WASHINGTON

As commander-in-chief of the American States, George Washington (1732-1799) led them to victory in the War of Independence. In 1789 he became the first President of the United States, governing for two terms until 1797. This jug was issued to celebrate the 250th anniversary of Washington's birth.

STYLE ONE: HANDLE — DECLARATION OF INDEPENDENCE

ROYAL DOULTON
TABLEWARE LTD. 1982
D6669

George Washington
1732-1799
**First Issued in 1982 to Celebrate
the 250th Anniversary of his Birth**

Backstamp B - Dates of Birth

Designer: Stanley J. Taylor
Handle: Declaration of Independence
Colourway: Black hat and coat; beige shirt

Backstamps: **A.** Doulton
    B. Doulton/George Washington 1732-1799/
      First Issued in 1982 to Celebrate the
      250th Anniversary of his Birth
    C. Doulton/George Washington/
      To Commemorate the 200th Anniversary
      of the Election of the First President
      of the United States of America

Doulton Number	Size	Backstamp	Height	Intro.	Discon.	Current Market Value U.K. £	U.S. $	Can. $
D6669	Large	A	7 ½"	1982	1994	100.00	200.00	225.00
D6669	Large	B	7 ½"	1989	1989	125.00	225.00	250.00
D6824	Small	A	4"	1989	1991	50.00	125.00	150.00
D6824	Small	B	4"	1989	1989	55.00	100.00	125.00
D6824	Small	C	4"	1989	1991	75.00	125.00	150.00
D6825	Miniature	A	2 ½"	1989	1994	50.00	150.00	175.00
D6825	Miniature	C	2 ½"	1989	1991	100.00	175.00	200.00

GEORGE WASHINGTON

PRESIDENTIAL SERIES
ONE OF THREE
PRESIDENTS OF THE UNITED STATES

This George Washington jug was issued in a limited edition of 2,500.

STYLE TWO: HANDLE — AXE, CHERRIES, LEAVES AND SCROLL

Designer: Stanley J. Taylor
Handle: Axe, cherries and leaves with scroll reading
"To the memory of the man, first in war, first
in peace, first in the hearts of his countrymen"
Colourway: Green, cream and red

Backstamp: Doulton

Doulton Number	Size	Backstamp	Height	Intro.	Discon.	Current Market Value		
						U.K. £	U.S. $	Can. $
D6965	Large	Doulton	7"	1995	Ltd. ed.	150.00	275.00	300.00

GERONIMO

THE WILD WEST COLLECTION
ONE OF SIX

Geronimo (1829-1909) was the last leader of the Apache Indians while they were still independent of American colonial rule. Although he fought many battles to protect the freedom of his people, in 1886 he surrendered to General Nelson Miles, and Apache territory became the state of Arizona.

Designer: Stanley J. Taylor
Handle: Indian game pieces
Colourway: Black, red and white

Backstamp: Doulton

Doulton Number	Size	Backstamp	Height	Intro.	Discon.	Current Market Value		
						U.K. £	U.S. $	Can. $
D6733	Mid	Doulton	5 ½"	1985	1989	125.00	250.00	300.00

GLADIATOR

From about 246 B.C., gladiatorial games were a popular form of entertainment for Roman audiences. The gladiators were most often slaves or prisoners condemned to fight, which they did to the death using sword, spear or trident. The most famous gladiator of the period was Spartacus, a slave who led an unsuccessful rebellion against Rome. Emperor Honorius banned the brutal games in 404 A.D.

Gladiator
D 6550
COPR 1960
DOULTON & CO LIMITED
Rd No 897939
Rd No 40889
Rd No 8598
Rd No 548A/60

Designer:	Max Henk	**Backstamp:** Doulton
Handle:	A dagger and shield	
Colourway:	Brown helmet; grey armour	

Doulton Number	Size	Backstamp	Height	Intro.	Discon.	Current Market Value U.K. £	U.S. $	Can. $
D6550	Large	Doulton	7 ¾"	1961	1967	400.00	900.00	1,000.00
D6553	Small	Doulton	4 ¼"	1961	1967	275.00	525.00	650.00
D6556	Miniature	Doulton	2 ¾"	1961	1967	275.00	525.00	650.00

Note: This jug was also issued in English Translucent China. These jugs command a premium of 50 to 100% over the earthenware variety.

GLENN MILLER

This jug commemorates the 50th anniversary of the disappearance of Glenn Miller in an airplane over the Bay of Biscay in 1944. Glenn wears his uniform and a pair of metal glasses. The backstamp includes his date of birth and death on the jugs issued in 1994.

Backstamp A - With
Dates

Backstamp B - Without
Dates

Designer: William K. Harper
Handle: Song sheet for "Moonlight Serenade"
Colourway: Browns and beige

Backstamps: **A:** Doulton/Dates of Miller's birth and death included.
B: Doulton/Without dates.

Doulton Number	Size	Backstamp	Height	Intro.	Discon.	Current Market Value U.K. £	U.S. $	Can. $
D6970	Large	Doulton/dates	7 ½"	1994	1994	150.00	300.00	425.00
D6970	Large	Doulton	7 ½"	1995	1998	125.00	275.00	375.00

GOLFER

This Golfer character jug was modelled in the likeness of W. J. Carey, the former chairman of Doulton U.S.A.

STYLE ONE: HANDLE — GOLD BAG AND CLUBS

VARIATION No. 1:   Colourway — Blue cap; brown sweater; brown golf bag

Royal Doulton
GOLFER
D 6623
Modelled by

David B Biggs

© ROYAL DOULTON TABLEWARE
LIMITED 1970

Designer: David B. Biggs
Handle: A golf bag and clubs
Colourway: Blue cap; brown sweater; brown golf bag

Backstamp: Doulton

Doulton Number	Size	Backstamp	Height	Intro.	Discon.	Current Market Value		
						U.K. £	U.S. $	Can. $
D6623	Large	Doulton	7"	1971	1995	65.00	125.00	150.00
D6756	Small	Doulton	4 ½"	1987	1990	50.00	85.00	110.00
D6757	Miniature	Doulton	2 ½"	1987	1991	50.00	100.00	125.00

VARIATION No. 2:   Colourway — Dark blue cap; blue striped sweater; light brown golf bag

Backstamp: Doulton
Commissioned by John Sinclair, Sheffield, England. Issued in 1987 in a limited edition of 1,000 pieces.

Doulton Number	Size	Backstamp	Height	Intro.	Discon.	Current Market Value U.K. £	U.S. $	Can. $
D6787	Large	Doulton	7"	1987	Ltd. ed.	100.00	260.00	250.00

THE GOLFER / THE MODERN GOLFER

CHARACTERS FROM LIFE
ONE OF SEVEN

In the United States, the Royal Doulton product list carried this jug as "The Modern Golfer."

STYLE TWO: HANDLE — 18TH-HOLE FLAG, BALL, TEE AND GOLF CLUB

Royal Doulton®
THE GOLFER
D 6865
Modelled by
Stanley James Taylor
© 1990 ROYAL DOULTON

Designer: Stanley J. Taylor
Handle: Golf club, 18th-hole flag, ball and tee
Colourway: Yellow sweater; green sun visor

Backstamp: Doulton

Doulton Number	Size	Backstamp	Height	Intro.	Discon.	Current Market Value		
						U.K. £	U.S. $	Can. $
D6865	Small	Doulton	4"	1990	1995	45.00	100.00	125.00

THE GOLFER

STYLE THREE: HANDLE — GOLF BAG, CLUBS, FLAG

Designer: David Biggs
Handle: Golf bag, clubs and flag
Colourway: Yellow shirt, white collar; blue visor

Backstamp: Doulton

Doulton Number	Size	Backstamp	Height	Intro.	Discon.	Current Market Value		
						U.K. £	U.S. $	Can. $
D7064	Small	Doulton	4 ¾"	1997	1999	53.00	145.00	285.00

GONDOLIER

The shallow, long craft the gondolier pilots through Venetian canals must be painted all black, according to ancient law. When not ferrying or serenading lovers on moonlight rides, the gondolier moors his gondola to a brightly striped pole by the waterside.

Designer:	David Biggs	**Backstamp:** Doulton
Handle:	Gondola	
Colourway:	Yellow hat; blue and white t-shirt; maroon and white pole	

Doulton Number	Size	Backstamp	Height	Intro.	Discon.	Current Market Value U.K. £	U.S. $	Can. $
D6589	Large	Doulton	8"	1964	1969	400.00	825.00	975.00
D6592	Small	Doulton	4"	1964	1969	300.00	575.00	700.00
D6595	Miniature	Doulton	2 ½"	1964	1969	275.00	550.00	600.00

Note: This jug was also issued in English Translucent China. These jugs command a premium of 50 to 100% over the earthenware variety.

GONE AWAY

This very British huntsman looks ready to give the traditional call signalling the loss of the quarry. His prey, the fox, has won this round!

```
Gone Away
D 6531
COPR 1959
DOULTON & CO LIMITED
Rd No 893844
Rd No 39652
Rd No 8316
Rd No 417/59
```

Designer: Garry Sharpe
Handle: A fox
Colourway: Red jacket; black cap

Backstamp: Doulton

Doulton Number	Size	Backstamp	Height	Intro.	Discon.	Current Market Value U.K. £	U.S. $	Can. $
D6531	Large	Doulton	7 ¼"	1960	1982	85.00	175.00	175.00
D6538	Small	Doulton	3 ¾"	1960	1982	50.00	80.00	115.00
D6545	Miniature	Doulton	2 ½"	1960	1982	45.00	90.00	90.00

THE GRADUATE (MALE)

Royal Doulton®
THE GRADUATE
D 6916
Modelled by

Stanley James Taylor

© 1991 ROYAL DOULTON

Designer: Stanley J. Taylor
Handle: Diploma
Colourway: Black and white

Backstamp: Doulton

Doulton Number	Size	Backstamp	Height	Intro.	Discon.	Current Market Value		
						U.K. £	U.S. $	Can. $
D6916	Small	Doulton	3 ½"	1991	1995	45.00	100.00	150.00

GRANNY

PROTOTYPE

This early coloured prototype of the toothless Grannny proved too expensive to produce. Only one copy is known to exist.

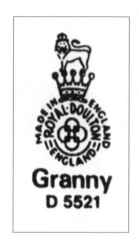

Designer: Harry Fenton	**Backstamp:** Doulton
Handle: Plain	
Colourway: Yellows	

Doulton Number	Size	Backstamp	Height	Intro.	Discon.	Current Market Value		
						U.K. £	U.S. $	Can. $
D5521	Large	Doulton	6 ¼"	1935	Unknown		Unique	

GRANNY

STYLE ONE: TOOTHLESS GRANNY

The wimple on this style does not show between the hat and the hair at the front of the head. There is no tooth showing between the lips.

Designer: Harry Fenton
Handle: Plain
Colourway: Dark green and white

Granny
D 6384

Backstamp: Doulton

Doulton Number	Size	Backstamp	Height	Intro.	Discon.	Current Market Value		
						U.K. £	U.S. $	Can. $
D5521	Large	Doulton	6 ¼"	1935	1941	500.00	1,100.00	1,300.00
D6384	Small	Doulton	3 ¼"	1935	Unknown		Extremely rare	

GRANNY

STYLE TWO: GRANNY WITH ONE TOOTH SHOWING

The wimple on this style of jugs is in waves under most of the hat.

For the tiny version of Granny character jug see the "Diamond Anniversary Set" page 214.

Granny
D 5521

Designer: Harry Fenton, large size
Max Henk, small and miniature sizes
Handle: Pink, blue, green and cream tied yarn
Colourway: Dark grey and white

Backstamp: Doulton

Doulton Number	Size	Backstamp	Height	Intro.	Discon.	Current Market Value U.K. £	U.S. $	Can. $
D5521	Large	Doulton	6 ¼"	1941	1983	60.00	125.00	150.00
D6384	Small	Doulton	3 ¼"	1953	1983	50.00	80.00	95.00
D6520	Miniature	Doulton	2 ¼"	1960	1983	55.00	100.00	125.00

Granny Derivative

Doulton Number	Item	Height	Intro.	Discon.	Current Market Value U.K. £	U.S. $	Can. $
D —	Table lighter	3 ½"	Unknown		Extremely Rare Only One Known to Exist		

Note: This jug was also issued in English Translucent China. These jugs command a premium of 50 to 100% over the earthenware variety.

GREAT BRITAIN'S
BRITANNIA

The Romans gave the name Britannia to England. Here she is depicted in shades of blues representing a distinguished naval history. This jug was commissioned by Travers Stanley Collections in a limited edition of 1,997.

Designer: William K. Harper
Handle: Crest of Helmet
Colourway: Blues

Backstamp: Doulton / Travers Stanley

Doulton Number	Size	Backstamp	Height	Intro.	Discon.	Current Market Value		
						U.K. £	U.S. $	Can. $
D7107	Small	Doulton/Travers	4 ¼"	1997	Ltd. ed.	60.00	120.00	175.00

GROUCHO MARX

PROTOTYPE

This design, with two of the Marx Brothers peering out from behind the cigar, was never put into production due to the complicated handle. Possibly only one is known to exist.

Designer: Stanley J. Taylor
Handle: Cigar with two other Marx Brothers
Colourway: Plain jacket, spotted bow tie

Backstamp: Doulton

Doulton Number	Size	Variation	Height	Intro.	Discon.	Current Market Value U.K. £	U.S. $	Can. $
D6710	Large	Prototype	7"	c.1984			Extremely Rare Last Sold March 12, 1997 Sotheby's Arcade Auction New York, $8,050.00	

GROUCHO MARX

THE CELEBRITY COLLECTION
ONE OF SIX

Julius Marx (1895-1977) was one of four brothers who became stars of American comedy. The Marx Brothers were known for their crazy slapstick antics and hilarious puns. Groucho led the gang, always smoking his trademark cigar.

Designer: Stanley J. Taylor   **Backstamp:** Doulton
Handle: Cigar
Colourway: Plain jacket; spotted bow tie

Doulton Number	Size	Backstamp	Height	Intro.	Discon.	Current Market Value U.K. £	U.S. $	Can. $
D6710	Large	Doulton	7"	1984	1988	100.00	200.00	225.00

GUARDSMAN

CHARACTERS FROM WILLIAMSBURG
ONE OF EIGHT

STYLE ONE: TRICORN HAT WITH PIKE

Designer: Max Henk
Handle: Pike
Colourway: Dark blue and yellow hat and jacket

Backstamp: Doulton

Doulton						Current Market Value		
Number	Size	Backstamp	Height	Intro.	Discon.	U.K. £	U.S. $	Can. $
D6568	Large	Doulton	6 ¾"	1963	1983	100.00	175.00	200.00
D6575	Small	Doulton	4 ¼"	1963	1983	60.00	110.00	135.00
D6582	Miniature	Doulton	2 ½"	1963	1983	55.00	110.00	125.00

Note: This jug was also issued in English Translucent China. These jugs command a premium of 50 to 100% over the earthenware variety.

THE GUARDSMAN

PROTOTYPE

This was the original design of The Guardsman jug, a prototype with the Union Jack.

Designer: Stanley J. Taylor   **Backstamp:** Doulton
Handle: A sword draped with the Union Jack
Colourway: Red tunic; black bearskin hat

Doulton Number	Size	Variation	Height	Intro.	Discon.	Current Market Value		
						U.K. £	U.S. $	Can. $
D —	Large	Prototype	8"		Unknown		Extremely rare	

THE GUARDSMAN

THE LONDON COLLECTION
ONE OF TEN

Long a fixture in London, the guardsman is easily identified by his tall bearskin hat and scarlet uniform. Today he still stands outside Buckingham Palace to protect the Queen. Guardsman models exist with white (gloss) tunics.

STYLE TWO: BEARSKIN HAT WITH SWORD

Designer: Stanley J. Taylor
Handle: Sword with draped brown flag
Colourway: Red tunic; black bearskin hat

Backstamp: Doulton

Royal Doulton®
THE GUARDSMAN
D 6755
Modelled by
Stanley James Taylor
© 1986 ROYAL DOULTON

Doulton Number	Size	Backstamp	Height	Intro.	Discon.	Current Market Value U.K. £	U.S. $	Can. $
D6755	Large	Doulton	8"	1986	Current	80.00	165.00	230.00
D6771	Small	Doulton	4"	1987	1999	40.00	90.00	130.00
D6772	Miniature	Doulton	2 ½"	1987	1991	50.00	110.00	125.00

GULLIVER

Jonathon Swift satirized society's leading men and institutions in his book, *Gulliver's Travels*, published in 1726. In it Gulliver the traveller sails to foreign lands, surviving shipwrecks, giants and the tiny people of Lilliput.

Designer: David Biggs
Handle: Castle tower with two Lilliputians in the turret
Colourway: Dark blue and grey hat; blue jacket; grey handle

Backstamp: Doulton

Doulton Number	Size	Backstamp	Height	Intro.	Discon.	Current Market Value		
						U.K. £	U.S. $	Can. $
D6560	Large	Doulton	7 ½"	1962	1967	500.00	950.00	1,100.00
D6563	Small	Doulton	4"	1962	1967	350.00	550.00	650.00
D6566	Miniature	Doulton	2 ½"	1962	1967	300.00	525.00	600.00

Note: This jug was also issued in English Translucent China. These jugs command a premium of 50 to 100% over the earthenware variety.

GUNSMITH

PROTOTYPE

This prototype has a different hat, hair style and handle from the design that was issued. Only one jug is known to exist.

Designer: David Biggs
Handle: Stock of a musket and flintlock
Colourway: Black hat; cream shirt; light brown apron

Backstamp: Doulton

Doulton Number	Size	Backstamp	Height	Intro.	Discon.	Current Market Value		
						U.K. £	U.S. $	Can. $
D —	Large	Doulton	7 ¼"	c. 1963			Unique	

GUNSMITH

CHARACTERS FROM WILLIAMSBURG
ONE OF EIGHT

Designer: David Biggs	**Backstamp:** Doulton
Handle: Stock of a musket	
Colourway: Black hat; cream shirt; light brown apron	

Doulton Number	Size	Backstamp	Height	Intro.	Discon.	Current Market Value		
						U.K. £	U.S. $	Can. $
D6573	Large	Doulton	7 ¼"	1963	1983	90.00	140.00	165.00
D6580	Small	Doulton	3 ½"	1963	1983	60.00	85.00	110.00
D6587	Miniature	Doulton	2 ½"	1963	1983	50.00	80.00	100.00

Note: This jug was also issued in English Translucent China. These jugs command a premium of 50 to 100% over the earthenware variety.

GUY FAWKES

Guy Fawkes (1570-1606) was part of the infamous "Gunpowder Plot," a plan by Catholic rebels to blow up the British Houses of Parliament and King James I on November 5, 1605. The conspiracy was leaked by a letter to Lord Monteagle, and Guy Fawkes was arrested and hanged. Every year on November 5, Guy Fawkes Day is celebrated with fireworks and the burning of Fawkes in effigy.

VARIATION No. 1:   Colourway — Black hat; red band; white collar on black coat

Designer: William K. Harper
Handle: A lantern above a barrel of gunpowder
Colourway: Black hat; red band; white collar; black coat

Backstamp: Doulton

Doulton Number	Size	Backstamp	Height	Intro.	Discon.	Current Market Value		
						U.K. £	U.S. $	Can. $
D6861	Large	Doulton	7"	1990	1996	75.00	175.00	200.00

VARIATION No. 2:   Colourway — Black hat; orange band; white collar on black coat

Designer: William K. Harper	**Backstamp:** Doulton / Canadian Art and
Handle: A lantern above a barrel of gunpowder	Collectables Show
Colourway: Black hat; orange band;	Pre-release was limited to 750 for
Annual Canadian Doulton Show and	the Third Sale in conjuction with
white collar; black coat	the 1990 Canadian Collectables
	Showcase, May 5 and 6, 1990,
	Durham, Ontario.

Doulton Number	Size	Backstamp	Height	Intro.	Discon.	Current Market Value		
						U.K. £	U.S. $	Can. $
D6861	Large	Doulton/Can.	7"	1990	Ltd. ed.	125.00	200.00	225.00

H. G. WELLS

Not just prolofic in his output, H. G. Wells was a futuristic writer, one of the earliest science fiction novelists. His character jug marks the centenary of the publication of the *War of the Worlds,* one of his best-known and celebrated works. This jug was issued in a limited edition of 1,998.

Designer: David B. Biggs
Handle: Martian fighting machine and an aeroplane
Colourway: Green jacket, yellow shirt, maroon tie

Backstamp: Doulton

Doulton Number	Size	Backstamp	Height	Intro.	Discon.	Current Market Value		
						U.K. £	U.S. $	Can. $
D7095	Large	Doulton	6 ¾"	1998	Ltd. ed.	100.00	200.00	395.00

HAMLET

THE SHAKESPEAREAN COLLECTION
ONE OF SIX

Probably Shakespeare's most famous play, *Hamlet, Prince of Denmark*, was first performed between 1599 and 1602. Hamlet became the quintessential tragic hero, driven by conscience and familial obligation to avenge his father's murder.

© ROYAL DOULTON TABLEWARE LIMITED 1982
D 6672

The
Shakespearean
Collection
HAMLET
A series of hand-made, hand-decorated Character Jugs by
Royal Doulton

Designer: Michael Abberley
Handle: A dagger and skull join the feather of the cap
Colourway: Black cap and robes; blond hair; grey feather

Backstamp: Doulton

Doulton Number	Size	Backstamp	Height	Intro.	Discon.	Current Market Value		
						U.K. £	U.S. $	Can. $
D6672	Large	Doulton	7 ¼"	1982	1989	100.00	175.00	200.00

THE HAMPSHIRE CRICKETER

The Hampshire Cricketer jug was developed and sold by the Hampshire Cricket Club to celebrate the centenary of the Hampshire cricket grounds. It was issued in 1985 in a limited edition of 5,000 pieces.

Designer: Harry Sales
Modeller: Graham Tongue
Handle: Cricket bat
Colourway: Navy blue cap; cream sweater with navy and yellow stripes

Backstamp: Doulton/
© Hampshire C. C. C. 1985

Doulton Number	Size	Backstamp	Height	Intro.	Discon.	Current Market Value		
						U.K. £	U.S. $	Can. $
D6739	Small	Doulton/ Hampshire	5"	1985	Ltd. ed.	75.00	150.00	175.00

HANDEL

GREAT COMPOSERS
ONE OF EIGHT

The great composer George Frederick Handel (1685-1759) resided in England for a great portion of his adult life, though he was born in Germany. The music score which forms part of the handle is from Handel's famous *Fireworks* composition.

Designer:	Stanley J. Taylor	**Backstamp:**	Doulton
Handle:	Music score, multi-coloured stars representing fireworks		
Colourway:	Green and gold jacket, blue-grey cravat, gey wig		

Doulton Number	Size	Backstamp	Height	Intro.	Discon.	Current Market Value		
						U.K. £	U.S. $	Can. $
D7080	Large	Doulton	7"	1997	Current	90.00	245.00	340.00

HAROLD DENNIS "DICKIE BIRD" MBE

Commissioned by Lawleys By Post in a limited edition of 9,500. This character jug pays homage to Dickie Bird who, for over a quarter century, was the top test match umpire in England.

Designer: Stanley J. Taylor
Handle: Cricket bat and TCCB banner
(Test and County Cricket Board)
Colourway: White and black

Backstamp: Doulton

Doulton Number	Size	Backstamp	Height	Intro.	Discon.	Current Market Value		
						U.K. £	U.S. $	Can. $
D7068	Small	Doulton	4 ½"	1996	Ltd. ed.	60.00	125.00	150.00

HENRY V

King Henry V (1387-1422) renewed the Hundred Years' War against France, and at the Battle of Agincourt in 1415, he won one of the most famous victories in English history. Henry married the daughter of King Charles VI of France and by the Treaty of Troyes became heir to the French throne.

For Henry V (style two) see "Kings and Queens of the Realm" page 328.

STYLE ONE: LARGE SIZE: HANDLE — ROYAL ENSIGN

VARIATION No. 1: Handle — Embossed
Colourway — Yellow crown with gold, turquoise and red design

© ROYAL DOULTON TABLEWARE LIMITED 1982
D 6671
The
Shakespearean
Collection
HENRY V̲
A series of hand-made, hand-decorated Character Jugs by
Royal Doulton

Designer: Robert Tabbenor
Handle: Royal Ensign
Colourway: Yellow crown with gold, turquoise and red design

Backstamp: Doulton

Doulton Number	Size	Variation	Height	Intro.	Discon.	Current Market Value U.K. £	U.S. $	Can. $
D6671	Large	Var. 1	7 ¼"	1982	c. 1984	150.00	275.00	300.00

VARIATION No. 2: Handle — Embossed
Colourway — Yellow crown; some blue colouring; no red or gold
This jug is actually a factory second, marked and sold as such.
One of the steps used when firing and painting the jugs was
missed. Hundreds are known to exist.

Doulton Number	Size	Variation	Height	Intro.	Discon.	Current Market Value U.K. £	Current Market Value U.S. $	Current Market Value Can. $
D6671	Large	Var. 2	7 ¼"	Unknown		1,000.00	1,750.00	2,000.00

VARIATION No. 3: Handle — Decorated with a decal
Colourway — Yellow crown with gold, blue and red design

Doulton Number	Size	Variation	Height	Intro.	Discon.	Current Market Value U.K. £	Current Market Value U.S. $	Current Market Value Can. $
D6671	Large	Var. 3	7 ¼"	c.1984	1989	100.00	175.00	200.00

HENRY VIII

HENRY VIII AND HIS SIX WIVES
ONE OF EIGHT

Henry VIII (1491-1547) was king of Great Britain from 1509 to 1547, during which time his infamous private life changed the course of history. Attempting to produce a male heir to the throne, he married six times, was excommunicated by the Pope for divorce and founded the Church of England.

For Henry VIII (Style two) see the "Kings and Queens of the Realm Set" page 328, for the character jug King Henry VIII see page 327, and for the toby jug King Henry VIII see page 73.

STYLE ONE: LARGE SIZE: HANDLE — TOWER

HENRY VIII
D.6642
© ROYAL DOULTON
TABLEWARE LTD. 1975

Designer:	Eric Griffiths	**Backstamp:** Doulton
Handle:	A tower joins the feather in the hat	
Colourway:	Black and gold hat; white plume; brown and maroon tunic	

Doulton Number	Size	Backstamp	Height	Intro.	Discon.	Current Market Value U.K. £	U.S. $	Can. $
D6642	Large	Doulton	6 ½"	1975	Current	60.00	165.00	230.00
D6647	Small	Doulton	3 ¾"	1979	1999	35.00	90.00	130.00
D6648	Miniature	Doulton	2 ¾"	1979	1991	50.00	125.00	150.00

HENRY COOPER

Henry Cooper, OBE, became British heavyweight champion in 1959 and held the title until 1971. During that time he won three Lonsdale belts in defence of his crown.
This jug was commissioned by Lawleys By Post in a limited edition of 9,500.

Designer:	Stanley J. Taylor	
Handle:	Lonsdale belt and boxing gloves	
Colourway:	Blue, white, brown and gold	

Backstamp: Doulton

Doulton Number	Size	Backstamp	Height	Intro.	Discon.	Current Market Value		
						U.K. £	**U.S. $**	**Can. $**
D7050	Small	Doulton	4"	1996	Ltd. ed.	60.00	125.00	150.00

HOME GUARD

HEROES OF THE BLITZ
ONE OF THREE

In the early part of World War II, young and old joined the Home Guard to protect the country from what was perceived as an imminent invasion by the German army, allowing the regular army to be used elsewhere. The Heroes of the Blitz series was available only from Lawleys By Post, in a limited edition of 9,500.

Designer:	Stanley J. Taylor					**Backstamp:**	Doulton	
Handle:	Sten gun with hand grenade							
Colourway:	Khaki uniform and cap							

Doulton Number	Size	Variation	Height	Intro.	Discon.	Current Market Value U.K. £	U.S. $	Can. $
D6886	Small	Doulton	4"	1991	Ltd. ed.	100.00	200.00	250.00

HUMPHREY BOGART

THE CELEBRITY COLLECTION

PROTOTYPE

Humphrey DeForest Bogart began his acting career in 1920 and enjoyed a prolific career, winning an Academy Award in 1952 for his performance in *The African Queen*. His best-known role, however, was that of Rick in *Casablanca*. The jug could not be issued due to copyright problems and is not known to be in private collections.

Designer: Eric Griffiths		**Backstamp:** Doulton
Handle: Movie camera pointing right		
Colourway: Black hat; brown coat; black bow tie		

Doulton Number	Size	Variation	Height	Intro.	Discon.	Current Market Value U.K. £	U.S. $	Can. $
D —	Large	Prototype	7"	Unknown		Extremely rare		

IAN BOTHAM OBE

This jug, of one of England's most famous all-round cricketers, was issued by Lawleys By Post in a limited edition of 9,500.

Designer: David B. Biggs
Handle: Shin pad and cricket ball
Colourway: White sweater with red, yellow and navy stripes

Backstamp: Doulton

Doulton Number	Size	Backstamp	Height	Intro.	Discon.	Current Market Value U.K. £	U.S. $	Can. $
D7091	Small	Doulton	4 ½"	1998	Ltd. ed.	50.00	100.00	175.00

IZAAK WALTON

The English writer Izaak Walton (1593-1683) is best known for his book *The Compleat Angler, or Contemplative Man's Recreation*. First published in 1653, this work became the most famous book written on the sport of fishing.

TO COMMEMORATE THE
300th ANNIVERSARY
OF THE
"COMPLEAT-ANGLER"
1653 - 1953

"IZAAK WALTON"
D 6404
COPR 1953
DOULTON & CO LIMITED
Rd No 871560
Rd No 31804
Rd No 6825
Rd No 237/53

Backstamp A - Doulton

CITY OF
STOKE-ON-TRENT
JUBILEE YEAR
1959-1960
WITH THE COMPLIMENTS OF
LORD MAYOR AND LADY MAYORESS
ALDERMAN HAROLD CLOWES O.B.E. J.P
AND
MISS CHRISTINE CLOWES

Backstamp B - City of
Stoke-on-Trent

Designer: Geoff Blower
Handle: A fishing rod resting on a tree trunk
Colourway: Brown hat and coat; white collar

Backstamps: **A.** Doulton
B. Doulton/City of Stoke-on-Trent Jubilee Year 1959-1960
With the compliments of Lord Mayor and Lady Mayoress
Alderman Harold Clowes, O.B.E., J.P. and Miss Christine Clowes

Doulton Number	Size	Backstamp	Height	Intro.	Discon.	Current Market Value U.K. £	U.S. $	Can. $
D6404	Large	Doulton	7"	1953	1982	85.00	125.00	150.00
D6404	Large	Doulton/City	7"	1959	1960	Extremely rare		

JANE EYRE AND MR ROCHESTER

DOUBLE CHARACTER JUGS
ONE OF TWO

The Charlotte Bronte characters from her 1847 *Jane Eyre* form the second in the double character jug series. This jug was issued by Lawleys By Post in a limited edition of 1,500 pieces.

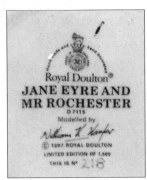

Designer: William K. Harper	**Backstamp:** Doulton
Handle: Jane Eyre — A book, rose and paint brushes	
Mr Rochester — Musical score and riding crop	
Colourway: Jane Eyre — Grey dress, white collar, yellow brooch	
Mr Rochester — Maroon smoking jacket with brown collar	

Doulton Number	Size	Backstamp	Height	Intro.	Discon.	U.K. £	U.S. $	Can. $
						Current Market Value		
D7115	Small	Doulton	4 ¾"	1998	Ltd. ed.	120.00	—	—

JANE SEYMOUR

HENRY VIII AND HIS SIX WIVES
ONE OF EIGHT

While serving as lady-in-waiting to both Catherine of Aragon and Anne Boleyn, Jane Seymour (1509-1537) attracted the attention of Henry VIII. She refused any proposal from the King except marriage, a factor leading to the trial of Anne. Two weeks after Anne Boleyn was beheaded, Jane Seymour became the third wife of Henry VIII, and the only one to bear him a male heir. She died shortly after Edward was born, and was the only wife to be buried at Henry's side.

For Jane Seymour, style two, see the "Six Wives of Henry VIII" page 478.

STYLE ONE: HANDLE: A MANDOLIN

Designer: Large size — Michael Abberley
Small and miniature sizes — Peter Gee
Handle: A mandolin
Colourway: Black and gold

Backstamp: Doulton

Doulton Number	Size	Backstamp	Height	Intro.	Discon.	Current Market Value U.K. £	U.S. $	Can. $
D6646	Large	Doulton	7 ¼"	1979	1990	100.00	175.00	200.00
D6746	Small	Doulton	4 ¼"	1986	1990	100.00	175.00	200.00
D6747	Miniature	Doulton	2 ¾"	1986	1990	115.00	190.00	200.00

JARGE

Jarge, the colloquial version of George, is a typical country bumpkin, with his polka-dot scarf and the piece of straw in his teeth.

"Jarge."

COPR. 1949
DOULTON & CO. LIMITED.
R⁴N⁰ 857577.
R⁴N⁰ 5904.
R⁴N⁰ 76/49.

Designer: Harry Fenton
Handle: The scarf extends upwards to the cap
Colourway: Green cap; white scarf with red polka-dots

Backstamp: Doulton

Doulton Number	Size	Backstamp	Height	Intro.	Discon.	Current Market Value		
						U.K. £	U.S. $	Can. $
D6288	Large	Doulton	6 ½"	1950	1960	250.00	450.00	500.00
D6295	Small	Doulton	3 ½"	1950	1960	150.00	250.00	375.00

Note: This jug was also issued in English Translucent China. These jugs command a premium of 50 to 100% over the earthenware variety.

JESSE OWENS

CHARACTER JUG OF THE YEAR

This jug was issued as the Character Jug of the Year for 1996, to commemorate both the Summer Olympic Games in Atlanta, Georgia, and the first African-American to win a gold medal in the Olympic Games. Owens won four gold medals in Berlin during the 1936 Summer Games.

Designer: Stanley J. Taylor
Handle: U.S. flag and olympic torch
Colourway: Black, brown and white

Backstamp: Doulton/Character
Jug of the Year, 1996
© The Jesse Owens Trust

Doulton Number	Size	Backstamp	Height	Intro.	Discon.	Current Market Value U.K. £	U.S. $	Can. $
D7019	Large	Doulton	7"	1996	1996	125.00	225.00	250.00

JESTER

The green and yellow colouring on either side of the hat may be reversed as a preference of the painter. Minor variations of this nature do not command a price differential.

For the tiny version of the Jester character jug see the "Diamond Anniversary Set" page 214.

Backstamp A - Doulton

Backstamp B - Bentalls

Backstamp C - Darley & Son

Designer: Charles Noke
Handle: Plain
Colourway: Brown, green and yellow

Backstamps: **A.** Doulton
    B. Doulton/Bentalls/Souvenir From Bentalls. 1936.
        Commissioned by Bentalls as an advertising piece.
    C. Doulton/Darley/Souvenir from Darley & Son,
        Sheffield & Rotherham

Doulton Number	Size	Backstamp	Height	Intro.	Discon.	Current Market Value U.K. £	U.S. $	Can. $
D5556	Small	Doulton	3 1/8"	1936	1960	75.00	125.00	150.00
D5556	Small	Doulton/Bentalls	3 1/8"	1936	1936	450.00	825.00	1,000.00
D5556	Small	Doulton/Darley	3 1/8"	1936	1936	450.00	825.00	1,000.00

Jester Derivative

Doulton Number	Item	Height	Intro.	Discon.	Current Market Value U.K. £	U.S. $	Can. $
D6111	Wall pocket	7 ¼"	1940	1941	1,000.00	1,750.00	2,000.00

JIMMY DURANTE

THE CELEBRITY COLLECTION
ONE OF SIX

James Francis Durante (1893-1980) began his entertaining career playing the piano, but it was his singing and clowning that brought him fame in Vaudeville theatre, night clubs, films, radio and television. Using his large nose as the object of jokes, Durante earned his nickname "Schnozzle."

Designer:	David Biggs	**Backstamp:** Doulton
Handle:	A piano keyboard	
Colourway:	Grey and black cap; yellow jacket; cream shirt	

Doulton Number	Size	Backstamp	Height	Intro.	Discon.	U.K. £	U.S. $	Can. $
						Current Market Value		
D6708	Large	Doulton	7 ½"	1985	1988	100.00	200.00	250.00

JOCKEY

Small and miniature sized jugs of the Jockey were test piloted but not produced. A small pilot jug is known to exist.

STYLE ONE: GOGGLES RESTING ON HIS CHEST
HANDLE — WINNING POLE

Designer: David Biggs
Handle: The winning pole
Colourway: Red and yellow striped cap and racing jersey

Backstamp: Doulton

Doulton Number	Size	Backstamp	Height	Intro.	Discon.	Current Market Value		
						U.K. £	U.S. $	Can. $
D6625	Large	Doulton	7 ¾"	1971	1975	275.00	475.00	650.00
D6629	Small	Doulton	4"	1974	1974		Unique	

THE JOCKEY

CHARACTERS FROM LIFE
ONE OF SEVEN

STYLE TWO: GOGGLES RESTING ON CAP
HANDLE — WINNING POLE AND HORSE HEAD

Designer: Stanley J. Taylor
Handle: Head of a horse and the winning pole
Colourway: Beige riding cap; yellow and black racing jersey

Backstamp: Doulton

Doulton Number	Size	Backstamp	Height	Intro.	Discon.	Current Market Value		
						U.K. £	U.S. $	Can. $
D6877	Small	Doulton	4"	1991	1995	45.00	100.00	150.00

JOHN BARLEYCORN

John Barleycorn is the personification of barley, the grain source of malt liquor. This character jug was the first design created by Charles Noke in 1934.

STYLE ONE: HANDLE — INSIDE JUG, 1934 TO 1939

JOHN BARLEYCORN.

Backstamp A - Doulton

R. No 782778

Coleman's Compliments

D 5327

Backstamp B - Coleman's

Designer: Charles Noke
Handle: Plain brown
Colourway: Brown rim with light brown body

Backstamps: **A.** Doulton
B. Doulton/Coleman's/
Coleman's Compliments
This large-size jug was commissioned by Coleman's as an advertising piece.
C. Doulton/Salt River Cement Works/
With Compliments From Salt River Cement Works
This large-size jug was commissioned by Salt River Cement Works as an advertising piece.

Doulton Number	Size	Backstamp	Height	Intro.	Discon.	Current Market Value U.K. £	U.S. $	Can. $
D5327	Large	Doulton	6 ½"	1934	1939	125.00	225.00	250.00
D5327	Large	Doulton/Coleman's	6 ½"	1938	1939	1,000.00	2,250.00	2,500.00
D5327	Large	Doulton/Salt River	6 ½"	Unknown		1,500.00	3,000.00	3,500.00
D5735	Small	Doulton	3 ½"	1937	1939	60.00	100.00	125.00
D6041	Mini	Doulton	2 ½"	Unknown		60.00	100.00	125.00

JOHN BARLEYCORN

STYLE TWO: HANDLE — OUTSIDE JUG, 1939 TO 1982

For the tiny version of John Barleycorn character jug see the "Diamond Anniversary Set" page 214.

VARIATION No. 1: Handle — Brown shading

Designer: Charles Noke
Handle: Plain, brown shading
Colourway: Brown rim; light brown face

Backstamp: Doulton

Doulton Number	Size	Backstamp	Height	Intro.	Discon.	Current Market Value U.K. £	U.S. $	Can. $
D5327	Large	Doulton	6 ½"	1939	1960	85.00	165.00	200.00
D5735	Small	Doulton	3 ½"	1939	1960	55.00	100.00	135.00
D6041	Miniature	Doulton	2 ½"	1939	1960	55.00	100.00	125.00

Note: This jug was also issued in English Translucent China. These jugs command a premium of 50 to 100% over the earthenware variety.

VARIATION No. 2:   Handle — Black shading
Issued from 1978 to 1982, this jug was similar to the previous variation, but a new mould had to be made because the original was not available. This special exhibition jug, modelled by Michael Abberley and limited to 7,500 pieces, was sold at Royal Doulton events.

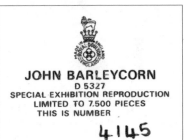

JOHN BARLEYCORN
D 5327
SPECIAL EXHIBITION REPRODUCTION
LIMITED TO 7,500 PIECES
THIS IS NUMBER
4145

Designer: Charles Noke
Modeller: Michael Abberley
Handle: Plain, black shading
Colourway: Brown rim; light brown face

Backstamp: Doulton/Special Exhibition Reproduction Limited to 7,500 Pieces

Doulton Number	Size	Backstamp	Height	Intro.	Discon.	Current Market Value		
						U.K. £	U.S. $	Can. $
D5327	Large	Doulton/Special	6"	1978	Ltd. ed.	125.00	200.00	225.00

John Barleycorn Derivative

Doulton Number	Item	Height	Intro.	Discon.	Current Market Value		
					U.K. £	U.S. $	Can. $
D5602	Ash bowl	4"	1936	1960	95.00	150.00	200.00

JOHN BARLEYCORN

Commissioned by American Express to form part of a 12-tankard set from various manufacturers, John Barleycorn was sold to between 500 and 600 card members.

This jug was issued only in English Translucent China.

STYLE THREE: BLUE HAT WITH BARLEY EARS

Designer:	Stanley J. Taylor
Handle:	Twisted barley stalk
Colourway:	Pale blue cap; light brown barley ears

Backstamp: Doulton/American Express

Doulton Number	Size	Backstamp	Height	Intro.	Discon.	Current Market Value		
						U.K. £	**U.S. $**	**Can. $**
D6780	Mid	Doulton/Amex	5 ½"	1988	Sp. ed.	200.00	325.00	425.00

JOHN DOULTON

ROYAL DOULTON INTERNATIONAL COLLECTORS CLUB

John Doulton (1793-1873) served a seven-year apprenticeship in the pottery industry as a thrower before fortune smiled on him and he was able to buy into a pottery partnership. In 1815 he bought a one-third share of a stoneware pot-house in Vauxhall Walk, Lambeth, and the company of Doulton and Watts was born.

To honour John Doulton, the Royal Doulton International Collectors Club made this jug available to all their original charter members in 1980.

This first style of this jug has the time shown on "Big Ben" as 8 o'clock.

VARIATION No. 1: TIME SHOWN ON BIG BEN IS EIGHT O'CLOCK

Designer: Eric Griffiths
Handle: The tower of Big Ben
Colourway: White cravat; Big Ben is grey

Backstamp: Doulton/RDICC

Doulton Number	Size	Backstamp	Height	Intro.	Discon.	Current Market Value U.K. £	U.S. $	Can. $
D6656	Small	Doulton/RDICC	4 ¼"	1980	c. 1982	75.00	135.00	150.00

JOHN DOULTON

ROYAL DOULTON INTERNATIONAL COLLECTORS CLUB

Starting in 1981 each new member joining the Royal Doulton International Collectors Club had the opportunity of purchasing the John Doulton jug; however, the time now shown on Big Ben is two o'clock.

VARIATION No. 2: TIME SHOWN ON BIG BEN IS TWO O'CLOCK

Backstamp: Doulton/RDICC

Designer: Eric Griffiths
Handle: The tower of Big Ben
Colourway: Yellow cravat; Big Ben is light brown

Doulton Number	Size	Backstamp	Height	Intro.	Discon.	Current Market Value		
						U.K. £	U.S. $	Can. $
D6656	Small	Doulton/RDICC	4 ¼"	1981	1994	45.00	85.00	100.00

JOHN GILPIN

PROTOTYPE

"The Diverting History of John Gilpin" is an 18th-century poem by Cowper. In it Gilpin, a "linen draper bold," and his wife go to Edmonton to celebrate their 20th wedding anniversary. His horse runs out of control, however, and John careens ten miles beyond Edmonton and back again.

Designer: David Biggs		**Backstamp:** Doulton
Handle: Brown wood sign post reading "Edmonton"		
Colourway: Dark green hat; maroon coat		

Doulton Number	Size	Backstamp	Height	Intro.	Discon.	Current Market Value U.K. £	U.S. $	Can. $
D —	Large	Doulton	7"	1968	1968	Extremely rare. Only two known.		

JOHN LENNON

THE BEATLES
ONE OF FOUR

John Winston Lennon (1940-1980) played guitar and wrote songs for the Beatles until the group disbanded in 1970. With his wife Yoko Ono, Lennon pursued a successful solo career until his tragic assassination in 1980.

VARIATION No. 1:   Colourway — Turquoise jacket with maroon collar and epaulettes

Royal Doulton
THE BEATLES
John Lennon
D 6725
Modelled by
Stanley James Taylor.
© ROYAL DOULTON TABLEWARE
LIMITED 1984

Designer: Stanley J. Taylor
Handle: Plain
Colourway: Turquoise jacket with
maroon collar and epaulettes

Backstamp: Doulton

Doulton Number	Size	Backstamp	Height	Intro.	Discon.	Current Market Value		
						U.K. £	U.S. $	Can. $
D6725	Mid	Doulton	5 ½"	1984	1991	125.00	300.00	350.00

VARIATION No. 2:   Colourway — Red jacket with yellow collar and epaulettes

Backstamp: Doulton/John Sinclair
New Colourway Special Edition of 1000 for John Sinclair, Sheffield
Commissioned by John Sinclair, Sheffield. Issued in 1987 in a limited edition of 1,000 pieces.

Doulton Number	Size	Backstamp	Height	Intro.	Discon.	U.K. £	U.S. $	Can. $
						Current Market Value		
D6797	Mid	Doulton/Sinclair	5 ½"	1987	Ltd. ed.	200.00	400.00	450.00

JOHN PEEL

John Peel (1776-1854) was a famous English huntsman, known for his enthusiasm, skill and hospitality. Fond of drink, he hosted large, popular post-hunt celebrations. Peel has been immortalized in the song "D'ye ken John Peel," written by John Woodcock Graves.

VARIATION No. 1:   Colourway — Grey handle

"John Peel."
Rᵈ Nº 809559.

Designer: Harry Fenton
Handle: Riding crop, with hunting horn forming top of handle
Colourway: Dark grey hat; maroon coat; dark blue bow tie

Backstamp: Doulton

Doulton Number	Size	Variation	Height	Intro.	Discon.	Current Market Value U.K. £	U.S. $	Can. $
D5612	Large	Var. 1	6 ½"	1936	1960	100.00	200.00	225.00
D5731	Small	Var. 1	3 ½"	1937	1960	50.00	80.00	100.00
D6130	Miniature	Var. 1	2 ¼"	1940	1960	50.00	75.00	95.00
D6259	Tiny	Var. 1	1 ¼"	1947	1960	125.00	260.00	275.00

VARIATION No. 2:   Colourway — Black and orange handle

Doulton Number	Size	Variation	Height	Intro.	Discon.	Current Market Value U.K. £	U.S. $	Can. $
D5612	Large	Var. 2	6 ½"	Unknown		125.00	225.00	250.00
D5731	Small	Var. 2	3 ½"	Unknown		55.00	85.00	120.00
D6130	Miniature	Var. 2	2 ¼"	c.1942	Unknown	60.00	90.00	110.00

Note: This jug was also issued in English Translucent China. These jugs command a premium of 50 to 100% over the earthenware variety.

JOHN SHORTER

Commissioned by the Character and Toby Jug Collectors Society of Australia, this depiction of Australian retailer John Shorter was released in 1991 in a limited edition of 1,500 pieces.

Royal Doulton®
JOHN SHORTER
D.6880
Modelled by

William K. Harper

© 1990 ROYAL DOULTON
Specially commissioned from Royal Doulton
by the Character and Toby Jug Collectors Society
of Australia to commemorate
the 10th anniversary of the Society 1980 – 1990.
ISSUED IN A WORLDWIDE
LIMITED EDITION OF 1,500.
THIS IS N⁰. **372**

Designer: William K. Harper
Handle: A kangaroo and joey
Colourway: Grey hair; black jacket; maroon
and white polka-dot bow tie

Backstamp: Doulton/CJCSA

Doulton Number	Size	Backstamp	Height	Intro.	Discon.	Current Market Value U.K. £	U.S. $	Can. $
D6880	Small	Doulton/CJCSA	4 ¼"	1991	Ltd. ed.	125.00	225.00	250.00

"JOHNNERS"
BRIAN JOHNSTON

Brian "Johnners" Johnston, 1912-1994, was a famous radio broadcaster. He was well liked for his test match commentaries. This jug was released by Lawleys by Post in a limited edition of 9,500.

Designer: Stanley J. Taylor
Handle: Microphone, cricket ball and bail
Colourway: White, blue, red and black

Backstamp: Doulton

Doulton Number	Size	Backstamp	Height	Intro.	Discon.	Current Market Value		
						U.K. £	U.S. $	Can. $
D7018	Small	Doulton	4"	1996	Ltd. ed.	50.00	125 .00	150.00

JOHNNY APPLESEED

John Chapman (1774-1845) was an American pioneer who sold and gave saplings and apple seeds to colonizing families. He travelled the eastern U.S., sowing apple orchards and tending his trees. After his death, Chapman became the hero of many legends.

"Johnny Appleseed."
D.6372
COPR.1952.
DOULTON & CO.LIMITED.
R⁴Nº 868196
R⁹Nº 98801
R⁹Nº 30304
R⁹Nº 6647.

Designer: Harry Fenton	**Backstamp:** Doulton
Handle: An apple tree and knapsack	
Colourway: Maroon and grey cap; brown robes	

Doulton Number	Size	Backstamp	Height	Intro.	Discon.	Current Market Value U.K. £	U.S. $	Can. $
D6372	Large	Doulton	6"	1953	1969	250.00	475.00	550.00

THE JUGGLER

THE CIRCUS
ONE OF FOUR

Royal Doulton®
THE JUGGLER
D 6835
Modelled by
Stanley James Taylor.
© 1988 ROYAL DOULTON

Designer: Stanley J. Taylor
Handle: Skittles and balls
Colourway: Brown hair; yellow, blue and red tunic; dark green head band

Backstamp: Doulton

Doulton Number	Size	Backstamp	Height	Intro.	Discon.	Current Market Value		
						U.K. £	U.S. $	Can. $
D6835	Large	Doulton	6 ½"	1989	1991	85.00	225.00	250.00

KING ARTHUR and GUINEVERE

THE STAR-CROSSED LOVERS COLLECTION (TWO-FACED JUG)
ONE OF FOUR

Arthur is the legendary fifth-century King of Britain, known for his courage and honesty. His 12 knights, with whom he ruled and planned his campaigns, sat at a round table, so that none had precedence. His best friend, the knight Lancelot, betrayed him by falling in love with his beautiful wife Guinevere. Arthur died at Camelford in a battle against his usurping nephew Mordred.

This jug was issued in 1989 in a limited edition of 9,500.

Designer: Stanley J. Taylor
Handle: King Arthur — Sword
Guinevere — Chalice
Colourway: Blue-grey, yellow and white

Royal Doulton®
THE
STAR-CROSSED LOVERS
COLLECTION
King Arthur & Guinevere
D.6836
Modelled by Stanley James Taylor
Stanley James Taylor.
Worldwide Limited Edition of 9,500
This is Number 792
© 1988 Royal Doulton

Backstamp: Doulton

Doulton Number	Size	Backstamp	Height	Intro.	Discon.	Current Market Value		
						U.K. £	U.S. $	Can. $
D6836	Large	Doulton	6 ½"	1989	Ltd. ed.	100.00	225.00	250.00

KING ARTHUR and MERLIN

The companion jugs King Arthur, releaseded in 1997, and Merlin in 1998, were issued in a limited edition of 1,500 each.

For Merlin (style one) see page 363.

STYLE TWO: MERLIN: HANDLE — DRAGON AND SWORD

Royal Doulton®
KING ARTHUR
D7055
Modelled by

ⓒ 1996 ROYAL DOULTON
LIMITED EDITION OF 1,500
THIS IS Nº

Photograph of this
backstamp not available
at press time

Designer: Robert Tabbenor	**Backstamp:** Doulton
Handle: King Arthur —A shield and an anvil	
Merlin — A dragon and sword Excalibur	
Colourway: King Arhtur — Red, brown, black and gold	
Merlin —White, red, gold and purple, platinum highlights	

Doulton Number	Name	Height	Intro.	Discon.	Current Market Value U.K. £	U.S. $	Can. $
D7055	King Arthur	7 ¼"	1997	Ltd. ed.	150.00	375.00	550.00
D7117	Merlin	7"	1998	Ltd. ed.	150.00	375.00	590.00

KING CHARLES I

This jug was issued in a limited edition of 2,500 to commemorate the 350th anniversary of the English Civil War in 1642. It is unusual in the sense that it is the first three-handled character jug ever produced by Doulton. On Charles's left Oliver Cromwell forms the handle, on his right, Queen Henrietta. The third handle, at the King's back and not seen in the photo below, is a plume.

For Charles I (style one) see the "Kings and Queens of the Realm" page 328, and for Charles I (style two) see page 184.

Royal Doulton®
KING CHARLES I
D 6917
Modelled by

William K. Harper

© 1992 ROYAL DOULTON
LIMITED EDITION OF 2,500
THIS IS № 1931
To commemorate the 350th
Anniversary of the start of
the English Civil War.1642

Designer: William K. Harper	**Backstamp:** Doulton
Handle: Three handles (see above)	
Colourway: Black, yellow and red	

Doulton Number	Size	Backstamp	Height	Intro.	Discon.	Current Market Value		
						U.K. £	U.S. $	Can. $
D6917	Large	Doulton	7"	1992	Ltd. ed.	250.00	450.00	500.00

KING EDWARD VII

ROYAL DOULTON INTERNATIONAL COLLECTORS CLUB EXCLUSIVE

In this jug, King Edward VII is shown wearing a crown and all his finery. The handle comprises the traditional Royal Doulton backstamp of the crown and lion. This piece had a limited edition of 2,500 and was issued exclusively for the Royal Doulton International Collectors Club.

For the character jug Edward VII see the "Kings and Queens of the Realm" page 328.

Designer: William K. Harper
Handle: Lion and crown of the Doulton backstamp
Colourway: Red, gold, and white

Backstamp: Doulton/RDICC

Doulton Number	Size	Backstamp	Height	Intro.	Discon.	Current Market Value		
						U.K. £	U.S. $	Can. $
D6923	Small	Doulton/RDICC	5 ½"	1992	Ltd. ed.	150.00	325.00	350.00

KING HENRY VIII

This is a two-handled jug and, strictly speaking, should be classified as a loving cup. It was issued in 1991 in a limited edition of 1,991 to commemorate the 500th anniversary of the birth of Henry VIII.

For the Henry VIII (style one), see page 295; for Henry VIII, style two, see the "Kings and Queens of the Realm", page 328, and for the toby jug King Henry VIII, see page 73.

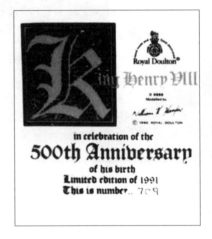

Royal Doulton®

King Henry VIII

in celebration of the
500th Anniversary
of his birth
Limited edition of 1991
This is number.. 709

Designer:	William K. Harper
Handle:	Double handle, three wives on either side
Colourway:	White and black with gold trim

Backstamp: Doulton

Doulton Number	Size	Backstamp	Height	Intro.	Discon.	Current Market Value		
						U.K. £	U.S. $	Can. $
D6888	Large	Doulton	7"	1991	Ltd. ed.	650.00	1,300.00	1,500.00

KING JOHN

For the character jug King John see page 426.

KINGS AND QUEENS OF THE REALM

This set of six tinies was issued by Lawleys By Post in a limited edition of 2,500 sets. Each set came with a wooden display stand and a certificate of authenticity.

Designer: William K. Harper	**Backstamp:** Doulton
Handles: Charles I — Crown and sceptre	**Colourways:** See below
Edward VII — Scroll reading "Entente Cordiale"	**Height:** 1 ½"
Elizabeth I — Orb and sceptre	**Issued:** 1994 in Ltd. ed. 2,500
Henry V — Royal standard	
Henry VIII — Bible and lute	
Victoria — Gold lion and crown	

Doulton Number	Name	Colourway	Current Market Value U.K. £	U.S. $	Can. $
D6995	Charles I	Black, yellow and red	50.00	90.00	110.00
D6993	Edward VII	Gold, white and yellow	50.00	90.00	110.00
D6992	Elizabeth I	Green, yellow and brown	50.00	90.00	110.00
D6994	Henry V	Gold, maroon and yellow	50.00	90.00	110.00
D6990	Henry VIII	Black, white and gold	50.00	90.00	110.00
D6991	Victoria	Yellow, brown and silver	50.00	90.00	110.00
		Complete set with stand	275.00	525.00	650.00

Note: Models exist without the gold highlights.

LAUREL AND HARDY

The Laurel and Hardy jugs were commissioned by Lawleys By Post and issued as a pair in a limited edition of 3,500.

For the Laurel and Hardey bookends see page 541.

Designer: William K. Harper
Handles: Early movie camera
Colourway: Browns, black, white and red

Backstamp: Doulton

Doulton Number	Name	Backstamp	Height	Intro.	Discon.	Current Market Value U.K. £	U.S. $	Can. $
7008	Laurel	Doulton	4"	1995	Ltd. ed.	75.00	135.00	175.00
7009	Hardy	Doulton	4"	1995	Ltd. ed.	75.00	135.00	175.00
	Pair					150.00	275.00	350.00

THE LAWYER

The Lawyer
D 6498
COPR 1958
DOULTON & CO LIMITED
Rd No 889569
Rd No 38225
Rd No 8035
Rd No 424/58

Backstamp - Large
Size Jug

Royal Doulton
THE LAWYER
D 6504
Modelled by

© ROYAL DOULTON TABLEWARE
LIMITED 1958

Backstamp - Small Size
Jug

Designer: Max Henk
Handle: Green feather quill
Colourway: Grey wig; black robes; white shirt

Backstamp: Doulton

Doulton Number	Size	Backstamp	Height	Intro.	Discon.	Current Market Value U.K. £	U.S. $	Can. $
D6498	Large	Doulton	7"	1959	1996	60.00	125.00	125.00
D6504	Small	Doulton	4"	1959	1996	35.00	70.00	90.00
D6524	Miniature	Doulton	2 ½"	1960	1991	35.00	80.00	90.00

The Lawyer Derivative

Doulton Number	Item	Height	Intro.	Discon.	Current Market Value U.K. £	U.S. $	Can. $
D6504	Table lighter	3 ½"	1962	1974	150.00	250.00	300.00

Note: This jug was also issued in English Translucent China. These jugs command a premium of 50 to 100% over the earthenware variety.

LEEDS UNITED (FOOTBALL CLUB)

THE FOOTBALL SUPPORTERS
ONE OF TEN

Backstamp: Doulton

Designer: Stanley J. Taylor
Handle: Team coloured scarf
Colourway: White, blue and yellow uniform

Doulton Number	Size	Backstamp	Height	Intro.	Discon.	Current Market Value U.K. £	U.S. $	Can. $
D6928	Mid	Doulton	5"	1992	Unknown	50.00	110.00	125.00

LEN HUTTON

Sir Leonard Hutton played for the Yorkshire County Cricket Club. The ribbon bearing the number 364, which is intertwined around the handle of the jug, represents his famous record innings against Australia at the Oval cricket grounds in 1938, a record which still stands in England today. The jug was commissioned by Lawleys By Post and was issued in a limited edition of 9,500. The first jug was presented to Her Royal Highness, the Duchess of Kent, who is patron of the Len Hutton 364 Appeal.

Designer: Stanley J. Taylor
Handle: Cricket bat, stumps and ball
Colourway: White shirt and sweater; black cap

Backstamp: Doulton

Doulton Number	Size	Backstamp	Height	Intro.	Discon.	Current Market Value U.K. £	U.S. $	Can. $
D6945	Mid	Doulton	4"	1993	Ltd. Ed.	65.00	150.00	175.00

LEPRECHAUN

This wizened little elf is a legendary Irish sprite with a mischievous nature. The Irish believed that leprechauns guarded hoards of treasure hidden at the end of rainbows.

Backstamp A - Doulton

Backstamp B - Site of the Green

Designer: William K. Harper
Handle: Rainbow with a sack of gold at the base
Colourway: Green cap; brown coat

Backstamps:
    A. Doulton
    For general release: large size — 1991, small size — 1992
    B. Doulton/The Site of the Green
    Large size commissioned by the Site of the Green and issued in 1990
    in a special edition of 500 pieces.
    C. Doulton/The Site of the Green
    Small size commissioned by the Site of the Green and issued in 1991
    in a special edition of 500 pieces.

Doulton Number	Size	Backstamp	Height	Intro.	Discon.	Current Market Value		
						U.K. £	U.S. $	Can. $
D6847	Large	Doulton	7 ½"	1991	1996	75.00	150.00	150.00
D6847	Large	Doulton/Site	7 ½"	1990	Sp. ed.	75.00	150.00	150.00
D6899	Small	Doulton	4 ½"	1992	1996	40.00	75.00	100.00
D6899	Small	Doulton/Site	4 ½"	1991	Sp. ed.	45.00	75.00	100.00

LEWIS CARROLL

CHARACTER JUG OF THE YEAR

One hundred years after the death of Lewis Carroll, creator of *Alice's Adventures in Wonderland*, he is celebrated with this Character Jug of The Year for 1998.

For the toby jug Lewis Carroll see page 76.

Royal Doulton®
CHARACTER JUG OF THE YEAR 1998
LEWIS CARROLL
D7096
Modelled by

David B Biggs

© 1997 ROYAL DOULTON

Designer:	David B. Biggs	
Handle:	A white rabbit and a clock	
Colourway:	Maroon jacket, white shirt, black bow tie	

Backstamp: Doulton/
Character Jug opf the Year, 1998

Doulton Number	Size	Backstamp	Height	Intro.	Discon.	Current Market Value		
						U.K. £	U.S. $	Can. $
D7096	Large	Doulton	8"	1998	1998	100.00	200.00	300.00

LITTLE MESTER MUSEUM PIECE

This jug was modelled on the likeness of Grinder Rowland Swindon, a grinder from Sheffield, England. It was commissioned by John Sinclair of Sheffield and issued in 1988 in a limited edition of 3,500 pieces. One thousand jugs were bought by the World Student Games to help launch the games in Sheffield.

Designer: Stanley J. Taylor
Handle: Bowie knife and grinder
Colourway: Black cap; blue jacket; white shirt; red scarf

Backstamp: Doulton

Doulton Number	Size	Backstamp	Height	Intro.	Discon.	Current Market Value U.K. £	U.S. $	Can. $
D6819	Large	Doulton	6 ¾"	1988	Sp. ed.	100.00	250.00	275.00

LITTLE NELL

For the character jug Little Nell see the "Charles Dickens Commemorative Set" page 185.

LIVERPOOL (FOOTBALL CLUB)

THE FOOTBALL SUPPORTERS
ONE OF TEN

Designer: Stanley J. Taylor
Handle: Team coloured scarf
Colourway: Red and white uniform

Backstamp: Doulton

Doulton Number	Size	Backstamp	Height	Intro.	Discon.	Current Market Value		
						U.K. £	U.S. $	Can. $
D6930	Mid	Doulton	5"	1992	Unknown	50.00	110.00	125.00

LIVERPOOL CENTENARY JUG (BILL SHANKLY)

Issued to commemorate the 100th anniversary of the Liverpool Football Club in 1992, this jug is a limited edition of 5,500.

LIVERPOOL CENTENARY JUG
D 6914
Specially Commissioned from
Royal Doulton®
by
LIVERPOOL F.C.
In celebration of
the clubs centenary
In 1992
Modelled by *William K. Harper*
© 1991 ROYAL DOULTON
A LIMITED EDITION OF 5,500
THIS IS N° 215

Designer: William K. Harper
Handle: Two footballs and flag
Colourway: Red jersey; white collar; grey hair

Backstamp: Doulton/Liverpool F.C.

Doulton Number	Size	Backstamp	Height	Intro.	Discon.	Current Market Value		
						U.K. £	U.S. $	Can. $
D6914	Small	Doulton/ Liverpool, F.C.	3 ½"	1992	Ltd. ed.	75.00	160.00	195.00

LOBSTER MAN

VARIATION No. 1: Colourway — Dark blue jacket and cap; white fisherman's jersey

LOBSTER MAN
D 6852
COPR 1967
DOULTON & CO LIMITED

Designer: David Biggs
Handle: Lobster
Colourway: Dark blue jacket and cap;
white fisherman's jersey

Backstamp: Doulton

Doulton Number	Size	Variation	Height	Intro.	Discon.	Current Market Value U.K. £	U.S. $	Can. $
D6617	Large	Var. 1	7 ½"	1968	1991	65.00	100.00	110.00
D6620	Small	Var. 1	3 ¾"	1968	1991	45.00	75.00	90.00
D6652	Miniature	Var. 1	2 ¾"	1980	1991	40.00	65.00	70.00

VARIATION No. 2: Colourway — Dark blue jacket and cap; blue-grey fisherman's jersey

Doulton Number	Size	Variation	Height	Intro.	Discon.	Current Market Value U.K. £	U.S. $	Can. $
D6783	Large	Var. 2	8"	1987	1989	75.00	200.00	250.00

VARIATION No. 3: Colourway — Light blue jacket

Doulton Number	Size	Variation	Height	Intro.	Discon.	Current Market Value U.K. £	U.S. $	Can. $
D —	Small	Var. 2	3 ¾"	1987	Unknown	85.00	150.00	185.00

Note: This jug was also issued in English Translucent China. These jugs command a premium of 50 to 100% over the earthenware variety.

THE LONDON 'BOBBY'

THE LONDON COLLECTION
ONE OF TEN

VARIATION No. 1: Hat badge embossed and hand painted

Royal Doulton®
THE LONDON 'BOBBY'
D 6744
Modelled by
Stanley James Taylor
© 1985 ROYAL DOULTON (UK)

Designer: Stanley J. Taylor
Handle: Tower of Big Ben and a whistle
Colourway: Black and white badge (see variations)

Backstamp: Doulton

Doulton Number	Size	Variation	Height	Intro.	Discon.	Current Market Value U.K. £	U.S. $	Can. $
D6744	Large	Var. 1	7"	1986	1987	185.00	325.00	350.00
D6762	Small	Var. 1	3 ½"	1987	1987	125.00	225.00	250.00
D6763	Miniature	Var. 1	2 ½"	1987	1987	125.00	250.00	275.00

VARIATION No. 2: Hat badge decal decorated

Doulton Number	Size	Variation	Height	Intro.	Discon.	Current Market Value U.K. £	U.S. $	Can. $
D6744	Large	Var. 2	7 ½"	1987	Current	90.00	165.00	230.00
D6762	Small	Var. 2	3 ½"	1987	Current	53.00	90.00	130.00
D6763	Miniature	Var. 2	2 ½"	1987	1991	45.00	120.00	145.00

LONG JOHN SILVER

CHARACTERS FROM LITERATURE
ONE OF 11

This scoundrel and pirate from Robert Louis Stevenson's *Treasure Island* had a wooden leg and a parrot companion. Together with the boy-hero Jim Hawkins, he set sail in a hair-raising search for buried treasure.

VARIATION No. 1: Colourway — Maroon shirt; green and grey parrot

Designer: Max Henk
Handle: A parrot
Colourway: Maroon shirt; green and grey parrot

" Long John Silver "
D.6335.
COPR. 1951.
DOULTON & CO LIMITED.
R⁴Nº 864843.
R⁴Nº 29156.
R⁴Nº 6404.
R⁴Nº 112/51

Backstamp: Doulton

Doulton Number	Size	Backstamp	Height	Intro.	Discon.	Current Market Value		
						U.K. £	U.S. $	Can. $
D6335	Large	Doulton	7"	1952	1998	85.00	160.00	230.00
D6386	Small	Doulton	4"	1952	1998	50.00	90.00	130.00
D6512	Miniature	Doulton	2 ½"	1960	1991	40.00	65.00	70.00

Note: This jug was also issued in English Translucent China. These jugs command a premium of 50 to 100% over the earthenware variety.

VARIATION No. 2: Colourway — Yellow shirt, yellow-green parrot

"LONG JOHN SILVER"
D 6799
Specially Commissioned
from
Royal Doulton®
by
D.H. HOLMES COMPANY LTD.
Celebrating the opening of
The Royal Doulton Room
D.H. Holmes, New Orleans, Louisiana, U.S.A.
HAND MODELLED AND HAND DECORATED
A LIMITED EDITION OF 250
THIS IS NO. 91
© 1987 ROYAL DOULTON

Backstamp: Doulton/D. H. Holmes/
Specially Commissioned from Royal Doulton by D. H. Holmes Company Ltd./
Celebrating the opening of The Royal Doulton Room D. H. Holmes, New Orleans, Louisiana, U.S.A.
Commissioned by D. H. Holmes Company Ltd. and issued in 1987 in a limited edition of 250 pieces.

Doulton Number	Size	Backstamp	Height	Intro.	Discon.	Current Market Value U.K. £	U.S. $	Can. $
D6799	Large	Doulton/Holmes	7"	1987	Ltd. ed.	225.00	400.00	475.00

VARIATION No. 3: Colourway — Dark brown shirt, crimson hat, green parrot

This special colourway of the small size Long John Silver jug was available only at the Michael Doulton Treasure Chest Events held during 1999. An incorrect backstamp reads 'We want that silver and we'll have it" on the first jugs issued. This was later corrected to read "We want that treasure and we'll have it."

Backstamp: Doulton/Michael Doulton Treasure Chest
Exclusive colourway for Treasure Chest Events

Doulton Number	Backstamp	Height	Intro.	Discon.	Current Market Value		
					U.K. £	U.S. $	Can. $
D7138	'Silver'	4"	1999	1999	50.00	—	—
D7138	'Treasure'	4"	1999	Current	45.00	—	—

Long John Silver Derivatives

Doulton Number	Item	Height	Intro.	Discon.	Current Market Value		
					U.K. £	U.S. $	Can. $
D6386	Lighter	3 ½"	1958	1973	125.00	225.00	225.00
D6853	Teapot	7"	1990	1991	125.00	225.00	225.00

LORD BADEN-POWELL

Commissioned by Travers Stanley Collections, and with permission from the Scout Association, this character jug, issued in a limited edition of 2,500, portrays the founder of the Boy Scout movement. A certificate of authenticity accompanies this jug.

Designer: William K. Harper
Handle: Kudu horn and Wood Badge
Colourway: Browns, black and red

Backstamp: Doulton/Travers Stanley Collections

Doulton Number	Size	Backstamp	Height	Intro.	Discon.	Current Market Value		
						U.K. £	U.S. $	Can. $
D7144	Small	Doulton/Travers	4 ¼"	1999	Ltd. ed.	60.00	125.00	175.00

LORD MAYOR OF LONDON

THE LONDON COLLECTION
ONE OF TEN

Designer: Stanley J. Taylor
Handle: Sceptre of office
Colourway: Black plume hat; red cloak; yellow chain of office

Backstamp: Doulton

Doulton Number	Size	Backstamp	Height	Intro.	Discon.	Current Market Value U.K. £	U.S. $	Can. $
D6864	Large	Doulton	7 ¼"	1990	1991	100.00	200.00	225.00

LORD NELSON

Horatio Nelson (1758-1805), a member of the navy since the age of 12, was made commander-in-chief of his own fleet in 1803. He saw action in the West Indies and in Canada, but is best remembered for his defeat of the French and Spanish navies at the Battle of Trafalgar in 1805. Nelson died during the battle.

For the character jug Nelson see page 380 and for the character jug Vice-Admiral Nelson see page 515.

Designer: Geoff Blower
Handle: Plain
Colourway: Blue tricorn and jacket with gold trim; white cravat

Backstamps: **A.** Doulton
             B. Doulton/Battle of Trafalgar/
                Commemorating the 150th Anniversary of the Battle of Trafalgar 21st October 1955
                Commissioned for the Admiralty to commemorate the 150th anniversary of Nelson's
                victory at Trafalgar, October 21, 1955.
             C. Three of the jugs carry an added line to the backstamp, either "First Lord," "First Sea Lord"
                or "Secretary," the intention being that these three jugs would be held in perpetuity at the
                respective offices. However one of the elected officials left office with a jug, which later
                appeared on the market.

Doulton Number	Size	Backstamp	Height	Intro.	Discon.	Current Market Value U.K. £	U.S. $	Can. $
D6336	Large	A	7"	1952	1969	300.00	600.00	700.00
D6336	Large	B	7"	1955	1955	Rare		
D6336	Large	C	7"	1955	1955	Extremely rare, only three issued and each with a different backstamp		

LORD NELSON AND LADY HAMILTON

DOUBLE CHARACTER JUG
ONE OF TWO

Lord Nelson led England to victory in the Battle of Trafalgar, but lost his own life. Lady Emma Hamilton secured supplies to Malta during its French occupation. Nelson and Lady Hamilton had a daughter, Horatia, born in 1801.

This jug was issued by Lawleys By Post in a limited edition of 1,500 pieces.

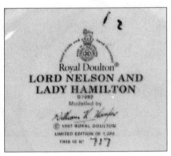

Designer:	William K. Harper
Handle:	Nelson — Admiralty flags and a telescope
	Lady Hamilton — Theatrical mask and a
	Maltese Cross
Colourway:	Nelson — Naval uniform, grey hair
	Lady Hamilton —White dress, auburn hair

Backstamp: Doulton

Doulton Number	Size	Backstamp	Height	Intro.	Discon.	Current Market Value U.K. £	U.S. $	Can. $
D7092	Small	Doulton	4"	1997	Ltd. ed.	120.00	—	—

LOUIS ARMSTRONG

THE CELEBRITY COLLECTION
ONE OF SIX

Daniel Louis "Satchmo" Armstrong (1900-1971) evolved from a self-taught cornet player to the first internationally famous soloist in jazz. He was well known for both his brilliant technique on the trumpet and for his deep throaty singing. Appearing in many live shows, Broadway musicals and films, Armstrong's music had a lasting influence on jazz.

Designer: David Biggs	**Backstamp:** Doulton
Handle: Trumpet and handkerchief	
Colourway: Brown and pink	

Doulton Number	Size	Backstamp	Height	Intro.	Discon.	Current Market Value U.K. £	U.S. $	Can. $
D6707	Large	Doulton	7 ½"	1984	1988	125.00	300.00	350.00

LUMBERJACK

CANADIAN CENTENNIAL SERIES, 1867-1967
ONE OF THREE

A small quantity of miniature Lumberjack prototypes are known to exist.
The Lumberjack is one of three jugs that received a special backstamp in 1967. The other two, the North American Indian and the Trapper, complete the three-jug Canadian Centennial Series.

Backstamp A - Doulton

Backstamp B
Doulton/Canadian
Centennial Series

Designer: Max Henk
Handle: Tree trunk and axe
Colourway: Red cap; green jacket; pink sweater

Backstamps: A. Doulton
B. Doulton/Canadian Centenary /Canadian Centennial Series 1867-1967 Available in North America during 1967 only.

| Doulton Number | Size | Backstamp | Height | Intro. | Discon. | Current Market Value | | |
						U.K. £	U.S. $	Can. $
D6610	Large	Doulton	7 ¼"	1967	1982	90.00	150.00	175.00
D6610	Large	Centenary	7 ¼"	1967	1967	150.00	300.00	325.00
D6613	Small	Doulton	3 ½"	1967	1982	45.00	75.00	100.00
—	Miniature	Doulton	2 ½"	Unknown		1,750.00	3,000.00	4,000.00

Note: This jug was also issued in English Translucent China. These jugs command a premium of 50 to 100% over the earthenware variety.

MACBETH

THE SHAKESPEAREAN COLLECTION
ONE OF SIX

First performed in 1606, this Shakespearean tragedy was based on Scottish history. With the help of his wife, Macbeth plots to usurp the throne. Three witches prophesy that he will succeed, but that the heirs of his enemy Banquo will one day rule the kingdom. In a series of grisly events, their dark predictions are fulfilled.

STYLE ONE: HANDLE — WITCHES FACING OUTWARD

The faces of the three witches on the outer side of the handle face outward (noses out). Only after the jug was in the initial stages of production did Doulton realize that the possibility of the handle being damaged during shipping was great, and thus the moulds were quickly modified resulting in the production of style two.

Designer: Michael Abberley
Handle: Three witches facing to the right
Colourway: Brown, yellow and green

Backstamp: Doulton

Doulton Number	Size	Backstamp	Height	Intro.	Discon.	U.K. £	Current Market Value U.S. $	Can. $
D6667	Large	Doulton	7 ¼"	1981	1981		Extremely rare	

MACBETH

THE SHAKESPEAREAN COLLECTION
ONE OF SIX

STYLE TWO: HANDLE — WITCHES FACING INWARD

Designer: Michael Abberley
Handle: The faces of the three witches are on the front of the handle facing forwards
Colourway: Brown, yellow and grey

Backstamp: Doulton

Doulton Number	Size	Backstamp	Height	Intro.	Discon.	Current Market Value		
						U.K. £	U.S. $	Can. $
D6667	Large	Doulton	7 ¼"	1982	1989	100.00	200.00	200.00

MAD HATTER

ALICE IN WONDERLAND
ONE OF SIX

A character from Lewis Carroll's *Alice's Adventures in Wonderland*, the Mad Hatter wears a watch that tells time in months, rather than in hours.

VARIATION No. 1: Colourway — Black hat; dark red bow tie

Mad Hatter
D 6598
COPR 1970
DOULTON & CO LIMITED
Rd No 917231
Rd No 46577
Rd No 10000
Rd No 592/64

Designer: Max Henk
Handle: A dormouse above a pocket watch
Colourway: Black hat, dark red bow tie

Backstamp: Doulton

Doulton Number	Size	Variation	Height	Intro.	Discon.	Current Market Value		
						U.K. £	U.S. $	Can. $
D6598	Large	Var. 1	7 ¼"	1965	1983	100.00	275.00	300.00
D6602	Small	Var. 1	3 ¾"	1965	1983	80.00	165.00	190.00
D6606	Miniature	Var. 1	2 ½"	1965	1983	75.00	140.00	160.00

Note: This jug was also issued in English Translucent China. These jugs command a premium of 50 to 100% over the earthenware variety.

VARIATION No. 2:   Colourway — Black hat; yellow bow tie

Backstamp B - Small
Size Jug

Backstamps: **A.** Doulton / Higbee's
The large-size jug was commissioned by the Higbee Company to celebrate the opening of the
first Royal Doulton Room. Issued on October 28, 1985, in a limited edition of 250 pieces.
B. Doulton/Higbee's
The small-size jug was commissioned by the Higbee Department Store to celebrate the second
anniversary of the opening of the Royal Doulton Room. Issued in 1987 in a limited edition of 500
pieces.

Doulton Number	Size	Backstamp	Height	Intro.	Discon.	Current Market Value U.K. £	U.S. $	Can. $
D6748	Large	Doulton/Higbee	7"	1985	Ltd. ed.	500.00	900.00	1,000.00
D6790	Small	Doulton/Higbee	3 ¼"	1987	Ltd. ed.	200.00	275.00	325.00

MAE WEST

THE CELEBRITY COLLECTION
ONE OF SIX

From her screen debut in 1932, Mae West (1892-1980) became an instant hit. She is best known for portraying tough, sophisticated characters who loved luxury and men. The public adored her and her witty quips, the most famous of which appears on the base of the jug: "When I'm good, I'm very good. But when I'm bad, I'm better."

Backstamp A - Doulton

Designer: Colin M. Davidson
Handle: Umbrella with a bow tied around the handle
Colourway: Yellow hair; white feather dress

Backstamps: **A.** Doulton
General issue, 1983.
B. Doulton/American Express/ Premier Edition for American Express. This series was first introduced in the U.S.A. as a promotional jug for the American Express Company. Approximately 500 jugs were given the special backstamp and were available only to the North American market.

Doulton Number	Size	Backstamp	Height	Intro.	Discon.	Current Market Value U.K. £	U.S. $	Can. $
D6688	Large	Doulton	7"	1983	1986	100.00	225.00	250.00
D6688	Large	Doulton/Amex	7"	1983	1983	300.00	475.00	600.00

MANCHESTER UNITED (FOOTBALL CLUB)

THE FOOTBALL SUPPORTERS
ONE OF TEN

Royal Doulton®
FOOTBALL SUPPORTER'S
CHARACTER JUG.
D 6924
Modelled by
Stanley James Taylor
© 1992 ROYAL DOULTON
"MANCHESTER UNITED"

Designer: Stanley J. Taylor
Handle: Team coloured scarf
Colourway: Red, white and black uniform

Backstamp: Doulton

Doulton Number	Size	Backstamp	Height	Intro.	Discon.	Current Market Value U.K. £	U.S. $	Can. $
D6924	Mid	Doulton	5"	1992	Unknown	50.00	110.00	125.00

MAORI

The Maori people of Polynesian descent were the first inhabitants of present-day New Zealand. Beginning as hunters and fishermen, the Maori later turned to agriculture and woodworking.

STYLE ONE: BLUE-GREY HAIR, FRIENDLY EXPRESSION

Designer: Unknown
Handle: Plain with plaque of Maori
Colourway: Brown and grey

Backstamp: Doulton

Doulton Number	Size	Backstamp	Height	Intro.	Discon.	Current Market Value		
						U.K. £	**U.S. $**	**Can. $**
D6080	Large	Doulton	7"	1939	1939	Extremely Rare. Only three known. Last sold May 1998. Phillips, New Bond Street London, England, £21,850.		

MAORI

STYLE TWO: DARK HAIR, TWO WHITE-TIPPED FEATHERS IN HAIR,
SERIOUS EXPRESSION

Designer: Unknown
Handle: Plain with plaque of Maori
Colourway: Brown and grey

Backstamp: Doulton

Doulton Number	Size	Backstamp	Height	Intro.	Discon.	Current Market Value U.K. £	U.S. $	Can. $
D6080	Large	Doulton	7"	1939	1939		Extremely rare	

THE MARCH HARE

ALICE IN WONDERLAND
ONE OF SIX

At the March Hare's home in Wonderland it is always six o'clock and time for tea. Not having a moment to tidy up, he and his friends, the Mad Hatter and the dormouse, sit at a table laid for a great number and change seats as they dirty the dishes. Alice makes herself unpopular by asking what they do when they arrive back at the beginning.

Designer: William K. Harper
Handle: One of the hare's ears
Colourway: Green hat; yellow bow tie with blue spots

Backstamp: Doulton

Doulton Number	Size	Backstamp	Height	Intro.	Discon.	Current Market Value U.K. £	U.S. $	Can. $
D6776	Large	Doulton	6"	1989	1991	125.00	300.00	350.00

MARCO POLO

For the character jug Marco Polo see the "Explorers Set" page 233.

MARILYN MONROE

THE CELEBRITY COLLECTION

PROTOTYPE

Norma Jean Baker (1926-1962) made her screen debut in 1948, and as Marilyn Monroe, her beauty and charisma established her as an international sex symbol. She died at the age of 36.

There are only two of these jugs known to exist. One is in the Doulton Museum, Stoke-on-Trent. The other came to auction in 1992 in Toronto and fetched $17,500.00. The jug was not issued due to copyright problems.

Designer: Eric Griffiths
Handle: A cine-camera encircled by a roll of film
Colourway: Yellow, white and grey

Backstamp: Doulton

Doulton Number	Size	Variation	Height	Intro.	Discon.	Current Market Value		
						U.K. £	U.S. $	Can. $
D6719	Large	Prototype	7 ¼"	1983	1983	Extremely Rare Last sold September 1992 Britannia Fair, Toronto,Canada $17,500.00		

MARK TWAIN

Born Samuel Langhorne Clemens (1835-1910), Mark Twain was an American writer and humourist. He was best loved for his classic adventure stories, *Tom Sawyer* (1876) and *The Adventures of Huckleberry Finn* (1884), which told of life in his native Mississippi.

The small jug was modelled for "The Queen's Table," Royal Doulton's exhibit at the United Kingdom Showcase at Walt Disney's Epcot Center in Orlando, Florida. The jug was sold exclusively to Epcot tourists visiting the exhibition during 1982.

Royal Doulton
MARK TWAIN
D 6654
Modelled by

© ROYAL DOULTON TABLEWARE
LIMITED 1979

Designer: Eric Griffiths	**Backstamp:** Doulton
Handle: Quill and ink pot	
Colourway: Black coat and bow tie; grey hair	

Doulton Number	Size	Backstamp	Height	Intro.	Discon.	Current Market Value		
						U.K. £	U.S. $	Can. $
D6654	Large	Doulton	7 ½"	1980	1990	100.00	175.00	200.00
D6694	Small	Doulton	4"	1983	1990	55.00	110.00	125.00
D6758	Miniature	Doulton	2 ½"	1986	1990	65.00	150.00	175.00

THE MASTER / EQUESTRIAN

This piece was released in the U.K. as The Master, and in North America as The Equestrian.

Designer: Stanley J. Taylor
Handle: Horse head
Colourway: Dark blue, red and white

Backstamp: Doulton

Doulton Number	Size	Backstamp	Height	Intro.	Discon.	Current Market Value U.K. £	Current Market Value U.S. $	Current Market Value Can. $
D6898	Small	Doulton	4"	1991	1995	50.00	100.00	150.00

McCALLUM

Produced as a promotional item for the D & J McCallum Distillery, Scotland, this jug exists in three different colour varieties, all in very limited quantities. This jug was also produced by other manufacturers from an almost identical design. The colourways and size are extremely close to the jug produced by Doulton. The backstamp is the best way to tell the difference.

Variation No. 1

Variation No. 2

Designer: McCallum
Handle: Plain

Colourway: See below
Backstamp: Doulton

VARIATION No. 1: Kingsware
Colourway — Light and dark browns
Approximately 1,000 to 1,500 pieces are thought to have been made

Doulton Number	Size	Variation	Height	Intro.	Discon.	Current Market Value U.K. £	U.S. $	Can. $
D —	Large	Kingsware glaze	7"	1930	Unknown	1,650.00	3,500.00	4,000.00

VARIATION No. 2: Colourway — Ivory glaze
Approximately 1,000 pieces were produced

Doulton Number	Size	Variation	Height	Intro.	Discon.	Current Market Value U.K. £	U.S. $	Can. $
D —	Large	White	7"	1930	Unknown	1,250.00	2,500.00	3,000.00

MEPHISTOPHELES

First found in 16th-century German legend, Mephistopheles became best known in Johann von Goethe's drama, *Faust* (1808). In it he is portrayed as an evil spirit or devil to whom Faust sells his soul in return for services.

Designer: Charles Noke
Harry Fenton
Handle: Plain
Colourway: Red and brown

Backstamps: A. Doulton — With verse
B. Doulton — Without verse

When the devil was sick
the devil a saint would be
When the devil got well
devil a saint was he

Backstamp A

Doulton Number	Size	Backstamp	Height	Intro.	Discon.	Current Market Value		
						U.K. £	U.S. $	Can. $
D5757	Large	With verse	7"	1937	1948	1,200.00	3,000.00	3,500.00
D5757	Large	Without verse	7"	1937	1948	1,000.00	2,500.00	3,000.00
D5758	Small	With verse	3 ¾"	1937	1948	750.00	1,600.00	1,850.00
D5758	Small	Without verse	3 ¾"	1937	1948	660.00	1,300.00	1,500.00

MERLIN

CHARACTERS FROM LITERATURE
ONE OF 11

In the legend of King Arthur of Camelot, Merlin appears as wizard and aide to the King. He is credited with the creation of the famous Round Table.

For Merlin (style two) see, King Arthur and Merlin, page 324.

STYLE ONE: HANDLE — AN OWL

Designer: Garry Sharpe
Handle: An owl
Colourway: Black, grey and brown

Backstamp: Doulton

Merlin
D 6543
COPR 1959
DOULTON & CO LIMITED
Rd No 893842
Rd No 39650
Rd No 8314
Rd No 41/959

Doulton Number	Size	Backstamp	Height	Intro.	Discon.	Current Market Value U.K. £	U.S. $	Can. $
D6529	Large	Doulton	7 ¼"	1960	1998	80.00	150.00	200.00
D6536	Small	Doulton	3 ¾"	1960	1998	45.00	80.00	125.00
D6543	Miniature	Doulton	2 ¾"	1960	1991	40.00	70.00	80.00

Note: This jug was also issued in English Translucent China. These jugs command a premium of 50 to 100% over the earthenware variety.

MICHAEL DOULTON

This jug was manufactured in an edition of 9,500 pieces. It was only available for sale at retail locations where and when Michael Doulton was present.

Backstamp: Doulton

Designer: William K. Harper
Handle: Flag bearing the Royal Doulton logo
Colourway: Black, brown and blue

Doulton Number	Size	Backstamp	Height	Intro.	Discon.	Current Market Value		
						U.K. £	U.S. $	Can. $
D6808	Small	Doulton	4 ¼"	1988	1989	45.00	65.00	75.00

THE MIKADO

"Mikado" is the ancient title for the emperor of Japan, beginning with the reign of the Mikado Jimmu in 660 B.C. Believed by many to have descended from the all-powerful Sun Goddess, the same family line has been traced through 124 reigns. The mikado is popularly known through the Gilbert and Sullivan operetta (1885) of the same name.

The Mikado
D.6501
COPR 1958
DOULTON & CO LIMITED
Rd No 889572
Rd No 38228
Rd No 8038
Rd No 421,58

Designer: Max Henk
Handle: A fan
Colourway: Black and turquoise hat; green and white robes

Backstamp: Doulton

Doulton Number	Size	Backstamp	Height	Intro.	Discon.	Current Market Value		
						U.K. £	U.S. $	Can. $
D6501	Large	Doulton	6 ½"	1959	1969	400.00	900.00	1,150.00
D6507	Small	Doulton	3 ¾"	1959	1969	275.00	500.00	650.00
D6525	Miniature	Doulton	2 ½"	1960	1969	275.00	525.00	675.00

Note: This jug was also issued in English Translucent China. These jugs command a premium of 50 to 100% over the earthenware variety.

MINE HOST

The forerunner of today's English publican, this cheerful man would hang a pine bough on the door of his home to let travellers know that refreshments were available. As the handle shows, these often ran to a good pint of strong ale!

Mine Host
D.6513
COPR 1957
DOULTON & CO LIMITED
Rd No 886230
Rd No 37212
Rd No 7854
Rd No 389/57

Designer: Max Henk
Handle: Evergreen bough and barrel
Colourway: Black tricorn; red coat; white bow tie with gold spots

Backstamp: Doulton

Doulton Number	Size	Backstamp	Height	Intro.	Discon.	Current Market Value U.K. £	U.S. $	Can. $
D6468	Large	Doulton	7"	1958	1982	85.00	150.00	175.00
D6470	Small	Doulton	3 ½"	1958	1982	50.00	80.00	100.00
D6513	Miniature	Doulton	2 ½"	1960	1982	55.00	90.00	100.00

Note: This jug was also issued in English Translucent China. These jugs command a premium of 50 to 100% over the earthenware variety.

MINNIE THE MINX

To celebrate the 60th anniversary of the Dandy and Beano comics in 1998 a special anniversary logo appeared on the base of the jug for that year.

Royal Doulton®
MINNIE THE MINX
D7036
Modelled by
Simon Ward
© 1996 ROYAL DOULTON
"MINNIE THE MINX" IS A TRADE MARK OF
D.C.THOMSON & Co., LTD.
© D.C.THOMSON & Co., LTD.,1996

Designer: Simon Ward
Handle: Cat, sling shot and apples
Colourway: Black, red and brown

Backstamp: **A.** Doulton/
© D.C. Thomson & Co. Ltd.
B. 60th Anniversary logo

Doulton Number	Size	Backstamp	Height	Intro.	Discon.	Current Market Value U.K. £	U.S. $	Can. $
D7036	Small	A. Doulton	4 ½"	1996	1999	55.00	125.00	150.00
D7036	Small	B. 60th Anniv.	4 ½"	1998	1998	55.00	125.00	150.00

MONTY

Bernard Law Montgomery (1887-1976), first Viscount Montgomery of Alamein, was referred to familiarly as Monty. The highlights of his long and distinguished military career include the first Allied victory of World War II in North Africa in 1942 and the acceptance of the German surrender at Luneburg Heath in 1945. He was Deputy Supreme Commander of the Allied Powers in Europe from 1951 to 1958.

In 1954 a minor colourway change occurred when the yellow highlighting on the cap badge was dropped.

For the character jug Field Marshall Montgomery, see page 241, and for the character jug Viscount Montgomery of Alamein, see page 518.

Designer:	Harry Fenton	**Backstamp:** Doulton
Handle:	Plain	
Colourway:	Brown beret; khaki uniform	
	Cap badge A. — Yellow highlights	
	Cap badge B. — No highlights	

Doulton Number	Size	Colourway	Height	Intro.	Discon.	Current Market Value U.K. £	U.S. $	Can. $
D6202	Large	Highlights	5 ¾"	1946	1954	90.00	100.00	100.00
D6202	Large	No highlights	5 ¾"	1954	1991	65.00	90.00	100.00

MOZART

GREAT COMPOSERS
ONE OF EIGHT

Designer: Stanley J. Taylor
Handle: Barber of Seville, bar of music and barber pole
Colourway: Black, white and red

Backstamp: Doulton

Doulton Number	Size	Backstamp	Height	Intro.	Discon.	Current Market Value		
						U.K. £	**U.S. $**	**Can. $**
D7031	Large	Doulton	7"	1996	Current	90.00	260.00	340.00

MR. BUMBLE

For the character jug Mr. Bumble see the "Charles Dickens Commemorative Set" page 185.

MR. MICAWBER

In Charles Dickens' classic, *David Copperfield*, Wilkins Micawber is Copperfield's landlord and friend. A sanguine idler, Micawber unmasks Uriah Heep as a villain and is rewarded with passage to Australia, where he settles happily in a prominent neighbourhood.

STYLE ONE: HANDLE — PLAIN

Designer: Leslie Harradine / Harry Fenton
Handle: Plain
Colourway: Black hat; green coat; blue polka-dot bow tie

Backstamp: Doulton

Doulton Number	Size	Backstamp	Height	Intro.	Discon.	Current Market Value U.K. £	U.S. $	Can. $
D5843	Mid	Doulton	5 ½"	1938	1948	135.00	250.00	275.00
D5843	Small	Doulton	3 ¼"	1948	1960	70.00	125.00	150.00
D6138	Miniature	Doulton	2 ¼"	1940	1960	45.00	65.00	70.00
D6143	Tiny	Doulton	1 ¼"	1940	1960	65.00	100.00	110.00

Mr. Micawber Derivatives

Doulton Number	Item	Height	Intro.	Discon.	Current Market Value U.K. £	U.S. $	Can. $
D5843	Table lighter	3 ½"	1958	1959	200.00	375.00	250.00
D6050	Bust	2 ¼"	1939	1960	85.00	125.00	125.00
HN1615	Bookend	4"	1934	c.1939	1,200.00	2,000.00	2,500.00
M58	Napkin ring	3 ½"	c.1935	1939	325.00	700.00	850.00

Note: This jug was also issued in English Translucent China. These jugs command a premium of 50 to 100% over the earthenware variety.

MR. MICAWBER

This jug was commissioned by Lawleys By Post in a limited edition of 2,500 and comes with a certificate of authenticity.

STYLE TWO: HANDLE — WALKING STICK AND GLOVES

Designer: David B. Biggs
Handle: Walking stick and gloves
Colourway: Mustard jacket, blue cravat, white shirt points, black hat with grey band

Backstamp: Doulton

Doulton Number	Size	Backstamp	Height	Intro.	Discon.	Current Market Value		
						U.K. £	U.S. $	Can. $
D7040	Large	Doulton	7 1/2"	1996	Ltd. ed.	150.00	350.00	450.00

MR. PICKWICK

Founder and chairman of the Pickwick Club, this gentleman is the elegant and genial hero of Charles Dickens' *The Posthumous Papers of the Pickwick Club*, first published in 1837.

STYLE ONE: HANDLE — PLAIN

Designer:	Leslie Harradine/Harry Fenton	**Backstamp:** Doulton
Handle:	Plain	
Colourway:	Green hat; brown coat; red bow tie	

Doulton Number	Size	Backstamp	Height	Intro.	Discon.	Current Market Value U.K. £	U.S. $	Can. $
D6060	Large	Doulton	7"	1940	1960	135.00	225.00	250.00
D5839	Mid	Doulton	4 ¼"	1938	1948	150.00	250.00	275.00
D5839	Small	Doulton	3 ½"	1948	1960	65.00	100.00	110.00
D6254	Miniature	Doulton	2 ¼"	1947	1960	55.00	90.00	100.00
D6260	Tiny	Doulton	1 ¼"	1947	1960	125.00	235.00	265.00

Mr. Pickwick Derivatives

Doulton Number	Item	Height	Intro.	Discon.	Current Market Value U.K. £	U.S. $	Can. $
D5839	Table lighter	3 ½"	1958	1961	200.00	400.00	300.00
D6049	Bust	3 ½"	1939	1960	90.00	125.00	125.00
HN1623	Bookend	4"	1934	c.1939	1,200.00	2,250.00	2,500.00
M57	Napkin ring	3 ½"	c.1935	c.1939	325.00	675.00	800.00

MR. PICKWICK

The large version of this jug was sold by Lawleys By Post in a limited edition of 2,500 pieces and the small version was released through the Royal Doulton International Collectors Club in a limited edition of 2,500. The Mr. Pickwick jugs were issued with metal spectacles, as was the Glenn Miller jug.

STYLE TWO: HANDLE — FIGURE OF SAM WELLER

MR PICKWICK
D 7025
Designed by *William K. Harper*
EXCLUSIVELY FOR
COLLECTORS CLUB
© 1995 ROYAL DOULTON

Designer: William K. Harper
Handle: The figure of Sam Weller
Colourway: Blue, black, green and cream

Backstamp: **A**. Large — Doulton
B. Small — Doulton/
R.D.I.C.C.

Doulton Number	Size	Backstamp	Height	Intro.	Discon.	Current Market Value		
						U.K. £	**U.S. $**	**Can. $**
D6959	Large	Doulton	7"	1994	Ltd. ed.	150.00	325.00	350.00
D7025	Small	Doulton	4"	1996	Ltd. ed.	75.00	150.00	175.00

MR. QUAKER

These jugs were made as an advertising piece for the internal use of Quaker Oats Limited, and a few were sold to members of the Royal Doulton International Collectors Club. They were issued with a certificate signed by Sir Richard Bailey and Michael Doulton.

Mr. Quaker was commissioned by Quaker Oats Limited and issued in 1985 in a limited edition of 3,500 pieces.

Designer:	Harry Sales
Modeller:	Graham Tongue
Handle:	A sheaf of wheat
Colourway:	Black, white and yellow

Backstamp: Doulton/Quaker Oats Ltd

Doulton Number	Size	Backstamp	Height	Intro.	Discon.	Current Market Value		
						U.K. £	U.S. $	Can. $
D6738	Large	Doulton/Quaker	7 ½"	1985	Ltd. ed.	375.00	900.00	1,000.00

MRS. BARDELL

For the character jug Mrs. Bardell see the "Charles Dickens Commemorative Set" page 185.

MRS. CLAUS

CHRISTMAS MINIATURES SERIES
ONE OF SIX

Commissioned for the North American market, Mrs. Claus has her handle to the left so she can be paired with her husband Santa Claus (D6900), whose handle points in the opposite direction.

Royal Doulton®

MRS. CLAUS

D 6922

© 1992 ROYAL DOULTON

Designer: Stanley J. Taylor
Handle: Holly wreath
Colourway: Red, cream and green

Backstamp: Doulton

Doulton Number	Size	Backstamp	Height	Intro.	Discon.	Current Market Value U.K. £	U.S. $	Can. $
D6922	Miniature	Doulton	2 3/8"	1992	Sp. ed.	75.00	125.00	150.00

MURRAY WALKER OBE

Murray Walker was famous for his enthusiastic lap-by-lap commentary of Formular One motor racing. This jug, commisioned by Lawleys By Post, was issued in a limited edition of 2,500 pieces.

Designer: Stanley J. Taylor
Handle: A checkered flag, microphone and racing tyre
Colourway: Tan, mustard, black and white

Backstamp: Doulton

Doulton Number	Size	Backstamp	Height	Intro.	Discon.	Current Market Value		
						U.K. £	U.S. $	Can. $
D7094	Small	Doulton	4"	1997	Ltd. ed.	60.00	125.00	175.00

NAPOLEON

Issued in a limited edition of 2,000 pieces, the Napoleon jug bears a special backstamp and comes with a certificate of authenticity.

STYLE ONE: HANDLE — AN EAGLE

Designer: Stanley J. Taylor
Handle: An eagle
Colourway: Black and gold

Backstamp: Doulton

Doulton Number	Size	Backstamp	Height	Intro.	Discon.	Current Market Value		
						U.K. £	U.S. $	Can. $
D6941	Large	Doulton	7"	1993	Ltd. ed.	150.00	325.00	400.00

NAPOLEON AND JOSEPHINE

STAR-CROSSED LOVERS (TWO-FACED JUG)
ONE OF FOUR

Napoleon (1769-1821) stood only 5 feet 2 inches tall, but he was a military genius who amassed an empire that covered most of western and central Europe. Josephine (1763-1814) married him in 1796, after her first husband, the Vicomte de Beauharnais, was killed during the French Revolution. Unable to produce an heir, Napoleon divorced Josephine in 1809 to marry a younger woman.

This jug was issued in 1986 in a limited edition of 9,500 pieces.

Designer: Michael Abberley
Handle: Napoleon: French Flag
Josephine: A fan and mirror
Colourway: Black, white, yellow and brown
Backstamp: Doulton

Doulton Number	Size	Backstamp	Height	Intro.	Discon.	Current Market Value		
						U.K. £	U.S. $	Can. $
D6750	Large	Doulton	7"	1986	Ltd. ed.	100.00	200.00	200.00

NAPOLEON AND WELLINGTON

These jugs were issued to commemorate the 180th anniversary of the Battle of Waterloo. The pair were commissioned by Lawleys By Post and issued in a limited edition of 2,500 sets.

For the character jug Duke of Wellington see page 224.

STYLE TWO: NAPOLEON: HANDLE — CROWN AND SCROLLS

Designer: William K. Harper	**Backstamp:** Doulton
Handles: Gold emblazoned crown atop scrolls showing the names of famous battles	
Colourway: Napoleon — Blue and white uniform; yellow and white handle	
Wellington — Red and gold uniform; yellow and white handle	

Doulton Number	Name	Height	Intro.	Discon.	Current Market Value		
					U.K. £	**U.S. $**	**Can. $**
D7001	Napoleon	4"	1995	Ltd. ed.	100.00	200.00	250.00
D7002	Wellington	4"	1995	Ltd. ed.	100.00	200.00	250.00
	Pair				200.00	400.00	500.00

NELSON

ROYAL DOULTON INTERNATIONAL COLLECTORS CLUB SERIES

Issued by the Royal Doulton International Collectors Club, the Nelson jug was available only to their members from 1994 to March 1995.

For the character jug Lord Nelson see page 345, and for the character jug Vice-Admiral Lord Nelson see page 515.

Designer: Warren Platt	**Backstamp:** Doulton/RDICC
Handle: The naval ensign	
Colourway: Black, white, red and gold	

Doulton Number	Size	Backstamp	Height	Intro.	Discon.	Current Market Value		
						U.K. £	**U.S. $**	**Can. $**
D—	Small	Doulton	4 ½"	1994	1995	85.00	175.00	200.00

NEPTUNE

In Roman mythology, Neptune is the god of the sea. According to legend Neptune married the sea nymph Amphitrite and together they had a son named Triton, who was half man and half fish.

Neptune
D 6552
COPR 1960
DOULTON & CO LIMITED
Rd No 897937
Rd No 40887
Rd No 8596
Rd No 547/60

Designer: Max Henk
Handle: Trident and fish
Colourway: Blue, grey and green

Backstamp: Doulton

Doulton Number	Size	Backstamp	Height	Intro.	Discon.	Current Market Value U.K. £	U.S. $	Can. $
D6548	Large	Doulton	6 ½"	1961	1991	75.00	135.00	150.00
D6552	Small	Doulton	3 ¾"	1961	1991	50.00	80.00	110.00
D6555	Miniature	Doulton	2 ½"	1961	1991	45.00	70.00	70.00

Note: This jug was also issued in English Translucent China. These jugs command a premium of 50 to 100% over the earthenware variety.

NIGHT WATCHMAN

CHARACTER JUGS FROM WILLIAMSBURG
ONE OF EIGHT

Character Jugs from Williamsburg
Night Watchman
D 6569
COPR 1962
DOULTON & CO LIMITED
Rd No 906339
Rd No 43446
Rd No 9225
Rd No 285/62

Designer: Max Henk
Handle: Lantern
Colourway: Black-purple tricorn and cloak

Backstamp: Doulton

Doulton Number	Size	Backstamp	Height	Intro.	Discon.	Current Market Value U.K. £	U.S. $	Can. $
D6569	Large	Doulton	7"	1963	1983	100.00	175.00	200.00
D6576	Small	Doulton	3 ½"	1963	1983	65.00	110.00	150.00
D6583	Miniature	Doulton	2 ½"	1963	1983	50.00	95.00	100.00

Note: This jug was also issued in English Translucent China. These jugs command a premium of 50 to 100% over the earthenware variety.

NORTH AMERICAN INDIAN

The North American Indian is one of three jugs which received a special backstamp in 1967. The other two, the Lumberjack and the Trapper form a three-jug Canadian Centennial Series.

VARIATION No. 1: Colourway — Red, white and black feathers; yellow and white band; green robes

Backstamp A - Doulton

Backstamp B - Canadian Centennial Series

Backstamp C - Okoboji

Designer: Max Henk
Handle: A totem pole
Colourway: Red, white and black feathers; yellow and white band; green robes
Handle: Dark brown

Backstamps: A. Doulton
B. Doulton/Canadian Centenary/ Canadian Centennial Series 1867-1967 Available only in North America during 1967
C. Doulton/Okoboji 75 Anniversary 1973 Issued for the 75th anniversary of the Okoboji Trap Shooting Club. 180 jugs were presented at the annual pow-wow.

Doulton Number	Size	Backstamp	Height	Intro.	Discon.	Current Market Value U.K. £	U.S. $	Can. $
D6611	Large	A	7 ¾"	1967	1991	85.00	150.00	165.00
D6611	Large	B	7 ¾"	1967	1967	150.00	300.00	300.00
D6611	Large	C	7 ¾"	1973	1973	1,250.00	2,750.00	3,000.00
D6614	Small	A	4 ¼"	1967	1991	45.00	85.00	110.00
D6665	Miniature	A	2 ¾"	1981	1991	40.00	75.00	85.00

Note: This jug was also issued in English Translucent China. These jugs command a premium of 50 to 100% over the earthenware variety.

VARIATION No. 2: Colourway —Yellow, blue, white and black feathers; green and white band; orange robes
Handle — Light brown

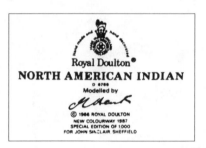

Backstamp: Doulton/John Sinclair
Commissioned by John Sinclair, Sheffield, England. Issued in 1987 in a special edition of 1,000 pieces

Doulton Number	Size	Backstamp	Height	Intro.	Discon.	Current Market Value U.K. £	U.S. $	Can. $
D—	Large	Doulton/Sinclair	7 ½"	1987	Sp. ed.	100.00	250.00	300.00
D—	Small	Doulton/Sinclair	4 ½"	1987	1987		Extremely Rare	
D—	Miniature	Doulton/Sinclair	2 ¾"	1987	1987		Extremely Rare	

Note: The small and miniature North American Indian jugs were sold at Sotheby's Arcade Auction, New York, on March 12, 1997. These two jugs carried the standard Royal Doulton backstamp plus the words "The property of Royal Doulton Tableware Ltd. Not produced for sale."

OLD CHARLEY

"Ten o'clock and all's well" was the familiar call of the Charlies, watchmen who originated during the reign of Charles II and were named after him. They enjoyed a history of almost two hundred years, before being replaced in the early 1800s by a version of the present-day policeman.

VARIATION No. 1: Colourway — Brown hat; dark green coat; blue polka-dot bow tie

Old Charley
D5420
DOULTON & CO. LIMITED

Backstamp A - Doulton

Backstamp B - Bentalls 1935   Backstamp C - Bentalls 1936

Designer: Charles Noke
Handle: Plain
Colourway: Brown hat; dark green coat; blue polka-dot bow tie

Backstamps: A. Doulton
B. Doulton/Bentalls/ Souvenir from Bentalls. Jubilee Year, 1935. Bentalls Ltd. is a London department store.
C. Doulton/Bentalls/ Souvenir from Bentalls. 1936.

Doulton Number	Size	Backstamp	Height	Intro.	Discon.	Current Market Value U.K. £	U.S. $	Can. $
D5420	Large	Doulton	5 ½"	1934	1983	75.00	125.00	125.00
D5527	Small	Doulton	3 ¼"	1935	1983	45.00	70.00	95.00
D5527	Small	Bentalls B	3 ¼"	1935	1935	500.00	900.00	1,100.00
D5527	Small	Bentalls C	3 ¼"	1936	1936	500.00	900.00	1,100.00
D6046	Miniature	Doulton	2 ¼"	1939	1983	30.00	65.00	70.00
D6144	Tiny	Doulton	1 ¼"	1940	1960	65.00	100.00	110.00

Note: 1. This jug was also issued in English Translucent China. These jugs command a premium of 50 to 100% over the earthenware variety.
2. Jugs exist without the polka-dots on the bow tie (colouring omission).

VARIATION No. 2: Colourway — Black hat; maroon coat; black polka-dot bow tie

Backstamp B

Backstamps: A. Doulton/Higbee/
Specially Commissioned from Royal Doulton by The Higbee Company
To Commemorate the First Anniversary of the Opening of the First Royal Doulton Room
Higbee's, Cleveland, Ohio, U.S.A.
Commissioned by the Higbee Department Store in 1985. Issued in 1986 in a limited edition of 250
pieces.

B. Doulton/Higbee/
Specially Commissioned from Royal Doulton by The Higbee Company
To Commemorate the Second Anniversary of the Opening of the First Royal Doulton Room
Higbee's, Cleveland, Ohio, U.S.A.
Commissioned by the Higbee Department Store and issued in a limited edition of 500 pieces.

Doulton Number	Size	Backstamp	Height	Intro.	Discon.	Current Market Value U.K. £	U.S. $	Can. $
D6761	Large	A. Higbee	5 ½"	1986	1986	325.00	350.00	400.00
D6791	Small	B. Higbee	3 ¼"	1987	1987	200.00	250.00	300.00

Old Charley Derivatives

Doulton Number	Item	Height	Intro.	Discon.	Current Market Value U.K. £	U.S. $	Can. $
D5227	Table lighter	3 ½"	1959	1973	150.00	175.00	175.00
D5844	Tobacco jar	5 ½"	1937	1960	900.00	1,750.00	2,000.00
D5858	Musical jug	5 ½"	1938	1939	525.00	1,100.00	1,100.00
D5599	Ashtray	2 ¾	1936	1960	85.00	150.00	175.00
D5925	Ash bowl	3"	1939	1960	85.00	150.00	175.00
D6012	Sugar bowl	2 ½"	1939	1960	450.00	800.00	800.00
D6017	Teapot	7"	1939	1960	1,000.00	1,900.00	2,000.00
D6110	Wall pocket	7 ¼"	1940	1960	1,000.00	1,750.00	2,000.00
D6152	Toothpick holder	2 ¼"	1940	1960	600.00	1,100.00	1,200.00

Note: The tune played on the musical jug is "Here's a Health Unto His Majesty."

OLD KING COLE

"Old King Cole was a merry old soul" are the words of the nursery rhyme that inspired the design of this jug. The collar frill was remodelled around 1939 and variation two can be found with both deep and shallow white ruff modellings.

VARIATION No. 1:   Colourway — Yellow crown; frills in the white ruff are deep and pronounced

Designer: Harry Fenton
Handle: Plain
Colourway: Yellow crown; frills in the white ruff are deep and pronounced

Backstamp: Doulton

Doulton Number	Size	Variation	Height	Intro.	Discon.	Current Market Value U.K. £	U.S. $	Can. $
D6036	Large	Var. 1	5 ½"	1938	1939	2,000.00	5,000.00	6,000.00
D6037	Small	Var. 1	3 ½"	1938	1939	1,500.00	3,500.00	4,000.00

VARIATION No. 2:   Colourway — Brown crown

Backstamps: A. Doulton
   B. Doulton/Royal Doulton International Collectors Club

Doulton Number	Size	Backstamp	Height	Intro.	Discon.	Current Market Value U.K. £	U.S. $	Can. $
D6036	Large	A	5 ¾"	1939	1960	200.00	325.00	350.00
D6037	Small	A	3 ½"	1939	1960	100.00	150.00	200.00
D6871	Tiny	B	1 ½"	1990	1990	125.00	175.00	200.00

Old King Cole Derivatives, Musical Jugs

Doulton Number	Variation	Height	Intro.	Discon.	Current Market Value U.K. £	U.S. $	Can. $
D —	Yellow crown	7 ½"	1939	1939	1,750.00	3,750.00	4,000.00
D6014	Brown crown	7 ½"	1939	1939	1,000.00	2,250.00	2,500.00

Note: 1. The tune played on the musical jugs is "Old King Cole was a Merry Old Soul."
   2. This jug was also issued in English Translucent China. These jugs command a premium of 50 to 100% over the earthenware variety.

OLD SALT

When the miniature Old Salt jug was launched in 1984, it had a hollow crook in the mermaid's arm. Later that year, because of production problems, the arm was moulded to the body. The first version of this miniature has attained near pilot status and commands a large premium over the general issue.

VARIATION No. 1:   Colourway — Dark blue fisherman's jersey
Handle — Mermaid has blue tail

Old Salt
D 6551
COPR 1960
DOULTON & CO LIMITED
Rd No 898030
Rd No 40938
Rd No 8616
Rd No 572/60

Designer: Gary Sharpe — Large and small
Peter Gee — Miniature
Handle: A mermaid
Colourway: Dark blue fisherman's jersey

Backstamp: Doulton

Doulton Number	Size	Variation	Height	Intro.	Discon.	Current Market Value U.K. £	U.S. $	Can. $
D6551	Large	Var. 1	7 ½"	1961	Current	70.00	165.00	230.00
D6554	Small	Var. 1	4"	1961	Current	35.00	90.00	130.00
D6557	Miniature	Open arm	2 ½"	1984	1984	800.00	1,400.00	1,600.00
D6557	Miniature	Closed arm	2 ½"	1984	1991	45.00	75.00	90.00

Note: This jug was also issued in English Translucent China. These jugs command a premium of 50 to 100% over the earthenware variety.

VARIATION No. 2: Colourway — Light and dark blue fisherman's jersey
Handle — Mermaid has yellow and black tail

Doulton Number	Size	Variation	Height	Intro.	Discon.	Current Market Value U.K. £	U.S. $	Can. $
D6782	Large	Var. 2	8"	1987	1990	100.00	200.00	250.00

Old Salt Derivative

Doulton Number	Item	Height	Intro.	Discon.	Current Market Value U.K. £	U.S. $	Can. $
D6818	Teapot	6 ¼"	1989	1989	135.00	275.00	300.00

OLIVER CROMWELL

This is a two-handled jug, with Colonel Fairfax and Charles I forming the handles. It was issued in a limited edition of 2,500 to celebrate the 350th Anniversary of the Battle of Marston Moor in 1644.

For the character jug Oliver Cromwell (style two) see Charles I and Oliver Cromwell page 184

STYLE ONE: LARGE-SIZE, TWO-HANDLED JUG

Designer: William K. Harper	**Backstamp:** Doulton
Handle: Colonel Fairfax and Charles I	
Colourways: Brown, cream, blue and black	

Doulton Number	Size	Backstamp	Height	Intro.	Discon.	Current Market Value U.K. £	U.S. $	Can. $
D6968	Large	Doulton	7"	1994	Ltd. ed.	225.00	400.00	475.00

OLIVER TWIST

For the character jug Oliver Twist see the "Charles Dickens Commemorative Set" page 185.

OTHELLO

THE SHAKESPEAREAN COLLECTION
ONE OF SIX

In Shakespeare's tragic play of 1604, Othello is a successful Venetian soldier who marries the attractive Desdemona. Out of spite and jealousy, his subordinate Iago convinces Othello that Desdemona has been unfaithful. Outraged, Othello kills her then commits suicide.

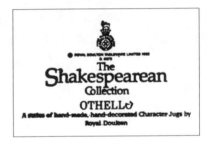

Designer: Michael Abberley
Handle: A figure of Iago
Colourway: Yellow turban; green, yellow and white robes

Backstamp: Doulton

Doulton Number	Size	Backstamp	Height	Intro.	Discon.	Current Market Value U.K. £	U.S. $	Can. $
D6673	Large	Doulton	7 ¼"	1982	1989	100.00	175.00	200.00

PADDY

Paddy, a colloquial term for an Irishman, is derived from St. Patrick, the country's patron saint. This gent is dressed in traditional green for St. Patrick's Day.

Designer: Harry Fenton
Handle: Plain
Colourway: Brown hat; green coat; yellow and red scarf

Backstamp: Doulton

Doulton Number	Size	Backstamp	Height	Intro.	Discon.	Current Market Value U.K. £	U.S. $	Can. $
D5753	Large	Doulton	6"	1937	1960	75.00	125.00	150.00
D5768	Small	Doulton	3 ¼"	1937	1960	40.00	75.00	100.00
D6042	Miniature	Doulton	2 ¼"	1939	1960	40.00	65.00	70.00
D6145	Tiny	Doulton	1 ¼"	1940	1960	65.00	100.00	110.00

Paddy Derivatives

Doulton Number	Item	Backstamp	Height	Intro.	Discon.	Current Market Value U.K. £	U.S. $	Can. $
D5845	Tobacco jar	Doulton	5 ½"	1939	1942	900.00	1,750.00	2,000.00
D5845	Tobacco jar	Salt River	5 ½"	1939	1942	1,000.00	2,000.00	2,250.00
D5845	Tobacco jar	Coleman's	5 ½"	1939	1942	900.00	1,750.00	2,000.00
D5887	Musical jug	Doulton	7"	1938	c..1939	525.00	1,100.00	1,200.00
D5926	Ash bowl	Doulton	3"	1938	1960	90.00	150.00	175.00
D6151	Toothpick holder	Doulton	2 ¼"	1940	1941	450.00	800.00	1,000.00

Note: The tune played on the musical jug is an Irish jig.

PARSON BROWN

For the tiny version of Parson Brown see the "Diamond Anniversary Set" page 214.

Backstamp C - Bentalls 1936

Backstamp D - Darley & Son

Designer: Charles Noke
Handle: Plain
Colourway: Dark grey

Backstamps: **A.** Doulton/Commissioned by Bentalls to celebrate Bentalls Jubilee Year 1935
B. Doulton/Bentalls/Souvenir from the silver jubilee of King George VI
C. Doulton/Bentalls/Souvenir from Bentalls. 1936.
D. Doulton/Darley/Souvenir from Darley & Son Sheffield & Rotherham

Doulton Number	Size	Backstamp	Height	Intro.	Discon.	Current Market Value U.K. £	U.S. $	Can. $
D5486	Large	Doulton	6 ½"	1935	1960	100.00	185.00	250.00
D5529	Small	Doulton	3 ¼"	1935	1960	50.00	90.00	125.00
D5529	Small	Bentalls/'35	3 ½"	1935	1935	450.00	800.00	1,000.00
D5529	Small	Bentalls/'36	3 ½"	1936	1936	450.00	800.00	1,000.00
D5529	Small	Doulton/Darley	3 ½"	1936	1936	450.00	800.00	1,000.00

Parson Brown Derivatives

Doulton Number	Size	Backstamp	Height	Intro.	Discon.	Current Market Value U.K. £	U.S. $	Can. $
D5600	Ashtray	Doulton	3 ½"	1936	1960	100.00	175.00	200.00
D6008	Ash bowl	Doulton	3"	1939	1960	100.00	175.00	200.00

Note: This jug was also issued in English Translucent China. These jugs command a premium of 50 to 100% over the earthenware variety.

PAUL McCARTNEY

THE BEATLES
ONE OF FOUR

Paul McCartney (b. 1942) was a singer, songwriter and the bass player with the Beatles, until they disbanded in 1970. He then performed with his own band, Wings, until 1981, and since then has remained active in the music field. This jug was issued only in Great Britain, due to copyright reasons.

Royal Doulton
THE BEATLES
Paul McCartney
D 6724
Modelled by
Stanley James Taylor.
© ROYAL DOULTON TABLEWARE
LIMITED 1984

Designer: Stanley J. Taylor
Handle: Plain
Colourway: Yellow tunic; blue collar and epaulettes

Backstamp: Doulton

Doulton Number	Size	Backstamp	Height	Intro.	Discon.	Current Market Value		
						U.K. £	U.S. $	Can. $
D6724	Mid	Doulton	5 ½"	1984	1991	90.00	225.00	225.00

PEARLY BOY

The Pearly Boy is a coster or costermonger, one who sells fruits and vegetables from a barrow in the streets of London. His finest attire consists of clothes covered in pearl buttons. 'Arry (page 132) is a costermonger without his buttons.

VARIATION No. 1:   Colourway — Brown hat with blue peak; blue coat; pearl buttons

Backstamp - A

Backstamp - B

Designer: Harry Fenton	**Backstamps:**	**A.** Doulton/Crown and lion
Handle: Plain		**B.** Doulton/'Arry and crown
Colourway: Brown hat with blue peak; blue coat; white buttons.		and lion

Doulton Number	Size	Variation	Height	Intro.	Discon.	Current Market Value U.K. £	U.S. $	Can. $
D —	Large	Var. 1	6 ½"	1947	Unknown	4,500.00	8,000.00	10,000.00
D —	Small	Var. 1	3 ½"	1947	Unknown	2,500.00	5,500.00	6,500.00
D —	Miniature	Var. 1	2 ½"	1947	Unknown	Extremely rare		

VARIATION No. 2:   Colourway — Brown hat and coat; pearl buttons

Doulton Number	Size	Variation	Height	Intro.	Discon.	Current Market Value U.K. £	U.S. $	Can. $
D —	Large	Var. 2	6 ½"	1947	Unknown	Extremely rare		
D —	Small	Var. 2	3 ½"	1947	Unknown	2,500.00	5,000.00	6,000.00
D —	Miniature	Var. 2	2 ½"	1947	Unknown	2,500.00	5,000.00	6,000.00

Variation No. 3

Variation No. 4

VARIATION No. 3: Colourway — Brown hat and coat; brown buttons

Doulton Number	Size	Variation	Height	Intro.	Discon.	Current Market Value		
						U.K. £	U.S. $	Can. $
D —	Large	Var. 3	6 ½"	1947	1947	1,250.00	2,500.00	2,750.00
D —	Small	Var. 3	3 ½"	1947	1947	550.00	1,200.00	1,400.00
D —	Miniature	Var. 3	2 ½"	1947	1947	450.00	1,000.00	1,200.00

VARIATION No. 4: Colourway — Beige hat; brown coat; pearl buttons

Doulton Number	Size	Variation	Height	Intro.	Discon.	Current Market Value		
						U.K. £	U.S. $	Can. $
D —	Large	Var. 4	6 ½"	1947	Unknown		Extremely rare	
D —	Small	Var. 4	3 ½"	1947	Unknown	2,500.00	5,000.00	6,000.00
D —	Miniature	Var. 4	2 ½"	1947	Unknown	2,500.00	5,000.00	6,000.00

PEARLY GIRL

Pearly Girl is the female counterpart of Pearly Boy. She was a costermonger who sold her produce in the streets of London. Pearly Girl is 'Arriet (page 131) dressed in her finest.

VARIATION No. 1: Colourway — Blue jacket; lime-green feather; maroon hat and button

Designer:	Harry Fenton
Handle:	Hat feather
Colourway:	Blue jacket; lime-green feather; maroon hat and button

Backstamp:	A. Doulton/Crown and lion
	B. Doulton/'Arriet and crown and lion

Doulton Number	Size	Variation	Height	Intro.	Discon.	Current Market Value U.K. £	U.S. $	Can. $
D —	Large	Var. 1	6 ½"	1946	Unknown	5,000.00	10,000.00	10,000.00
D —	Small	Var. 1	3 ¼"	1946	Unknown	2,500.00	4,750.00	5,000.00
D —	Miniature	Var. 1	2 ½"	1946	Unknown	Extremely rare		

VARIATION No. 2: Colourway — Dark brown jacket; lime-green feather; pink hat and button

Doulton Number	Size	Variation	Height	Intro.	Discon.	Current Market Value U.K. £	U.S. $	Can. $
D —	Large	Var. 2	6 ½"	1946	Unknown	Extremely rare		
D —	Small	Var. 2	3 ¼"	1946	Unknown	Extremely rare		

PEARLY KING

THE LONDON COLLECTION
ONE OF TEN

The Pearly King is the head spokesman for the street-market costers of London. Over a hundred years ago, his chief mandate was as a go-between for the costers and the London police. Today the Pearlies have turned their energy to raising money for charity.

Backstamp: Doulton

Designer: Stanley J. Taylor
Handle: The Bow Bells; pearl buttons
Colourway: Black cap and jacket with silver buttons; yellow scarf with red polka dots

Doulton Number	Size	Backstamp	Height	Intro.	Discon.	Current Market Value		
						U.K. £	U.S. $	Can. $
D6760	Large	Doulton	6 ¾"	1987	1991	100.00	200.00	225.00
D6844	Small	Doulton	3 ½"	1987	1991	55.00	125.00	150.00

PEARLY QUEEN

THE LONDON COLLECTION
ONE OF TEN

The Pearly Queen, like the Pearly King, is the chief spokesperson for the street-market costers of London. The office is both hereditary and elected.

Royal Doulton®
PEARLY QUEEN
D 6759
Modelled by
Stanley James Taylor.
© 1986 ROYAL DOULTON

Designer: Stanley J. Taylor
Handle: The Bow Bells and pink and blue feathers
Colourway: Black coat with silver buttons; black hat with white, pink and blue feathers

Backstamp: Doulton

Doulton Number	Size	Backstamp	Height	Intro.	Discon.	Current Market Value U.K. £	U.S. $	Can. $
D6759	Large	Doulton	7"	1987	1991	100.00	200.00	225.00
D6843	Small	Doulton	3 ½"	1987	1991	55.00	125.00	150.00

THE PENDLE WITCH

This jug was the first and only jug issued in the proposed series, Myths, Fantasies and Legends. It was commissioned and distributed by Kevin Francis Ceramics in 1989 in a special edition of 5,000 pieces.

Original Design and Concept by Alison Faulds of My Fair Lady

Royal Doulton®
THE PENDLE WITCH
D 6826
Modelled by
Stanley James Taylor.
A Special Edition of 5000
Produced by Royal Doulton
for Kevin Francis Ceramics
© 1988 ROYAL DOULTON
AND KEVIN FRANCIS CERAMICS

Designer: Stanley J. Taylor
Handle: A Hound
Colourway: Grey hair; black dress

Backstamp: Doulton

Doulton Number	Size	Backstamp	Height	Intro.	Discon.	Current Market Value U.K. £	U.S. $	Can. $
D6826	Large	Doulton	7 ¼"	1989	Sp. ed.	175.00	350.00	400.00

THE PHANTOM OF THE OPERA

Commissioned by Lawleys By Post to commemorate Gaston Leroux's 1910 novel *Le antome de L'Opera*, this jug was issued in a limited edition of 2,500.

Designer: David B. Biggs
Handle: A stage curtain and lantern
Colourway: Black, white, red and blue

Backstamp: Doulton

Doulton Number	Size	Backstamp	Height	Intro.	Discon.	Current Market Value		
						U.K. £	U.S. $	Can. $
D7017	Large	Doulton	7"	1995	Ltd. ed.	200.00	400.00	450.00

THE PHARAOH

FLAMBÉ SERIES
ONE OF THREE

This was the last flambé character jug to be produced by Royal Doulton at Stoke. The jug was issued in 1996 in a limited edition of 1,500.

Designer: Robert I. Tabbenor
Handle: The symbol ankh; Shawabtwy (funerary figure); Head of Anubis (jackal-god of mummification)
Colourway: Flambé

Backstamp: Doulton

Doulton Number	Size	Backstamp	Height	Intro.	Discon.	Current Market Value		
						U.K. £	U.S. $	Can. $
D7028	Large	Doulton	8"	1996	Ltd. ed.	400.00	800.00	900.00

PIED PIPER

PROTOTYPE

STYLE ONE: HANDLE — ONE WHITE RAT, FLUTE

Designer: Geoff Blower
Handle: White rat at the top of a dark brown flute
Colourway: Light brown hat; blond hair

Backstamp: Doulton

Doulton Number	Size	Variation	Height	Intro.	Discon.	Current Market Value		
						U.K. £	U.S. $	Can. $
D6403	Large	Prototype	7"		Unknown		Unique	

PIED PIPER

In German legend, a stranger came to the town of Hamelin and told the mayor he would rid the village of rats for a sum of money. The Pied Piper walked through town playing a flute, and the rats followed him to the Weser River, where they drowned. When the mayor refused to pay him, the Pied Piper played his flute again, and this time the village children followed him into a cave, never to be seen again.

STYLE TWO: HANDLE — THREE BROWN RATS, FLUTE

Pied Piper
D 6403
COPR 1953
DOULTON & CO LIMITED

Designer: Geoff Blower
Handle: Three brown rats atop a flute
Colourway: Green cap; maroon and yellow tunic

Backstamp: Doulton

Doulton Number	Size	Backstamp	Height	Intro.	Discon.	Current Market Value U.K. £	U.S. $	Can. $
D6403	Large	Doulton	7"	1954	1981	90.00	150.00	175.00
D6462	Small	Doulton	3 ¾"	1957	1981	50.00	95.00	110.00
D6514	Miniature	Doulton	2 5/8"	1960	1981	50.00	85.00	110.00

Note: This jug was also issued in English Translucent China. These jugs command a premium of 50 to 100% over the earthenware variety.

PIERRE ELLIOT TRUDEAU

PROTOTYPE

Joseph Philippe Pierre Yves Elliott Trudeau (b. 1919) became Canada's Minister of Justice and Attorney General in 1967. He was elected Prime Minister from 1968 to 1979 and from 1980 to 1984.

Doulton was unable to obtain permission to issue this jug.

Designer: William K. Harper
Handle: The Canadian flag
Colourway: Black and grey

Backstamp: Doulton

Doulton Number	Size	Variation	Height	Intro.	Discon.	U.K. £	Current Market Value U.S. $	Can. $
D —	Large	Prototype	7"	Unknown			Unique	

PILGRIM FATHER

PROTOTYPE

Designer: David Biggs
Handle: The Mayflower
Colourway: Black suit; white collar; brown and white ship

Backstamp: Doulton

Doulton Number	Size	Variation	Height	Intro.	Discon.	Current Market Value		
						U.K. £	U.S. $	Can. $
D —	Large	Prototype	8 ¼"	1969	1969		Unique	

THE PIPER

The Piper jug was issued in a limited edition of 2,500 pieces.

Royal Doulton®
THE PIPER
D 6918
Modelled by
Stanley James Taylor.
© 1992 ROYAL DOULTON
LIMITED EDITION OF 2,500
THIS IS N° 425

Designer: Stanley J. Taylor
Handle: Bagpipes
Colourway: Black, red, white and yellow

Backstamp: Doulton

Doulton Number	Size	Backstamp	Height	Intro.	Discon.	Current Market Value		
						U.K. £	U.S. $	Can. $
D6918	Large	Doulton	8 ¼"	1992	Ltd. ed.	200.00	400.00	450.00

PLUG OF THE BASH STREET KIDS

To celebrate the 60th anniversary of the Dandy and Beano comics in 1998, a special anniversary logo appeared on the base of the jug for that year.

Designer: Simon Ward
Handle: Banana, arrows and quiver
Colourways: Red, yellow and brown

Backstamp: A. Doulton/
     © D.C. Thomson & Co., Ltd.
    B. 60th Anniversary logo

Doulton Number	Size	Backstamp	Height	Intro.	Discon.	Current Market Value		
						U.K. £	U.S. $	Can. $
D7035	Small	A. Doulton	4 ½"	1996	1999	55.00	125.00	150.00
D7035	Small	B. 60th Anniv.	4 ½"	1998	1998	55.00	125.00	150.00

THE POACHER

VARIATION No. 1: Colourway — Green coat; red scarf; light brown hat

Designer: Max Henk
Handle: A salmon
Colourway: Green coat; red scarf; light brown hat

Backstamp: Doulton

"The Poacher"
D 6429
COPR 1954
DOULTON & CO LIMITED
Rd No 875201
Rd No 33325
Rd No 7095
Rd No 321/54

Doulton Number	Size	Variation	Height	Intro.	Discon.	Current Market Value U.K. £	U.S. $	Can. $
D6429	Large	Var. 1	7"	1955	1995	60.00	125.00	150.00
D6464	Small	Var. 1	4"	1957	1995	45.00	70.00	90.00
D6515	Miniature	Var. 1	2 ½"	1960	1991	45.00	60.00	70.00

Note: This jug was also issued in English Translucent China. These jugs command a premium of 50 to 100% over the earthenware variety.

VARIATION No 2:   Colourway — Maroon coat; yellow striped scarf; black hat

Doulton Number	Size	Variation	Height	Intro.	Discon.	Current Market Value		
						U.K. £	U.S. $	Can. $
D6781	Large	Var. 2	7"	1987	1989	100.00	200.00	250.00

The Poacher Derivative

Doulton Number	Item	Height	Intro.	Discon.	Current Market Value		
					U.K. £	U.S. $	Can. $
D6464	Table lighter	4 ¾"	c. 1960	1973	135.00	200.00	250.00

THE POLICEMAN

JOURNEY THROUGH BRITAIN
ONE OF FOUR

The Policeman was commissioned by Lawleys By Post and issued in 1989 in a limited edition of 5,000 pieces. The Doulton backstamp is set within the design of a policeman's badge.

Designer: Stanley J. Taylor
Handle: Handcuffs and truncheon
Colourway: Black and white

Backstamp: Doulton

Doulton Number	Size	Backstamp	Height	Intro.	Discon.	Current Market Value		
						U.K. £	U.S. $	Can. $
D6852	Small	Doulton	4"	1989	Ltd. ed.	100.00	250.00	300.00

PORTHOS

THE THREE MUSKETEERS, ONE OF FOUR
NOW PART OF THE CHARACTERS FROM LITERATURE, ONE OF 11

One of the much-loved three musketeers in the 1844 novel by Alexandre Dumas, Porthos roamed Europe with his merry band in search of adventure. "One of the Three Musketeers" was included in the early backstamp to indicate that Porthos was one of the famous Musketeers.

VARIATION No. 1:   Colourway — Black hat; red cloak; black hair and moustache

Backstamp A - Doulton

Backstamp B -
Doulton/"One of"

Designer: Max Henk
Handle: A sword
Colourway: Black hat; red cloak; black hair and moustache

Backstamps: **A.** Doulton
B. Doulton/
(One of the "Three Musketeers")

Doulton Number	Size	Backstamp	Height	Intro.	Discon.	Current Market Value		
						U.K. £	U.S. $	Can. $
D6440	Large	Doulton	7 ¼"	1956	1991	85.00	100.00	110.00
D6440	Large	Doulton/One...	7 ¼"	1956	1970	85.00	110.00	125.00
D6453	Small	Doulton	4"	1956	1991	75.00	65.00	80.00
D6453	Small	Doulton/One...	4"	1956	1970	75.00	75.00	90.00
D6516	Miniature	Doulton	2 ¾"	1960	1991	40.00	70.00	75.00
D6516	Miniature	Doulton/One...	2 ½"	1960	1970	40.00	70.00	75.00

Note: This jug was also issued in English Translucent China. These jugs command a premium of 50 to 100% over the earthenware variety.

VARIATION No. 2:   Colourway — Maroon hat; blue cloak; ginger hair and moustache

Backstamp: Doulton/Peter Jones China Ltd.
Commissioned by Peter Jones China Ltd., Sheffield, England.
Issued in 1988 in a limited edition of 1,000 pieces.

Doulton Number	Size	Backstamp	Height	Intro.	Discon.	Current Market Value U.K. £	U.S. $	Can. $
D6828	Large	Doulton	7 ¼"	1988	1988	100.00	225.00	250.00

Porthos Derivative

Doulton Number	Item	Height	Intro.	Discon.	Current Market Value U.K. £	U.S. $	Can. $
D6453	Table lighter	3 ½"	1958	Unknown	425.00	800.00	500.00

THE POSTMAN

JOURNEY THROUGH BRITAIN
ONE OF FOUR

The Postman was commissioned by Lawleys By Post and issued in 1988 in a limited edition of 5,000 pieces. The Doulton backstamp is set within the design of a postage stamp.

Designer: Stanley J. Taylor
Handle: A pillar box
Colourway: Black jacket and cap; white shirt; red pillar box

Backstamp: Doulton

Doulton Number	Size	Backstamp	Height	Intro.	Discon.	Current Market Value		
						U.K. £	U.S. $	Can. $
D6801	Small	Doulton	4"	1988	Ltd. ed.	150.00	325.00	375.00

PUNCH AND JUDY

ROYAL DOULTON INTERNATIONAL COLLECTORS CLUB SERIES

This two-faced jug was created exclusively for the Royal Doulton International Collectors Club, in a limited edition of 2,500.

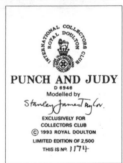

PUNCH AND JUDY
D 6946
Modelled by
Stanley James Taylor
EXCLUSIVELY FOR
COLLECTORS CLUB
© 1993 ROYAL DOULTON
LIMITED EDITION OF 2,500
THIS IS No. 1174

Designer: Stanley J. Taylor
Handle: Punch — dog; Judy — crocodile
Colourway: Red, yellow, blue, white and green

Backstamp: Doulton/RDICC

Doulton Number	Size	Backstamp	Height	Intro.	Discon.	Current Market Value U.K. £	U.S. $	Can. $
D6946	Large	Doulton/RDICC	7"	1994	Ltd. ed.	325.00	450.00	450.00

PUNCH AND JUDY MAN

Coming to England in the 17th century by way of Italy and France, the Punch and Judy puppet show features Punch, the hunchbacked boastful husband, who beats his shrew-like wife Judy.

The colours on Punch's bat are occasionally reversed with no effect on the market value.

Punch & Judy Man
D 6590
COPR 1963
DOULTON & CO LIMITED
Rd No 9 1 3 1 3 8
Rd No 4 5 3 5 8
Rd No 9 6 8 3
Rd No 8 1 3 / 6 3

Designer: David Biggs
Handle: Punch
Colourway: Brown hat; green coat; yellow scarf

Backstamp: Doulton

Doulton Number	Size	Backstamp	Height	Intro.	Discon.	Current Market Value		
						U.K. £	U.S. $	Can. $
D6590	Large	Doulton	7"	1964	1969	450.00	925.00	1,100.00
D6593	Small	Doulton	3 ½"	1964	1969	300.00	600.00	700.00
D6596	Miniature	Doulton	2 ½"	1964	1969	275.00	600.00	700.00

Note: This jug was also issued in English Translucent China. These jugs command a premium of 50 to 100% over the earthenware variety.

QUASIMODO

Quasimodo was the hunchback featured in Victor Hugo's 1831 novel *Notre Dame de Paris*. The handle represents the belfry of the Notre Dame Cathedral, and the bell it was his job to ring, even as his heart yearned in vain for the beautiful gypsy girl. This jug was issued by Lawleys By Post in a limited edition of 2,500 pieces.

Designer: David B. Biggs
Handle: Cathedral belefry and bell
Colourway: Green, orange and tan

Backstamp: Doulton

Doulton Number	Size	Backstamp	Height	Intro.	Discon.	Current Market Value		
						U.K. £	U.S. $	Can. $
D7108	Large	Doulton	7"	1997	Ltd. ed.	100.00	250.00	350.00

QUEEN ELIZABETH I *and* KING PHILIP OF SPAIN

Daughter of Anne Boleyn, the second wife of Henry VIII, Elizabeth (1533-1603) enjoyed a 45 year reign. With the leadership of Sir Francis Drake, her Royal Navy defeated the Spanish Armada and Philip's attempted invasion of England. Issued by Lawleys By Post in 1988, this jug was one of a pair (with King Philip of Spain) that was produced to celebrate the 400th anniversary of the defeat of the Spanish Armada in 1588. Both jugs were issued in limited editions of 9,500 pieces.

For Elizabeth I see the "Kings and Queens of the Realm Set" page 328.

Designer: William K. Harper	**Backstamp:** Doulton
Handle: Warship	
Colourway: Grey, dark red and white	

Doulton Number	Size	Backstamp	Height	Intro.	Discon.	Current Market Value		
						U.K. £	**U.S. $**	**Can. $**
D6821	Queen Elizabeth I		4"	1988	Ltd. ed.	100.00	175.00	200.00
D6822	King Philip of Spain		4"	1988	Ltd. ed.	100.00	175.00	200.00
	Pair					200.00	350.00	400.00

QUEEN VICTORIA

Alexandrina Victoria (1819-1901) succeeded her uncle William IV to the throne on her eighteenth birthday in 1837. Reigning until her death in 1901, she had a longer rule than any other British monarch, and her reign became known as one of the most peaceful in English history.

For Victoria see the "Kings and Queens of the Realm Set" page 328.

STYLE ONE: HANDLE — SCEPTRE

VARIATION No. 1: Colourway — Dark blue and yellow crown; beige and pink veil

Backstamp A - Large Size Jug

Backstamp B - Small Size Jug

Designer:	Stanley J. Taylor
Handle:	Yellow sceptre
Colourway:	Dark blue and yellow crown; beige and pink veils; yellow jewel in sceptre

Backstamps: **A.** Doulton
B. Special Limited Edition of 1500
The small size jug was commissioned by
Pascoe & Co. in a special edition of 1,500.

Doulton Number	Size	Backstamp	Height	Intro.	Discon.	Current Market Value U.K. £	U.S. $	Can. $
D6816	Large	Doulton	7 ¼"	1989	1991	100.00	250.00	275.00
D6913	Small	Doulton	3 ½"	1992	Sp. ed.	75.00	200.00	225.00

VARIATION No. 2:   Colourway — Purple and yellow crown; grey veil with white frills; red jewel in sceptre

Backstamp: The Guild of Specialist China & Glass Retailers
Commissioned by the Guild of Specialist China & Glass Retailers in 1988 and issued in a special edition of 3,000 pieces.

Doulton Number	Size	Backstamp	Height	Intro.	Discon.	Current Market Value U.K. £	U.S. $	Can. $
D6788	Large	Doulton	7 ¼"	1988	Sp. ed.	100.00	250.00	300.00

QUEEN VICTORIA and PRINCE ALBERT

Issued in 1997 by Lawleys by Post in a limited edition of 2,500 pairs, these character jugs commemorate the marriage of Victoria and Albert in 1840.

STYLE TWO: QUEEN VICTORIA: HANDLE — UNION JACK AND CROWN

Designer:	William K. Harper	**Backstamp:** Doulton
Handle:	Victoria — Union Jack and crown	
	Albert — The Great Exhibition of 1851 banner	
Colourway:	Victoria — Brown, red, white, blue and yellow	
	Albert — Black, red, yellow and white	

Doulton Number	Name	Height	Intro.	Discon.	Current Market Value U.K. £	Current Market Value U.S. $	Current Market Value Can. $
D7072	Queen Victoria	4"	1997	Ltd. ed.	65.00	175.00	200.00
D7073	Prince Albert	4"	1997	Ltd. ed.	65.00	175.00	200.00
	Pair				125.00	350.00	400.00

RANGERS (FOOTBALL CLUB)

THE FOOTBALL SUPPORTERS
ONE OF TEN

Royal Doulton®
FOOTBALL SUPPORTER'S
CHARACTER JUG.
D 6929
Modelled by
Stanley James Taylor
© 1992 ROYAL DOULTON
"RANGERS"

Designer: Stanley J. Taylor   **Backstamp:** Doulton
Handle: Team coloured scarf
Colourway: Blue, white and red uniform

Doulton Number	Size	Backstamp	Height	Intro.	Discon.	Current Market Value U.K. £	U.S. $	Can. $
D6929	Mid	Doulton	5"	1992	Unknown	50.00	110.00	125.00

THE RED QUEEN

ALICE IN WONDERLAND
ONE OF SIX

A character from Lewis Carroll's *Alice's Adventures in Wonderland,* the Queen of Hearts shows her suit on the blade of an axe and cries, "Off with his head." Issued in 1987, it was the first in the Alice in Wonderland series.

Designer: William K. Harper
Handle: An axe
Colourway: Yellow, red and blue

Backstamp: Doulton

Doulton Number	Size	Backstamp	Height	Intro.	Discon.	Current Market Value U.K. £	U.S. $	Can. $
D6777	Large	Doulton	7 ¼"	1987	1991	100.00	200.00	250.00
D6859	Small	Doulton	3"	1990	1991	75.00	175.00	200.00
D6860	Miniature	Doulton	2"	1990	1991	55.00	175.00	200.00

REGENCY BEAU

The regency of the Prince of Wales lasted from 1811 to 1820, when the Prince became George IV. The Regency Period, however, is a term loosely applied to the years from 1805 to 1830, when classical mythology and Greek and Roman authors were popular.

Regency Beau
D 6559
COPR 1961
DOULTON & CO LIMITED
Rd No 902090
Rd No 42142
Rd No 8925
Rd No R84/6'

Designer: David Biggs
Handle: Cane and handkerchief
Colourway: Green coat; green and yellow hat

Backstamp: Doulton

Doulton Number	Size	Backstamp	Height	Intro.	Discon.	Current Market Value U.K. £	U.S. $	Can. $
D6559	Large	Doulton	7 ¼"	1962	1967	650.00	1,500.00	1,750.00
D6562	Small	Doulton	4 ¼"	1962	1967	450.00	1,000.00	1,200.00
D6565	Miniature	Doulton	2 ¾"	1962	1967	550.00	1,400.00	1,600.00

Note: This jug was also issued in English Translucent China. These jugs command a premium of 50 to 100% over the earthenware variety.

RICHARD III and KING JOHN

ROYAL DOULTON INTERNATIONAL COLLECTORS CLUB SERIES

These companion piece jugs, issued in a limited edition of 1,500 each, were available exclusively through the Royal Doulton International Collectors Club. Richard II was introduced in 1998, with Merlin being introduced in 1999.

Designer:	Robert Tabbenor	**Backstamp:** Doulton/RDICC
Handle:	Richard III — Tower and boar	
	King John — Magna Carta manuscript, sack of taxes	
Colourway:	Richard III — Navy, brown, black and red	
	King John — Brown, yellow, green, red and blue	

Doulton Number	Size	Backstamp	Height	Intro.	Discon.	Current Market Value U.K. £	U.S. $	Can. $
D7099	Richard III	Doulton/RDICC	7"	1998	Ltd. ed.	150.00	310.00	410.00
D7125	King John	Doulton/RDICC	7 ¼"	1999	Lrd. ed.	150.00	310.00	410.00

THE RING MASTER

THE CIRCUS
ONE OF FOUR

Backstamp A - Doulton

Backstamp B - Doulton/ Maple
Leaf Edition

Designer: Stanley J. Taylor
Handle: Horse's head and plume
Colourway: Black top hat with a light blue ribbon; red jacket;
black lapel; green plume atop horses head

Backstamps: **A.** Doulton
For general release, 1991.
B. Doulton/The Maple Leaf Edition/The International Royal Doulton Collectors
Weekend 1990. Toronto, Ontario, Canada/The Maple Leaf Edition
Commissioned to commemorate the International Royal Doulton Collectors Weekend,
September 14, 15 and 16, 1990. The design incorporates a red maple leaf in honour of the
25th anniversary of Canada's flag. Issued with a certificate of authenticity.
Pre-released in 1990 in a special edition of 750 pieces.

Doulton Number	Size	Backstamp	Height	Intro.	Discon.	Current Market Value U.K. £	U.S. $	Can. $
D6863	Large	Doulton	7 ½"	1991	1993	100.00	225.00	250.00
D6863	Large	Doulton/Maple	7 ½"	1990	Sp. ed.	175.00	275.00	300.00

RINGO STARR

THE BEATLES
ONE OF FOUR

Richard Starkey (b. 1940) was the drummer for the Beatles until they disbanded in 1970.

Royal Doulton
THE BEATLES
Ringo Starr
D 6726
Modelled by

© ROYAL DOULTON TABLEWARE
LIMITED 1984

Designer: Stanley J. Taylor
Handle: Plain
Colourway: Black tunic; yellow collar and epaulettes

Backstamp: Doulton

Doulton Number	Size	Backstamp	Height	Intro.	Discon.	Current Market Value U.K. £	U.S. $	Can. $
D6726	Mid	Doulton	5 ½"	1984	1991	125.00	275.00	300.00

RIP VAN WINKLE

CHARACTERS FROM LITERATURE
ONE OF 11

In 1820, the American writer Washington Irving wrote the story of Rip Van Winkle, based on legends he had heard from Dutch settlers. While walking in the Catskill Mountains of New York, Rip drinks a fairy potion and falls asleep for 20 years. He wakes to find an unrecognizable world.

VARIATION No. 1: Colourway — Grey-blue cap; brown robes; figure dressed in blue resting against tree

"Rip Van Winkle".
D.6438.
COPR.1954.
DOULTON & CO.LIMITED.
R⁴N° 874255.
R⁴N° 32854.
R⁴N° 7022.
R⁴N° 193/54.

Designer:	Geoff Blower
Handle:	A man resting against the trunk of a tree, with a blackbird sitting atop it
Colourway:	Grey-blue cap; brown robes; figure dressed in blue resting against tree

Backstamp: Doulton

Doulton Number	Size	Backstamp	Height	Intro.	Discon.	Current Market Value U.K. £	U.S. $	Can. $
D6438	Large	Doulton	6 ½"	1955	1995	65.00	125.00	150.00
D6463	Small	Doulton	4"	1957	1995	40.00	75.00	90.00
D6517	Miniature	Doulton	2 ½"	1960	1991	35.00	65.00	70.00

Note: This jug was also issued in English Translucent China. These jugs command a premium of 50 to 100% over the earthenware variety.

VARIATION No. 2: Colourway — Black cap; green robes; figure dressed in black resting against tree

Backstamp: Doulton/John Sinclair
Commissioned by John Sinclair, Sheffield, England. Issued in 1987 in a special edition of 1,000 pieces.

Doulton Number	Size	Backstamp	Height	Intro.	Discon.	Current Market Value		
						U.K. £	U.S. $	Can. $
D6785	Large	Doulton/Sinclair	7"	1987	Sp. ed.	100.00	200.00	275.00

Rip Van Winkle Derivative

Doulton Number	Item	Height	Intro.	Discon.	Current Market Value		
					U.K. £	U.S. $	Can. $
D6463	Table lighter	3 ½"	1958	Unknown	500.00	850.00	1,000.00

ROBIN HOOD

PROTOTYPE

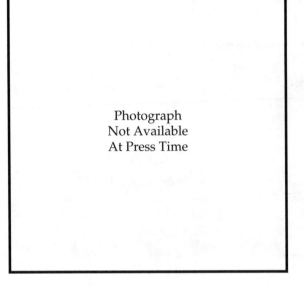

Photograph
Not Available
At Press Time

Designer: Eric Griffiths   **Backstamp:** Doulton
Handle: Plain
Colourway: Black, brown and green

Doulton Number	Size	Variation	Height	Intro.	Discon.	Current Market Value U.K. £	U.S. $	Can. $
D —	Large	Prototype	6 ½"	1987	1987		Unique	

ROBIN HOOD

A legendary figure from the reign of Richard I in 12th-century England, Robin Hood and his group of benevolent bandits had many adventures while robbing the rich to help the poor.

STYLE ONE: HAT WITH NO FEATHER
HANDLE — PLAIN

Designer: Harry Fenton
Handle: Two feathers
Colourway: Brown hat; green robes

Backstamp: Doulton

Doulton Number	Size	Backstamp	Height	Intro.	Discon.	Current Market Value		
						U.K. £	U.S. $	Can. $
D6205	Large	Doulton	6 ¼"	1947	1960	100.00	200.00	225.00
D6234	Small	Doulton	3 ¼"	1947	1960	60.00	100.00	125.00
D6252	Miniature	Doulton	2 ¼"	1947	1960	50.00	85.00	100.00

Note: This jug was also issued in English Translucent China. These jugs command a premium of 50 to 100% over the earthenware variety.

ROBIN HOOD

CHARACTERS FROM LITERATURE
ONE OF 11

STYLE TWO: HAT WITH FEATHER
HANDLE — BOW, QUIVER AND ARROWS

Backstamp - Large Size Jug

Backstamp - Miniature Size
Jug

Designer:	Max Henk
Handle:	Bow and quiver of arrows
Colourway:	Brown hat with white feather on one side and oak leaves and acorns on the other; green robes
Backstamp:	Doulton

Doulton Number	Size	Backstamp	Height	Intro.	Discon.	Current Market Value		
						U.K. £	U.S. $	Can. $
D6527	Large	Doulton	7 ½"	1960	1992	80.00	150.00	150.00
D6534	Small	Doulton	4"	1960	1992	45.00	80.00	100.00
D6541	Miniature	Doulton	2 ¾"	1960	1991	40.00	75.00	80.00

Note: This jug was also issued in English Translucent China. These jugs command a premium of 50 to 100% over the earthenware variety.

ROBIN HOOD

Style three was issued in a limited edition of 2,500.

STYLE THREE: HANDLE — FIGURES OF MAID MARION, FRIAR TUCK,
LITTLE JOHN AND THE SHERIFF OF NOTTINGHAM

Royal Doulton®
ROBIN HOOD
D 6998
Modelled by
William K. Harper
© 1995 ROYAL DOULTON
LIMITED EDITION OF 2,500
THIS IS N° 101

Designer: William K. Harper
Handle: Figures of Maid Marion, Friar Tuck
Little John and the Sheriff of Nottingham
Colourway: Green hat and tunic collar with brown

Backstamp: Doulton

Doulton Number	Size	Backstamp	Height	Intro.	Discon.	Current Market Value		
						U.K. £	U.S. $	Can. $
D6998	Large	Doulton	7"	1995	Ltd. ed.	275.00	550.00	800.00

ROBINSON CRUSOE

In 1719, Daniel Defoe wrote *Robinson Crusoe*, based on the experiences of Alexander Selkirk, who was marooned on a deserted Pacific island for five years.

VARIATION No. 1: Without footprint on shoulder

Variation No. 2 - Footprint on shoulder

Designer: Max Henk
Handle: The man Friday peers from behind a palm tree
Colourway: Brown and green

Backstamp: Doulton

Doulton Number	Size	Backstamp	Height	Intro.	Discon.	Current Market Value U.K. £	U.S. $	Can. $
D6532	Large	Doulton	7 ½"	1960	1982	75.00	150.00	175.00
D6539	Small	Doulton	4"	1960	1982	50.00	75.00	100.00
D6546	Miniature	Doulton	2 ¾"	1960	1982	45.00	70.00	100.00

VARIATION No. 2: With footprint on shoulder

Doulton Number	Size	Backstamp	Height	Intro.	Discon.	Current Market Value U.K. £	U.S. $	Can. $
D6532	Large	Doulton	7 ½"	1960	1982	100.00	175.00	200.00
D6539	Small	Doulton	4"	1960	1982	55.00	90.00	115.00
D6546	Miniature	Doulton	2 ¾"	1960	1982	50.00	85.00	110.00

Note: This jug was also issued in English Translucent China. These jugs command a premium of 50 to 100% over the earthenware variety.

ROMEO

PROTOTYPE

STYLE ONE: HANDLE — A VIAL OF POISON SPILLS OVER A DAGGER BELOW

Designer: David Biggs
Handle: A vial of poison spills over a dagger below
Colourway: Brown and white

Backstamp: Doulton

Doulton Number	Size	Variation	Height	Intro.	Discon.	Current Market Value		
						U.K. £	U.S. $	Can. $
D6670	Large	Prototype	7"	1981	1981	Extremely rare		

ROMEO

THE SHAKESPEAREAN COLLECTION
ONE OF SIX

The hero of Shakespeare's 1596 romantic play, Romeo falls in love with Juliet, the daughter of a Verona family feuding with his own. The lives of these two clandestine lovers end tragically and, with bitter irony, cause the reconciliation of the two families.

STYLE TWO: HANDLE — A DAGGER SUPERIMPOSED ON THE COLUMN SUPPORTING A BALCONY

Designer: David Biggs
Handle: A dagger superimposed on the column supporting a balcony
Colourway: Brown and white

Backstamp: Doulton

Doulton Number	Size	Backstamp	Height	Intro.	Discon.	Current Market Value		
						U.K. £	**U.S. $**	**Can. $**
D6670	Large	Doulton	7 ½"	1983	1989	75.00	125.00	150.00

RONALD REAGAN

PROTOTYPE

STYLE ONE: THE U.S. FLAG WITH GREEN CORD AND NO CAP

Photograph
Not Available
At Press Time

Designer: Eric Griffiths   **Backstamp:** Doulton
Handle: The U.S. flag with green cord, no cap
Colourway: Blue grey suit; dark blue tie

Doulton Number	Size	Variation	Height	Intro.	Discon.	U.K. £	U.S. $	Can. $
						Current Market Value		
D6718	Large	Prototype	7 ¾"	1984	1984		Unique	

RONALD REAGAN

Ronald Wilson Reagan (b. 1911) began as an Iowa sports announcer, then worked as a movie actor for 30 years. In 1966 Reagan was elected governor of California, then he became President of the United States in 1980 and served two terms until 1988.

This jug was commissioned for the Republican National Committee. Originally planned as a limited edition of 5,000 pieces, the jug did not sell well and only 2,000 pieces were said to have been produced. It was issued with a certificate and photograph of President Reagan in a decorative folio.

STYLE TWO: THE U.S. FLAG WITH YELLOW CORD AND GOLD CAP

THE PRESIDENT'S SIGNATURE EDITION
1984 PRESIDENTIAL ELECTION

Ronald Reagan

D 6718
Royal Doulton
Worldwide Limited Edition of 5000
This is number 1166.
© Royal Doulton Tableware Ltd. 1984

Designer: Eric Griffiths
Handle: The U.S. flag with yellow cord, gold cap
Colourway: Dark blue suit; white shirt; purple striped tie

Backstamp: Doulton/Reagan

Doulton Number	Size	Backstamp	Height	Intro.	Discon.	Current Market Value		
						U.K. £	U.S. $	Can. $
D6718	Large	Doulton/Reagan	7 ¾"	1984	Ltd. ed.	425.00	850.00	1,000.00

RONNIE CORBETT O.B.E. and RONNIE BARKER O.B.E.
(THE TWO RONNIES)

Ronnie Corbett and Ronnie Barker, the comic duo whose television show, The Two Ronnies, enthralled viewers for seventeen years, gain enduring recognition in this companion pair of character jugs, issued in a limited edition of 5,000. This jug was commissioned by Lawleys By Post.

Designer: David B. Biggs
Handle: Scripts: Ronnie Corbett "It's goodnight from me."
Ronnie Barker "And it's goodnight form him."
Colourway: Ronnie Corbett — Browns, red and black
Ronnie Barker — Grey, blue and black

Backstamp: Doulton

Doulton Number	Name	Size	Height	Intro.	Discon.	U.K. £	U.S. $	Can. $
						Current Market Value		
D7113	R. Corbett	Small	4"	1998	Ltd. ed.	125.00	—	—
D7114	R. Barker	Small	4 ½"	1998	Ltd. ed.	Pair		

THE SAILOR

THE ARMED FORCES
ONE OF THREE

STYLE ONE: HANDLE — BINOCULARS

Variation No. 1: Without "R.C.N." on Binoculars

Designer: William K. Harper	**Backstamp:** Doulton
Handle: Binoculars	
Colourway: White Royal Navy cap; light brown coat; white sweater	

Doulton Number	Size	Backstamp	Height	Intro.	Discon.	Current Market Value U.K. £	U.S. $	Can. $
D6875	Small	Doulton	4 ½"	1991	1996	45.00	100.00	125.00

THE SAILOR

THE CANADIANS
ONE OF THREE

The Sailor was commissioned by The British Toby in a limited edition of 250 pieces. The set sold originally for $465.00 Canadian.

STYLE ONE: HANDLE — BINOCULARS

Variation No. 2: With "R.C.N." on Binoculars

Designer: William K. Harper
Handle: R.C.N. binoculars
Colourway: White Royal Canadian Navy cap; dark brown coat; white sweater

Backstamp: Doulton

Doulton Number	Size	Backstamp	Height	Intro.	Discon.	Current Market Value U.K. £	U.S. $	Can. $
D6904	Small	Doulton/British	4 ½"	1991	Ltd. ed.	150.00	300.00	350.00

THE SAILOR

NATIONAL SERVICE EDITION
ONE OF THREE

Commissioned by Lawleys By Post, it was possible to have a National Service number incorporated within the accompanying certificate.

STYLE TWO: HANDLE — AN ANCHOR

NATIONAL SERVICE EDITION

Royal Doulton®
THE SAILOR
D 6984
Modelled by

William K. Harper.

© 1990 ROYAL DOULTON

Designer: William K. Harper
Handle: Anchor
Colourway: White, black, brown and gold

Backstamp: Doulton

Doulton Number	Size	Backstamp	Height	Intro.	Discon.	Current Market Value U.K. £	U.S. $	Can. $
D6984	Small	Doulton	4 ½"	1994	Sp. ed.	50.00	125.00	150.00

SAIREY GAMP

In Charles Dickens' 1843 novel, *Martin Chuzzlewit*, Sairey Gamp is a gossiping, gin-drinking midwife and nurse. Misnumbered large-size jugs exist with the number D5528, which is the number allocated to the small-size jug. This does not add any premium to the price.

VARIATION No. 1: Colourway — Black hair; light green band; dark green coat; yellow and burgundy bow
Handle — green umbrella

Backstamp B - Bentalls 1935

Backstamp C - Darley & Son

Designer: Leslie Harradine/Harry Fenton
Handle: A green umbrella with brown handle
Colourway: Black hair; light green band; dark green coat; yellow and burgundy bow

Backstamp: **A.** Doulton
B. Doulton/Bentalls/
Souvenir From Bentalls. Jubilee Year, 1935.
Commissioned by Bentalls to commemorate the silver jubilee in 1935 of King George V.
C. Doulton/Darley/
Souvenir from Darley & Son Sheffield & Rotherham

Doulton Number	Size	Backstamp	Height	Intro.	Discon.	Current Market Value		
						U.K. £	U.S. $	Can. $
D5451	Large	Doulton	6 ¼"	1935	1986	65.00	100.00	100.00
D5528	Small	Doulton	3 1/8"	1935	1986	40.00	70.00	70.00
D5528	Small	Doulton/Bentalls	3 1/8"	1935	1935	700.00	1,200.00	1,500.00
D5528	Small	Doulton/Darley	3 1/8"	1936	1936	700.00	1,200.00	1,500.00
D6045	Miniature	Doulton	2 1/8"	1939	1986	35.00	55.00	60.00
D6146	Tiny	Doulton	1 ¼"	1940	1960	60.00	90.00	100.00

Note: This jug was also issued in English Translucent China. These jugs command a premium of 50 to 100% over the earthenware variety.

VARIATION No. 2: Colourway —Yellow band on hat; yellow bow; maroon umbrella

Backstamp A

Backstamps: **A.** Strawbridge and Clothier/
Celebrating the opening of The Royal Doulton Room at Strawbridge and Clothier, Philadelphia, U.S.A.
Commissioned by Strawbridge and Clothier, Philadelphia.
Issued in 1986 in a limited edition of 250 pieces.
B. Strawbridge and Clothier/
Made for the First Anniversary of the Royal Doulton Room at Strawbridge and Clothier
Commissioned by Strawbridge and Clothier in 1987 and issued in a limited edition of 500 pieces.

Doulton Number	Size	Variation	Height	Intro.	Discon.	Current Market Value U.K. £	U.S. $	Can. $
D6770	Large	Var. 2A	6 ¼"	1986	Ltd. ed.	225.00	350.00	400.00
D6789	Small	Var. 2B	3"	1987	Ltd. ed.	200.00	225.00	250.00

Sairey Gamp Derivatives

Doulton Number	Item	Height	Intro.	Discon.	Current Market Value U.K. £	U.S. $	Can. $
D6009	Ash bowl	3"	1939	1960	85.00	150.00	175.00
D6011	Sugar bowl	2 ½"	1939	1942	400.00	750.00	850.00
D6015	Teapot	7"	1939	1942	900.00	2,000.00	2,500.00
D6047	Bust	2 ¼"	1939	1960	75.00	100.00	125.00
D6150	Toothpick holder	2 ¾"	1940	1942	275.00	500.00	600.00
HN1625	Bookend	3 ½"	1934	1939	1,250.00	2,250.00	2,500.00
M62	Napkin ring	3 ½"	c.1935	1939	375.00	750.00	900.00

SAM JOHNSON

A celebrated poet, essayist and lexicographer, Dr. Johnson (1709-1784) published his *Dictionary* in 1755, which was the first systematic study of the English language. His literary club met regularly at a London pub and included such famous figures as David Garrick, Oliver Goldsmith and Edmund Burke.

"Sam Johnson."

COPR.1949.
DOULTON & CO.LIMITED.
R⁰N⁰ 857579
R⁰N⁰ 5906.
R⁰N⁰ 77/49

Designer: Harry Fenton
Handle: Plain
Colourway: Dark brown hat; light brown,
maroon and white robes

Backstamp: Doulton

Doulton Number	Size	Backstamp	Height	Intro.	Discon.	Current Market Value		
						U.K. £	U.S. $	Can. $
D6289	Large	Doulton	6 ¼"	1950	1960	225.00	400.00	450.00
D6296	Small	Doulton	3 ¼"	1950	1960	125.00	250.00	350.00

SAM WELLER

In the 1837 Charles Dickens novel, *The Pickwick Papers*, Sam Weller was a boots employed at the White Hart Inn. He became a faithful aide and valet to Mr. Pickwick and eventually married Napkins's housemaid.

This character jug is unusual in that its modelling changes dramatically between the large and smaller versions.

Designer:	Leslie Harradine / Harry Fenton
Handle:	Plain
Colourway:	Dark brown hat; light brown coat; red kerchief with white spots

Backstamp: Doulton

Doulton Number	Size	Backstamp	Height	Intro.	Discon.	Current Market Value U.K. £	U.S. $	Can. $
D6064	Large	Doulton	6 ½"	1940	1960	100.00	175.00	175.00
D5841	Mid	Doulton	4 ½"	1938	1948	125.00	225.00	250.00
D5841	Small	Doulton	3 ¼"	1948	1960	65.00	125.00	140.00
D6140	Miniature	Doulton	2 ¼"	1940	1960	50.00	80.00	85.00
D6147	Tiny	Doulton	1 ¼"	1940	1960	65.00	110.00	125.00

Sam Weller Derivatives

Doulton Number	Item	Height	Intro.	Discon.	Current Market Value U.K. £	U.S. $	Can. $
D6052	Bust	2 ½"	1939	1960	75.00	100.00	125.00
M61	Napkin ring	3 ½"	c. 1939	1939	375.00	650.00	800.00

Note: This jug was also issued in English Translucent China. These jugs command a premium of 50 to 100% over the earthenware variety.

SAMSON AND DELILAH

THE STAR-CROSSED LOVERS COLLECTION (TWO-FACED JUG)
ONE OF FOUR

Samson was an Israelite judge from Biblical times, famous for his strength. Delilah, a Philistine, was paid to find the secret of Samson's strength, so that her people could overthrow their Israelite enemies. Samson fell in love with Delilah and told her that his strength lay in his hair. She shaved his head while he slept and the Philistines captured and blinded him. When his hair grew back, Samson avenged himself by pulling down a Philistine temple, killing himself and many of his enemies.

This jug was issued in 1988 in a limited edition of 9,500 pieces.

Designer: Stanley J. Taylor
Handle: Samson — Jawbone of an ass
Delilah — A broken column
Colourway: Brown, black and cream

Backstamp: Doulton

Doulton Number	Size	Backstamp	Height	Intro.	Discon.	Current Market Value U.K. £	U.S. $	Can. $
D6787	Large	Doulton	7"	1988	Ltd. ed.	100.00	200.00	200.00

SANCHO PANÇA

This amiable peasant was employed as the squire to Don Quixote in Cervantes's 17th-century novel. Accompanying Quixote on many adventures, his down-to-earth common sense acted as a foil to his master's romantic musing.

Sancho Panca
(A Servant to Don Quixote)
D 6461
COPR 1956
DOULTON & CO LIMITED
Rd No 881510
Rd No 35706
Rd No 7561
Rd No 332/56

Backstamp A - Doulton

Designer: Geoff Blower
Handle: Light brown donkey
Colourway: Black hat with a white feather; black coat with a white collar

Backstamps: **A.** Doulton
B. Doulton/Sancho Panca/(A Servant to Don Quixote)
Produced from 1957 to the early 1970s, with no cedilla.
C. Doulton/Sancho Pança
The spelling of the name Pança with the cedilla gives a soft "s" sound in pronunciation.
Early versions of the backstamp included the cedilla, but it was dropped in the late fifties.
The incised name shows that the cedilla was included in the modelling.

Doulton Number	Size	Backstamp	Height	Intro.	Discon.	Current Market Value U.K. £	U.S. $	Can. $
D6456	Large	Doulton	6 ½"	1957	1983	85.00	185.00	200.00
D6456	Large	A Servant ...	6 ½"	1957	1970	100.00	185.00	225.00
D6456	Large	Cedilla	6 ½	1957	1959	100.00	185.00	225.00
D6461	Small	Doulton	3 ¼"	1957	1983	50.00	95.00	100.00
D6461	Small	A Servant ...	3 ¼"	1957	1970	50.00	95.00	135.00
D6461	Small	Cedilla	3 ¼"	1957	1959	50.00	95.00	135.00
D6518	Miniature	Doulton	2 ½"	1960	1983	45.00	90.00	90.00
D6518	Miniature	A Servant ...	2 ½"	1960	1970	45.00	90.00	110.00
D6518	Miniature	Cedilla	2 ½"	1960	Unknown	45.00	90.00	110.00

Note: 1. The dates for the discontinuance of the backstamp varieties are only approximate.
2. This jug was also issued in English Translucent China. These jugs command a premium of 50 to 100% over the earthenware variety.

SANTA CLAUS

The Santa Claus jug was introduced in 1981 and was the first to undergo annual design changes. Featuring different well-known Christmas themes, the handle has changed several times since 1981.

STYLE ONE: HANDLE — A DOLL AND DRUM

Designer: Michael Abberley	**Backstamp:** Doulton
Handle: A doll stands on a drum	
Colourway: Red, white and light brown	

Doulton Number	Size	Backstamp	Height	Intro.	Discon.	Current Market Value U.K. £	U.S. $	Can. $
D6668	Large	Doulton	7 ½"	1981	1981	125.00	300.00	325.00

SANTA CLAUS

STYLE TWO: HANDLE — THE HEAD OF A REINDEER

Designer: Michael Abberley
Handle: The head of a reindeer
Colourway: Red, white and brown

Backstamp: Doulton

Doulton Number	Size	Backstamp	Height	Intro.	Discon.	Current Market Value		
						U.K. £	U.S. $	Can. $
D6675	Large	Doulton	7 ¼"	1982	1982	150.00	350.00	375.00

SANTA CLAUS

STYLE THREE: HANDLE — A SACK OF TOYS

Designer: Michael Abberley
Handle: A sack of toys
Colourway: Red, white and light brown

Backstamp: Doulton

Doulton Number	Size	Backstamp	Height	Intro.	Discon.	Current Market Value U.K. £	U.S. $	Can. $
D6690	Large	Doulton	7 ½"	1983	1983	200.00	450.00	475.00

SANTA CLAUS

STYLE FOUR: HANDLE — PLAIN RED

Backstamp A - Doulton

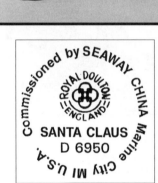

Backstamp B -
Doulton/Seaway China

Designer: Michael Abberley, Large, small, miniature
William K. Harper, Tiny
Handle: Plain
Colourway: Red and white

Backstamps: **A.** Doulton
B. Doulton/Seaway China
Commissioned by Seaway
China Marine City MI U.S.A.
Issued in a special edition of 2,500.

Doulton Number	Size	Backstamp	Height	Intro.	Discon.	Current Market Value U.K. £	U.S. $	Can. $
D6704	Large	Doulton	7 ½"	1984	Current	80.00	165.00	230.00
D6705	Small	Doulton	3 ¼"	1984	Current	43.00	90.00	130.00
D6706	Miniature	Doulton	2 ½"	1984	1991	75.00	125.00	135.00
D6950	Tiny	Doulton/Seaway	1 ¼"	1994	Sp. ed.	45.00	65.00	90.00

SANTA CLAUS

CHRISTMAS MINIATURE SERIES
ONE OF FIVE

STYLE FIVE: HANDLE — A HOLLY WREATH

Backstamp A - Doulton

Designer: Michael Abberley
Handle: A holly wreath
Colourway: Red, white and green

Backstamps: **A.** Doulton
Issued in a limited edition
of 5,000 for Christmas 1991.
B. Doulton/Home Shopping
Commissioned by the Home
Shopping Network, Florida
Issued in a special edition of
5,000.

Doulton Number	Size	Backstamp	Height	Intro.	Discon.	U.K. £	U.S. $	Can. $
						Current Market Value		
D6794	Large	Doulton/Home	7"	1988	Sp. ed.	300.00	550.00	650.00
D6900	Miniature	Doulton	2 ½"	1991	Ltd. ed.	65.00	100.00	120.00

SANTA CLAUS

STYLE SIX: HANDLE — A CANDY CANE

VARIATION No. 1: Handle — Candy cane with red and white stripes

Royal Doulton
SANTA CLAUS
D6793
Modelled by

© 1987 ROYAL DOULTON

Designer:	Michael Abberley, Large William K. Harper, Tiny
Handle:	Candy cane with red and white stripes
Colourway:	Red and white

Backstamp: A. Doulton/Cable Value Commissioned by the Cable Value Network. Issued in a special edition of 1,000.
B. Doulton/Seaway China Commissioned by Seaway China Marine City MI U.S.A. Issued in a special edition of 2,500.

Doulton Number	Size	Backstamp	Height	Intro.	Discon.	Current Market Value		
						U.K. £	U.S. $	Can. $
D6793	Large	A. Doulton/Cable	7 ½"	1988	Sp. ed.	1,000.00	1,500.00	2,000.00
D6980	Tiny	B. Doulton/ Seaway	1 ¼"	1995	Sp. ed.	45.00	60.00	90.00

VARIATION No. 2: Handle — Candy cane with red, white and green stripes

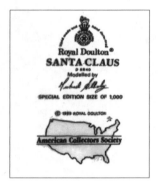

Backstamp: Doulton/American Collectors Society
Commissioned by the American Collectors Society. Issued in 1989 in a special edition of 1,000 pieces.

| Doulton | | | | | | Current Market Value | | |
Number	Size	Backstamp	Height	Intro.	Discon.	U.K. £	U.S. $	Can. $
D6840	Large	Doulton/ American	7 ½"	1989	Sp. ed.	300.00	625.00	700.00

SANTA CLAUS

STYLE SEVEN: HANDLE — CHRISTMAS PARCELS

Designer: William K. Harper
Handle: Blue and green Christmas parcels
Colourway: Red and white

Backstamp: Doulton/Seaway China
Commissioned by Seaway China
Marine City MI U.S.A. Issued
in a special edition of 2,500.

Doulton Number	Size	Backstamp	Height	Intro.	Discon.	Current Market Value		
						U.K. £	U.S. $	Can. $
D7020	Tiny	Doulton/Seaway	1 ¼"	1996	Sp. ed.	45.00	70.00	85.00

SANTA CLAUS

STYLE EIGHT: HANDLE — TEDDY BEAR

Designer:	William K. Harper
Handle:	Teddy bear
Colourway:	Red and white

Backstamp: Doulton/Seaway China
Commissioned by Seaway China
Marine City MI U.S.A. Issued
in a special edition of 2,500.

Doulton Number	Size	Backstamp	Height	Intro.	Discon.	Current Market Value		
						U.K. £	U.S. $	Can. $
D7060	Tiny	Doulton/Seaway	1 ¼"	1997	Sp. ed.	45.00	65.00	80.00

SANTA CLAUS

This jug was sold through the Home Shopping Network in the U.S.A. and was limited to 1,000 jugs.

STYLE NINE: HANDLE — CHRISTMAS BELLS

Designer: Michael Abberley
Handle: Christmas Bells
Colourway: Red and white

Backstamp: Doulton

Doulton Number	Size	Backstamp	Height	Intro.	Discon.	Current Market Value U.K. £	U.S. $	Can. $
D6964	Small	Doulton	4 ½"	1996	Ltd. ed.	350.00	675.00	775.00

SANTA CLAUS

This jug was commissione by Pascoe and Company in a special edition of 1,500 pieces.

STYLE TEN: HANDLE — CHRISTMAS TREE AND PARCELS

Designer: David B. Biggs

Handle: Christmas tree and parcels

Colourway: Red, white, blue and grey

Backstamp: Doulton/Pascoe

Doulton Number	Size	Backstamp	Height	Intro.	Discon.	Current Market Value		
						U.K. £	U.S. $	Can. $
D7123	Large	Doulton/Pascoe	7"	1998	Spec. ed.	175.00	250.00	375.00

SCARAMOUCHE

In the 17th-century comedy, written by Edward Ravenscroft, Scaramouche appears as a boastful, foolish character, dressed in the old Spanish style.

STYLE ONE HANDLE — A GUITAR WITH THE TWO MASKS OF COMEDY AND TRAGEDY

Designer: Max Henk
Handle: A guitar
Colourway: Blue-black, brown and green

Backstamp: Doulton

Doulton Number	Size	Backstamp	Height	Intro.	Discon.	Current Market Value		
						U.K. £	U.S. $	Can. $
D6558	Large	Doulton	7"	1962	1967	625.00	1,150.00	1,350.00
D6561	Small	Doulton	3 ¼"	1962	1967	400.00	725.00	850.00
D6564	Miniature	Doulton	2 ½"	1962	1967	375.00	650.00	750.00

Note: This jug was also issued in English Translucent China. These jugs command a premium of 50 to 100% over the earthenware variety.

SCARAMOUCHE

CHARACTERS FROM LITERATURE,
ONE OF 11

STYLE TWO: HANDLE —A CURTAIN WITH THE TWO MASKS
OF COMEDY AND TRAGEDY

VARIATION No. 1: Colourway —Yellow hat; turquoise tunic; white ruff; light brown hair
Handle — Lavender

Royal Doulton®
SCARAMOUCHE
D 6814
Modelled by
Stanley James Taylor.
© 1987 ROYAL DOULTON
NEW COLOURWAY 1988

Designer: Stanley J. Taylor
Handle: The masks of tragedy and comedy
rest against a curtain
Colourway: Yellow hat; turquoise tunic; white ruff;
light brown hair; lavender handle

Backstamp: Doulton

Doulton Number	Size	Variation	Height	Intro.	Discon.	Current Market Value		
						U.K. £	U.S. $	Can. $
D6814	Large	Var. 1	6 ¾"	1988	1991	125.00	250.00	275.00

VARIATION No. 2: Colourway — Black hat; green tunic; white ruff; dark brown hair; yellow handle

Designer: Stanley J. Taylor
Handle: The masks of tragedy and comedy rest against a curtain
Colourway: Black hat; green tunic; white ruff; dark brown hair; yellow handle

Backstamp: Doulton/Guild Commissioned by the Guild of Specialist China & Glass Retailers in 1987 and issued in a special edition of 1,500 pieces.

Doulton Number	Size	Variation	Height	Intro.	Discon.	Current Market Value U.K. £	U.S. $	Can. $
D6774	Large	Var. 2	6 ¾"	1987	Sp. ed.	100.00	325.00	350.00

SCARLET PIMPERNEL

PROTOTYPE

In the 1905 novel by the Hungarian Baroness Orczy, the Scarlet Pimpernel was a group of Englishmen dedicated to the rescue of victims of the Reign of Terror in Paris. Sir Percy Blakeney, the group's leader, bested his opponents by clever wit and courage while disguising his identity from his friends back in England.

Designer: Geoff Blower
Handle: Characters in assorted disguises
Colourway: Black, white and blue

Backstamp: Doulton

Doulton Number	Size	Variation	Height	Intro.	Discon.	U.K. £	U.S. $	Can. $
							Current Market Value	
D —	Large	Prototype	7"	Unknown			Unique	

SCHUBERT

Franz Schubert (1797-1828) was a prolific composer in his short life, and is best remembered for his songs and the famous "Unfinished" symphony.

Designer: Stanley J. Taylor
Handle: Music rack and an excert from "Cradle Song"
Colourway: Black, green, brown and yellow

Backstamp: Doulton

Doulton Number	Size	Backstamp	Height	Intro.	Discon.	Current Market Value		
						U.K. £	U.S. $	Can. $
D7056	Large	Doulton	6 ¾"	1996	Current	90.00	260.00	340.00

SCROOGE

For the character jug Scrooge see the "Charles Dickens Commemorative Set" page 185.

SHAKESPEARE

For William Shakespeare see page 523.

Designer: William K. Harper
Handle: Inkwell and books
Colourway: Black coat; yellow collar; light brown hair and beard; burgundy books; grey inkwell and quill

Backstamp: Doulton

Doulton Number	Size	Backstamp	Height	Intro.	Discon.	Current Market Value		
						U.K. £	U.S. $	Can. $
D6938	Small	Doulton	3 ½"	1993	Current	60.00	125.00	165.00

SHEFFIELD WEDNESDAY (FOOTBALL CLUB)

THE FOOTBALL SUPPORTERS
ONE OF TEN

This jug was sold exclusively through John Sinclair of Sheffield, England.

Designer: Stanley J. Taylor
Handle: Team coloured scarf
Colourway: Blue and cream striped uniform

Backstamp: Doulton

Doulton Number	Size	Backstamp	Height	Intro.	Discon.	Current Market Value		
						U.K. £	U.S. $	Can. $
D6958	Mid	Doulton	5"	1993	Unknown	50.00	100.00	120.00

SHERLOCK HOLMES SET

These six tiny character jugs were issued in a tribute to Sir Arhur Conan Doyle, the creator of Sherlock Holmes. They were released by Lawleys By Post in a limited edition of 2,500. Each set has matching edition numbers and was issued with a presentation stand.

For the toby jug Sherlock Holmes see page 98, and for the Sherlock Holmes and Dr. Watson bookends see page 540.

Designer: William K. Harper	**Backstamp:** Doulton
Height: 1 ½"	**Handle:** Miscellaneous
Colourway: See below	**Issued:** 1996 in a Ltd. ed. of 2,500
Size: Tiny	

Doulton Number	Name	Colourway	Current Market Value U.K. £	U.S. $	Can. $
D7011	Doctor Watson	Brown, white and grey	40.00	70.00	85.00
D7012	Inspector Lestrade	Brown, white and grey	40.00	70.00	85.00
D7013	Jefferson Hope	Black, white and red	40.00	70.00	85.00
D7014	Mrs. Hudson	Black, white and yellow	40.00	70.00	85.00
D7015	Professor Moriarty	Black, white and green	40.00	70.00	85.00
D7016	Sherlock Holmes	Brown, white and grey	40.00	70.00	85.00
	Complete set with display stand		225.00	425.00	525.00

SIMON THE CELLARER

Simon was the subject of a 19th-century English folksong. The keys on the handle are those to his cellar, full of great wines and ales. He was always good for standing a drink for his friends.

The tiny version of Simon the Cellarer was one of a set of six tinies issued in 1994, in a limited edition of 2,500, to commemorate the diamond anniversary of the first character jug. The set, modelled by William K. Harper, was sold out within the first year. Other tinies in this series are Dick Turpin, Granny, the Jester, John Barleycorn and Parson Brown. The issue price was £150.00.

For the tiny version of Simon the Cellarer see the "Diamond Anniversary Set" page 214.

Backstamp A - Doulton

Backstamp B - Bentalls

Designer:	Charles Noke / Harry Fenton					**Backstamps:**	**A.** Doulton	
Handle:	A bunch of keys						**B.** Doulton/Bentalls/	
Colourway:	Maroon hat; white ruff						Souvenir from Bentalls. 1936.	

Doulton Number	Size	Backstamp	Height	Intro.	Discon.	Current Market Value U.K. £	U.S. $	Can. $
D5504	Large	Doulton	6 ½"	1935	1960	100.00	175.00	200.00
D5616	Small	Doulton	3 ½"	1936	1960	50.00	80.00	100.00
D5616	Small	Doulton/Bentalls	3 ½"	1936	1936	425.00	825.00	975.00

SIMPLE SIMON

The subject of this jug dates back to a 17th-century nursery rhyme of Simon meeting a pieman.

Designer: Geoff Blower
Handle: Plain
Colourway: Green, brown and white

Backstamp: Doulton

Doulton Number	Size	Backstamp	Height	Intro.	Discon.	Current Market Value		
						U.K. £	U.S. $	Can. $
D6374	Large	Doulton	7"	1953	1960	400.00	750.00	850.00

SIR FRANCIS DRAKE

This version of the Drake jug was produced to celebrate the 400th anniversary of the defeat of the Spanish Armada in 1588. Commissioned by the Guild of Specialist China & Glass Retailers, this jug was issued in 1988 in a special edition of 6,000 pieces.

For the character jug Drake see page 221 and for the toby jug Sir Francis Drake see page 99.

Designer: Peter A. Gee
Handle: The Golden Hind's bow and sails
Colourway: Black and white

Backstamp: Doulton/Guild

Doulton Number	Size	Backstamp	Height	Intro.	Discon.	Current Market Value		
						U.K. £	U.S. $	Can. $
D6805	Large	Doulton/Guild	7"	1988	Sp. ed.	100.00	200.00	225.00

SIR HENRY DOULTON

ROYAL DOULTON INTERNATIONAL COLLECTORS CLUB SERIES

In the mid 1830s, Henry Doulton (1820-1897) joined his father's firm just in time to capitalize on the expanding market that was developing in London for modern sanitation products. The manufacture of stoneware sewer and water pipes led Doulton and Company, as they were known after 1854, to become a large and flourishing concern. John Doulton retired around this time leaving Doulton and Company in the hands of his son Henry. In the 1860s, with decorative wares expanding, Henry Doulton was persuaded to hire students from the Lambeth School of Art as designers and decorators of the new ornamental wares his company was introducing. Their outstanding creations heralded the beginning of the studio-art pottery movement.

STYLE ONE: SINGLE HANDLE — ART POTTERY VASE

Designer: Eric Griffiths	**Backstamp:** Doulton/RDICC
Handle: A Doulton art pottery vase	
Colourway: Black coat; yellow cravat; grey hair; brown and blue vase	

Doulton Number	Size	Backstamp	Height	Intro.	Discon.	Current Market Value U.K. £	U.S. $	Can. $
D6703	Small	RDICC	4 ½"	1984	1984	85.00	150.00	175.00

SIR HENRY DOULTON

ROYAL DOULTON INTERNATIONAL COLLECTOR'S CLUB SERIES

This was the Royal Doulton International Collector's Club Character Jug of the Year for 1997. The jug was issued in a limited edition of 1,997 and carries the special Sir Henry Doulton Centenary 1897-1997 backstamp.

STYLE TWO: SINGLE HANDLE — ART POTTERY EWER

Designer: William K. Harper
Handle: Ewer and ribbon "Doulton & Co."
Colourway: Black, brown, yellow and gold

Backstamp: Doulton/RDICC
Sir Henry Doulton Centenary
1897-1997

Doulton Number	Size	Backstamp	Height	Intro.	Discon.	Current Market Value U.K. £	U.S. $	Can. $
D7057	Small	RDICC	5"	1997	1997	75.00	150.00	175.00

SIR HENRY DOULTON

This large size two-handled jug was issued to commemorate the 100th anniversary of the death of Sir Henry Doulton in 1897. The jug carries a special backstamp for the centenary year and was issued in a limited edition of 1,997.

STYLE THREE: TWO HANDLED JUG

Designer: William K. Harper
Handles: Lambeth product on the right and Burslem product on the left with Hannah Barlow and a rabbit modelled by Mark Marshall
Colourway: Blue, black, yellow and brown

Backstamp: Doulton/Sir Henry Doulton Centenary 1897-1997

Doulton Number	Size	Backstamp	Height	Intro.	Discon.	Current Market Value		
						U.K. £	U.S. $	Can. $
D7054	Large	Doulton	7"	1997	1997	125.00	300.00	500.00

SIR HENRY DOULTON AND MICHAEL DOULTON

This two-faced jug was a special edition jug issued to mark Michael Doulton's personal appearances at retail locations. This piece is one of the few two-faced jugs made in the small size.

Designer: William K. Harper
Handle: Flag bearing the lion and crown backstamp of Royal Doulton
Colourway: Henry — Grey hair; yellow cravat
Michael — Brown hair; dark blue suit; white shirt; light blue tie
Backstamp: Doulton

Doulton Number	Size	Backstamp	Height	Intro.	Discon.	Current Market Value U.K. £	U.S. $	Can. $
D6921	Small	Doulton	4 ½"	1992	Sp. ed.	60.00	100.00	100.00

SIR THOMAS MORE

HENRY AND HIS SIX WIVES
ONE OF EIGHT

Thomas More (1478-1535) entered the service of King Henry VIII in 1518 as royal councillor. He was knighted and became Lord Chancellor after the dismissal of Cardinal Wolsey in 1529. At this time Henry was embroiled in a battle with Rome over his decision to divorce Catherine of Aragon. Unable to support his King, More resigned.

In 1534 More was arrested for high treason when he refused to swear an oath of supremacy, stating that Henry VIII ranked above all foreign leaders, including the Pope. He was beheaded in 1535 and canonized by the Catholic Church 400 years later, in 1935.

Royal Doulton®
SIR THOMAS MORE
D 6792
Modelled by
Stanley James Taylor
© 1987 ROYAL DOULTON

Designer: Stanley J. Taylor	**Backstamp:** Doulton
Handle: A window arch and a bible	
Colourway: Dark green hat; brown fur-trimmed collar; gold chain of office	

Doulton Number	Size	Backstamp	Height	Intro.	Discon.	Current Market Value U.K. £	U.S. $	Can. $
D6792	Large	Doulton	6 ¾"	1988	1991	125.00	275.00	300.00

SIR WINSTON CHURCHILL

HEROIC LEADERS
ONE OF THREE

This Churchill jug was a new design, commissioned by Lawleys By Post. It was issued in 1989 as part of a set of three, and limited to 9,500 pieces.

For the character jug Churchill see page 197, and for the character jug Winston Churchill see page 527. For the toby jug Winston Churchill see page 105.

Designer:	Stanley J. Taylor	
Handle:	The Union Jack flag	
Colourway:	Black, grey and white	

Backstamp: Doulton

Doulton Number	Size	Backstamp	Height	Intro.	Discon.	Current Market Value		
						U.K. £	U.S. $	Can. $
D6849	Small	Doulton	3 ¼"	1989	Ltd. ed.	125.00	250.00	275.00

THE SIX WIVES OF HENRY VIII

This set was commissioned by Lawleys By Post in a limited edition of 2,500.

STYLE TWO: HANDLES INITIALS

Anne Boleyn	Anne of Cleves	Catherine of Aragon	Catherine Howard	Catherine Parr	Jane Seymour
D 7042	D 7044	D 7041	D 7045	D 7046	D 7043

Designer: William K. Harper
Height: 1 ½"
Size: Tiny
Colourway: See below

Backstamp: Doulton
Handle: Plain
Issued: 1994 in a Ltd. ed. of 2,500

Doulton Number	Size	Colourway	Current Market Value		
			U.K. £	U.S. $	Can. $
D7042	Anne Boleyn	Black and pink	45.00	80.00	100.00
D7044	Anne of Cleves	Beige	45.00	80.00	100.00
D7041	Catherine of Aragon	Yellow and green	45.00	80.00	100.00
D7045	Catherine Howard	Yellow and green	45.00	80.00	100.00
D7046	Catherine Parr	Brown and white	45.00	80.00	100.00
D7043	Jane Seymour	Yellow and black	45.00	80.00	100.00
	Complete set with stand		250.00	475.00	600.00

THE SLEUTH

Arthur Conan Doyle (1859-1930), an unsuccessful doctor, published the first of his widely popular detective stories in 1887. The amateur sleuth Sherlock Holmes shared rooms on Baker Street, as well as many adventures, with his friend and foil, Dr. Watson.

VARIATION No. 1:   Colourway — Black deerstalker hat, brown cloak

The Sleuth
D 6631
© DOULTON & CO. LIMITED 1972
REGISTRATION APPLIED FOR

Designer: Alan Moore
Handle: A pipe and magnifying glass
Colourway: Dark green deerstalker hat; brown cloak

Backstamp: Doulton

Doulton Number	Size	Backstamp	Height	Intro.	Discon.	Current Market Value		
						U.K. £	U.S. $	Can. $
D6631	Large	Doulton	7"	1973	1996	75.00	130.00	150.00
D6635	Small	Doulton	3 ¼"	1973	1996	50.00	75.00	100.00
D6639	Miniature	Doulton	2 ¾"	1973	1991	45.00	85.00	90.00

Note: This jug was also issued in English Translucent China. These jugs command a premium of 50 to 100% over the earthenware variety.

VARIATION No. 2:   Colourway — Brown deerstalker hat; red cloak

Backstamp: Doulton/Lawleys/
This Limited Edition of 5,000 Commemorates The Centenary of the Publication
of the First Sherlock Holmes story "A Study In Scarlet"
Commissioned by Lawleys By Post and issued in 1987 in a limited edition of 5,000 pieces.

Doulton Number	Size	Backstamp	Height	Intro.	Discon.	Current Market Value U.K. £	U.S. $	Can. $
D6773	Small	Lawleys	3 ¼"	1987	Ltd. ed.	125.00	275.00	300.00

SMUGGLER

The detailing on the barrel of the small-size jug is often less distinguishable than that on the large jug.

Designer: David Biggs
Handle: Lantern above a barrel
Colourway: Green hat; red scarf

Backstamp: Doulton

Doulton Number	Size	Backstamp	Height	Intro.	Discon.	Current Market Value		
						U.K. £	U.S. $	Can. $
D6616	Large	Doulton	7 ¼"	1968	1981	125.00	225.00	250.00
D6619	Small	Doulton	3 ¼"	1968	1981	60.00	125.00	135.00

Note: This jug was also issued in English Translucent China. These jugs command a premium of 50 to 100% over the earthenware variety.

SMUTS

A South African attorney, military man and politician, Jan Christiaan Smuts (1870-1950) served as a member of the British War Cabinet in World War I and was one of the authors of the Covenant of the League of Nations. In 1945, after again serving the Allies in World War II, Smuts is credited with writing the preamble to the Charter of the United Nations. He became the Prime Minister of South Africa in 1919 and again in 1939.

Designer:	Harry Fenton	**Backstamp:** Doulton
Handle:	Springbok	
Colourway:	Light brown	

Doulton Number	Size	Backstamp	Height	Intro.	Discon.	Current Market Value		
						U.K. £	U.S. $	Can. $
D6198	Large	Doulton	6 ½"	1946	1948	1,200.00	2,250.00	2,750.00

THE SNAKE CHARMER

This jug was issued in a limited edition of 2,500 pieces.

Designer:	Stanley J. Taylor		**Backstamp:**	Doulton
Handle:	Cobra, basket and pipe			
Colourway:	Yellow turban with blue and pink jewel; burgundy and yellow robes			

Doulton Number	Size	Backstamp	Height	Intro.	Discon.	Current Market Value		
						U.K. £	**U.S. $**	**Can. $**
D6912	Large	Doulton	7"	1992	Ltd. ed.	200.00	325.00	350.00

THE SNOOKER PLAYER

CHARACTERS FROM LIFE
ONE OF SEVEN

Designer: Stanley J. Taylor
Handle: Cue with chalk and red and black cue balls
Colourway: Black hair; white shirt; black bow tie and vest

Backstamp: Doulton

Doulton Number	Size	Backstamp	Height	Intro.	Discon.	Current Market Value		
						U.K. £	U.S. $	Can. $
D6879	Small	Doulton	4"	1991	1995	50.00	100.00	150.00

SNOWMAN

CHRISTMAS MINIATURES SERIES
ONE OF SIX

This jug was commissioned by Royal Doulton (U.S.A.) Limited. It is also listed in the *Charlton Standard Catalogue of Royal Doulton Beswick Storybook Figurines*, under the Snowman series.

STYLE ONE: HANDLE — A SCARF

Designer: Graham Tongue	**Backstamp:** Doulton
Modeller: Martyn Alcock	
Handle: Scarf	
Colourway: White, green and black	

Doulton Number	Size	Backstamp	Height	Intro.	Discon.	Current Market Value		
						U.K. £	U.S. $	Can. $
D6972	Miniature	Doulton	2 ¾"	1994	1994	100.00	175.00	200.00

SNOWMAN

SNOWMAN MINIATURES SERIES
ONE OF FOUR

A series of four snowman character jugs was commissioned by John Sinclair, England. One jug to be year to be issued each year in a special edition of 2,000 each, with a special gold edition being issued for the millennium in 2000.

STYLE TWO: HANDLE — HOLLY AND BERRIES

Designer:	William K. Harper	
Handle:	Holly and berries	
Colourway:	White; red hat, white and green striped scarf	

Backstamp: Doulton/Sinclair

Doulton Number	Size	Backstamp	Height	Intro.	Discon.	Current Market Value		
						U.K. £	**U.S. $**	**Can. $**
D7062	Miniature	Doulton/Sinclair	2 ¾"	1997	Spec. ed.	40.00	100.00	150.00

SNOWMAN

SNOWMAN MINIATURE SERIES
ONE OF FOUR

This is the second jug in the Snowman series, issued in a special edition of 2,000.

STYLE THREE: HANDLE — CHRISTMAS STOCKING AND PARCELS

Designer: William K. Harper
Handle: Christmas stocking and parcels
Colourway: White; blue hat, red and white striped scarf

Backstamp: Doulton/Sinclair

Doulton Number	Size	Backstamp	Height	Intro.	Discon.	Current Market Value		
						U.K. £	U.S. $	Can. $
D —	Miniature	Doulton/Sinclair	2 ¾"	1998	Spec. ed.	40.00	100.00	150.00

SNOWMAN

SNOWMAN MINIATURES SERIES
ONE OF FOUR

The third in the series of Snowman jugs issued in a special edition of 2,000.

STYLE FOUR: HANDLE — CHRISTMAS CRACKER

Designer: William K. Harper
Handle: Christmas cracker
Colourway: White; green hat, white and blue striped scarf

Backstamp: Doulton/Sinclair

Doulton Number	Size	Backstamp	Height	Intro.	Discon.	Current Market Value		
						U.K. £	U.S. $	Can. $
D —	Miniature	Doulton/Sinclair	2 ¾"	1999	Spec. ed.	40.00	100.00	150.00

SNOWMAN

SNOWMAN MINIATURES SERIES
ONE OF FOUR

This jug, to be issued in a special gold edition of 2,000, will be issued to commemorate the millenium. It will be the final jug in the Snowman series.

STYLE FIVE: HANDLE — WREATH AND ROBIN

Designer: William K. Harper   **Backstamp:** Doulton/Sinclair
Handle: A wreath and a robin
Colourway: White; grey hat,olive and white striped scarf

Doulton Number	Size	Backstamp	Height	Intro.	Discon.	Current Market Value		
						U.K. £	U.S. $	Can. $
D —	Miniature	Doulton/Sinclair	2 ¾"	2000	Spec. ed.	50.00	N/A	N/A

THE SOLDIER

THE ARMED FORCES
ONE OF THREE

STYLE ONE: HANDLE — BAYONET AND WATER CANTEEN

Variation No. 1: Desert Rat Patch On Canteen

Designer: William K. Harper
Handle: Bayonet and water canteen
Colourway: Army steel helmet with netting; khaki tunic

Backstamp: Doulton

Doulton Number	Size	Backstamp	Height	Intro.	Discon.	Current Market Value U.K. £	U.S. $	Can. $
D6876	Small	Doulton	4 ½"	1991	1996	45.00	100.00	150.00

THE SOLDIER

THE CANADIANS
ONE OF THREE

Commissioned by The British Toby in a limited edition of 250 pieces, the Soldier originally sold in a set for $465.00 Canadian.

STYLE ONE: HANDLE — BAYONET AND WATER CANTEEN

Variation No. 2: Red Patch On Canteen

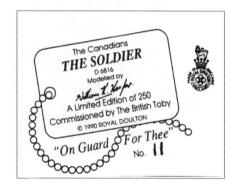

Designer: William K. Harper	
Handle: Bayonet and water canteen with red patch	
Colourway: Army steel helmet with netting; khaki tunic	

Backstamp: Doulton/The British Toby
The backstamp illustrated
shows an incorrect 'D' number

Doulton Number	Size	Backstamp	Height	Intro.	Discon.	Current Market Value		
						U.K. £	U.S. $	Can. $
D6905	Small	Doulton/ British Toby	4 ½"	1991	Ltd. ed.	175.00	350.00	400.00

THE SOLDIER

NATIONAL SERVICE EDITION
ONE OF THREE

The Soldier (style three) was a special edition for Lawleys By Post and paid tribute to all those who were called up for national service in the U.K.

STYLE TWO: HANDLE — JERRY CAN AND HAVERSACK

NATIONAL SERVICE
EDITION

Royal Doulton®
THE SOLDIER
D 6983
Modelled by

William K. Harper
© 1990 ROYAL DOULTON

Designer: William K. Harper
Handle: A jerry can and haversack
Colourways: Black and brown

Backstamp: Doulton

Doulton Number	Size	Backstamp	Height	Intro.	Discon.	Current Market Value U.K. £	U.S. $	Can. $
D6983	Small	Doulton	4 ½"	1994	Sp. ed.	50.00	150.00	175.00

ST. GEORGE

The patron saint of England since the 13th century, George is the hero of a legend which describes him as a chivalrous knight who single-handedly slayed a huge dragon, saving the princess Melisande.

STYLE ONE: HANDLE — A DRAGON

Designer: Max Henk
Handle: A dragon
Colourway: Grey helmet; turquoise armour

Backstamp: Doulton

Doulton Number	Size	Backstamp	Height	Intro.	Discon.	Current Market Value U.K. £	U.S. $	Can. $
D6618	Large	Doulton	7 ½"	1968	1975	200.00	400.00	550.00
D6621	Small	Doulton	3 ¾"	1968	1975	150.00	300.00	450.00

Note: This jug was also issued in English Translucent China. These jugs command a premium of 50 to 100% over the earthenware variety.

ST. GEORGE

This jug was commissioned by Lawleys By Post and issued in a limited edition of 2,500.

STYLE TWO: HANDLE — FLAG OF ST. GEORGE AND DRAGON

Designer: Robert Tabbenor
Handle: A dragon and the flag of St. George
Colourway: Grey-brown, gold and red

Backstamp: Doulton

Doulton Number	Size	Backstamp	Height	Intro.	Discon.	Current Market Value		
						U.K. £	U.S. $	Can. $
D7129	Large	Doulton	7 ½"	1998	Ltd. ed.	125.00	.00	.00

STRAUSS II

GREAT COMPOSERS
ONE OF EIGHT

Famous for his waltzes, especially the *Blue Danube* composition featured on the handle of this jug, Johann Strauss II (1825-1899) is known as the Waltz King.

Designer: Stanley J. Taylor
Handle: Violin, waves, Blue Danube score
Colourway: Brown, black and yellow

Backstamp: Doulton

Doulton Number	Size	Backstamp	Height	Intro.	Discon.	Current Market Value U.K. £	U.S. $	Can. $
D7097	Large	Doulton	7"	1998	Current	90.00	185.00	375.00

TAM O'SHANTER

In a poem written by Robert Burns in 1791, Tam O'Shanter is a drunken farmer who happens upon witches who pursue him and his horse. He escapes, but his horse doesn't quite make it—one witch pulls its tail off. The Scottish woollen cap is reputedly named after this poem's hero.

Tam o'Shanter
D. 6632
©DOULTON & CO. LIMITED 1972
REGISTRATION APPLIED FOR.

Designer: Max Henk
Handle: Witch holding horse's tail
above a mug of ale
Colourway: Dark blue tam; green cloak

Backstamp: Doulton

Doulton Number	Size	Backstamp	Height	Intro.	Discon.	Current Market Value		
						U.K. £	U.S. $	Can. $
D6632	Large	Doulton	7"	1973	1980	100.00	200.00	200.00
D6636	Small	Doulton	3 ¼"	1973	1980	65.00	120.00	150.00
D6640	Miniature	Doulton	2 ½"	1973	1980	60.00	120.00	125.00

Note: This jug was also issued in English Translucent China. These jugs command a premium of 50 to 100% over the earthenware variety.

TCHAIKOVSKY

GREAT COMPOSER
ONE OF EIGHT

Designer: Stanley J. Taylor
Handle: Swans and music from Swan Lake
Colourway: Black, grey and white

Backstamp: Doulton

Doulton Number	Size	Backstamp	Height	Intro.	Discon.	Current Market Value		
						U.K. £	U.S. $	Can. $
D7022	Large	Doulton	7"	1996	Current	90.00	260.00	340.00

TERRY FOX

Canadian Terrance Stanley Fox (1958-1981) was a student and athlete until diagnosed with a rare form of bone cancer. While recovering from the amputation of most of one leg, Fox conceived the idea of a "Marathon of Hope," a run across Canada to raise money for cancer research. He began on April 12, 1980, but had to abort his run on September 1, after being diagnosed with lung cancer. He raised over $24 million and became a source of inspiration for millions of people. Only three jugs were produced. One was given to his family, one resides in the Sir Henry Doulton Gallery and one was put up for auction at the International Royal Doulton Collectors Weekend, September 14 to 16, 1990, which realized $21,000 for charity.

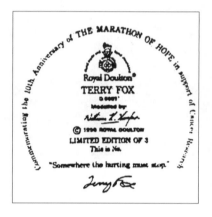

Designer: William K. Harper
Handle: Fox's artificial leg
Colourway: Brown and white

Backstamp: Doulton

Doulton Number	Size	Backstamp	Height	Intro.	Discon.	Current Market Value		
						U.K. £	U.S. $	Can. $
D6881	Large	Doulton	7"	1990	Ltd. ed.	Extremely rare. Only 3 known. Last sold at auction, Toronto, 1990 $21,000.00 Can.		

THOMAS JEFFERSON

PRESIDENTIAL SERIES
ONE OF THREE
PRESIDENTS OF THE UNITED STATES

This jug was issued in a limited edition of 2,500 to commemorate the 250th anniversary of Thomas Jefferson's birth in 1743. It was available only within the U.S.A., with an allocation of jugs for overseas members of the Royal Doulton International Collectors Club.

Designer: Stanley J. Tayler	**Backstamp:** Doulton
Handle: "Life, Liberty and the pursuit of happiness" on scroll, feather quill and ink pot	
Colourway: Grey hair; dark blue coat; grey cravat	

Doulton Number	Size	Backstamp	Height	Intro.	Discon.	Current Market Value U.K. £	Current Market Value U.S. $	Current Market Value Can. $
D6943	Large	Doulton	6 ¾"	1994	Ltd. ed.	175.00	250.00	300.00

TOBY GILLETTE

Jimmy Saville's British television show, "Jim'll Fix It," invites public requests and it received one from Toby Gillette to have a character jug created in his likeness.

In 1984 three were produced: one was given to Toby Gillette, one remains in the Sir Henry Doulton Gallery, and the third was auctioned by Sotheby's, with the proceeds ($30,000) going to one of the charities Jimmy Saville supported. In 1986 Toby Gillette sold his own jug at a Sotheby's auction.

Royal Doulton
TOBY GILLETTE
D6717
Modelled by

Eric Griffiths

© ROYAL DOULTON TABLEWARE
LIMITED 1983
WORLDWIDE
LIMITED EDITION OF 3
This is No. 1

Designer: Eric Griffiths
Handle: Plain
Colourway: Brown

Backstamp: Doulton

Doulton Number	Size	Backstamp	Height	Intro.	Discon.	Current Market Value		
						U.K. £	U.S. $	Can. $
D6717	Large	Doulton	7"	1984	Ltd. ed.	Extremely rare. Only 3 known.		

TOBY PHILPOTS

A "thirsty old soul" in an 18th-century drinking song, Toby is thought by some to be the source of the traditional British toby jug, in which a character sits astride a barrel of ale. Popular opinion suggests his name is a derivation of the French *topé*, to toast.

Backstamp A - Doulton

Backstamp B - Philpotts

Backstamp C - Philpots

Designer: Charles Noke
Colourway: Green hat; brown coat; blue scarf with white spots
Handle: Plain

Backstamps:
 A. Doulton
 B. Doulton/Toby Philpotts.
  Incised name on jug is "Toby Philpots," but on the backstamp "Toby Philpotts," which is incorrect.
 C. Doulton/Toby Philpots
  Incised name on jug is "Toby Philpots," and the backstamp has been corrected to "Toby Philpots."

Doulton Number	Size	Backstamp	Height	Intro.	Discon.	Current Market Value U.K. £	U.S. $	Can. $
D5736	Large	A. Doulton	6 ¼"	1937	1951	90.00	150.00	175.00
D5736	Large	B. Philpotts	6 ¼"	1937	1951	100.00	175.00	200.00
D5736	Large	C. Philpots	6 ¼"	1952	1969	90.00	150.00	175.00
D5737	Small	A. Doulton	3 ¼"	1937	1951	40.00	65.00	90.00
D5737	Small	B. Philpotts	3 ¼"	1937	1951	45.00	75.00	110.00
D5737	Small	C. Philpots	3 ¼"	1952	1969	40.00	65.00	90.00
D6043	Miniature	A. Doulton	2 ¼"	1939	1951	40.00	65.00	75.00
D6043	Miniature	B. Philpotts	2 ¼"	1939	1951	40.00	65.00	75.00
D6043	Miniature	C. Philpots	2 ¼"	1952	1969	40.00	65.00	75.00

Note: This jug was also issued in English Translucent China. These jugs command a premium of 50 to 100% over the earthenware variety.

TONY WELLER

Backstamp - B Darley & Sons

Backstamp D - Bentalls

Designer: Leslie Harradine/Harry Fenton
Handle: Plain
Colourway: Grey hat; maroon coat; white bow with yellow spots

Backstamps: **A.** Doulton
B. Doulton/Darley & Son/Souvenir From Darley & Son/Sheffield & Rotherham
Commissioned by Darley & Son, Sheffield and Rotherham.
C. Doulton/Bentalls/Souvenir From Bentalls Jubilee Year 1935
Commissioned by Bentalls to commemorate the silver jubilee in 1935 of King George V.
D. Doulton/Bentalls/Souvenir from Bentalls. 1936.

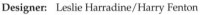

Doulton Number	Size	Backstamp	Height	Intro.	Discon.	Current Market Value U.K. £	U.S. $	Can. $
D5531	Ext. Large	Doulton	8 ½"	1936	1942	225.00	400.00	500.00
D5531	Large	Doulton	6 ½"	1936	1960	100.00	225.00	250.00
D5530	Small	Doulton	3 ¼"	1936	1960	45.00	75.00	100.00
D5530	Small	Doulton/Darley	3 ¼"	1936	1936	500.00	875.00	975.00
D5530	Small	Doulton/Bentalls	3 ¼"	1935	1935	500.00	875.00	975.00
D5530	Small	Doulton/Bentalls	3 ¼"	1936	1936	500.00	875.00	975.00
D6044	Miniature	Doulton	2 ¼"	1939	1960	40.00	70.00	85.00

Tony Weller Derivatives

Doulton Number	Item	Height	Intro.	Discon.	Current Market Value U.K. £	U.S. $	Can. $
D5888	Musical jug	6 ½"	1937	1939	500.00	1,000.00	1,100.00
D6013	Sugar bowl	2 ½"	1939	1960	500.00	800.00	1,000.00
D6016	Teapot	7"	1939	1960	1,200.00	2,000.00	2,500.00
D6051	Bust	4"	1939	1960	75.00	100.00	125.00
HN1616	Bookend	4"	1934	1939	1,500.00	3,500.00	4,000.00
M60	Napkin ring	3 ½"	1935	1939	350.00	625.00	750.00

TOTTENHAM HOTSPUR (FOOTBALL CLUB)

THE FOOTBALL SUPPORTERS
ONE OF TEN

Designer: Stanley J. Taylor
Handle: Team coloured scarf
Colourway: White shirt with navy collar,
navy scarf with yellow amd white stripe

Backstamp: Doulton

Doulton Number	Size	Backstamp	Height	Intro.	Discon.	Current Market Value		
						U.K. £	U.S. $	Can. $
D6960	Small	Doulton	5"	1995	Unknown	65.00	125.00	150.00

TOUCHSTONE

In Shakespeare's comedy, *As You Like It*, Touchstone is a jester to the court of the exiled Duke of Frederick. The Duke accompanies Rosalind and Celia into the Forest of Arden.

Designer: Charles Noke	**Backstamp:** Doulton
Handle: Head of a clown	
Colourway: Maroon, green and light brown	

Doulton Number	Size	Backstamp	Height	Intro.	Discon.	Current Market Value		
						U.K. £	U.S. $	Can. $
D5613	Large	Doulton	7"	1936	1960	200.00	375.00	475.00

TOWN CRIER

STYLE ONE: HANDLE — BELL ON SCROLL

Designer: David Biggs
Handle: Bell on scroll
Colourway: Black hat trimmed with gold;
scarlet coat trimmed with gold

Backstamp: Doulton

Town Crier
D 6530
COPR 1959
DOULTON & CO LIMITED
Rd No 893943
Rd No 39651
Rd No S 315
Rd No 41859

Doulton Number	Size	Backstamp	Height	Intro.	Discon.	Current Market Value		
						U.K. £	U.S. $	Can. $
D6530	Large	Doulton	7"	1960	1973	175.00	300.00	325.00
D6537	Small	Doulton	3 ¼"	1960	1973	100.00	185.00	225.00
D6544	Miniature	Doulton	2 ½"	1960	1973	135.00	250.00	275.00

Note: This jug was also issued in English Translucent China. These jugs command a premium of 50 to 100% over the earthenware variety.

TOWN CRIER

STYLE TWO: HANDLE — SCROLL WRAPPED AROUND BELL

Royal Doulton®
TOWN CRIER
D 6895
Modelled by
Stanley James Taylor
© 1991 ROYAL DOULTON

Designer: Stanley J. Taylor
Handle: Scroll wrapped around bell
Colourway: Black, maroon and white

Backstamp: Doulton

Doulton Number	Size	Backstamp	Height	Intro.	Discon.	Current Market Value		
						U.K. £	U.S. $	Can. $
D6895	Large	Doulton	7"	1991	1994	110.00	200.00	225.00

THE TRAPPER

CANADIAN CENTENNIAL SERIES, 1867-1967
ONE OF THREE

An integral part of Canadian history, the early trappers, or voyageurs, were largely responsible for the early exploration of the country. In search of animal pelts for export to the European market, these rugged men spent the winter travelling by canoe, snowshoe and foot through the wild Canadian north.

The miniature version of the Trapper character jug was put into production briefly in 1983; however, before any quantity was produced, the decision was made to withdraw the character. Several dozen have appeared on the market.

The Trapper is one of three jugs that received a special backstamp in 1967. The other two, the Lumberjack and the North American Indian, complete the three-jug Canadian Centennial Series.

Backstamp A - Doulton

Backstamp B - Canadian
Centennial Series

Designer: Max Henk / David Biggs
Handle: A horn and a pair of snowshoes
Colourway: Dark green and white hat; brown and green clothing

Backstamps: **A.** Doulton
B. Doulton/Canadian Centennial Series 1867-1967

Doulton Number	Size	Backstamp	Height	Intro.	Discon.	Current Market Value U.K. £	Current Market Value U.S. $	Current Market Value Can. $
D6609	Large	Doulton	7 ¼"	1967	1983	85.00	150.00	150.00
D6609	Large	Doul/Cent	7 ¼"	1967	1967	175.00	375.00	425.00
D6612	Small	Doulton	3 ¾"	1967	1983	55.00	75.00	100.00
D —	Miniature	Doulton	2 ½"	1983	1983	2,000.00	3,500.00	4,000.00

Note: This jug was also issued in English Translucent China. These jugs command a premium of 50 to 100% over the earthenware variety.

TUTANKHAMEN and ANKHESENAMUN

This pair of jugs was issued by Lawleys By Post in a limited edition of 1,500.

Photograph of
Ankhesenmun
not available
at presstime

Designer: William K. Harper
Handle: Tutankhamen — Horus, Hawk God of the Sun
Ankhesenamun — Unknown
Colourway: Tutankhamen — Blue, gold and coral
Ankhesenamun — Unknown

Backstamp: Doulton

Doulton Number	Name	Height	Intro.	Discon.	Current Market Value U.K.£	U.S. $	Can. $
D7127	Tutankhamen	4 ½"	1998	Ltd. ed.	95.00	—	—
D7128	Ankhesenamun	4 ½"	1999	Ltd. ed.	95.00	—	—

UGLY DUCHESS

ALICE IN WONDERLAND
ONE OF SIX

The Ugly Duchess lives in Wonderland and plays croquet with the Queen. Alice found the game a curious one, with live hedgehogs for balls, flamingos for mallets and playing-cards soldiers, who doubled over to serve as the arches.

Designer: Max Henk
Handle: A flamingo
Colourway: Green, purple and pink

Backstamp: Doulton

Doulton Number	Size	Backstamp	Height	Intro.	Discon.	Current Market Value		
						U.K. £	U.S. $	Can. $
D6599	Large	Doulton	6 ¾"	1965	1973	450.00	850.00	950.00
D6603	Small	Doulton	3 ½"	1965	1973	275.00	475.00	525.00
D6607	Miniature	Doulton	2 ½"	1965	1973	250.00	450.00	475.00

Note: This jug was also issued in English Translucent China. These jugs command a premium of 50 to 100% over the earthenware variety.

ULYSSES S. GRANT AND ROBERT E. LEE

PROTOTYPE

Differences between the prototype and issued jug — the eyes on the Grant prototype look ahead, while on the limited edition jug show the eyes looking to the left; the section of the flag bearing the stars is larger on the prototype jug and there are only four stipes on the prototype jug as apposed to seven on the limited edition jug.

Designer: Michael Abberley

Handle: Grant — Flag of the Union

Lee — Flag of the Confederacy

Colourway: Black, grey, brown and red

Backstamp: Doulton

Doulton Number	Size	Backstamp	Height	Intro.	Discon.	Current Market Value		
						U.K. £	U.S. $	Can. $
D6698	Large	Doulton	6 ½"	1983	1983	Extremely Rare Sold at Sotheby's Arcade Auction New York, March 12, 1997, $2,415.00		

ULYSSES S. GRANT AND ROBERT E. LEE

THE ANTAGONISTS' COLLECTION (TWO-FACED JUG)
ONE OF FOUR

Ulysses Samuel Grant (1822-1885), a native of Ohio, was made Lieutenant General by President Lincoln and put in command of the Union Army in the American Civil War. His successes led to his election as president in 1868.

Robert E. Lee (1807-1870) was the general in command of the Confederate Army. He was ruthlessly pursued by General Grant, who forced him to retreat from his defence of Richmond, Virginia, in 1865. Lee's troops were surrounded at the great battle of Appomattox, where he and the Confederate Army surrendered.

This jug was issued in 1983 in a limited edition of 9,500 pieces.

 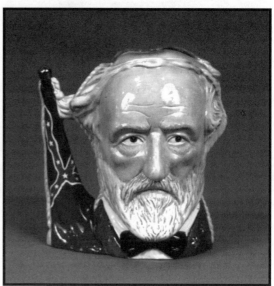

Designer: Michael Abberley	**Backstamp:** Doulton
Handle: Grant — Flag of the Union	
Lee — Flag of the Confederacy	
Colourway: Black, grey, brown and red	

Doulton						Current Market Value		
Number	Size	Backstamp	Height	Intro.	Discon.	U.K. £	U.S. $	Can. $
D6698	Large	Doulton	7"	1983	Ltd. ed.	200.00	400.00	450.00

UNCLE TOM COBBLEIGH

In the popular 18th-century Devonshire song, Tom Cobbleigh and six friends borrow Tom Pearse's old mare to ride to the fair. Unable to support so many, the mare becomes sick and dies and still haunts the night-time moors to this day.

Designer: Max Henk
Handle: Horseshoe
Colourway: Dark brown hat; green coat; dark grey horseshoe

Backstamp: Doulton

Doulton Number	Size	Backstamp	Height	Intro.	Discon.	Current Market Value		
						U.K. £	U.S. $	Can. $
D6337	Large	Doulton	7"	1952	1960	250.00	500.00	575.00

URIAH HEEP

For the tiny character jug Uriah Heep see the "Charles Dickens Commemorative Set" page 185.

VETERAN MOTORIST

Veteran Motorist
D.6637
© DOULTON & CO. LIMITED.1972
REGISTRATION APPLIED FOR.

Designer: David Biggs
Handle: A horn
Colourway: Yellow hat; green coat; white scarf

Backstamp: Doulton

Doulton Number	Size	Backstamp	Height	Intro.	Discon.	Current Market Value		
						U.K. £	U.S. $	Can. $
D6633	Large	Doulton	7 ½"	1973	1983	125.00	200.00	250.00
D6637	Small	Doulton	3 ¼"	1973	1983	65.00	125.00	175.00
D6641	Miniature	Doulton	2 ½"	1973	1983	75.00	150.00	175.00

VICAR OF BRAY

In a popular song of the 18th century, this very adaptable parson boasted that he was able to accommodate himself to the religious views of Charles, James, William, Anne and George, and that "whosoever King may reign, he would always be the Vicar of Bray."

Prior to 1940 these jugs had a distinctive yellow rim.

"Vicar of Bray."
R·N·807475.

Designer: Charles Noke/Harry Fenton
Handle: Plain
Colourway: Brown hat; green coat

Backstamp: Doulton

Doulton Number	Size	Backstamp	Height	Intro.	Discon.	Current Market Value		
						U.K. £	U.S. $	Can. $
D5615	Large	Doulton	6 ¾"	1936	1960	175.00	325.00	375.00

VICE-ADMIRAL LORD NELSON

CHARACTER JUG OF THE YEAR

This was the Character Jug of the Year for 1993. It was issued to commemorate the Battle of Trafalgar, on October 21, 1805.

For the character jug Nelson see page 380, and for the character jug Lord Nelson see page 345.

Designer: Stanley J. Taylor
Handle: The Victory
Colourway: Black, gold and cream

Backstamp: Doulton/Character Jug of the Year, 1993

Doulton Number	Size	Backstamp	Height	Intro.	Discon.	Current Market Value U.K. £	Current Market Value U.S. $	Current Market Value Can. $
D6932	Large	Doulton	8"	1993	1993	150.00	275.00	325.00

VIKING

The large-size Viking character jug is reported to also carry the Stoke-on-Trent backstamp.

Designer: Max Henk
Handle: The prow of a Viking long ship
Colourway: Black, green and brown

Backstamp: Doulton

Doulton Number	Size	Backstamp	Height	Intro.	Discon.	Current Market Value U.K. £	U.S. $	Can. $
D6496	Large	Doulton	7 ¼"	1959	1975	175.00	325.00	350.00
D6502	Small	Doulton	4"	1959	1975	120.00	200.00	225.00
D6526	Miniature	Doulton	2 ½"	1960	1975	130.00	225.00	250.00

Note: This jug was also issued in English Translucent China. These jugs command a premium of 50 to 100% over the earthenware variety.

THE VILLAGE BLACKSMITH

PROTOTYPE

Designer: Max Henk
Handle: Tree above anvil, wheel and horseshoe
Colourway: Blue, brown, black and green

Backstamp: None shown

Doulton Number	Size	Backstamp	Height	Intro.	Discon.	U.K. £	U.S. $	Can. $
						Current Market Value		
D6549	Large	None	7 ½"	1961	1961	Only One Known Sold at Philipps, London, England, May 1993 — £6,000.00.		

Note: Prototype character jugs are extremely rare and the price is solely between the buyer and the seller.

VISCOUNT MONTGOMERY OF ALAMEIN

HEROIC LEADERS
ONE OF THREE

This new design was specially commissioned by Lawleys By Post and was produced in a limited edition of 9,500 pieces. It was sold in a set of three: Montgomery, Mountbatten and Churchill.

For the character jug Field Marshall Montgomery see page 241, and for the character jug Monty see page 368.

Royal Doulton®
VISCOUNT MONTGOMERY OF ALAMEIN
1887-1976
D 6850
Modelled by
Stanley James Taylor
© 1989 ROYAL DOULTON
A LIMITED EDITION OF 9500
THIS IS NO. 1609

Designer:	Stanley J. Taylor	**Backstamp:**	Doulton
Handle:	Imperial Army flag		
Colourway:	Black beret, khaki uniform, red flag		

Doulton Number	Size	Backstamp	Height	Intro.	Discon.	Current Market Value		
						U.K. £	U.S. $	Can. $
D6850	Small	Doulton	3 ¼"	1990	Ltd. ed.	125.00	200.00	225.00

W. C. FIELDS

THE CELEBRITY COLLECTION
ONE OF SIX

Born Claude William Dukenfield (1880-1946), W.C. Fields began his entertainment career at the age of 11 as a juggler. Much later he appeared in the Ziegfeld Follies and then in 1925 began his work in film. With his rasping voice and bulbous nose, he became a very successful satiric comedian.

The following quote appears on the base of the jug: "I was in love with a beautiful blonde once. She drove me to drink — 'tis the one thing I'm indebted to her for."

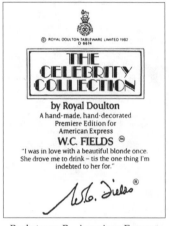

Backstamp B - American Express

Designer: David Biggs
Handle: A walking cane
Colourway: Black, grey and yellow

Backstamps: **A.** Doulton
B. Doulton/American Express/ Premier Edition for American Express. Introduced in the U.S.A. as a promotional jug for American Express. Approximately 1,500 jugs bore the special backstamp.

Doulton Number	Size	Backstamp	Height	Intro.	Discon.	U.K. £	U.S. $	Can. $
D6674	Large	Doulton	7"	1983	1986	125.00	250.00	275.00
D6674	Large	Doulton/Amex	7 ½"	1983	Sp. ed.	200.00	400.00	450.00

W. G. GRACE

William Gilbert Grace (1848-1915) began playing professional cricket at the age of 16 and rose quickly to the status of England's best batsman, earning the title of "The Champion." Throughout his long career, he set many records, retiring at the age of 60 after 44 seasons.

The small jug was commissioned by Lawleys By Post and issued in 1989 in a limited edition of 9,500 pieces.

Designer: Stanley J. Taylor	**Backstamp:** Doulton
Handle: Cricket bat and ball	
Colourway: Yellow and orange striped cap; black beard	

Doulton Number	Size	Backstamp	Height	Intro.	Discon.	Current Market Value		
						U.K. £	U.S. $	Can. $
D7032	Large	Doulton	7"	1996	Ltd. ed.	100.00	225.00	300.00
D6845	Small	Doulton	3 ¼"	1989	Ltd. ed.	85.00	150.00	175.00

THE WALRUS & CARPENTER

ALICE IN WONDERLAND
ONE OF SIX

On a beach in Wonderland, the walrus and carpenter invited a number of oysters for evening conversation, which the walrus promptly ate.

The Walrus & Carpenter
D 6600
COPR 1964
DOULTON & CO LIMITED
Rd No 917233
Rd No 46579
Rd No 10002
Rd No 591/64

Designer: Max Henk
Handle: A walrus
Colourway: Black, green and red

Backstamp: Doulton

Doulton Number	Size	Backstamp	Height	Intro.	Discon.	Current Market Value		
						U.K. £	U.S. $	Can. $
D6600	Large	Doulton	7 ¼"	1965	1980	150.00	275.00	300.00
D6604	Small	Doulton	3 ¼"	1965	1980	100.00	175.00	250.00
D6608	Miniature	Doulton	2 ½"	1965	1980	100.00	175.00	225.00

Note: This jug was also issued in English Translucent China. These jugs command a premium of 50 to 100% over the earthenware variety.

WILD BILL HICKOCK

THE WILD WEST COLLECTION
ONE OF SIX

After serving as a Union scout in the American Civil War, James Butler Hickock (1837-1876) became a marshall and then sheriff of several western frontier towns. An excellent gunman, he earned his nickname from his trigger-happy method of upholding the law at the many shootouts that erupted from poker games. He toured briefly with Buffalo Bill's Wild West Show (1872-1873) and was later murdered at Deadwood.

Designer:	Michael Abberley
Handle:	An upturned whiskey bottle flowing into a glass
Colourway:	Black, brown and white

Backstamp: Doulton

Doulton Number	Size	Backstamp	Height	Intro.	Discon.	Current Market Value		
						U.K. £	U.S. $	Can. $
D6736	Mid	Doulton	5 ½"	1985	1989	85.00	175.00	200.00

WILLIAM SHAKESPEARE

THE SHAKESPEAREAN COLLECTION
ONE OF SIX

Shakespeare (1564-1616) was born in Stratford-upon-Avon. Apparently he moved to London in 1585 and by 1592 had emerged as a promising actor and playwright. He was a part of the theatre company, the King's Men of James I, throughout his London career, and in 1599, he became the new owner of the Globe Theatre. Immensely successful as a playwright, director, poet and actor, Shakespeare was said to have been quite wealthy by the time he returned to Stratford in 1613.

For the character jug Shakespeare see page 466.

STYLE ONE: HANDLE — INK WELL WITH THE APPEARANCE OF THE GLOBE THEATRE

Royal Doulton
The
Shakespearean
Collection
WILLIAM SHAKESPEARE
D6689
Modelled by

© ROYAL DOULTON TABLEWARE LIMITED 1982

Designer: Michael Abberley
Handle: A feather quill with an inkwell of the appearance of the Globe Theatre
Colourway: White, grey and yellow

Backstamp: Doulton

Doulton Number	Size	Backstamp	Height	Intro.	Discon.	Current Market Value		
						U.K. £	U.S. $	Can. $
D6689	Large	Doulton	7 ¾"	1983	1991	100.00	175.00	200.00

WILLIAM SHAKESPEARE

STYLE TWO: HANDLE — CHARACTERS FROM DIFFERENT PLAYS

This jug was issued in a limited edition of 2,500 pieces.

Designer: William K. Harper
Handle: Two handles, characters from different plays
Colourway: Brown

Backstamp: Doulton

Doulton Number	Size	Backstamp	Height	Intro.	Discon.	Current Market Value		
						U.K. £	U.S. $	Can. $
D6933	Large	Doulton	7"	1992	Ltd. ed.	300.00	500.00	600.00

WILLIAM SHAKESPEARE

CHARACTER JUG OF THE YEAR

This jug was commemorates the 400th anniversary of the opening of William Shakepeares Globe Theatre in London, England. The handle is fashioned from the masks of Comedy and Tragedy, as well as a replica of the Globe Theatre.

For the character jug Shakespeare, see page 466.

STYLE THREE: HANDLE — GLOBE THEATRE, MASKS OF COMEDY AND TRAGEDY

Designer:	Robert Tabbenor	
Handle:	Masks of Comedy and Tragedy; a replica of the Globe theatre	
Colourway:	Cream, brown, red and yellow	

Backstamp: Doulton

Doulton Number	Size	Backstamp	Height	Intro.	Discon.	Current Market Value		
						U.K. £	U.S. $	Can. $
D7136	Large	Doulton	7 ¾"	1999	1999	100.00	205.00	395.00

WILLIE CARSON

Born in Stirling in 1942, Willie Carson was the first Scotsman to become Champion Jockey. Among his many racing achievements are his first major Classic win in 1977 in the 2,000 Guineas, also in that year the Oaks and St. Leger, and in 1980 the Derby. This jug was issued by Lawleys By Post in a limited edition of 2,500 pieces.

Royal Doulton®
WILLIE CARSON O.B.E.
D.7111
Modelled by
Stanley James Taylor
© 1998 ROYAL DOULTON
LIMITED EDITION OF 2,500
THIS IS N?

Designer: Stanley J. Taylor
Handle: Riding crop, boot, horshoe and ribbon
Colourway: Blue and white jockey silks

Backstamp: Doulton

Doulton Number	Size	Backstamp	Height	Intro.	Discon.	Current Market Value		
						U.K. £	U.S. $	Can. $
D7111	Small	Doulton	4"	1998	Ltd. ed.	60.00	125.00	175.00

WINSTON CHURCHILL

CHARACTER JUG OF THE YEAR

STYLE ONE: HANDLE — UNION JACK AND BULLDOG

For the character jug Churchill, see page 197, and for the character jug Sir Winston Churchill, see page 477. For the toby jug Winston Churchill, see page 105.

Royal Doulton®
CHARACTER JUG OF THE YEAR
WINSTON CHURCHILL
D 6907
Modelled by

Stanley James Taylor.

This special edition will only
be available during the year
1992
© 1991 ROYAL DOULTON

Designer: Stanley J. Taylor
Handle: Union Jack and bulldog
Colourway: Black, brown and white

Backstamp: Doulton/
Character Jug of the Year, 1992

Doulton Number	Size	Backstamp	Height	Intro.	Discon.	Current Market Value		
						U.K. £	U.S. $	Can. $
D6907	Large	Doulton	7"	1992	1992	175.00	350.00	450.00

WINSTON CHURCHILL

STYLE TWO: HANDLE — NEWS CHRONICLE VICTORY ISSUE

Backstamp: Doulton

Designer: Stanley J. Taylor
Handle: News Chronicle victory issue
Colourway: Black, grey, white and cream

Backstamp: Doulton

Doulton Number	Size	Backstamp	Height	Intro.	Discon.	Current Market Value		
						U.K. £	U.S. $	Can. $
D6934	Small	Doulton	4"	1992	Current	43.00	125.00	155.00

THE WITCH

MYSTICAL SERIES
ONE OF THREE

Designer: Stanley J. Taylor
Handle: Part of the witch's hat
Colourway: Black and greys

Backstamp: Doulton

Doulton Number	Size	Backstamp	Height	Intro.	Discon.	Current Market Value		
						U.K. £	U.S. $	Can. $
D6893	Large	Doulton	7"	1991	1991	150.00	275.00	325.00

THE WIZARD

MYSTICAL SERIES
ONE OF THREE

Royal Doulton®
THE WIZARD
D 6862
Modelled by

Stanley James Taylor.

© 1990 ROYAL DOULTON

Designer: Stanley J. Taylor   **Backstamp:** Doulton
Handle: Black cat and a magic wand
Colourway: Blue-grey cap; black coat; red collar

Doulton Number	Size	Backstamp	Height	Intro.	Discon.	Current Market Value U.K. £	U.S. $	Can. $
D6862	Large	Doulton	6 ¾"	1990	1996	95.00	200.00	275.00
D6909	Small	Doulton	3 ¾"	1992	1998	50.00	85.00	125.00

WYATT EARP

THE WILD WEST COLLECTION
ONE OF SIX

Wyatt Berry Stapp Earp (1848-1929) was an expert gunfighter. He worked as a police officer and armed guard and, in 1881, was involved in the famous shootout at the O.K. Corral. Later Earp travelled around the West, operating a number of saloons.

Designer: Stanley J. Taylor
Handle: A gun and sheriff's badge
Colourway: Brown coat; light brown hat with red band

Backstamp: Doulton

Doulton Number	Size	Backstamp	Height	Intro.	Discon.	Current Market Value		
						U.K. £	U.S. $	Can. $
D6711	Mid	Doulton	5 ½"	1985	1989	100.00	200.00	225.00

YACHTSMAN

The small and miniature jugs of the Yachtsman were piloted, but never put into production.

STYLE ONE: YACHTSMAN WITH LIFE JACKET

Yachtsman
D6626
COPR 1970
DOULTON & CO LIMITED
Rd No 949549
Rd No 57980
Rd No 12385
Rd No 914/70

Designer: David Biggs
Handle: A yacht sailing from the front to back
Colourway: Blue cap and jersey; yellow lifejacket

Backstamp: Doulton

Doulton Number	Size	Backstamp	Height	Intro.	Discon.	Current Market Value		
						U.K. £	U.S. $	Can. $
D6626	Large	Doulton	8"	1971	1980	125.00	200.00	225.00
D —	Small	Doulton	3"	Unknown			Extremely rare	

YACHTSMAN

STYLE TWO: YACHTSMAN WITH PEAK CAP AND SCARF

Royal Doulton®
YACHTSMAN
D 6820
Modelled by
Stanley James Taylor
© 1988 ROYAL DOULTON

Backstamp A - Doulton

Designer: Stanley J. Taylor
Handle: Sailboat with white sails and green trim sailing back to front
Colourway: Navy blue cap; dark blue jacket; yellow shirt; grey scarf

Backstamps: **A.** Doulton
For general release, 1989.
B. Doulton/Canadian Doulton Show and Sale
Issued to commemorate the first Canadian Doulton Show and Sale at Durham, Ontario, July 29 to 31, 1988. Issued in a special edition of 750 pieces.

Doulton Number	Size	Backstamp	Height	Intro.	Discon.	Current Market Value		
						U.K. £	U.S. $	Can. $
D6820	Large	Doulton	6 ½"	1989	1991	75.00	175.00	200.00
D6820	Large	Doulton/Durham	6 ½"	1988	Sp. ed.	175.00	225.00	250.00

THE YEOMAN OF THE GUARD

THE LONDON COLLECTION
ONE OF TEN

In 1485 Henry VIII organized the Yeomen of the Guard, bodyguards to the monarch of England. Today the Yeomen, or Beefeaters as they are more commonly known, serve only as ceremonial guards.

Backstamp A - Doulton

Designer: Stanley J. Taylor
Handle: Raven and tree trunk
Colourway: Black hat; white frills; red jacket

Backstamp C - Doulton/Horne

Backstamp D -
Doulton/Strawbridge

Backstamps: **A.** Doulton

The jugs bearing backstamps B, C, D and E were released in the U.S.A. to commemorate the anniversaries of the opening of the four Royal Doulton Rooms in the U.S.A. They were issued in a limited edition of 450 pieces total and bore a special backstamp.

    B. Doulton/Dillards/
        To Commemorate the third anniversary of the opening of the Royal Doulton Room Dillards, New Orleans, Louisiana, U.S.A.
        Issued in a limited edition of 50 pieces.

    C. Doulton/Joseph Horne/
        To Commemorate the third anniversary of the opening of the Royal Doulton Room Joseph Horne, Pittsburgh, Pennsylvania, U.S.A.
        Issued in a limited edition of 75 pieces.

    D. Doulton/Strawbridge and Clothier/
        To Commemorate the fourth anniversary of the opening of the Royal Doulton Room Strawbridge and Clothier, Philadelphia, Pennsylvania, U.S.A.
        Issued in a limited edition of 75 pieces.

    E. Doulton/Higbee/
        To Commemorate the fifth anniversary of the opening of the Royal Doulton Room Higbee Cleveland, Ohio, U.S.A.
        Issued in a limited edition of 250 pieces.

Doulton Number	Size	Backstamp	Height	Intro.	Discon.	Current Market Value		
						U.K. £	U.S. $	Can. $
D6873	Large	Doulton	7"	1991	1997	100.00	150.00	200.00
D6883	Large	Dillards	7"	1990	Ltd. ed.	225.00	375.00	450.00
D6882	Large	Horne	7"	1990	Ltd. ed.	200.00	350.00	425.00
D6885	Large	Strawbridge	7"	1990	Ltd. ed.	200.00	350.00	425.00
D6884	Large	Higbee	7"	1990	Ltd. ed.	175.00	300.00	400.00

BOOKENDS

HENRY V and FALSTAFF

Designer: David B. Biggs

Colourway: Henry V — Grey maroon, yellow and gold
Falstaff — Maroon, white, grey and gold
Red book covers

Backstamp: Doulton

Doulton Number	Name	Height	Intro.	Discon.	Current Market Value		
					U.K. £	U.S. $	Can. $
D7088	Henry V	7 1/2"	1998	Current	75.00	205.00	340.00
D7089	Falstaff	7 1/2"	1998	Current	75.00	205.00	340.00

SHERLOCK HOLMES AND DOCTOR WATSON

VARIATION No. 1: BOOK TITLES
Sherlock Holmes — "The Adventures of Sherlock Holmes" "The Hound of the Baskervilles"
Dr. Watson —"The Adventures of Sherlock Holmes " "The Last Problem"

VARIATION No. 2: BOOK TITLES
Sherlock Holmes — "The Memoirs of Sherlock Holmes"
Dr. Watson — "The Memoirs of Sherlock Holmes" "The Final Problem"

Designer: Martyn C. R. Alcock
Colourway: Sherlock Holmes — Brown coat and deerstalker
Dr. Watson — Grey jacket and tie, brown hat
Green book covers

Backstamp: Doulton

Doulton Number	Variation	Name	Height	Intro.	Discon.	U.K. £	U.S. $	Can. $
D7038	Var. 1	Sherlock Holmes	7 ½"	1996	1997	95.00	250.00	375.00
D7038	Var. 2	Sherlock Holmes	7 ½"	1997	Current	75.00	220.00	340.00
D7039	Var. 1	Doctor Watson	7 ½"	1996	1997	95.00	250.00	375.00
D7039	Var. 2	Doctor Watson	7 ½"	1997	Current	75.00	220.00	340.00

STAN LAUREL AND OILVER HARDY

These bookends were issued in a limited edition of 2,500.

Designer: William K. Harper

Colourway: Stan Laurel — Grey jacket, black bow tie with white spots, black bowler with grey band "You've Gotten Us Into."
Oliver Hardy — Grey jacket, red tie with white spots black bowler with grey band "Here's Another Nice Mess"

Backstamp: Doulton/TM & © 1998 Larry Harmon Pictures Corporation All Rights Reserved

Doulton Number	Name	Height	Intro.	Discon.	Current Market Value		
					U.K. £	U.S. $	Can. $
D7119	Stan Laurel	7 ¾"	1998	Ltd. ed.	150.00	340.00	680.00
D7120	Oliver Hardy	7 ¾"	1998	Ltd. ed.		Pair	

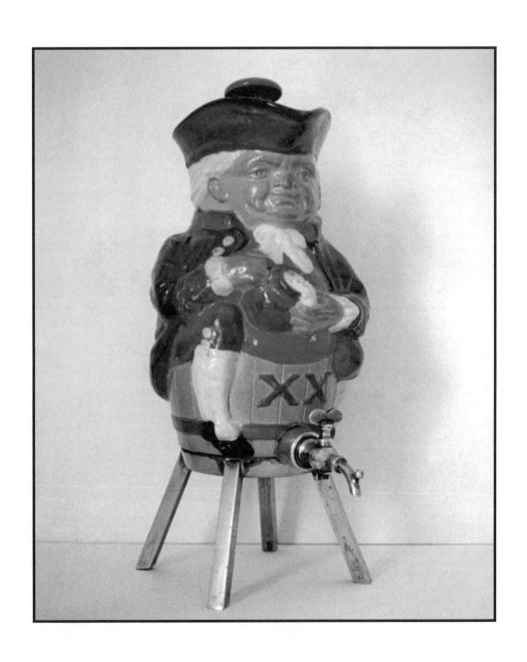

LIQUOR CONTAINERS AND JUGS

The Pickwick Collection

ASPREY & CO. LTD.

WHISKEY DECANTERS

Two whisky flasks, one depicting an Irishman and the other a Scotsman, were made in the 1920s for Asprey and Co. Ltd, New Bond Street, London, England. Each was set within a wooden tantalus, and the head of the flask was detachable. The Irishman contained Irish whiskey, and the Scotsman, Scottish whisky. These two flasks are usually traded as a set.

Designer: Harry Fenton   **Backstamp:** Doulton
Colourway: Black hat and coat; green cravat; maroon vest

Doulton Number	Name	Backstamp	Height	Intro.	Discon.	Current Market Value		
						U.K. £	**U.S. $**	**Can. $**
D —	Irishman	Doulton	9 ½"	1920	1930	900.00	2,250.00	2,750.00
D —	Scotsman	Doulton	9 ½"	1920	1930	900.00	2,250.00	2,750.00

CAPTAIN COOK

THE INTERNATIONAL COLLECTION
ONE OF FOUR

LIQUOR CONTAINER

This Captain Cook liquor container was commissioned by Pick-Kwik Wines and Spirits in a limited edition of 2,000 pieces.

THIRD OF A SERIES
THE INTERNATIONAL COLLECTION
Specially Commissioned
from
Royal Doulton®
200ml. **JIM BEAM BOURBON WHISKEY** 40% Vol.
PICK-KWIK WINES & SPIRITS
MICKLEOVER. DERBY. ENGLAND
with special permission from
JAMES B. BEAM DISTILLING INTERNATIONAL CO.

Designer: Harry Sales
Modeller: Graham Tongue
Handle: Scroll
Colourway: Black hat; black and yellow uniform
Inscription around Base: "Captain Cook" "The World's Finest Bourbon since 1795"

Backstamp: Doulton/Pick-Kwik

Doulton Number	Size	Backstamp	Height	Intro.	Discon.	Current Market Value		
						U.K. £	U.S. $	Can. $
D —	Small	Doulton	4 ¾"	1985	Ltd. ed.	65.00	125.00	150.00

FALSTAFF

LIQUEUR CONTAINER

The Falstaff, Poacher and Rip Van Winkle character jugs were adapted by RoyalDoulton as liqueur containers for Bols liqueur for the bottling firm of W. Walklate Ltd. The small-size jugs were commissioned c.1960 by W. Walklate Ltd.

Designer: Harry Fenton
Handle: Plain
Colourway: Rose tunic; black hat trimmed
with rose plumes; grey beard

Backstamp: Doulton

Doulton Number	Size	Backstamp	Height	Intro.	Discon.	Current Market Value U.K. £	U.S. $	Can. $
D6385	Small	Falstaff	4"	c. 1960	c. 1960	60.00	150.00	175.00

JOHN BULL

THE INTERNATIONAL COLLECTION
ONE OF FOUR

LIQUOR CONTAINER

The John Bull liquor container was commissioned by Pick-Kwik Wines and Spirits in a limited edition of 2,000 pieces.

SECOND OF A SERIES
THE INTERNATIONAL COLLECTION
*Specially Commissioned
from*
Royal Doulton®
200ml. JIM BEAM BOURBON WHISKEY 40% Vol.
PICK-KWIK WINES & SPIRITS
MICKLEOVER, DERBY, ENGLAND
with special permission from
JAMES B. BEAM DISTILLING INTERNATIONAL CO.

Designer: Harry Sales
Modeller: Graham Tongue
Handle: Cane with bull dog head
Colourway: Black hat with yellow band, red coat
Inscription around Base: "John Bull"

Backstamp: Doulton/Pick-Kwik

Doulton Number	Size	Backstamp	Height	Intro.	Discon.	U.K. £	U.S. $	Can. $
						Current Market Value		
D —	Small	Doulton	5"	1985	Ltd. ed.	85.00	175.00	200.00

MR. MICAWBER

STYLE ONE: LIQUOR CONTAINER

This liquor container was commissioned by Pick-Kwik Wines and Spirits.

VARIATION No. 1: Colourway — Brown hat; dark blue blazer; maroon cravat
Handle — Dewar's
Inscription on Base —"Dewar's"
Issued — 2,000 pieces

Designer: Harry Sales
Modeller: Graham Tongue
Handle: Dewar's
Colourway: Brown hat; dark blue blazer; maroon cravat
Inscription around Base: "Dewar's"

Backstamp: Doulton/Pick-Kwik

Doulton Number	Size	Variation	Height	Intro.	Discon.	Current Market Value		
						U.K. £	U.S. $	Can. $
D —	Small	Var. 1	5"	1983	Ltd. ed.	70.00	150.00	175.00

VARIATION No. 2: Colourway — Grey hat; green blazer; light blue cravat
Handle — Pickwick Deluxe
Inscription around Base — "Pickwick Deluxe Whiskey"
Issued — 2,000 pieces

Doulton Number	Size	Variation	Height	Intro.	Discon.	Current Market Value		
						U.K. £	U.S. $	Can. $
D —	Small	Var. 2	5"	1983	Ltd. ed.	65.00	125.00	150.00

VARIATION No. 3: Colourway — White
Handle — Pickwick Deluxe
Inscription around Base — "Pickwick Deluxe Whiskey"
Issued — 100 pieces

Doulton Number	Size	Variation	Height	Intro.	Discon.	Current Market Value		
						U.K. £	U.S. $	Can. $
D —	Small	Var. 3	5"	1985	Ltd. ed.	150.00	250.00	300.00

MR. MICAWBER

STYLE TWO: CHARACTER JUG

This jug was commissioned by Pick-Kwik Wines and Spirits.

VARIATION No. 1: Colourway — Brown hat; blue blazer; maroon cravat
Handle — Dewar's
Inscription around Base — "Dewar's"
Issued — 100 pieces

Designer: Harry Sales	**Backstamp:** Doulton/Pick-Kwik
Modeller: Graham Tongue	
Handle: Dewar's	
Colourway: Brown hat; blue blazer; maroon cravat	
Inscription around Base: "Dewar's"	

Doulton Number	Size	Variation	Height	Intro.	Discon.	Current Market Value U.K. £	U.S. $	Can. $
D —	Small	Var. 1	4"	1985	Ltd. ed.	150.00	250.00	275.00

Variation No. 2   Variation No. 3   Variation No. 3

VARIATION No. 2:   Colourway — White
Handle — Dewar's
Inscription around Base — "Dewar's" in red
Issued — 100 pieces

Doulton Number	Size	Variation	Height	Intro.	Discon.	Current Market Value		
						U.K. £	U.S. $	Can. $
D —	Small	Var. 2	4"	1985	Ltd. ed.	150.00	275.00	300.00

VARIATION No. 3:   Colourway — Grey hat; green blazer; light blue cravat
Handle — Pickwick Deluxe
Inscription around Base — "Pickwick Deluxe Whiskey"
Issued — 100 pieces

Doulton Number	Size	Variation	Height	Intro.	Discon.	Current Market Value		
						U.K. £	U.S. $	Can. $
D —	Small	Var. 3	4"	1985	Ltd. ed.	150.00	275.00	300.00

VARIATION No. 4:   Colourway — White
Handle — Pickwick Deluxe
Inscription around Base — "Pickwick Deluxe Whiskey"
Issued — 100 pieces

Doulton Number	Size	Variation	Height	Intro.	Discon.	Current Market Value		
						U.K. £	U.S. $	Can. $
D —	Small	Var. 4	4"	1985	Ltd. ed.	150.00	275.00	300.00

MR. PICKWICK

CHARACTER JUG

Pick-Kwik Wines and Spirits commissioned the Mr. Pickwick jug.

VARIATION No. 1:   Colourway — Green hat; black coat
Handle — No label / "Whisky"
Inscription around Base — "Pick-Kwik Derby Whiskies Wines Ales"
Issued — 2,000 pieces

MR PICKWICK
(FOUNDER & GENERAL CHAIRMAN
OF THE PICKWICK CLUB)
THE MOST FAMOUS OF
CHARLES DICKENS' CHARACTERS FROM
"PICKWICK PAPERS"
FIRST PUBLISHED IN 1846

Designer: Harry Sales
Modeller: Graham Tongue
Handle: Pick-Kwik
Colourway: Green hat; black coat
Inscription around Base: "Pick-Kwik Derby Whiskies Wines Ales"

Backstamp: Doulton/Pick-Kwik

Doulton Number	Size	Variation	Height	Intro.	Discon.	Current Market Value U.K. £	Current Market Value U.S. $	Current Market Value Can. $
D —	Small	Var. 1	4"	1982	Ltd. ed.	85.00	150.00	175.00

VARIATION No. 2:   Colourway — Brown hat; dark brown coat
Handle — Jim Beam
Inscription around Base — "Pick-Kwik Derby Sells Jim Beam Whiskey"
Issued — 2,000 pieces

Doulton Number	Size	Variation	Height	Intro.	Discon.	Current Market Value		
						U.K. £	U.S. $	Can. $
D —	Small	Var. 2	4"	1984	Ltd. ed.	75.00	175.00	200.00

VARIATION No. 3:   Colourway — Beige hat; brown coat
Handle — Beam's White Label
Inscription around Base —"Beam Whiskey" "The World's Finest Bourbon"
Issued — 1,000 pieces

Doulton Number	Size	Variation	Height	Intro.	Discon.	Current Market Value		
						U.K. £	U.S. $	Can. $
D —	Small	Var. 3	5 ¼"	1984	Ltd. ed.	75.00	175.00	200.00

VARIATION No. 4:   Colourway — Beige hat; brown coat
Handle — Beam's Black Label
Inscription around Base — "Beam Whiskey"
Issued — 1,000 pieces

Doulton Number	Size	Variation	Height	Intro.	Discon.	Current Market Value		
						U.K. £	U.S. $	Can. $
D —	Small	Var. 4	5 ¼"	1984	Ltd. ed.	75.00	175.00	200.00

VARIATION No. 5:   Colourway — White
Handle — No label / "Whiskey"
Inscription around Base — "Pick Kwik Derby"
Issued — 100 pieces

Doulton Number	Size	Variation	Height	Intro.	Discon.	Current Market Value U.K. £	U.S. $	Can. $
D —	Small	Var. 5	5 ¼"	1985	Ltd. ed.	125.00	275.00	300.00

VARIATION No. 6:   Colourway — White with red transfers
Handle — Jim Beam
Inscription around Base — "Pick Kwik Derby Sells Jim Beam Whiskey"
Issued — 100 pieces

Doulton Number	Size	Variation	Height	Intro.	Discon.	Current Market Value U.K. £	U.S. $	Can. $
D —	Small	Var. 6	5 ¼"	1985	Ltd. ed.	125.00	275.00	300.00

VARIATION No. 7:   Colourway — Brown hat, green coat
Handle — Beam's White Label
Inscription around Base — "Pick Kwik Derby Sells Jim Beam Whiskey"
Issued — 2000 pieces

Doulton Number	Size	Variation	Height	Intro.	Discon.	Current Market Value U.K. £	U.S. $	Can. $
D —	Small	Var. 7	4"	1985	Ltd. ed.	125.00	275.00	300.00

MR. PICKWICK AND SAM WELLER

THE PICKWICK COLLECTION

LIQUOR CONTAINER

This two-faced liquor container was commissioned by Pick-Kwik Wines and Spirits in a limited edition of 2,000 pieces.

Designer: Harry Sales
Modeller: Graham Tongue
Handle: Jim Beam, plain bottle
Colourway: Mr. Pickwick — Dark green coat; pink bow tie
Sam Weller — Dark green coat; yellow cravat
with red dots

Inscription on Base: "Beam Whiskey" and "The World's Finest Bourbon"

Backstamp: Doulton/Pick-Kwik

Doulton Number	Size	Backstamp	Height	Intro.	Discon.	Current Market Value U.K. £	U.S. $	Can. $
D —	Small	Doulton	5"	1985	Ltd. ed.	75.00	200.00	225.00

OLD MR. TURVERYDROP

LIQUOR CONTAINER

Commissioned by Pick-Kwik Wines and Spirits, Old Mr. Turverydrop was produced in a limited edition of 2,000 pieces.

THE PICKWICK COLLECTION
Specially Commissioned from
Royal Doulton®
200ml.   JIM BEAM BOURBON WHISKEY   40% Vol.
PICK-KWIK WINES & SPIRITS
MICKLEOVER, DERBY, ENGLAND
with special permission from
JAMES B. BEAM DISTILLING INTERNATIONAL CO.

Designer:	Harry Sales
Modeller:	Graham Tongue
Handle:	Jim Beam
Colourway:	Yellow hat; dark brown coat

Backstamp: Doulton/Pick-Kwik

Inscription on Base: "Beam Whiskey" "Famous for quality since 1795"

Doulton Number	Size	Backstamp	Height	Intro.	Discon.	Current Market Value U.K. £	U.S. $	Can. $
D —	Small	Doulton	5"	1985	1985	65.00	175.00	175.00

THE POACHER

LIQUEUR CONTAINER

The Falstaff, Poacher and Rip Van Winkle character jugs were adapted by Doulton to liqueur containers for Bols liqueurs for the bottling firm W. Walklate Ltd. The small-size jugs were commissioned about 1960 by W. Walklate Ltd.

Designer: Max Henk   **Backstamp:** Doulton
Handle: A salmon
Colourway: Green coat; red scarf; light brown hat

Doulton Number	Size	Backstamp	Height	Intro.	Discon.	Current Market Value		
						U.K. £	U.S. $	Can. $
D6464	Small	Doulton	4"	c. 1960	c. 1960	60.00	150.00	150.00

RIP VAN WINKLE

LIQUEUR CONTAINER

The Falstaff, Poacher and Rip Van Winkle character jugs were adapted by Doulton to liqueur containers for Bols liqueurs for the bottling firm W. Walklate Ltd. The small-size jugs were commissioned about 1960 by W. Walklate Ltd.

Designer: Geoff Blower	**Backstamp:** Doulton	
Handle: A man resting against a tree		
Colourway: Grey-blue cap; brown robes; figure resting against tree dressed in blue		

Doulton Number	Size	Backstamp	Height	Intro.	Discon.	Current Market Value U.K. £	U.S. $	Can. $
D6463	Small	Doulton	4"	c. 1960	c. 1960	60.00	150.00	150.00

SAMURAI WARRIOR

THE INTERNATIONAL COLLECTION
ONE OF FOUR

LIQUOR CONTAINER

Commissioned by Pick-Kwik Wines and Spirits, the Samurai Warrior was produced in a limited edition of 2,000 pieces.

Designer:	Harry Sales	**Backstamp:**	Doulton/Pick-Kwik
Modeller:	Graham Tongue		
Handle:	Sword		
Colourway:	Black hair; white face		

Inscription on Base: "Samurai Warrior" "Famous for quality since 1795"

Doulton Number	Size	Backstamp	Height	Intro.	Discon.	Current Market Value		
						U.K. £	**U.S. $**	**Can. $**
D —	Small	Doulton	5"	1986	1986	75.00	150.00	150.00

SGT. BUZ FUZ

CHARACTER JUG

This character jug was commissioned by Pick-Kwik Wines and Spirits.

VARIATION No. 1:   Colourway — White hair; black coat
Handle — Dewar's
Inscription around Base — "Pick-Kwik Derby Sells Dewar's Whisky"
Issued — 2,000 pieces

Designer: Harry Sales
Modeller: Graham Tongue
Handle: Dewar's
Colourway: White hair; black coat
Inscription around Base: "Pick-Kwik Derby Sells Dewar's Whisky"

Backstamp: Doulton/Pick-Kwik

Doulton Number	Size	Variation	Height	Intro.	Discon.	Current Market Value U.K. £	Current Market Value U.S. $	Current Market Value Can. $
D —	Small	Var. 1	4"	1982	Ltd. ed.	75.00	200.00	200.00

VARIATION No. 2: Colourway — White with red transfers
Handle — Dewar's
Inscription around Base — "Pick-Kwik Derby Sells Dewar's Whisky"
Issued — 100 pieces

Doulton Number	Size	Variation	Height	Intro.	Discon.	Current Market Value U.K. £	U.S. $	Can. $
D —	Small	Var. 2	4"	1985	Ltd. ed.	125.00	275.00	300.00

VARIATION No. 3: Colourway — White
Handle — Plain bottle
Inscription around Base — "Pick-Kwik Derby Sells Whisky"
Issued — 100 pieces

Doulton Number	Size	Variation	Height	Intro.	Discon.	Current Market Value U.K. £	U.S. $	Can. $
D —	Small	Var. 3	4"	1985	Ltd. ed.	125.00	275.00	300.00

TOWN CRIER OF EATANSWILL

LIQUOR CONTAINER

This Town Crier was commissioned by Pick-Kwik Wines and Spirits and was issued in a limited edition of 2,000 pieces.

Designer: Harry Sales
Modeller: Graham Tongue
Handle: Jim Beam
Colourway: Black hat; maroon coat with yellow trim
Inscription around Base: "Beam Whiskey"

Backstamp: Doulton/Pick-Kwik

Doulton Number	Size	Backstamp	Height	Intro.	Discon.	Current Market Value U.K. £	U.S. $	Can. $
D —	Small	Doulton	5"	1986	Ltd. ed.	85.00	175.00	200.00

UNCLE SAM

THE INTERNATIONAL COLLECTION
ONE OF FOUR

STYLE ONE: HANDLE — JIM BEAM BOTTLE

Commissioned by Pick-Kwik Wines and Spirits, Uncle Sam was issued in a limited edition of 2,000 pieces.

VARIATION No. 1:   Inscription around Base — "Uncle Sam" "Famous for quality since 1795"

Designer: Harry Sales	
Modeller: Graham Tongue	**Backstamp:** Doulton/Pick-Kwik
Handle: Jim Beam bottle	
Colourway: Red, white and blue hat, blue brim	

Doulton Number	Size	Variation	Height	Intro.	Discon.	Current Market Value U.K. £	U.S. $	Can. $
D —	Small	Var. 1	5 ¼"	1984	Ltd. ed.	75.00	175.00	200.00

VARIATION No. 2:   Inscription around base — "Beam Whiskey"

Doulton Number	Size	Variation	Height	Intro.	Discon.	Current Market Value U.K. £	U.S. $	Can. $
D —	Small	Var. 2	5 ¼"	1984	Ltd. ed.	75.00	175.00	200.00

UNCLE SAM

STYLE TWO: HANDLE: EAGLE

Commissioned by Pick-Kwik Wines and Spirits, Uncle Sam was issued as promotional item in a limited edition of 500 pieces.

VARIATION No. 1:   Inscription around base — "In God We Trust"

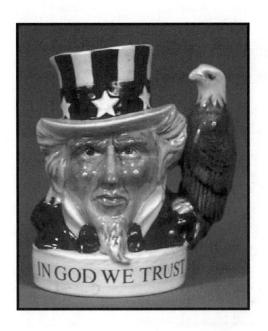

Designer: Harry Sales	**Backstamp:** Doulton/Pick-Kwik
Modeller: Graham Tongue	
Handle: Eagle	
Colourway: Red, white and blue hat, white brim	

Doulton						Current Market Value		
Number	Size	Variation	Height	Intro.	Discon.	U.K. £	U.S. $	Can. $
D —	Small	Var. 1	5 ¼"	1986	Ltd. ed.	100.00	250.00	300.00

VARIATION No. 2:   Inscription around base —"Beam Whiskey" "The World's Finest Bourbon"

Doulton						Current Market Value		
Number	Size	Variation	Height	Intro.	Discon.	U.K. £	U.S. $	Can. $
D —	Small	Var. 2	5 ¼"	1986	Ltd. ed.	100.00	250.00	300.00

WILLIAM GRANT

LIQUOR CONTAINER

STYLE ONE: HANDLE — FOUR OAK CASKS

Issued to commemorate the centenary of the founding of the Glenfiddich Distillery, this jug contains 750 ml of 25-year-old Grants Whisky. The uniform is that of a major of the 6th Volunteer Battalion of the Gordon Highlanders. The Glengarry cap features the symbol of a stag's head, which also appears on all of the company's bottles of whisky.

Backstamp A - 100th
Anniversary Foundation Stone

Backstamp B - Christmas 1987

Designer: Graham Tongue
Handle: Four oak casks
Colourway: Scarlet

Backstamps:　**A.** Doulton/William Grant 100th Anniversary
　　　　　　　Issued in 1986 in a limited edition of 500 pieces to commemorate
　　　　　　　the 100th anniversary of the laying of the foundation stone.
　　　　　　B. Special commission by Grant & Sons for employees on
　　　　　　　Christmas 1987
　　　　　　C. Doulton / William Grant 100 Years
　　　　　　　Issued in 1987 in a limited edition of 2,500 pieces to celebrate the
　　　　　　　100 years since whisky first flowed from the stills.

Backstamp C - 100th
Anniversary of Production

Doulton Number	Size	Backstamp	Height	Intro.	Discon.	Current Market Value U.K. £	U.S. $	Can. $
D —	Large	A	7"	1986	Ltd. ed.	300.00	500.00	550.00
D —	Large	B	7"	1987	Ltd. ed.		Rare	
D —	Large	C	7"	1987	Ltd. ed.	200.00	375.00	375.00

WILLIAM GRANT

LIQUOR CONTAINER

STYLE TWO: HANDLE — FIELD OFFICERS' SWORD

Commissioned by Grants Glenfiddich Distillery, this liquor container was issued in 1988 in a limited edition of 5,000 pieces.

William Grant
Founder of William Grant & Sons Ltd
An independent family company for five generations
Specially Commissioned from
Royal Doulton®
Hand Modelled and Hand Painted
Designed and Modelled by:
William Grant's 25 Year Old
Very Rare Blended Scotch Whisky
One of a limited edition of 5000
William Grant Character Jugs specially styled
with a Field Officer's sword handle
Blended and Bottled by
William Grant & Sons Ltd
The Glenfiddich Distillery, Banffshire, Scotland
Product of Scotland
750ml 43% vol.

Designer: Graham Tongue
Handle: Field officers' sword
Colourway: Scarlet

Backstamp: Doulton/William Grant

Doulton Number	Size	Backstamp	Height	Intro.	Discon.	Current Market Value U.K. £	U.S. $	Can. $
D —	Large	Doulton/Grant	7"	1988	Ltd. ed.	250.00	525.00	600.00

The International Collection

LOVING CUPS AND JUGS

ADMIRAL LORD NELSON

This cup was issued in a limited edition of 600 pieces.

Designer: Charles Noke / Harry Fenton
Handles: Block and tackles
Main Colours: Brown, blue, yellow and green
Inscription around base: "England Expects" and "It was in Trafalgar Bay"

Backstamp: Doulton

Doulton Number	Type	Backstamp	Height	Intro.	Discon.	Current Market Value		
						U.K. £	U.S. $	Can. $
—	Cup	Doulton	10 ½"	1935	Ltd. ed.	1,250.00	2,200.00	2,500.00

THE APOTHECARY

The Apothecary was issued in a limited edition of 600.

Designer: Charles Noke/Harry Fenton
Handles: Distorted faces
Main Colours: Green, red, yellow

Backstamp: Doulton

Doulton Number	Type	Backstamp	Height	Intro.	Discon.	Current Market Value		
						U.K. £	U.S. $	Can. $
—	Cup	Doulton	6"	1934	Ltd. ed.	800.00	1,450.00	1,600.00

CAPTAIN COOK

The Captain Cook loving cup was issued in a limited edition of 350 pieces.

Designer: Charles Noke/Harry Fenton
Handles: Coconut palms with the flags of
St. George and the Union Jack
Main Colours: Green, blue, yellow and red

Backstamp: Doulton

Doulton Number	Type	Backstamp	Height	Intro.	Discon.	Current Market Value		
						U.K. £	U.S. $	Can. $
—	Cup	Doulton	9 ½"	1933	Ltd. ed.	3,000.00	5,500.00	6,500.00

CAPTAIN PHILLIP

This jug was issued in a limited edition of 350 pieces.

Designer: Charles Noke/Harry Fenton
Handle: Eucalyptus tree trunk
Main Colours: Yellow, blue, red and green
Spout: Face of Captain Phillip
Inscription around base: "Colony New South Wales founded January 1788 Sydney"

Backstamp: Doulton

Doulton Number	Type	Backstamp	Height	Intro.	Discon.	Current Market Value		
						U.K. £	U.S. $	Can. $
—	Jug	Doulton	9 ¼"	1938	Ltd. ed.	3,000.00	5,000.00	6,500.00

CHARLES DICKENS

This jug was issued in a limited edition of 1,000.

Designer: Charles Noke/Harry Fenton
Handle: Open book
Spout: Face of Charles Dickens
Main Colours: Brown, green and red

Backstamp: Doulton

Doulton Number	Type	Backstamp	Height	Intro.	Discon.	Current Market Value		
						U.K. £	U.S. $	Can. $
—	Jug	Doulton	10 ½"	1936	Ltd. ed.	1,000.00	1,850.00	2,500.00

DICKENS DREAM

Although Dickens Dream was issued in an unlimited edition, probably only 1,000 pieces were produced.

Designer: Charles Noke
Handle: Poor Jo
Main Colours: Brown, green and red

Backstamp: Doulton

Doulton Number	Type	Backstamp	Height	Intro.	Discon.	Current Market Value		
						U.K. £	U.S. $	Can. $
—	Jug	Doulton	10 ½"	1933	Unknown	2,000.00	3,500.00	4,500.00

GEORGE WASHINGTON

PROTOTYPE

The handle of this prototype differs from the production model in that the stars are moulded in relief and set atop a striped background.

Photograph
Not Available
At Press Time

Designer: Charles Noke/Harry Fenton
Handle: Stars and Stripes
Main Colours: Brown, blue, red and cream
Spout: Face of George Washington
Inscription around base: "Declaration of Independence"

Backstamp: Doulton

Doulton Number	Type	Backstamp	Height	Intro.	Discon.	Current Market Value U.K. £	U.S. $	Can. $
—	Jug	Doulton	10 ¼"	1932	1932	Extremely rare		

GEORGE WASHINGTON

This jug was issued in a limited edition of 1,000 pieces.

STYLE ONE: JUG

Designer: Charles Noke/Harry Fenton	**Backstamp:** Doulton
Handle: The Stars and Stripes	
Main Colours: Brown, blue, red and cream	
Spout: Face of George Washington	
Inscription around base: "Declaration of Independence"	

Doulton Number	Type	Backstamp	Height	Intro.	Discon.	Current Market Value		
						U.K. £	U.S. $	Can. $
—	Jug	Doulton	10 ¼"	1932	Ltd. ed.	7,000.00	12,500.00	14,500.00

GEORGE WASHINGTON

This George Washington loving cup was issued to commemorate the 200th anniversary of his birth.

STYLE TWO: LOVING CUP

Designer: C. J. Noke
Handle: Laurel leaves
Main Colours: Browns, green and red

Backstamp: Doulton

Doulton Number	Type	Backstamp	Height	Intro.	Discon.	Current Market Value		
						U.K. £	**U.S. $**	**Can. $**
—	Cup	Doulton	8 ¼"	1932	Unknown	Extremely rare. Only four known. Sold October 29, 1998 Phillips, London, England, £6,325.00		

Note: A pitcher, 9" high, with the same design as the George Washington, style two, loving cup is known.

GUY FAWKES

The Guy Fawkes jug was issued in a limited edition of 600 pieces.

Designer: Harry Fenton	**Backstamp:** Doulton
Handle: Flaming torch	
Main Colours: Green, brown and red	

Doulton Number	Type	Backstamp	Height	Intro.	Discon.	Current Market Value U.K. £	U.S. $	Can. $
—	Jug	Doulton	7 ½"	1934	Ltd. ed.	1,000.00	1,500.00	1,750.00

I.T. WIGG, BROOM-MAN

This is believed to have been a trial piece only. There are no production pieces known to exist.

Designer: Unknown	**Backstamp:** Unknown
Handle: Unknown	
Main Colours: Unknown	

Doulton Number	Type	Backstamp	Height	Intro.	Discon.	Current Market Value U.K. £	U.S. $	Can. $
—	Jug	Doulton	Unknown	Unknown			Unique	

Note: We have no information or photographs for this jug. We would appreciate anyone with further particulars contacting the Charlton Press.

JACKDAW OF RHEIMS

This jug is believed to have been a trial piece only. No evidence exists that this jug actually went into production.

Designer: Unknown
Handle: Candle, candlestick and candle-snuffer
Main Colours: Brown, red and green

Backstamp: Doulton

Doulton Number	Type	Backstamp	Height	Intro.	Discon.	Current Market Value U.K. £	U.S. $	Can. $
—	Jug	Doulton	11"		c. 1934	Extremely rare. Only one known.		

JAN VAN RIEBEECK

This cup was issued in limited edition of 300 pieces.

Designer: Charles Noke / Harry Fenton
Handles: Van Riebeeck figures
Main Colours: Yellow, green, blue and red

Backstamp: Doulton

Doulton Number	Type	Backstamp	Height	Intro.	Discon.	Current Market Value		
						U.K. £	U.S. $	Can. $
—	Cup	Doulton	10 ¼"	1935	Ltd. ed.	4,000.00	6,000.00	7,000.00

JOHN PEEL

The John Peel cup was issued in a limited edition of 500 pieces.

Designer: Unknown
Handles: Fox heads on riding whips
Main Colours: Green, red and brown

Backstamp: Doulton

Doulton Number	Type	Backstamp	Height	Intro.	Discon.	Current Market Value		
						U.K. £	U.S. $	Can. $
—	Cup	Doulton	9"	1933	Ltd. ed.	1,250.00	2,500.00	2,750.00

KING EDWARD VIII CORONATION

STYLE ONE: ENGLISH EDITION, LARGE SIZE

This coronation cup was issued in a limited edition of 2,000 pieces, of which 1,080 were sold.

Designer: Charles Noke/Harry Fenton
Handle: Names of Commonwealth countries
Main Colours: Green, yellow and red

Backstamp: Doulton

Doulton Number	Type	Backstamp	Height	Intro.	Discon.	Current Market Value		
						U.K. £	U.S. $	Can. $
—	Cup	Doulton	10"	1937	Ltd. ed.	700.00	1,250.00	1,500.00

KING EDWARD VIII CORONATION

STYLE TWO: ENGLISH EDITION, SMALL SIZE

This small cup was issued in a limited edition of 1,000 pieces, of which only 454 were sold because the coronation never took place.

Designer: Charles Noke
Handle: Names of Commonwealth countries
Main Colours: Green, red and yellow

Backstamps: Doulton

Doulton Number	Type	Backstamp	Height	Intro.	Discon.	Current Market Value		
						U.K. £	U.S. $	Can. $
—	Cup	Doulton	6 ½"	1937	Ltd. ed.	Extremely Rare		

KING EDWARD VIII CORONATION

STYLE THREE: WELSH EDITION, SMALL SIZE

Style three was issued in limited edition of 2,000 pieces and made especially for the Welsh market. The portrait of Edward, Prince of Wales, differs from that on the previous cup. The words "I am still the same man" appear on the jug, taken from a speech Edward made while on his first visit to Wales as sovereign.

Designer:	Charles Noke
Handle:	Names of Commonwealth countries
Main Colours:	Green, red and brown

Backstamps: Doulton

Doulton Number	Type	Backstamp	Height	Intro.	Discon.	Current Market Value		
						U.K. £	U.S. $	Can. $
—	Cup	Doulton	6 ½"	1937	Ltd. ed.	1,200.00	2,000.00	2,500.00

KING GEORGE V AND
QUEEN MARY SILVER JUBILEE

This jubilee cup was issued in a limited edition of 1,000 pieces.

STYLE ONE: CROWNED CONJOINED PORTRAITS

Designer: Charles Noke/Harry Fenton	**Backstamp:** Doulton
Handles: Names of Commonwealth countries and provinces	
Main Colours: Green and brown	

Doulton Number	Type	Backstamp	Height	Intro.	Discon.	Current Market Value		
						U.K. £	**U.S. $**	**Can. $**
—	Cup	Doulton	10"	1935	Ltd ed.	800.00	1,500.00	1,750.00

KING GEORGE V AND
QUEEN MARY SILVER JUBILEE

STYLE TWO: UNCROWNED CONJOINED PORTRAITS

Designer: Charles Noke/Harry Fenton   **Backstamp:** Doulton
Handles: Plain
Main Colours: Yellow, red and green

Doulton Number	Type	Backstamp	Height	Intro.	Discon.	Current Market Value U.K. £	U.S. $	Can. $
—	Cup	Doulton	10 ½"	1935	Unknown	800.00	1,350.00	1,600.00

KING GEORGE VI AND
QUEEN ELIZABETH CORONATION

STYLE ONE: LARGE DESIGN — CROWNED CONJOINED PORTRAITS

Style one was issued in a limited edition of 2,000 pieces.

Designer: Charles Noke / Harry Fenton
Handles: Plain
Main Colours: Yellow, red and green

Backstamp: Doulton

Doulton Number	Type	Backstamp	Height	Intro.	Discon.	Current Market Value U.K. £	U.S. $	Can. $
—	Cup	Doulton	10 ½"	1937	Ltd. ed.	750.00	1,300.00	1,500.00

KING GEORGE VI AND
QUEEN ELIZABETH CORONATION

STYLE TWO: SMALL DESIGN — CROWNED SINGLE PORTRAITS

Style two was issued in a limited edition of 2,000 pieces.

Designer:	Charles Noke/Harry Fenton	
Handles:	Plain	
Main Colours:	Yellow, green, blue and red	

Backstamp: Doulton

Doulton Number	Type	Backstamp	Height	Intro.	Discon.	Current Market Value		
						U.K. £	**U.S. $**	**Can. $**
—	Cup	Doulton	6 ½"	1937	Ltd. ed.	600.00	900.00	1,200.00

MASTER OF FOXHOUNDS

This presentation jug was issued in a limited edition of 500 pieces.

Designer: Charles Noke
Handle: Whip
Main Colours: Green, red and brown
Spout: Rooster's head

Backstamp: Doulton

Doulton Number	Type	Backstamp	Height	Intro.	Discon.	Current Market Value		
						U.K. £	U.S. $	Can. $
—	Presentation jug	Doulton	13"	1930	Ltd. ed.	1,250.00	2,600.00	3,000.00

PIED PIPER

The Pied Piper jug was issued in a limited edition of 600 pieces.

Designer: Charles Noke/Harry Fenton
Handle: Tree
Main Colours: Yellow, brown and green
Spout: Window

Backstamp: Doulton

Doulton Number	Type	Backstamp	Height	Intro.	Discon.	Current Market Value		
						U.K. £	U.S. $	Can. $
—	Jug	Doulton	10"	1934	Ltd. ed.	1,250.00	2,250.00	2,500.00

POTTERY IN THE PAST

The Pottery in the Past cup was issued exclusively for the members of the Royal Doulton International Collectors Club.

Designer: Graham Tongue
Handles: Plain
Main Colours: Brown and green

Backstamp: Doulton/RDICC

Doulton Number	Type	Backstamp	Height	Intro.	Discon.	Current Market Value		
						U.K. £	U.S. $	Can. $
D6696	Cup	Doulton	6"	1983	1983	150.00	250.00	275.00

QUEEN ELIZABETH II CORONATION

Elizabeth became Queen of England on February 6, 1952. This commemorative cup features depictions of both Queen Elizabeth II and Elizabeth I. The handles are plain. It was issued in a limited edition of 1,000 pieces.

LOVING CUP

Designer: Cecil J. Noke / Harry Fenton
Handles: Plain
Main Colour: Brown

Backstamp: Doulton

Doulton Number	Type	Backstamp	Height	Intro.	Discon.	Current Market Value		
						U.K. £	**U.S. $**	**Can. $**
—	Cup	Doulton	10 ½"	1953	Ltd. ed.	500.00	1,000.00	1,250.00

QUEEN ELIZABETH II CORONATION

This small jug features a portrait of Queen Elizabeth II flanked by the Union Jack and the royal standard, with "Elizabeth R" underneath. A scene of Windsor Castle is on the other side. This piece was not issued in a limited edition.

JUG

Designer:	Unknown	**Backstamp:** Doulton
Handles:	Plain	
Main Colour:	Brown	

Doulton Number	Type	Backstamp	Height	Intro.	Discon.	Current Market Value U.K. £	U.S. $	Can. $
—	Jug	Doulton	6 ¼"	1953	1953	150.00	300.00	350.00

QUEEN ELIZABETH II SILVER JUBILEE

This Queen Elizabeth II Silver Jubilee cup was issued in a limited edition of 250 pieces.

Designer: Reg Johnson
Handles: Lion heads
Main Colours: Red, brown and green

Backstamp: Doulton

Doulton Number	Type	Backstamp	Height	Intro.	Discon.	Current Market Value		
						U.K. £	U.S. $	Can. $
—	Cup	Doulton	10 ½"	1977	Ltd. ed.	1,400.00	2,750.00	3,000.00

REGENCY COACH

The Regency Coach jug was issued in a limited edition of 500 pieces.

Designer: Charles Noke
Handle: Tree branch
Main Colours: Green and brown
Spout: A parchment and inn sign

Backstamp: Doulton

Doulton Number	Type	Backstamp	Height	Intro.	Discon.	Current Market Value		
						U.K. £	U.S. $	Can. $
—	Jug	Doulton	10"	1931	Ltd. ed.	1,200.00	2,000.00	2,500.00

ROBIN HOOD

This cup was issued in a limited edition of 600 pieces.

Designer:	Charles Noke/Harry Fenton	**Backstamp:** Doulton
Handles:	Plain, incised names of "The Merry Men"	
Main Colours:	Green, red and brown	

Doulton Number	Type	Backstamp	Height	Intro.	Discon.	Current Market Value U.K. £	U.S. $	Can. $
—	Cup	Doulton	8 ½"	1938	Ltd. ed.	1,400.00	2,000.00	2,500.00

ROGER SOLEMEL, COBBLER

TRIAL PIECE

This is believed to have been a trial piece only. There are no production pieces known to exist.

Designer:	Geoff Blower	**Backstamp:** Doulton
Handle:	Unknown	
Main Colours:	Unknown	

Doulton Number	Type	Backstamp	Height	Intro.	Discon.	Current Market Value U.K. £	U.S. $	Can. $
—	Jug	Doulton	10 ½"		Unknown		Unique	

SIR FRANCIS DRAKE

The Sir Francis Drake jug was issued in a limited edition of 500 pieces.

Designer: Charles Noke/Harry Fenton
Handle: Rope and lantern
Main Colours: Brown, red, green and blue

Backstamp: Doulton

Doulton Number	Type	Backstamp	Height	Intro.	Discon.	Current Market Value		
						U.K. £	U.S. $	Can. $
—	Jug	Doulton	10 ¼"	1933	Ltd. ed.	1,200.00	1,850.00	2,250.00

THE THREE MUSKETEERS

This cup was issued in a limited edition of 600 pieces.

Designer: Charles Noke/Harry Fenton
Handles: Trophies of war and the accoutrements of pleasure
Main Colours: Yellow, green, brown and red

Backstamp: Doulton

Doulton Number	Type	Backstamp	Height	Intro.	Discon.	Current Market Value		
						U.K. £	U.S. $	Can. $
—	Cup	Doulton	10"	1936	Ltd. ed.	800.00	1,850.00	2,250.00

TOWER OF LONDON

This jug was issued in a limited edition of 500 pieces.

Designer: Charles Noke/Harry Fenton
Handle: Axes, pikes, chains and armour
Spout: Shield bearing the lions of England
Main Colours: Red, green, grey and brown

Backstamp: Doulton

Doulton Number	Type	Backstamp	Height	Intro.	Discon.	Current Market Value		
						U.K. £	U.S. $	Can. $
—	Jug	Doulton	10"	1933	Ltd. ed.	1,000.00	2,000.00	2,250.00

TREASURE ISLAND

The Treasure Island jug was issued in a limited edition of 600 pieces.

Designer: Charles Noke/Harry Fenton
Handle: Palm tree
Spout: Palm leaves
Main Colours: Yellow, green and brown

Backstamp: Doulton

Doulton Number	Type	Backstamp	Height	Intro.	Discon.	Current Market Value		
						U.K. £	U.S. $	Can. $
—	Jug	Doulton	7 ½"	1934	Ltd. ed.	850.00	1,375.00	1,650.00

THE VILLAGE BLACKSMITH

This jug was issued in a limited edition of 600 pieces.

Designer: Charles Noke
Handle: Branch with milestone at base of handle; milestone incised "Longfellow" on one side and "Long-fellow 1842" on the other
Spout: Leaves
Main Colours: Brown, green and red

Backstamp: Doulton

Doulton Number	Type	Backstamp	Height	Intro.	Discon.	Current Market Value		
						U.K. £	U.S. $	Can. $
—	Jug	Doulton	7 ¾"	1936	Ltd. ed.	1,000.00	1,650.00	2,000.00

THE WANDERING MINSTREL

The Wandering Minstrel cup was issued in a limited edition of 600 pieces.

Designer: Charles Noke/Harry Fenton
Handles: Trees
Main Colours: Green, brown and yellow

Backstamp: Doulton

Doulton Number	Type	Backstamp	Height	Intro.	Discon.	Current Market Value U.K. £	U.S. $	Can. $
—	Cup	Doulton	5 ½"	1934	Ltd. ed.	1,000.00	1,650.00	2,000.00

WILLIAM SHAKESPEARE

The William Shakespeare jug was issued in a limited edition of 1,000 pieces.

Designer: Charles Noke
Handle: Masks of tragedy and comedy; swords
Spout: Face of Shakespeare
Main Colours: Green, brown and red

Backstamp: Doulton

Doulton Number	Type	Backstamp	Height	Intro.	Discon.	Current Market Value		
						U.K. £	U.S. $	Can. $
—	Jug	Doulton	10 ½"	1933	Ltd. ed.	1,100.00	1,850.00	2,250.00

WILLIAM WORDSWORTH

This cup was issued in an unlimited edition, but few are known to exist.

Designer: Charles Noke
Handles: Tied vines
Main Colours: Green, yellow and red

Backstamp: Doulton

Doulton Number	Type	Backstamp	Height	Intro.	Discon.	Current Market Value		
						U.K. £	U.S. $	Can. $
—	Cup	Doulton	6 ½"	1933	Unknown	2,000.00	3,750.00	5,000.00

BESWICK
TOBY JUGS

MARTHA GUNN

VARIATION No. 1:   Colourway — Lilac dress

Variation No. 1   Variation No. 2

Designer: Arthur Gredington
Handle: Plain
Colourway: Lilac dress with turquoise collar, red hat with
yellow pattern, red shoes, yellow base

Backstamp: Impressed
Beswick England
1113

Beswick Number	Size	Backstamp	Height	Intro.	Discon.	Current Market Value		
						U.K. £	U.S. $	Can. $
1113	Small	Beswick	3 ½"	1948	1966	150.00	275.00	325.00

VARIATION No. 2:   Colourway — Deep purple dress

Designer: Arthur Gredington
Handle: Plain
Colourway: Deep purple dress with green collar, red hat with
yellow pattern, green shoes, beige base

Backstamp: Impressed
Beswick England
1113

Beswick Number	Size	Backstamp	Height	Intro.	Discon.	Current Market Value		
						U.K. £	U.S. $	Can. $
1113	Small	Beswick	3 ½"	1948	1966	150.00	275.00	325.00

MIDSHIPMAN TOBY

Designer: Arthur Gredington
Handle: Plain
Colourway: Purple coat; red trousers; blue shirt and socks; dark blue hat; green and yellow waistcoat

Backstamp: Impressed —
Midshipman
Beswick England 1,112
Black ink stamp — Old Castle

Beswick Number	Size	Backstamp	Height	Intro.	Discon.	Current Market Value U.K. £	U.S. $	Can. $
1112	Medium	Beswick	5 ¼"	1948	1973	150.00	350.00	400.00
—	Small	Beswick	3 ½"	1948	1966	125.00	300.00	300.00

TOBY PHILLPOT

STYLE ONE: WITH JUG

Designer: Arthur Gredington
Handle: Plain
Colourway: Green coat with maroon cuffs; yellow
waistcoat; brown trousers and
hat; blue cravat and socks; brown jug

Backstamp: Impressed —
Beswick England
(model no.)

Beswick Number	Size	Backstamp	Height	Intro.	Discon.	Current Market Value		
						U.K. £	U.S. $	Can. $
1110	Large	Beswick	8"	1948	1973	165.00	350.00	375.00
1114	Small	Beswick	3 ½"	1948	1966	125.00	275.00	325.00

TOBY PHILLPOT

STYLE TWO: WITH GLASS AND JUG

Designer: Arthur Gredington
Handle: Plain
Colourway: Red coat with yellow cuffs; green waistcoat; purple trousers and hat; blue cravat and socks; brown jug and glass

Backstamp: Impressed —
Toby Phillpot Beswick
England (model no.)
Black ink stamp —
Beswick England

Beswick Number	Size	Backstamp	Height	Intro.	Discon.	Current Market Value U.K. £	U.S. $	Can. $
1111	Medium	Beswick	6 ½"	1948	1973	100.00	200.00	225.00

WINSTON CHURCHILL

The inscription reads "We shall fight them on the beaches, the landing grounds in the fields, in the streets, and on the hills, we shall never surrender. Churchill 1940."

Designer:	Mr. Watkin	**Backstamp:**	Gold ink stamp
Handle:	Lion		Beswick Ware
Colourway:	Navy jactet and trousers, blue bow tie,		Made in England
	red, white and blue Union Jack, yellow lion		

Beswick Number	Size	Backstamp	Height	Intro.	Discon.	Current Market Value		
						U.K. £	U.S. $	Can. $
931	Large	Beswick	7"	1941	1954	650.00	1,250.00	1,500.00

BESWICK
CHARACTER JUGS

AIR FORCE

ARMED FORCES
ONE OF THREE

This Air Force jug is one of a set of three. The others are the Army jug and the Navy jug.

Designer: Mr. Watkin
Handle: Flying bird
Colourway: Dark brown hair; blue hat and bird

Backstamp: Impressed —
Made in England
Beswick
737

Beswick Number	Size	Backstamp	Height	Intro.	Discon.	Current Market Value		
						U.K. £	U.S. $	Can. $
737	Medium	Beswick	5"	1939	1954	250.00	450.00	500.00

ARMY — OLD BILL

ARMED FORCES
ONE OF THREE

Designer:	Mr. Watkin					**Backstamp:**	Impressed	
Handle:	Swagger stick					**Colourway:**	Brown, khaki, white, yellow	

Beswick Number	Size	Backstamp	Height	Intro.	Discon.	Current Market Value		
						U.K. £	U.S. $	Can. $
735	Medium	Beswick	5"	1939	1954	250.00	550.00	675.00

BARNABY RUDGE

Designer: Arthur Gredington
Handle: Black crow
Colourway: Light brown hair; reddish brown coat;
blue shirt; grey hat; black bird with yellow beak

Backstamp: Impressed —
Barnaby Rudge
Beswick England
1,121
Black ink stamp —
Beswick England

Beswick Number	Size	Backstamp	Height	Intro.	Discon.	Current Market Value		
						U.K. £	U.S. $	Can. $
1121	Small	Beswick	4 ½"	1948	1969	50.00	150.00	200.00

BETSY TROTWOOD

Designer: Albert Hallam
Handle: Knitting needles and wool
Colourway: Dark green dress with mauve collar and cuffs; light blue mobcap with pink ribbon; dark brown hair; light brown needles; yellow wool

Backstamp: Impressed —
Beswick England
2075
Betsy Trotwood

Beswick Number	Size	Backstamp	Height	Intro.	Discon.	Current Market Value		
						U.K. £	U.S. $	Can. $
2075	Medium	Beswick	5"	1966	1973	75.00	200.00	300.00

CAPTAIN CUTTLE

Designer: Arthur Gredington
Handle: Hook
Colourway: Black hat and coat; white collar;
light blue cravat; brown hair

Backstamp: Impressed —
Captain Cuttle
Beswick England
1120
Black ink stamp —
Beswick England Circle

Beswick Number	Size	Backstamp	Height	Intro.	Discon.	Current Market Value		
						U.K. £	U.S. $	Can. $
1120	Small	Beswick	4 ½"	1948	1973	50.00	175.00	250.00

FALSTAFF

Designer: Albert Hallam
Handle: Feather from cap
Colourway: Red cap; green coat with gold trim

Backstamp: Impressed —
Beswick England
2095
Falstaff

Beswick Number	Size	Backstamp	Height	Intro.	Discon.	Current Market Value		
						U.K. £	U.S. $	Can. $
2095	Medium	Beswick	6 ¾"	1965	1973	65.00	300.00	350.00

HENRY VIII

Designer: Albert Hallam
Handle: Garter
Colourway: Brown coat; light brown shirt;
black hat with white trim and feather

Backstamp: Impressed —
Beswick England
2099
Henry VIII

Beswick Number	Size	Backstamp	Height	Intro.	Discon.	Current Market Value U.K. £	U.S. $	Can. $
2099	Large	Beswick	7"	1967	1973	85.00	300.00	325.00

LITTLE NELL'S GRANDFATHER

Designer: Albert Hallam
Handle: Candle snuffer
Colourway: Grey-green hat and coat; red shirt;
light brown hair; yellow handle

Backstamp: Impressed —
Made In England
2031
Little Nell's Grandfather
Black ink stamp —
Beswick England Circle

Beswick Number	Size	Backstamp	Height	Intro.	Discon.	Current Market Value		
						U.K. £	U.S. $	Can. $
2031	Medium	Beswick	5 ½"	1965	1973	85.00	300.00	375.00

MARTIN CHUZZLEWIT

Designer: Albert Hallam	**Backstamp:** Impressed —
Handle: "Last will and testamony Martin Chuzzlewit"	Made in England
Colourway: Brown hat and hair; green coat; white shirt	2030

Beswick Number	Size	Backstamp	Height	Intro.	Discon.	Current Market Value U.K. £	U.S. $	Can. $
2030	Small	Beswick	4 ¾"	1965	1973	65.00	300.00	350.00

MICAWBER

STYLE ONE: MAROON CRAVAT WITH CREAM DOTS, EYES LOOK DOWN

VARIATION No. 1:   Colourway — Green hat and coat

Designer: Mr. Watkin
Handle: Scroll reading "Title Deeds" (painted black)
Colourway: Green hat and coat; white collar;
maroon cravat with cream dots

Backstamp: Impressed —
Beswick England
310
Micawber
Beswick ink stamp:
Beswick Ware
Made in England

Beswick Number	Variation	Backstamp	Height	Intro.	Discon.	Current Market Value		
						U.K. £	U.S. $	Can. $
310	Var. 1	Beswick	9"	1935	1970	65.00	150.00	200.00

VARIATION No. 2:   Colourway — Black hat and coat

Designer: Mr. Watkin
Handle: Scroll reading "Title Deeds"(not painted)
Colourway: Black hat and coat; white collar;
white cravat

Backstamp: Impressed —
310
Made in England
Micawber
Beswick ink stamp —
Beswick Ware

Beswick Number	Variation	Backstamp	Height	Intro.	Discon.	Current Market Value U.K. £	U.S. $	Can. $
310	Var. 2	Beswick	9"	1935	1970	85.00	250.00	300.00

Micawber Derivatives

Photograph not
available at press time

Designer: Mr. Watkin
Handle: Walking cane (on cream jug)
Colourway: Cream jug — Brown coat; green hat; brown and yellow walking cane on cream jug
Cream jug —Dark brown coat, grey hat, orange walking cane
Salt — Brown coat; green hat; brown and yellow walking cane on cream jug
Wall plaque — Black hat and coat collar; white bow tie
Backstamp: Impressed — Beswick * England Micawber

Beswick Number	Item	Colour	Height	Intro.	Discon.	Current Market Value U.K. £	U.S. $	Can. $
674	Cream	Yellow cane	3 ¼"	1939	1973	35.00	60.00	90.00
674	Cream	Orange cane	3 ¼	1939	1973	35.00	60.00	90.00
690	Salt	Yellow cane	3 ½"	1939	1973	30.00	60.00	90.00
7800	Wall plaque	Black/white	9"	1939	1973	95.00	300.00	350.00

MICAWBER

STYLE TWO: MAROON CRAVAT, EYES LOOK TO THE RIGHT

Designer:	Mr. Watkin		**Backstamp:**	Impressed —
Handle:	Scroll reading "Title Deeds"			Beswick England
Colourway:	Green hat and coat; white collar;			310
	maroon cravat			Micawber
				Black ink stamp —
				Beswick Ware
				Made in England

Beswick Number	Size	Backstamp	Height	Intro.	Discon.	Current Market Value		
						U.K. £	**U.S. $**	**Can. $**
310	Large	Beswick	9"	1970	1973	100.00	225.00	250.00

MR. BUMBLE THE BEADLE

Designer:	Albert Hallam
Handle:	Walking cane
Colourway:	Black hat with yellow trim; light brown hair; light green cravat

Backstamp: Impressed —
Beswick England
2032
Mr Bumble Parish Beadle

Beswick Number	Size	Backstamp	Height	Intro.	Discon.	Current Market Value		
						U.K. £	U.S. $	Can. $
2032	Medium	Beswick	5"	1965	1973	50.00	200.00	300.00

NAVY HMS WINK

ARMED FORCES
ONE OF THREE

The Navy jug is one of a set of three, the Army and Air Force jugs being the other two.

Designer: Mr. Watkin
Handle: Rope
Colourway: Brown hair; blue and white hat with "H.M.S. Wink" printed in black; light brown rope

Backstamp: Impressed —
Made in England
Beswick
736

Beswick Number	Size	Backstamp	Height	Intro.	Discon.	Current Market Value		
						U.K. £	U.S. $	Can. $
736	Medium	Beswick	5"	1939	1954	250.00	500.00	650.00

PECKSNIFF

Derivatives

Designer: Arthur Gredington	**Backstamp:** Impressed —
Handle: Plain (cream jug)	Pecksniff
Colourway: Reddish brown coat with black trim;	Beswick England
blue shirt; brown hair; light brown	(model no.)
handle on cream jug	Black ink stamp —
	Beswick England

Beswick Number	Item	Backstamp	Height	Intro.	Discon.	Current Market Value U.K. £	U.S. $	Can. $
1117	Cream	Beswick	3 ½"	1948	1973	35.00	50.00	70.00
1129	Sugar	Beswick	3 ½"	1948	1973	35.00	60.00	80.00

P. G. W. COLONEL

This jug was produced by Beswick in 1967 for the 35th anniversary of Peter, Griffin, Woodward, Inc.

Designer: Unknown
Handle: Plain, Peters, Griffin, Woodward, Inc.
Colourway: Black, white and red

Backstamp: Black ink stamp —
Beswick

Beswick Number	Size	Backstamp	Height	Intro.	Discon.	Current Market Value		
						U.K. £	U.S. $	Can. $
—	Medium	Beswick	5 1/8"	1967	1967	80.00	300.00	375.00

PICKWICK

Derivatives

Designer: Arthur Gredington
Handle: Plain (on cream jug)
Colourway: Reddish brown coat; green shirt;
blue bow tie; brown hair;
grey hat; yellow glasses

Backstamp: Impressed —
Pickwick
Beswick England
(model no.)
Black ink stamp —
Beswick England

Beswick Number	Item	Backstamp	Height	Intro.	Discon.	Current Market Value		
						U.K. £	U.S. $	Can. $
1118	Sugar	Beswick	3"	1948	1973	30.00	80.00	100.00
1119	Cream	Beswick	3 ¼"	1948	1973	30.00	80.00	110.00

SAIREY GAMP

Designer: Mr. Watkin
Handle: Umbrella
Colourway: Green hat with cream polka dots; maroon coat; maroon umbrella with brown handle

Backstamp: Impressed —
Made in England
371
Sairey Gamp
Black ink stamp

Beswick Number	Size	Backstamp	Height	Intro.	Discon.	Current Market Value		
						U.K. £	U.S. $	Can. $
371	Large	Beswick	7"	1936	1973	60.00	150.00	250.00

Derivatives

Beswick Number	Item	Backstamp	Height	Intro.	Discon.	Current Market Value		
						U.K. £	U.S. $	Can. $
689	Pepper	Beswick	2 ½"	1939	1973	30.00	75.00	100.00
691	Teapot	Beswick	5 ¾"	1939	1973	80.00	175.00	250.00
1206	Preserve and lid	Beswick	3"	1950	1973	30.00	75.00	100.00

SCROOGE

Designer: Mr. Watkin
Handle: Part of hat and tassle
Colourway: Green hat with white dots; maroon coat and scarf; light brown hair

Backstamp: Impressed —
Made in England
372
Black or green ink stamp —
Beswick Ware
Made in England

Beswick Number	Size	Backstamp	Height	Intro.	Discon.	Current Market Value		
						U.K. £	U.S. $	Can. $
372	Large	Beswick	7"	1936	1973	65.00	200.00	275.00

TONY WELLER

STYLE ONE: HANDLE TOUCHES HAT, GREEN CRAVAT

Designer: Mr. Watkin   **Backstamp:** Beswick
Handle: Whip
Colourway: Green hat; red-brown coat; patterned green cravat

Beswick Number	Size	Backstamp	Height	Intro.	Discon.	Current Market Value		
						U.K. £	U.S. $	Can. $
281	Large	Beswick	6 ¾"		Unknown	85.00	150.00	275.00

TONY WELLER

STYLE TWO: WHIP TOUCHES EAR, SMILE SHOWS TEETH

VARIATION No. 1: Colourway — Gloss

Designer: Mr. Watkin
Handle: Whip
Colourway: Green hat; maroon coat; white shirt; green polka-dot cravat with cream horseshoe-shaped pin on scarf (gloss)

Backstamp: Impressed —
Made in England
281
Tony Weller
Black ink stamp

Beswick Number	Variation	Backstamp	Height	Intro.	Discon.	Current Market Value		
						U.K. £	U.S. $	Can. $
281	Var. 1	Beswick	7 ¼"	1935	1973	75.00	150.00	200.00

Tony Weller Derivative

Designer: Unknown
Colourway: Sugar and jam pot — Brown coat; green hat; green and cream scarf
Wall plaque — Tan hat with black band; brown tie; brown horseshoe pin

Backstamp: Impressed —
Beswick * England
Tony Weller
Black ink stamp —
Beswick England

Beswick Number	Item	Backstamp	Height	Intro.	Discon.	Current Market Value		
						U.K. £	U.S. $	Can. $
673	Sugar	Beswick	2 ¾"	1939	1973	35.00	75.00	90.00
1207	Jam pot	Beswick	3"	1950	1973	35.00	100.00	150.00
7776	Wall plaque	Beswick	7	1939	1973	95.00	250.00	300.00

VARIATION No. 2:   Colourway — Matt

Designer: Mr. Watkin	**Backstamp:** Impressed —
Handle: Whip	Made in England
Colourway: Beige hat with dark blue band; dark	281
blue coat with light green collar;	Dark blue ink stamp —
brown bow tie with gold horseshoe-	7796
shaped pin (matt)	Beswick Ware
	Made in England

Beswick Number	Variation	Backstamp	Height	Intro.	Discon.	Current Market Value U.K. £	U.S. $	Can. $
281	Var. 2	Beswick	6 ¾"		Unknown	95.00	200.00	300.00

TONY WELLER

STYLE TWO: WHIP TOUCHES EAR

VARIATION No. 3:   Closed-mouth smile

Designer: Mr. Watkin
Remodeller: Mr. Tangeel
Handle: Whip
Colourway: Green collar; black coat;
yellow hat with black band;
yellow bow tie and horseshoe pin

Backstamp: Impressed —
Made in England
Ink stamp —
Beswick Ware

Beswick Number	Variation	Backstamp	Height	Intro.	Discon.	Current Market Value		
						U.K. £	U.S. $	Can. $
281	Var. 3	Beswick	7"	1969	1973	95.00	200.00	350.00

BESWICK
MISCELLANEOUS

CAT TEAPOT

Designer: Martyn C. R. Alcock
Handle: Cat's tail
Colourway: Variation No. 1 — White
Variation No. 2 — Black and white

Backstamp: Beswick

Beswick Number	Item	Variation	Height	Intro.	Discon.	Current Market Value U.K. £	U.S. $	Can. $
3138	Teapot	Var. 1	7 ¼"	1989	1990	65.00	125.00	175.00
3138	Teapot	Var. 2	7 ¼"	1989	1990	75.00	200.00	225.00

DOLLY VARDEN TEAPOT

Designer: Arthur Gredington
Handle: Feather
Colourway: Yellow hat; blue bow and ribbons with dark blue polka dots; bow tie with blue and dark blue dots

Backstamp: Impressed —
Beswick England
1203
Dolly Varden

Beswick Number	Item	Backstamp	Height	Intro.	Discon.	Current Market Value		
						U.K. £	U.S. $	Can. $
1203	Teapot	Beswick	6 ¼"	1950	1973	150.00	400.00	500.00

FALSTAFF

Designer: Arthur Gredington, Albert Hallam
Handle: Plain
Main Colours: Browns, green and maroon
Inscription Around Jug Base: "'Falstaff' Myself & skirted page"
Inscription Around Mug Base: "Pistol with Wit or Steel Merry Wives of Windsor"

Backstamp: Impressed —
Beswick England
(Model number)
Falstaff

Beswick Number	Item	Backstamp	Height	Intro.	Discon.	Current Market Value		
						U.K. £	U.S. $	Can. $
1126	Jug	Beswick	8"	1948	1973	100.00	300.00	300.00
1127	Mug	Beswick	4"	1948	1973	45.00	90.00	90.00

HAMLET

Designer: Unknown
Handle: Plain
Main Colours: Browns, greens, black and yellow
Inscription Around Jug Base: "Hamlet-Be Thou A Spirit of Health"
Inscription Around Mug Base: "To Be or Not To Be"

Backstamp: Beswick

Beswick Number	Item	Backstamp	Height	Intro.	Discon.	Current Market Value U.K. £	U.S. $	Can. $
1146	Jug	Beswick	8 ¼"	1949	1973	100.00	250.00	300.00
1147	Mug	Beswick	4 ¼"	1949	1973	45.00	100.00	100.00

JULIET

Designer: Unknown
Handle: Plain
Main Colours: Browns, greens, maroon and blue
Inscription Around Jug Base: "Romeo and Juliet"
Inscription Around Mug Base: "Sweet Sorrow"

Backstamp: Beswick

Beswick Number	Item	Backstamp	Height	Intro.	Discon.	Current Market Value		
						U.K. £	U.S. $	Can. $
1214	Jug	Beswick	8 ¼"	1951	1973	100.00	300.00	300.00
1215	Mug	Beswick	4"	1951	1973	45.00	90.00	90.00

LAUREL AND HARDY CRUET SET

Photograph not available
at press time

Designer: Mr. Watkin
Colourway: Black and fleshtone

Backstamp: Beswick

Beswick Number	Item	Backstamp	Height	Intro.	Discon.	Current Market Value		
						U.K. £	U.S. $	Can. $
575	Cruet set	Beswick	4 ½"	1938	1969	75.00	150.00	200.00

Note: Cruet Set = 3 pieces - salt, pepper and tray

MIDSUMMER NIGHTS DREAM

Designer: Unknown   **Backstamp:** Beswick
Handle: Plain
Main Colours: Greens, browns, blue and maroon
Inscription Around Jug Base: "A Midsummer Nights Dream"
Inscription Around Mug Base: "A Midsummer Nights Dream"

Beswick Number	Item	Backstamp	Height	Intro.	Discon.	Current Market Value U.K. £	U.S. $	Can. $
1366	Jug	Beswick	8"	1955	1973	125.00	400.00	500.00
1368	Mug	Beswick	4 ¼"	1955	1973	75.00	150.00	175.00

MOUSE TEAPOT

Designer: Warren Platt
Handle: Mouse's tail
Colourway: Brown and white mouse, pink tail

Backstamp: Beswick

Beswick Number	Item	Backstamp	Height	Intro.	Discon.	Current Market Value		
						U.K. £	U.S. $	Can. $
3139	Teapot	Beswick	7"	1989	1990	65.00	150.00	225.00

MR VARDEN CREAMER

Designer:	Arthur Gredington	
Handle:	Key	
Colourway:	Purple coat; dark brown hair; blue ribbon; green hat; yellow key	

Backstamp: Impressed —
Beswick * England
1204
Mr Varden
Black ink stamp —
Beswick England

Beswick Number	Item	Backstamp	Height	Intro.	Discon.	Current Market Value		
						U.K. £	**U.S. $**	**Can. $**
1204	Creamer	Beswick	3 ½"	1950	1973	35.00	70.00	110.00

MRS VARDEN SUGAR BOWL

Photograph not available
at this time

Designer:	Arthur Gredington	
Colourway:	Unknown	

Backstamp: Beswick

Beswick Number	Item	Backstamp	Height	Intro.	Discon.	Current Market Value		
						U.K. £	**U.S. $**	**Can. $**
1205	Sugar bowl	Beswick	3"	1950	1973	35.00	70.00	90.00

PANDA TEAPOT

Panda Teapot - Variation No. 1   Panda Teapot - Variation No. 2

Variation No. 1:   Small head; bamboo shoot equal to mouth

Designer: Mr. Watkin   **Backstamp:**   Beswick
Handle: Bamboo shoot
Colourway: Black and white panda

Beswick Number	Item	Backstamp	Height	Intro.	Discon.	Current Market Value U.K. £	U.S. $	Can. $
742	Teapot	Beswick	6"	1939	1954	65.00	200.00	250.00

Variation No. 2:   Large head; bamboo shoot lower than mouth

Designer: Warren Platt and Martyn C. R. Alcock

Beswick Number	Item	Backstamp	Height	Intro.	Discon.	Current Market Value U.K. £	U.S. $	Can. $
3015/3105	Teapot	Beswick	6"	1989	1990	65.00	125.00	175.00

PEGGOTY TEAPOT

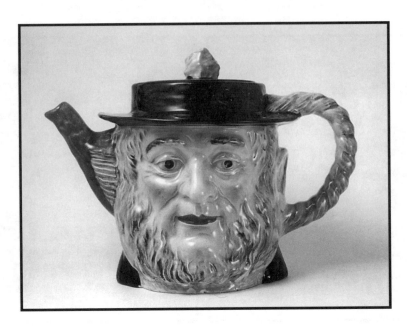

Designer: Arthur Gredington	**Backstamp:** Impressed —
Handle: Rope	Peggotty
Colourway: Light brown hair and rope; black coat	Beswick England
and hat; light blue shirt; grey spout	1,116
	Green ink stamp —
	Beswick Ware
	Made in England

Beswick Number	Item	Backstamp	Height	Intro.	Discon.	Current Market Value		
						U.K. £	U.S. $	Can. $
1116	Teapot	Impressed	6"	1948	1973	120.00	250.00	300.00

ROBERT BURNS

Photograph not available
at press time

Designer: Unknown	**Backstamp:** Beswick
Handle: Plain	
Colourway: Unknown	
Inscription Around Base: Unknown	

Beswick Number	Item	Backstamp	Height	Intro.	Discon.	Current Market Value		
						U.K. £	U.S. $	Can. $
1045	Jug	Beswick	8"	1946	1967	120.00	300.00	400.00
1596	Mug	Beswick	4 ½"	1959	1967	95.00	200.00	200.00

SAM WELLER TEAPOT

Designer: Arthur Gredington
Handle: Umbrella handle
Colourway: Green, brown, maroon and yellow

Backstamp: Beswick

Beswick Number	Item	Backstamp	Height	Intro.	Discon.	Current Market Value		
						U.K. £	U.S. $	Can. $
1369	Teapot	Beswick	6 ¼"	1955	1973	165.00	400.00	450.00

SQUIRREL TEAPOT

Designer: Amanda Hughes-Lubeck   **Backstamp:** Beswick
Handle: Squirrel's tail
Colourway: Red-brown and white squirrel

Beswick Number	Item	Backstamp	Height	Intro.	Discon.	Current Market Value U.K. £	U.S. $	Can. $
3142	Teapot	Beswick	7 ¼"	1989	1990	65.00	150.00	200.00

COLLECTING BY SERIES

Double Character Jugs (limited)

Jane Eyre and Mr Rochester	301
Lord Nelson and Lady Hamilton	346

Doultonville Tobies

Albert Sagger the Potter	37
Alderman Mace the Mayor	38
Betty Bitters the Barmaid	40
Captain Prop the Pilot	42
Capt. Salt the Sea Captain	43
Charlie Cheer the Clown	46
Dr. Pulse the Physician	51
Flora Fuchsia the Florist	56
Fred Fearless the Fireman	57
Fred Fly the Fisherman	58
Len Lifebelt the Lifeboatman	74
Madam Crystal the Clairvoyant	77
Major Green the Golfer	78
Mike Mineral the Miner	80
Miss Nostrum the Nurse	81
Miss Studious the Schoolmistress	82
Monsieur Chasseur the Chef	83
Mr. Brisket the Butcher	84
Mr. Furrow the Farmer	85
Mr. Litigate the Lawyer	86
Mr. Tonsil the Town Crier	89
Mrs. Loan the Librarian	90
Pat Parcel the Postman	93
Rev. Cassock the Clergyman	94
Sgt. Peeler the Policeman	97

Flambé, (limited)

Aladdin's Genie	113
Confucius	205
The Pharaoh	403

Football Supporters

Arsenal	133
Aston Villa	134
Celtic	183
Everton	232
Leeds United	331
Liverpool	336
Manchester United	354
Rangers	423
Sheffield Wednesday	467
Tottenham Hotspur	503

Great Composers

Beethoven	151
Chopin	194
Elgar	229
Handel	291
Mozart	369
Schubert	465
Strauss II	495
Tchaikovsky	497

Great Generals (limited)

Duke of Wellington	224
General Eisenhower	253
General Gordon	254
General Patton	255

Henry VIII and his Six Wives

Anne Boleyn (style one)	119
Anne of Cleves (style one)	120
Catherine of Aragon (style one)	178
Catherine Howard (style one)	179
Catherine Parr (style one)	180
Henry VIII (style one)	295
Jane Seymour (style one)	302
(Sir Thomas More)	476

Heroes of the Blitz (limited)

A.R.P. Warden	130
Auxiliary Fireman	140
Home Guard	297

Heroic Leaders (limited)

Earl Mountbatten of Burma (style one)	225
Sir Winston Churchill	477
Viscount Montgomery of Alamein	518

Journey through Britain (limited)

The Engine Driver	231
The Fireman (style two)	243
The Policeman	412
The Postman	415

London Collection

Beefeater	148
The Busker	164
Chelsea Pensioner	190
City Gent	199
The Guardsman (style two)	282
The London 'Bobby'	339
Lord Mayor of London	344
Pearly King	399
Pearly Queen	400
Yeoman of the Guard	534

Mystical Characters

The Genie	256
The Witch	529
The Wizard	530

National Service

The Airman (style two)	112
The Sailor (style two)	443
The Soldier (style two)	492

Presidential Series (limited)
(Presidents of the United States)

Abraham Lincoln	109
George Washington (style two)	263
Thomas Jefferson	499

Royal Doulton
International Collectors Club

Albert Sagger the Potter (toby)	37
Beefeater (tiny)	150
Charles Dickens (style two)	186
Christopher Columbus (style two)	196
Earl Mountbatten of Burma (style two)	226
George Tinworth	261

NUMERICAL
INDEX

ROYAL DOULTON SERIES

BESWICK SERIES

ROYAL DOULTON
OUTLET STORES

Join our Royal Doulton International Collector's Club or renew your membership at any of our Royal Doulton Outlet Stores.

Phoenix, **AZ** .....(602) 465-7371	Calhoun, **GA** .....(706) 602-2066	Aurora, **OH** ....(330) 995-0202
Barstow, **CA** ....(760) 253-2161	Darien, **GA** ....(912) 437-3295	Jeffersonville, **OH** ..(740) 948-9200
Cabazon, **CA** .....(909) 849-4222	Dawsonville, **GA** ...(706) 216-1480	Lincoln City, **OR** ...(541) 996-5065
Camarillo, **CA** .....(805) 987-6208	Huntley, **IL** ....(847) 669-1671	Lancaster, **PA** .....(717) 291-9370
Carlsbad, **CA** ....(760) 804-0159	Michigan City, **IN** ..(219) 872-7916	Grove City, **PA** ....(724) 748-4990
Gilroy, **CA** ....(408) 842-1653	Worcester, **MA** .....(508) 792-2499	Hilton Head, **SC** .....(843) 837-9157
Lake Elsinore, **CA** ..(909) 674-5884	Kittery, **ME** ....(207) 439-4770	Myrtle Beach, **SC** ...(843) 236-5703
Vacaville, **CA** .....(707) 448-2793	Birch Run, **MI** .....(517) 624-1011	Pigeon Forge, **TN** ...(423) 428-0977
Castle Rock, **CO** ...(303) 660-1601	Howell, **MI** ....(517) 545-3712	Conroe, **TX** ....(409) 856-7383
Clinton, **CT** ....(860) 669-3496	Blowing Rock, **NC** ..(828) 295-9230	San Marcos, **TX** ....(512) 754-0555
Rehoboth, **DE** .....(302) 226-9335	Smithfield, **NC** .....(919) 934-0101	Prince William, **VA** ...(703) 497-6845
Ellenton, **FL** ....(941) 729-2076	Flemington, **NJ** ....(908) 788-5677	Williamsburg, **VA** ...(757) 565-0752
Orlando, **FL** .....(407) 352-5578	Las Vegas, **NV** .....(702) 260-4192	Burlington, **WA** ......(360) 757-6660
Sunrise, **FL** ....(954) 845-9521	Central Valley, **NY** .....(914) 928-2434	
Vero Beach, **FL** .....(561) 563-9663	Riverhead, **NY** .....(516) 369-6940	

 ROYAL DOULTON

Visit our web site at: www.royal-doulton.com